Trauma and the Therapist

Countertransference and Vicarious
Traumatization in Psychotherapy
with Incest Survivors

By Laurie Anne Pearlman
(with I. L. McCann)

Psychological Trauma and the Adult Survivor:
Theory, Therapy, and Transformation

A NORTON PROFESSIONAL BOOK

TRAUMA AND THE THERAPIST

Countertransference and Vicarious
Traumatization in Psychotherapy
with Incest Survivors

LAURIE ANNE PEARLMAN, Ph.D.

KAREN W. SAAKVITNE, Ph.D.

W. W. Norton & Company
New York • London

Printed in the United States of America

First Edition

Manufacturing by Haddon Craftsmen, Inc.

Library of Congress Cataloging-in-Publication Data

Pearlman , Laurie A.
    Trauma and the therapist : countertransference and vicarious
traumatization in psychotherapy with incest survivors / Laurie Anne
Pearlman, Karen W. Saakvitne.
        p.   cm.
    "A Norton professional book".
    Includes bibliographical references and index.
    ISBN 0-393-70183-2
    1. Incest victims—Rehabilitation.   2. Countertransference
(Psychology)   3. Adult child sexual abuse victims—Rehabilitation.
4. Psychic trauma.   I. Saakvitne, Karen W.   II. Title.
RC560.I53P43   1995
616.85'83690651—dc20   95-8213   CIP

W. W. Norton & Company, Inc., 500 Fifth Avenue, New York, NY 10110
W. W. Norton & Company, Ltd., 10 Coptic Street, London WC1A 1PU

1 2 3 4 5 6 7 8 9 0

To our clients, the courageous women and men who have allowed us the honor of accompanying them in their process of healing and reclaiming their lives. Their lives have touched our lives and we are deeply grateful.

Contents

Acknowledgments

WE WANT TO THANK the many individuals who contributed their energy, time, and love to this project. Vicki Garvin, Bruce Reis, and Maggie Ziegler read and provided us with detailed feedback for which we are most grateful. Paul Adler, Susan Fortgang, JoAnn Griffin, Lynn Matteson, Lake McClenney, and Rob Neiss also read and gave us very useful commentary. Our colleagues at The Traumatic Stress Institute read chapters, and they also supported us in many other ways: encouraging us, bringing us lunches, expressing their esteem for our work. They include Daniel J. Abrahamson, Amy Ehrlich Charney, Sarah J. Gamble, J. Mark Hall, Sandra Hartdagen, Debra A. Neumann, Anne C. Pratt, and Dena Rosenbloom. We particularly thank Dan Abrahamson, our Administrative Director, for all of his support. Others who read and provided very helpful discussion include Vivian Carr-Allen, Carol Bozena, Barbara Eler, Marci Korwin, Sandra Streifender, and Carol Thompson.

Our administrative helpers, Prudence Duzan and Judy Vonasek, and research assistants, Anna Maria Lucca, Paula Mac Ian, and Regina Wilson, have been wonderful, and we thank them for all of their support and patience. Finally, we thank our editors, Susan Barrows Munro and Regina Dahlgren Ardini, at Norton Professional Books for their help shaping this book.

We also thank our friends, partners, and families for their nurturance, love, and support. We are grateful to our many teachers, supervisors, and mentors and to our own therapists for all they have taught and shown us. This book is dedicated to our clients who have been our best teachers. From them we have learned about humility, emotional honesty, the courage to change, and the privilege of connection.

In both its content and its process, this is a book about relationships. The content of course is an examination of the therapist's role in the therapeutic relationship. The process is one of collaboration between two women who share many roles. We are cotherapists for three sexual abuse survivor groups. We are both administrators at The Traumatic Stress Institute. We supervise one another's clinical work, and consult to one another endlessly about our many shared projects. And we are friends. In writing this book together, we have attempted to blend our voices, while allowing each to speak clearly. We hope the result for the reader is harmonious. For us, the book represents a celebration of these relationships.

Preface

AT HEART, PSYCHOTHERAPY IS a relationship between two people. This relationship is deeply intimate and personal for both participants. In psychotherapy with adult survivors of incest and childhood sexual abuse, the shared goal is nothing less than the client's reclaiming of her life, body, and self. Both participants make a commitment to bring themselves to this endeavor with honesty and courage; however ambivalently, they agree to risk trusting and connecting with one another. Over the years, theorists, mental health professionals, and researchers have devoted enormous effort to understanding one member of the therapy relationship—the client. Far less attention has been paid to the therapist, what he or she brings to the work, and the effect the work has on him or her. This oversight has been not only misleading, but dangerous to both client and therapist.

This book reflects two important aspects of trauma and the therapist. First, trauma therapy requires that the therapist be aware of his or her countertransference. Countertransference in psychotherapy with trauma survivors is powerful and can profoundly influence the development of the therapeutic relationship. When identified and used appropriately, countertransference responses inform and enrich the treatment; if unacknowledged or unexamined, they can damage both client and therapist.

Second, the work of trauma therapy has a major impact on the therapist, through a process we call vicarious traumatization (McCann & Pearlman, 1990a). Vicarious traumatization refers to alterations in the therapist's identity and usual ways of understanding and experiencing herself and her world. While this impact may be inevitable, therapists can manage and address it in a variety of constructive ways both to enhance their work with their clients and improve the quality of their personal and professional lives.

Our goal is to elaborate the processes and effects of countertransference and vicarious traumatization in psychotherapy with adult incest survivors. In doing so, we integrate psychoanalytic premises of personality and therapeutic action and technique with trauma-specific personality theories and empirical research. The fields of psychoanalysis and trauma are closely related; each enriches the other. In this book, we highlight the contribution of each body of knowledge and theory to the other.

THE AUTHORS' CONTEXT

Our desire to write this book grows from three sources: our recognition of the relative inattention to the therapist in the current trauma treatment literature, our awareness of the relative neglect of childhood sexual trauma in psychoanalytic literature, and our observations as clinicians and supervisors about the needs of survivors and their therapists. Yet neither strictly academic nor professional concerns alone have shaped this manuscript. We also chose to write this book for personal reasons.

Both of us have committed our professional lives to practicing, supervising, learning, and teaching about psychotherapy with trauma survivor clients. We feel passionate about the work we do and its effects — effects which are not only restorative and inspiring, but also discouraging and potentially damaging to client and therapist. We have seen clients damaged by mismanaged therapies with therapists not sufficiently educated about psychological trauma or adequately trained in psychotherapy in general and trauma therapy in particular. We have also seen many clients whose lives were transformed by psychotherapy with sensitive and knowledgeable therapists able to address issues of childhood trauma with them in respectful and informed ways. We have seen therapists who failed to address their own needs outside of their therapeutic relationships and so knowingly or unwittingly used clients to meet these needs.

This book is also inspired by our observations of therapist friends and colleagues who have ignored their own vicarious traumatization, believed they could continue to give to others without replenishing themselves, worked beyond the limits of their internal and external resources, or remained exquisitely attuned to their clients' needs while ignoring their own. We have seen therapists suffering from distressing symptoms related to their exposure to clients' trauma material, or from burnout, chronic anhedonia, or cynicism related to overwork and lack of self-care. We have known therapists who became entangled in difficult or traumatic situations with clients because they were working alone, without a collegial network for support and consultation or without a theoretical framework for their work. We have known therapists to leave the profession because they had lost too much of themselves and their peace of mind as a direct result of the work they were doing. We have also seen profound relief when the painful aspects of this work are acknowledged and expressions of gratitude for validation and support for therapist self-care.

We have seen profound and painful changes in ourselves, our beliefs about the world, our ways of being in the world, and our relationships with ourselves and others as a result of our work as trauma therapists. At the same time, we experience on a daily basis the rewards and joy of meaningful trauma therapy. We see the benefits to clients and therapists of psychotherapy that is grounded in theory and that offers the potential for growth, healing, and hope. We have seen the rewards for therapists who take care of themselves and are able to bring the best of themselves to their clients and their psychotherapeutic work. We acknowledge the rewards our work gives us—the opportunities for learning, human connection, personal growth, inspiration, and the creation of meaning in our lives.

In our teaching—locally, nationally, and internationally—we hear repeatedly how desperately therapists need guidance in this difficult work and permission to take care of themselves. As they make the courageous choice to accompany their survivor clients on painful, sometimes torturous, healing journeys, therapists need to make commitments to both their clients and themselves. To their clients, they need to make a commitment to bring themselves to the work with integrity and genuineness, and to be open to learning what they need to know to be helpful. To themselves, they need to make a commitment to attend to their whole self, particularly emotional, spiritual, and interpersonal needs, and not to do this work alone, without collegial support.

At a personal level, we have a deep commitment to making available to survivors treatment of the highest quality and integrity. We strongly believe that unless we and our colleagues attend to our own contributions to these therapies and to their impact upon us, we will no longer be available emotionally to work with our clients.

An important context for this book is our work as clinical psychologists at The Traumatic Stress Institute, a private mental health organization. In our roles as research director (LAP) and clinical director (KWS), we conduct psychotherapy with adult survivors of traumatic life events, particularly with adult survivors of childhood sexual abuse; supervise trauma therapists both within our organization and in the community; train psychotherapists and other mental health care providers; and undertake clinical research on survivor issues. Our organization has provided both a context and major support for this work. This book emerges from ongoing discussions with our colleagues, continuing study of the psychoanalytic and trauma literatures, detailed attention to the therapy process with our clients, and a persistent and deepening awareness of our own experience as trauma therapists. We owe an enormous debt to our clients, who have taught us much of what we think important to pass on in the pages of this book.

We acknowledge our significant debt to the clinicians and researchers who studied and wrote about sexual abuse and incest before these topics gained acceptance and popularity, including but not limited to Diana Russell (1984, 1986), David Finkelhor (1979, 1986), and Albert Kinsey and his colleagues (1953), for their epidemiological work; Christine Courtois (1979, 1988), Judith Herman (1981, 1992), Denise Gelinas (1983), Jean Goodwin (1989), Richard Ulman and Doris Brothers (1988), Suzanne Sgroi (1982, 1988, 1989), Leonard Shengold (1989), Alice Miller (1981, 1984, 1988), Bessel van der Kolk (1984, 1987, 1988, 1989), and Mardi Horowitz (1986) for contemporary clinical writing; and to Sigmund Freud, Pierre Janet, and Sandor Ferenczi for their initial exploration of the impact of childhood trauma on later adult psychological functioning. In addition, we owe an incalculable debt to the social activists and reformers who have done so much to bring the issues of childhood sexual abuse into the public awareness. From crusaders like Bertha Pappenheim (Anna O.) to the leaders of the women's movement, rape crisis centers, shelters for victims of domestic violence, and advocacy groups for children and families, grass roots organizers have led the way in addressing the shattering social and personal impact of abuse and violence. In the area of childhood sexual abuse, these contributions to the field have included Ellen Bass and Laura Davis's book, *The Courage to Heal* (1988).

Trauma and the Therapist reflects the integration of the authors' distinct theoretical orientations, beliefs, languages, and ideas. While our theoretical backgrounds differ, we have both worked to evaluate and integrate our professional training with our clinical experience and observations. This process requires us to move beyond our education and training to address the role of interpersonal trauma in psychological functioning and psychopathology.

While our orientations reflect different language and focus, they are compatible and enhance one another. One of us (KWS) comes from a strong psychoanalytic background, while the other (LAP) comes from a cognitive, social learning, and object relations based theoretical background. We work collaboratively as clinicians as well as coauthors and in both clinical and academic realms find that our differences heighten the clarity of our thinking and increase the complexity and flexibility of our work. Over time we have developed a shared language and shared ideas. Because our theoretical meeting place reflects the process of the developing field of trauma theory and therapy, we elaborate in early chapters our theoretical frameworks and evolution to set the context of this book. The book reflects the integration of these paths of development, specifically the integration of psychoanalytic and trauma theories and psychotherapy.

TRAUMA AND THE THERAPIST

Countertransference and Vicarious
Traumatization in Psychotherapy
with Incest Survivors

Introduction

BACKGROUND OF THE BOOK

While the body of literature on psychotherapy with trauma survivors has flourished over the past 15 years, little of that literature addresses the role and needs of the therapist. As early as 1974, Sarah Haley wrote about the difficulties therapists experienced with Vietnam veteran clients' reports of atrocities they suffered or witnessed. Yet to date only a handful of authors have written specifically about the countertransference issues faced by psychotherapists working with adult survivors of childhood sexual abuse and even fewer about the cumulative transformative effects of such work upon the self of the therapist that we call vicarious traumatization. The need is great for both theoretical elucidation and applied clinical techniques.

While most psychotherapists working with trauma survivor clients are well-intentioned, many work in isolation. Too often, therapists, counselors, trauma workers, and researchers lack conceptual frameworks, practical approaches, and supportive environments for either examining their role in relationships with trauma survivors or for understanding the impact their work has on them. Lack of information and training increases the likelihood that therapists will impose their needs and conflicts on their clients and psychotherapies. To date, few training programs for mental health

1

professionals offer education about psychological trauma; even fewer address details of the complex process of trauma therapy, including issues of developing a therapeutic alliance, establishing a therapeutic frame, understanding and using transference and countertransference, managing traumatic memories, and addressing common post-trauma adaptations in the context of a developmental trauma theory and psychoanalytic theory.

Without an understanding of these issues and techniques, both trauma clients and therapists are at risk for harm. Clients who have been abused in childhood are extremely vulnerable to reinjury by therapists who do not understand their own responses to these clients (Armsworth, 1989). The field of psychotherapy suffers when a therapy fails or a client is reinjured by a therapy. Furthermore, the entire field of trauma therapy is at risk of extinction if overtaxed professionals are unable to mitigate the deleterious effects of their work upon themselves. The need for further education and training is indicated by the current demand for consultation and supervision.

The danger of returning to silence, denial, and failure to recognize and know the prevalence and effects of childhood sexual abuse is real. Herman (1992) refers to the history of the field of psychological trauma as one of "periodic amnesia." While child abuse has existed for centuries, it emerges into cultural consciousness episodically, only to be again dissociated, repressed, or denied (Brett, 1993). We cannot afford to again "forget" the reality of child abuse and its deleterious effects. Our work as trauma therapists is subversive work; we name and address society's shame. There are and will continue to be forces within society that work to silence us and our clients. When we do not recognize the social and political context for our work, we unwittingly participate in this return to silence, denial, and neglect.

The well-publicized controversies in the early 1990s concerning the validity of survivors' memories, the fear that therapists can by suggestion "implant memories" into their clients' minds, and disagreements about the mechanisms of traumatic forgetting and repression (Loftus, 1993; van der Kolk & McFarlane, in press; Olio, 1994; Terr, 1994; van der Kolk, 1994) each reflects our society's great ambivalence about recognizing the reality of childhood sexual abuse. The current debate confuses several issues, including (1) the reality of childhood sexual abuse; (2) the process of traumatic forgetting; (3) the scientific defensibility of retroactively created false memories; (4) the need for standards for and training in ethical clinical practice; and (5) the difference between legal and clinical standards of evidence. In effect, this confusion leads survivors and observers to question an incontrovertible reality: that children in our society are commonly victims of sexual abuse (Olio, 1993; Olio, Schwartz, Courtois, & Bloom, 1994). In this way, as a society, we repeat the childhood trauma of calling reality into question; the requirement not to know one's truth leads to a chronic state of dissociation.

This volume is written in the context of two paradigm shifts in the field of mental health and psychotherapy. First, our growing recognition of the importance of psychological trauma in the lives of our clients has profoundly changed the way we understand psychopathology. Second, within psychodynamic conceptualizations of the therapeutic relationship, there is a concurrent paradigm shift. Elkind writes, "Psychotherapists are currently making an effort to shift our reliance upon a medical model to a relational model that encompasses the interaction of both therapist and patient and their mutual impact upon each other" (1992, p. 9). The growth of our awareness of intersubjectivity, the centrality of the self of the therapist, and the relational context of the therapeutic work all speak to fundamentally altered concepts of psychotherapy and the role of the psychotherapist. A related shift is the emergence of a feminist relational perspective reflected in the work of the Stone Center and other feminist texts (Brown & Ballou, 1992; Jordan, Kaplan, Miller, Stiver, & Surrey, 1991; Miller, 1976).

WHY INCEST SURVIVORS?

We have chosen to focus specifically on countertransference and vicarious traumatization in psychotherapy with adult survivors of incest and other childhood sexual abuse for a variety of reasons. First, the striking prevalence of child sexual abuse in the general population tells us that many psychotherapists will be seeing adult survivors in their offices. Current estimates are that one in three women have had unwanted sexual experiences (which included physical contact) before the age of 17 (Russell, 1984), and one in six men have had sexual experiences before age 15 involving someone at least five years older (Finkelhor, Hotaling, Lewis, & Smith, 1990). The prevalence of childhood sexual abuse in clinical populations is even higher (Briere, 1992; Briere & Zaidi, 1989; Brown & Anderson, 1991; Browne & Finkelhor, 1986; Mas, 1992). Current research suggests that between 68 and 86 percent of hospitalized patients with a diagnosis of borderline personality disorder have childhood histories of sexual abuse, physical abuse, or witnessing severe violence (Bryer, Nelson, Miller, & Krol, 1987; Herman, Perry, & van der Kolk, 1989; Ogata et al., 1990; Westen, Ludolph, Misle, Ruffins, & Block, 1990). Among outpatients with the borderline personality disorder diagnosis, rates of childhood sexual abuse reported in the literature range from 67 to 76 percent (Herman et al., 1989; Wagner, Linehan, & Wasson, 1989).

Second, survivors of childhood incest and sexual abuse are often challenging psychotherapy clients. Their post-trauma symptomatology and adaptations can be confusing and anxiety-provoking, and their level of psychological disruption significant (Gelinas, 1983; Neumann, in press). Their affective and interpersonal style is intense and compelling. These therapies are uniquely challenging because of the inevitability that sexual abuse survivors will engage in unconscious or dissociated reenactments of traumatic interpersonal experiences that invite therapists to respond in complementary ways. As Davies and Frawley write,

> These reenactments are not "clinical errors" but the essence of the material to be analyzed within the treatment. Such reenactments involve the unconscious recreation in the treatment setting of dissociatively unavailable aspects of self and object representations—aspects that cannot be verbally described but can, via projective-introjective mechanisms, particularly projective-identification, volley back and forth between patient and therapist in startling reconstructions of early trauma, their fantasied elaborations, and their ultimate infiltration into present-day interpersonal relationships. . . . Successful treatment, therefore, depends on the therapist's ability to freely engage in these transference-countertransference reenactments and then disengage sufficiently to observe, contain, and process with the patient what has occurred between them. Treatment is threatened both when the therapist resists participation and when he is so enmeshed in enacting that the capacity to observe is lost. (1994, pp. 3–4)

Third, for survivors of childhood interpersonal trauma, the development of a therapeutic relationship is the central process of healing; at the same time to the survivor client it feels enormously threatening. This paradox requires that the therapist possess great patience, skill, and understanding. While navigating the often stormy therapeutic waters, the therapist needs support, humility, and self-confidence.

Fourth, in work with adult survivors of childhood sexual abuse, countertransference and vicarious traumatization issues are particularly complicated and difficult. Child sexual abuse and incest are topics overladen with powerful cultural taboos and related affects and defenses, which directly affect the therapist, who is also part of the larger culture that allows such abuse to continue (Saakvitne, 1990; Saakvitne & Pearlman, 1993). The complex and conflictual interplay of transference and countertransference paradigms will challenge the therapist at all levels of her personal and professional identity. At the same time, our countertransference is an absolutely invaluable tool in these therapies.

Fifth, and finally, the percentage of therapists who are themselves survivors of childhood sexual abuse is higher than the percentage of survivors in the general population (Elliott & Guy, 1993; Follette, Polusny, & Milbeck, 1994; Pope & Feldman-Summers, 1992; Schauben & Frazier, in press). It is not uncommon for survivors to pursue a healing mission, such as helping other survivors, as part of their own recovery. Survivor therapists face unique challenges in this work related to both countertransference and vicarious traumatization.

REVIEW OF THE LITERATURE

Countertransference and Vicarious Traumatization with Trauma Survivors

While the literature on countertransference and vicarious traumatization with survivors of childhood sexual abuse, which we review below, is still relatively sparse, there is an early literature on therapist responses to trauma survivors in general. Initially this literature focused on therapist responses to war veterans, and usually did not distinguish between responses to individual clients and the cumulative responses to clinical work that can be understood within the vicarious traumatization framework. These authors noted such responses as numbing, fear, and sadistic and retaliatory wishes (Haley, 1974); existential or spiritual issues (Blank, 1985a; Margolin, 1984); judgmental and aggressive feelings, as well as grief, horror, rage, and vulnerability (Scurfield, 1985); and classic symptoms of posttraumatic stress disorder (Lindy, 1988).

More recently, Herman (1992) elaborated some specific countertransference hazards to which trauma therapists may be vulnerable, including taking the part of rescuer or developing a sense of omnipotence to defend against feelings of helplessness, violating therapeutic boundaries, and identifying with the victim's rage and grief. Within Wilson and Lindy's volume on *Countertransference in the Treatment of PTSD* (Wilson & Lindy, 1994b), Lindy, Wilson, and Raphael (1994) provide a categorical model for understanding types of therapist responses to working with trauma survivors. They elaborate responses that are primarily avoidant and those that involve overidentification with survivor clients. Other contributors to the volume apply their model to psychotherapists' countertransference responses with various traumatized populations. Wilson and Lindy (1994a) also explore the connection between these phenomena as they affect the treatment of trauma survivors.

In one of the few research studies on countertransference in trauma therapy, Danieli (1982) examined therapists' responses to working with

Nazi Holocaust survivors and their children. She found such responses as guilt, rage, dread, grief, shame, inability to contain intense emotions, and the use of defenses, including numbing, denial, and avoidance.

Another empirical study, conducted by Lindy, Green, Grace, MacLeod, and Spitz (1988), also found "excessive affect" in therapists working with Vietnam veterans. Lindy et al. identified a range of feelings of subjective distress and a variety of behaviors (including excitement, voyeurism, sado-masochism, and prosocial action) in these therapists.

Countertransference with Survivors of Childhood Sexual Abuse

In 1991, Wolf and Alpert reviewed the psychoanalytic literature on treatment issues for clients sexually abused as children and concluded that "there is a need for literature on treatment issues, specifically whether and how analysis should be modified with the sexually abused population" (1991, p. 323). With the few notable exceptions discussed below, the psychoanalytic literature on transference and countertransference with survivors consists largely of case studies describing thematic patterns of responses for client and therapist.

Virtually everyone who writes about psychotherapy with adult survivors of childhood sexual abuse acknowledges the significance of countertransference. Those who write about countertransference with incest survivors have primarily identified the many strong (and often negative) feelings elicited in the course of work with survivors (Courtois, 1988; Ganzarain & Buchele, 1988; Herman, 1992; Marvasti, 1992; Renshaw, 1982). Marcus (1989) and Ganzarain and Buchele discussed a range of countertransference responses and emphasized the potential for therapist to "act out" of her countertransference and divert the therapy. Some have provided models for examining specific sources of countertransference, whether focusing primarily on the client and his material or on the therapist. Several authors address briefly the special issues of survivor therapists (Briere, 1989; Courtois, 1988; Davies & Frawley, 1991, 1994; Friedrich, 1990; Marvasti, 1992).

While thoughtful and interesting, the majority of these works are incomplete in their examination of countertransference, as they focus largely on affective responses and do not address in depth the interaction of transference and countertransference, the complexity of conscious and unconscious processes, and fluctuating self and object representations that represent the full range of countertransference responses to these clients in the context of the therapeutic relationship.

There are a few notable exceptions in the very recent literature. Courtois and Chefetz (1993) provide a creative model for conceptualizing the inter-action of erotic and traumatic transference and countertransference. They describe the interaction between the survivor client's need to create bound-aries between self and other, desire to be special, and need for control and the therapist's strong responses to clinical themes presented by sexual abuse survivors, transference responses to their clients, and their own sexuality and aggression.

In their important volume *Treating the Adult Survivor of Childhood Sexual Abuse: A Psychoanalytic Perspective*, Davies and Frawley (1994) have added substantially to the literature by elaborating the complex coun-tertransference responses and specifically the transference-countertransfer-ence matrix (Ogden, 1986) in analytic therapy with incest survivors. They elegantly outline the role of reenactments in analytic treatment and the centrality of countertransference in the unfolding of such reenactments. They elaborate the process and working through of the fluid identifications represented in these reenactments—among the child and adult self of the client and the perpetrator, rescuer, and helpless bystander identities avail-able to the therapist; these shifting identities have been identified by others (Lindy & Wilson, 1994; McCann & Pearlman, 1990b; Miller, 1994), but their lucid elaboration of the careful interpretive working through of the transference and countertransference dynamics is particularly helpful. Da-vies and Frawley emphasize the centrality of dissociative and projective identification processes in the transference and countertransference unfold-ing; they identify the task of the therapy as the participation in *and* interpre-tation of these reenactments of the symbolic encoding of traumatic memo-ries.

However, Wolf and Alpert's conclusion to their review of 48 articles on psychoanalysis and childhood sexual abuse remains true:

> Despite the impact that countertransference issues might be expected to have on treatment, they received relatively little discussion in the literature reviewed here. Most such writing addressed concerns such as errors which promote acting out only in a general way; there was little discussion of specific feelings, particularly incestuous and sexual ones and anger at offenders. . . . [These phenomena] point to a need for further writing and exploration of the issues to promote a more accepting attitude. (1991, pp. 322–323)

Vicarious Traumatization

While many authors address the difficulty of this work, there have been few systematic ways to describe and measure vicarious traumatization, the

enduring deleterious effects of trauma therapy on the therapist. Some authors have noted therapists' responses across trauma survivor clients. Figley
and his colleagues have written about secondary traumatic stress disorder,
which refers to the effects of trauma upon psychotherapists as well as upon
relatives and friends of the victims and those who are more indirectly affected by a traumatic event (Figley, 1991; Figley, in press). Others have
also noted the emergence of symptoms of post-traumatic stress disorder in
therapists (Hartman & Jackson, 1994; Lindy & Wilson, 1994). Kauffman
(1994) describes "cumulative countertransference," the daily impact upon
the therapist of holding multiple transference identities and countertransference responses in sequential therapy sessions with trauma clients.

Figley (1994) has recently reconceptualized secondary traumatic stress
disorder as compassion fatigue, emphasizing the strain therapists experience on their ability to remain in empathic connection with trauma survivor
clients over time. This empathic strain is the focus of many of the chapters
in Wilson and Lindy's (1994b) edited volume.

The nature of the psychotherapist's role is such that it puts us at a
particular emotional risk. Much research is beginning, and some studies are
providing early data on this phenomenon (Follette, Polusny, & Milbeck,
1994; Gamble, Pearlman, Lucca, & Allen, 1994; Hollingsworth, 1993;
Munroe, 1990; Pearlman & Mac Ian, 1994; Schauben & Frazier, in press).
In general, these researchers are finding that working with survivors takes a
special toll on helpers.

Unfortunately, the literature has not yet provided a systematic theoretical framework for understanding the complex interplay of therapist, client,
and contextual factors that impact upon both the work and the self of the
therapist in psychotherapies with adult survivors of childhood sexual abuse.
We hope to build upon the extant literature, as well as our clinical experience, to provide such a framework.

LANGUAGE

The focus of this book is the therapist who works with adult survivors of
childhood incest and sexual abuse. In this book, we use the term *incest*
broadly to refer to all experiences of childhood sexual contact with a trusted
significant adult or older person (e.g., parent, grandparent, sibling, cousin,
neighbor). We emphasize that the trauma of childhood sexual abuse and
incest is not simply an event; rather, it occurs in an interpersonal and
familial context that often includes emotional and physical abuse or neglect
and psychological abuse (assaults on a person's perceptions of reality, psychological identity and separateness, and attempts to drive someone crazy
or convince him that he is crazy). As Denise Gelinas has written, "it is the
relationship, not the biology, that is betrayed" (1983, p. 313).

We choose to use the term *client* rather than patient because it reflects our clinical context of outpatient work and philosophical emphasis on the therapeutic relationship as a partnership with shared goals. We believe the term client reflects an interactive relationship rather than a one-way process in which the clinician is doing something to a patient.

We use the term *survivor* because all of the victim clients who make it to psychotherapy are, in an important sense, survivors. They have shown remarkable courage, persistence, adaptability, and creativity in enduring and living in a world that has betrayed them. A pattern of identity development takes place in the healing process in which a person moves from recognizing his victimization, to acknowledging his survivorship, and finally to reclaiming his personhood. The latter identity reflects that the client has recognized and mourned his experiences of abuse and integrated their meaning into his narrative and identity, but they no longer fully define him.

Our clinical experience is as female therapists with a preponderance of female clients. However, we have also drawn upon the experiences of our male colleagues and the male clients with whom we have worked directly or as supervisors. To honor all survivors and therapists, we will at times use female and at times male pronouns to refer to therapist and to client. We hope to maximize clarity while remaining consistent with the dictates of usage. We are consistent in our assignment of gender to therapist and client within each section of the book.

Finally, in the service of protecting readers from further vicarious traumatization, we offer information about the material you will find in this book. Clearly, the reality of childhood sexual abuse and its aftermath in adulthood is deeply painful and distressing. The ideas presented in this book may stir strong feelings in the reader. We give many examples of intensely painful feelings, beliefs, and relationships that people experience as a result of childhood sexual abuse. However, as part of our professional commitment to eliminating unnecessary vicarious traumatization, we do not emphasize graphic, explicit details of traumatic and abusive acts.

OVERVIEW OF THE BOOK

Our goal has been to cover the breadth of issues for the therapist working with survivors of childhood sexual abuse in enough depth to be useful clinically and theoretically. We strive to address the issues with enough clarity to be useful to therapists new to psychotherapy with trauma survivors and with enough complexity to be thought-provoking for experienced therapists and experienced trauma therapists.

While each chapter can stand alone, each of the five sections of the book incorporates different aspects of this complex work. The three chapters in Part I provide an introduction to intensive psychotherapy with trauma survivors. Here we provide the theoretical context for the rest of the book. Chapter 1 sets the stage with a discussion of the therapist and the therapeutic relationship. This chapter elaborates the historical context for our interpretation of countertransference and introduces the notion of vicarious traumatization. Chapter 2 provides a discussion of the contributions of psychoanalytic theory to our thinking and to trauma theory and therapy, specifically identifying its major contributions and impediments. Chapter 3 describes constructivist self development theory, or CSDT (McCann & Pearlman, 1990b), an integrative, developmental, relational theory that forms a foundation for clinical work with survivors and the basis for our conceptualization of the impact of trauma therapy upon the therapist.

Each of the nine chapters in Part II addresses a specific countertransference issue that arises in intensive psychotherapy with incest survivors. These chapters introduce particular countertransference dynamics and discuss clinical and technical implications. Chapters 4 and 5 provide the broadest overview of countertransference responses in work with survivors. In chapter 4, we discuss therapists' responses to the meanings of childhood sexual abuse. In chapter 5, we address countertransference to transference paradigms that commonly emerge in psychotherapy with survivors of childhood sexual abuse. In chapter 6, we discuss therapists' responses to the process of dissociation in the therapeutic relationship, so common with survivors of childhood sexual abuse. Chapter 7 addresses the complexities of establishing boundaries and working therapeutically within the therapeutic frame. In chapter 8, we discuss special countertransference issues for the many therapists who are survivors of childhood sexual abuse. Chapter 9 explores gender-related countertransference issues for different gender pairings of therapist and client, as well as some of the gender issues related to childhood sexual abuse. Chapter 10 provides an exploration of therapeutic impasses with survivor clients and related countertransference responses. We devote chapter 11 to an exploration of countertransference issues that arise in group therapy conducted by cotherapists. Finally, chapter 12 speaks to the unique responses therapists may experience in treating survivor clients who report abuse by a previous therapist.

Part III focuses on vicarious traumatization. In chapter 13, we talk about the ways trauma therapy affects the therapist. In chapter 14, we discuss the factors in the therapist and in the therapeutic situation that contribute to vicarious traumatization.

Part IV highlights the interaction between countertransference and vicarious traumatization. Chapter 15 examines ways in which unaddressed vicarious traumatization can set the stage for particular countertransference responses which, unanalyzed, can lead to therapeutic errors and impasses, as well as the ways in which countertransference contributes to vicarious traumatization. In chapter 16, we discuss countertransference and vicarious traumatization in the context of the therapist's ongoing professional development and changing identity.

Part V focuses on therapist self-care. Chapter 18 is written for supervisors and teachers of trauma therapists. Chapter 19 addresses specific ways of responding to and ameliorating vicarious traumatization. In chapter 20, we discuss the rewards of doing trauma therapy.

The book ends with an appendix in which we provide two measures developed at The Traumatic Stress Institute. The TSI Belief Scale is a measure of disrupted cognitive schemas (Pearlman, Mac Ian, Johnson, & Mas, 1992). The Life Orientation Inventory is a measure of spirituality (Neumann & Pearlman, 1994).

In the interest of protecting clients' privacy and confidentiality, where we use case material the cases are either fictional or composites drawn from our clinical and supervision experience. We invite you to bring to mind your own clinical experience as you consider what we have written. While we have attempted to generalize, each therapeutic relationship is unique.

Part One

THEORETICAL UNDERPINNINGS

1

The Therapeutic Relationship as the Context for Countertransference and Vicarious Traumatization

THE PRIMARY HEALING of psychotherapy with adult survivors of childhood sexual abuse occurs in the context of the therapeutic relationship. The client and the therapist create and develop the therapeutic relationship over time, consciously and unconsciously, intentionally and unintentionally, through their interactions and ways of relating to one another. The therapeutic relationship includes the interpersonal interactions in the therapy (feelings, words, behaviors), conscious and unconscious transference and counter-transference responses and their interpretation, traumatic and other reenactments and the examination of them, and the complex relational context that develops between the person of the therapist and that of the client.

The focus on the therapeutic relationship, rather than a more limited focus on transference (i.e., the client), allows us to use countertransference and therefore the self of the therapist as a rich resource and fundamental tool of the work (Jacobs, 1991). This shift in attention from an exclusive focus on the client to a more complicated view of the client, the therapeutic relationship, and the therapist makes available the fertile, intersubjective field of the therapeutic process. Thus, a focus on the therapeutic relationship requires that we examine our subjectivity; the relational space of the psychotherapy is shaped by what we bring to it, specifically our personal history, feelings, attitudes, defenses, unconscious processes, conscious reac-

tions, and behaviors, all of which will inform and be reflected in our countertransference.

Historically, the development of greater focus on the interpersonal aspects of the therapeutic relationship is paralleled by the development and
exploration of the concept of countertransference (Kahn, 1991; Wolstein,
1988). The concept of a therapeutic relationship began with Freud's early
conceptualization of transference (1905, 1915). But the complexity of the
concept and the blend of conscious (here-and-now relationship) factors
with unconscious (transference, projective identifications) factors did not
receive extensive attention until the confluence of several developmental
lines with psychology and psychoanalysis (see chapter 2). Over the last
three decades, psychoanalytic theory has benefited enormously from the
clarification of the role and use of the therapeutic relationship in the process
of healing (Elkind, 1992; Kahn, 1991).

For clients who are survivors, it is within this new relationship that
opportunities emerge to rework and heal damage done in the context of
early, trusting relationships. Because his current distress is rooted in historical, often chronic, interpersonal trauma, for the survivor the new interpersonal environment of the therapeutic relationship is terrifying as well as
promising. Establishing safety and trust is both essential and inherently
challenging in these therapeutic relationships. Yassen (in press) has said
that the process of building the therapeutic relationship *is* the therapy with
trauma survivors. This premise frames the psychotherapy as an evolution-
ary relational process, rather than a series of either crises and their solutions, or dramatic mutative interpretations.

Survivors of childhood interpersonal traumas will bring fear, profound
mistrust, and anger, as well as yearning, intense loneliness, and fragile hope
to the therapeutic relationship. They will be acutely attuned to the most
subtle signs of inattention, abandonment, or betrayal in their therapist's
demeanor; they will also be influenced by her communication of compassion and respect. Our clients' attunement requires that our self-awareness
be as acute. We invite our clients' awareness of us because it opens the door
to conscious negotiation of the interpersonal space of the therapy, and
thus allows the client to make conscious the unconscious object relational
paradigms and schemas that guide his present life.

The opportunity for this new relationship to be different, specifically for
events and perceptions in the therapy to be open for nondefensive naming
and discussion, is part of the healing context of psychotherapy. What does
this require of the therapist? Self-esteem, an identity as a "good-enough"
therapist, and a theoretical perspective that recognizes this process as the
work of the therapy.

Example   Picture this scenario. Your survivor client is describing a particularly horrific experience of childhood abuse. You know it is coming and brace yourself to listen, yet after a few minutes you realize you are staring out the window behind him feeling numb and inattentive. Your mind has wandered to planning your garden. As you notice your (inner) departure from the relationship, you can acknowledge your feelings—perhaps dread, revulsion, anger—in response to the trauma material, and your wish not to hear or know it. This inner process will allow you to reenter your body and the room.

What if your client has noticed and says that you "spaced out" at a critical moment, and he is hurt and feels abandoned? You can acknowledge that you indeed spaced out, and that you are back. As you and your client discuss this response to his story and his feelings about it, the relationship will move forward. The client will feel heard and acknowledged by the straightforward acknowledgment that you were not fully present, and his own feelings of horror may be validated by your need to distance from the material. At the same time, he is supported by your commitment to reconnect with him. This process reinforces the truth that psychotherapy does not promise perfect attunement or mirroring, but entails repeated cycles of connections and disconnections and then repair and reconnection.

These acknowledgments require the therapist's consciousness and non-defensive honesty. This example also speaks to a fundamental truth of trauma therapy: Trauma material is difficult to hear and both parties will be affected by it. Clients know this, but therapists often feel they must deny it.

THE THERAPEUTIC RELATIONSHIP IN TRAUMA THERAPY

The therapeutic relationship is unique in certain key ways. It is always founded on basic respect for the personhood of the client. It is organized around the premise that events in the therapy have meaning and can be examined to understand the client and recognize his striving for connection, safety, and meaning in his life. The premise that there is nothing that cannot be spoken and that events in the therapy and the therapeutic relationship itself are open to observation and discussion is central. The relationship exists primarily to address the client's needs and occurs within an explicit therapeutic structure or frame that reflects the theoretical premises of the psychotherapy and the ethical principles of the therapist's profession. These premises ensure the safety, integrity, and therapeutic efficacy of the therapeutic relationship.

Clearly, the therapy relationship has unique properties. It has a specific purpose and primary focus on the growth and healing of the client through elucidation of the client's experience. The therapist brings herself and her experience to the relationship with this purpose and responsibility. The relationship has a relatively fixed structure, an economic basis, certain power inequities, and legal constraints that must be acknowledged. However, when the therapy relationship is working well, client and therapist come to a sense of shared purpose, a working together which implies commitment and emotional investment in the relationship as an arena for growth and change. (Miller, Jordan, Kaplan, Stiver, & Surrey, 1991, p. 10)

The defining assumptions of psychoanalytic psychotherapy* are: (1) an individual's personality is related developmentally to his past; (2) unconscious processes influence the individual's thoughts, feelings, and behaviors; and (3) both client and therapist bring to the therapeutic relationship assumptions and expressions of internalized object representations from previous relationships (i.e., transference and countertransference). Countertransference is an aspect of every psychotherapy; a defining aspect of analytic interpersonal therapies is that we bring our countertransference responses into conscious awareness for analysis in order to enhance and deepen the therapeutic work.

As we recognize the subjectivity of our experience in the therapeutic relationship, our understanding of our role as therapists shifts. We use our observations in the service of a journey of shared discovery, rather than a tour on which we believe ourselves to be the guide. We move away from a position of *authoritative knowing* of the client, the implications of his history, and his needs to a position of collaboration and mutual endeavor. We are not suggesting that our training and theories give us no guideposts; we draw upon these resources to help identify our path as we follow our client's lead. The therapy will be unique for the interaction between the person of client and the person of therapist; the therapist's self is elemental to the unfolding therapeutic relationship.

In the mental health care climate today there is diminishing financial support for psychotherapy. Yet helping a person reexamine his entire early context and overcome and rework lifelong patterns of managing affect and relationships is long-term work. Childhood sexual abuse survivors require and deserve this commitment to heal from their traumatic injuries. Trauma

---

*We use the term "psychoanalytic psychotherapy" to refer to an integrated model combining classic psychoanalysis with later techniques informed by object relations theory, self psychology, ego psychology, and interpersonal psychiatry.

researchers and clinicians have worked hard to discover and develop effective ways of helping survivors. Our task now is to create an environment that supports this work.

SPECIFIC COMPONENTS OF TRAUMA THERAPY

Good trauma therapy is first and foremost good theory-based psychotherapy. Such psychotherapy is based on psychological theories of development and incorporates an understanding of the mechanisms of psychological change and relational development. A therapist must understand personality development and adaptation, as well as the interpersonal and intrapsychic process of psychotherapy itself. Our model of psychotherapy is relational and analytic; its goals are consistent with those outlined by Davies and Frawley (1994):

> An integrated model for the psychoanalytically oriented treatment of adult survivors of childhood sexual abuse is thus based on the progressive unfolding of five specific and heretofore foreclosed intrapsychic capacities. They are (1) the therapeutic containment of the physiological and psychological hyperarousal and disorganization secondary to chronic trauma; (2) the recovery of pathogenic memories and fantasied elaborations; (3) the symbolization of memory and fantasied elaborations; (4) the integration of dissociated self and object representations; and finally (5) the internalization of a new object relationship, within which these capacities will be enfolded and by dint of which they will become internalized. (p. 60)

However, there are modifications of traditional insight-oriented psychotherapy that are essential to transformative work with adult survivors of childhood sexual abuse. We identify seven specific components of an analytic trauma therapy that is relational and constructivist.

1. *An emphasis on the development of self capacities* (McCann & Pearlman, 1990b; see chapter 3), that is, development of affect tolerance and modulation, object constancy, and stability of benign self-regard. Survivors often have great difficulty tolerating their own emotional experience. In response to strong affect, they may feel flooded, dissociate, or "go numb." Powerful affects, which are experienced physiologically as well as emotionally, may lead to intense self-loathing and fears of abandonment or annihilation. Many survivors have little ability to self-soothe and turn to self-destructive or self-abusive behaviors to manage or eradicate disturbing affects. Attention to developing affect tolerance is a key element of psychotherapy with childhood abuse survivors.

2. *The therapist must be genuine and present emotionally.* Affective availability is not comfortable for all therapists. Therapists whose preferred demeanor is uninvolved, silent, expert, affectively distant, or completely anonymous will face a conflict between their manner and the demands of the therapy. Being genuine and affectively available means being open to our own and our clients' observation, acknowledging our mistakes, making countertransference disclosures when helpful, and being willing to be known by and vulnerable to a client as the work unfolds. It does not mean abandoning one's role as a therapist, or asking the client to take care of us, or bringing our needs into the relationship at the expense of our clients. However, it may mean being more disclosive of one's experience in the here and now.

3. *A primary focus on the development of the therapeutic relationship, rather than an exclusive focus on transference.* Survivors of severe childhood abuse cannot take the development of a healthy relationship for granted. Childhood sexual abuse often takes place in a context of neglect and physical, verbal, emotional, and psychological* abuse. The psychotherapy relationship becomes a forum for identifying relational losses, practicing relationship skills, and experiencing rewarding relationships that can offset despair learned long ago. This suggests a greater emphasis on the "real relationship" (Greenson, 1967) than is customary in classical therapies. Inviting the survivor client to notice the developing relationship contradicts his powerfully learned lessons not to notice, question, or challenge events in a relationship. As Balint (1969) argued, we have two major therapeutic methods: interpretation and the creation of the therapeutic relationship. "Compared with the first, the techniques for the second method have been much less well studied" (p. 435).

4. *The therapist must recognize that the management of transference differs somewhat in therapies with survivors of severe abuse from that with other clients.* In trauma therapy, the interpretation of transference should occur earlier, within the context of inviting the client to notice the process of bringing the past into the present. It is not generally useful to encourage a transference reaction to reach full affective force. Childhood trauma survivors' transferences are often malevolent or include feelings of terror,

---

*Psychological abuse includes attempting to drive someone crazy, to discredit someone's perceptions of reality or of his own experience, and to undermine his psychic integrity, psychological separateness, and ability to trust his own judgment (Nicarthy, 1982). Whereas emotional abuse includes verbal abuse and tirades of criticism, hurtful words, and actions designed to inflict emotional pain and shame, psychological abuse is similar to brainwashing, as its intent is to eradicate someone's autonomy and reality base and to assault his basic psychological functions.

dread, shame, rage, masochism, or sadism. They may reflect dissociated aspects of the client's self or of the perpetrator. Because of the undeveloped self capacities of many childhood abuse survivors, tolerating such intense affects may be impossible until much later in treatment and can severely disrupt the safety and trust being established. The process of sorting out transference- and present-based responses to people is part of the developmental work of psychotherapy for survivor clients.

5. *The therapist must understand the role of dissociation in trauma responses.* A therapist's awareness of the potential for dissociative processes permits her to notice dissociation when it occurs, to educate the client, and to recognize the interpersonal and intrapsychic anxiety that may provoke dissociative defenses. Without the premise of dissociation, many occurrences in these therapies remain unfathomable, or invite inaccurate and often pathologizing or shaming interpretations (Davies & Frawley, 1994). It is essential to integrate this understanding of dissociation into interpretations of interpersonal events in the therapy. Dissociation is an interpersonal event in the psychotherapy. Further, the client's complex and varied transference responses may be occurring outside of the client's awareness and reflect highly disconnected experiences of self and other.

6. *Psychoeducation* is extremely important, particularly information about the normal effects of traumatic events; management of common post-trauma symptoms and adaptations (flashbacks, memory fragments, dissociation); resources for survivors and their loved ones; expectable reactions to the treatment process itself (e.g., people often feel worse before they feel better); and normal child development, that is, typical behavior and psychological abilities at particular developmental stages. Imparting this information to survivor clients often helps them understand their adaptations to developmental conditions. Over time, the recognition of "symptoms" or "weaknesses" as adaptations to difficult circumstances creates a profound shift in a survivor's relationship to self and in his sense of meaning.

Survivors often have distorted expectations of themselves in both the present and the past. As they reconstruct their past, they often hold themselves as children to adult standards (or super-adult, i.e., to magical standards of omnipotence) without recognizing the real developmental limitations and abilities of a child of a given age. Clients are often brought up short when we ask whether they would expect a five-year-old child (for example) to be able to protect himself from an assaultive 200-pound adult male. For survivors who are parents, a broad understanding of normal child development is also very helpful. Because of a deep sense of not being normal, many survivors feel at sea when raising their own children. It is enormously reassuring to survivor parents to understand the natural course of children's growing awareness and exploration of their bodies, their sexuality, their fantasy lives, and intimate relationships.

7. *Frame and boundary negotiation.* Major therapeutic work with trauma survivor clients takes place in the process of negotiating therapeutic frame and boundaries. These therapies require a clear frame and boundaries that ideally are developed by client and therapist. Clients with severe damage in trust and safety in interpersonal relationships will struggle to have some control over closeness and distance and develop ways to maintain some control over their terror and their vulnerable self-esteem in the therapies. Therapists who work with survivors must address and negotiate respectfully certain boundary questions that arise (e.g., gifts, touch, length of sessions). This process of negotiation is clinically useful and enlightening to both client and therapist.

COUNTERTRANSFERENCE: A TOOL FOR UNDERSTANDING

Definitions of Countertransference

The extensive countertransference literature has been ably reviewed by many authors (e.g., Lane, 1986; Maroda, 1991; Racker, 1957; Wolstein, 1988). This literature is characterized by an ongoing debate about the definition and the components of countertransference. The more inclusive interpretations define countertransference as any response the therapist has to her client, positive or negative, conscious or unconscious, spoken or unspoken. The more focused interpretations define countertransference as those responses that are unconscious, that inhibit the therapist's ability to be therapeutic with the client, or that reflect the therapist's transference onto the client of significant relationships from the therapist's past.

Despite these differences, most definitions of countertransference include:

1. The therapist's affective response to her client (i.e., to client's identity, presentation, material, interpersonal style, history) (Ferenczi, 1950; Heimann, 1950; Maroda, 1991; Reik, 1948; Winnicott, 1949)
2. The therapist's transference to her client, based upon her own history (Cohen, 1952; Gitelson, 1952; Jacobs, 1991; Little, 1957; Reich, 1951)
3. The therapist's responses to the client's transference to the therapist (Jacobs, 1991; Little, 1957)
4. The therapist's defenses against her own affects or intrapsychic conflicts

aroused by her client and his material in the session (Freud, 1910; Jacobs, 1991; Maroda, 1991)

5. Any responses that hinder a therapist's ability to be therapeutic to her client or impede the therapy (Cohen, 1952)
6. The therapist's unconscious responses to her client (Little, 1957)

Our definition of countertransference includes two components: (1) the affective, ideational, and physical responses a therapist has to her client, his clinical material, transference, and reenactments, and (2) the therapist's conscious and unconscious defenses against the affects, intrapsychic conflicts, and associations aroused by the former. All of a client's responses and our responses to the client arise in the context of our role and professional identity as therapist, the unique nature of the therapeutic relationship, and our own personal histories.

Countertransference emerges at multiple levels of awareness, not only in our conscious thoughts and feelings, but also in conscious manifestations of unconscious and preconscious processes. Our attunement to our countertransference requires the same evenly hovering attention with which we listen to our clients' material.

Countertransference is part of every therapeutic relationship (regardless of the therapist's theoretical orientation). By definition, unrecognized and unanalyzed countertransference impedes our ability to be fully and actively present in the room with the client. Clinical work within the therapeutic relationship is predicated on our awareness of ourselves in the relationship, which requires countertransference attunement and analysis.

Countertransference can serve to make conscious that which is unconscious and bring dissociated affects into the room and the relationship. Dissociation is, of course, a front-line defense against trauma and therefore a central component of the psychological style of many adult survivors of interpersonal childhood trauma (van der Kolk & van der Hart, 1991). Thus, survivor clients are often unaware of their affective experience so that we, as therapists, are often first aware of our client's feelings through our own (Reik, 1937). We often hold rage, fear, grief, shame, and self-doubt for them. These affects are intense and often intolerable; if we cannot acknowledge and process them, we risk acting out in the therapy.

Countertransference responses can reflect projective identification processes through which we come to hold the client's rejected affects or aspects of self (Tansey & Burke, 1989). Our experience of the client's pain allows us to understand in a profound human way the client's early and current reality in relationships. This process can be very disturbing in psychother-

apy with adult survivors of childhood abuse; we are asked to feel threatened, terrified, devalued, objectified, ignored, and hated—on the other
hand we may be idealized and revered, and required to maintain a standard
of perfection that splits off any disconfirming aspect of our selves (Davies
& Frawley, 1994).

  To respond therapeutically to often intolerable interpersonal assaults
requires understanding of the subtle unconscious processes of the therapeutic relationship in trauma therapy as well as self-knowledge.

Example   One client started each therapy session with a complaint
about the therapist, usually suggesting that the therapy wasn't helping and
that it was probably the therapist's ineptitude that explained this. This
client's mother had blamed her for every negative event and feeling in the
family, including the sexual abuse she had experienced as a little girl. After
many months of feeling shame, guilt, defensiveness, and anger, sadistic
wishes to retaliate, and exhaustion, the therapist sought consultation. As
she came to recognize that devaluing the therapist was a reflection of the
client's self-loathing and certainty that the therapist was bound to reject her
eventually—and to blame her in the process, she could help her client also
recognize the fear and painful memories embedded in the reenactment. By
complaining about the therapist and the treatment, the client unconsciously
set a self-protective stage for the therapist's anticipated abandonment of
her. In addition, the client reenacted an aspect of her trauma by identifying
with her mother and projecting her faulty self onto the therapist. The therapist's subjective experience of failure, shame, and anger could easily have
led to blaming or rejecting the client had she failed to seek consultation and
identify a framework for understanding the projective identification and
reenactment.

  Countertransference is a part of all psychotherapy. However, psychotherapists who work with adult survivors of childhood abuse know that
this work evokes particularly powerful and complicated countertransference responses.

Factors Contributing to Countertransference
in Trauma Therapies

There are six significant contributing factors in any countertransference
response to a client with a history of childhood sexual trauma:

1. The therapist's response to the reality of incest and child abuse; the
   facts of child abuse and rape invite a variety of responses (see chapters 4
   and 6)

2. The therapist's responses to the client's transference, which will vary with both the nature of the transference and its consistency with her own experience of self (see chapters 5, 9, 10, 11, and 12)
3. The therapist's response to the client's particular post-trauma adaptation, e.g., numbing, flooding, dissociation, intrusive imagery and memories, repression, anxiety, chronic suicidal wishes, depression, despair, interpersonal mistrust, revictimization, self-loathing, etc. (see chapters 6, 7, 11, and 12)
4. The therapist's history, personality, coping style, and transference to the client (see chapters 8, 9, and 10)
5. The therapist's response to her own vicarious traumatization (see chapters 13, 14, and 15)
6. The therapist's theoretical perspective on trauma and relationship to her teachers and mentors in the field (Davies & Frawley, 1994) (see chapters 4, 12, 16)

Interwoven, these six threads create the fabric of our experience as therapists in psychotherapies with survivors of childhood sexual abuse.

The Therapist's Awareness
of Countertransference

Countertransference provides therapists with invaluable information to inform and shape their clinical interventions. Therapists can gather crucial diagnostic information through responses to unspoken, unconscious events in the therapy relationship. Our subjective experience of confusion and disorientation during history-taking, for example, often provides early clues about a client's lack of access to basic information or about his discomfort as he tries to hold contradictory pieces of information simultaneously. Awareness of our own dissociated affects after a session provides important diagnostic clues about the presence and use of dissociation in the client's psychological presentation.

In order to use countertransference productively, a therapist must be able to identify it without shame. Ongoing supervision or consultation ideally provides necessary opportunities to reflect on our own process. Greenson (1967) noted, "working alone with his patient and thus shielded from the scrutiny of his peers, [the analyst] is predisposed to a biased and uncritical attitude toward his own technique" (p. 4). In trauma therapy this isolation is dangerous to both the client and the therapist. In addition, the therapist's own extended insight-oriented personal psychotherapy is essential to self-knowledge, self-observation, and empathy for the vulnerability inherent in being a client.

ANALYZING COUNTERTRANSFERENCE

What does it mean to analyze one's countertransference? The first step is noticing one's full range of responses to a given client and psychotherapy relationship. The process of naming one's countertransference, initially to oneself, transforms an unconscious process into a conscious one. Once it is conscious, the therapist can analyze the countertransference by *tracing its sources*.

Noticing Countertransference

Countertransference is not simply manifest in the therapist's conscious thoughts and feelings; the therapist becomes aware of unconscious countertransference responses through noticing her own associational paths in sessions, fantasies in and out of sessions, parapraxes (slips of the tongue, etc.), clinical errors, dreams about the client, bodily sensations in sessions, identifications and desire not to identify with the client and his significant objects, and the client's responses to and observations about the therapist. Countertransference is evident in positive and negative thoughts and feelings about a client, which may run the gamut from sympathetic to pejorative, from love to hatred.

The therapist's unconscious defenses against her feelings are manifest in anxiety, behaviors that reflect conflict (forgetting appointment times or scheduled phone contacts, violating boundaries with the client, saying thoughtless things to or about the client, and so forth), dreams about the client, unprocessed frame changes (such as letting sessions run over or touching the client without discussing the meaning of these behaviors). Noticing these signs of conflict or countertransference creates an opportunity to move to a deeper level in the therapy. By reflecting on them and all of their possible sources and meanings, the therapist gains invaluable information about herself, the client, *and* their relationship.

Countertransference can also be detected in parallel process enactments in supervision. For example, the therapist may begin asking the supervisor for extra time or arriving late for supervision sessions, reflecting current dynamics or interactions in the therapeutic relationship. Countertransference may be detected in the therapist's use of language. The uncharacteristic use of certain words, whether in therapy sessions or in consultation about the therapy, may indicate a therapist's disowned responses to her client. This may be the language of love, of mothering, of fear, of dislike or disgust, or war or violence, of intimidation, of sensuality, or of any other feeling that one human may evoke in another.

Sometimes the therapist may become aware of split-off countertransference through her supervisor's language or responses to the client.

Example   A therapist had been working with a survivor client for two years, and was primarily aware of feelings of fondness and admiration for the client. When she presented the client in supervision, she was surprised by the supervisor's annoyance with the client. As her supervisor described her response to the client's need for control and subtle but constant denigration of the therapist and the therapy, the therapist realized how she herself regularly dismissed her responses to certain events in order to maintain the positive regard she felt the client needed from her. She realized she had colluded with the client's experience that anger would destroy connection (a belief that was also held in the therapist's family of origin), and thus deprived her client of the reparative work of negotiating anger in a relationship. Now the therapist could examine her previously disavowed anger at the client, first in the supervision and then in the therapy, and be open to the client's anger.

Exploring one's countertransference involves asking oneself whether this response feels unfamiliar, significant, unusual. What does the response tell you about feelings that may be out of your awareness? Does a particular dream stay with you? Are you behaving differently with this client than previously? than with other clients? Are the feelings more familiar to you in a different (e.g., nonclinical or historical) context? Do they seem alien or distressing or syntonic and comfortable? These questions invite the therapist's awareness and self-exploration which both deepen and expand her use of countertransference.

Sources of Countertransference

Countertransference responses spring from a variety of sources. The therapist may respond to the client's presentation, including his physical appearance, interpersonal style, and affective style; she may respond to the way the client relates to himself (e.g., a self-deprecating style in the client may evoke a flattering or reassuring response from the therapist), or the way he responds to her. Over time, each therapist becomes familiar with the responses and transferences she typically evokes in clients. She may then have noteworthy responses to unique or unfamiliar client responses. The particular trauma material or the client's adaptation to his traumatic experiences often evoke powerful countertransference responses.

Within the therapist, countertransference responses arise from specific aspects of the self of the therapist, such as (1) the therapist's identity (including gender and body image), inner life, personal history (including trauma history), personality, defensive style, psychological needs, morals and values, and spirituality, (2) the therapist's current life context, and (3) the therapist's professional identity, context and particular theories of trauma and therapy.

The therapist's identity includes her gender and gender identity (i.e., beliefs about her gender, what it means to her to be female), her relationship with her body, her experience of herself as a person, mother (father), daughter (son), a person of worth, her ego ideal, and so forth. A therapist's degree of comfort and familiarity with her own inner life, fantasies, and affects, particularly strong experiences of longing, aggression, sexuality, grief, rage, terror, love, and hate, will influence her awareness and acknowledgment of countertransference responses.

Personal history includes the therapist's family context, key early relationships, sibling order and role, childhood abuse history, and other life experiences (both traumatic and otherwise). Her moral principles, assumptions about causality, values, and sense of spirituality influence her response to events in the therapeutic relationship. These elements, tempered by the therapist's internalization of her social and cultural context, also inform countertransference responses.

Current life context includes the therapist's intrapsychic and interpersonal contexts, including her level of satisfaction with intimate relationships with herself and others, family life, parenting, partner roles, psychological health, physical health, substance use—in short, her current experience and contentment with herself and her relationships. Clearly, life crises such as personal illness or family illness, marriage or commitment, divorce or separation, deaths, childbirth or adoption, job condition changes, home changes, and crises for friends, partners, or family members all contribute to stress, vulnerability, and distractibility and may emerge in a variety of overt and covert ways in our ongoing therapy relationships (Fromm-Reichmann, 1960).

Finally, the therapist's professional identity and place in her professional development influence her responses to her clients.* The new trauma therapist will have different responses to her clients than the seasoned therapist. The clinician's internalized professional ego ideal will influence her responses as well. Therapists struggle at times with conflicts between their natural responses and those they deem worthy of or appropriate to themselves as psychotherapists, that is, those responses they learned from mentors or fantasies of idealized mentors as role models (Casement, 1991; Davies & Frawley, 1994).

Another aspect of the professional self of the therapist influencing countertransference is theory.† A therapist may accept more calmly those client behaviors that fit within her theory; conversely, she may react with confu-

---

*Discussed in detail in chapter 16.
†Thanks to Andrew Chirchirillo, Ph.D. for suggesting this specific source of countertransference.

sion or distress to behaviors not predicted or described by her theory. If the theory deems certain adaptations "pathological" or "psychotic," the therapist will respond to their emergence differently than if she views them as a normal adaptation. In fact, theoretical paradigm shifts in the field, create a climate ripe for this countertransference dilemma.*

Of course, a key source of countertransference is the interaction between client and therapist within the therapeutic relationship. A therapist's countertransference to a client's transference is a relational countertransference. When a therapist identifies a specific countertransference response, she needs to consider its relational context. Is it a time of deepening connection between therapist and client? Is a separation anticipated (e.g., vacation or other break)? Has an important piece of work begun or been completed recently? Examining the contextual factors of a particular countertransference response provides clues to its meaning.

Using Countertransference

As the therapist identifies the various sources of her countertransference, she can reconnect her response to a particular client and therapeutic relationship. She can explore how her response either facilitates or inhibits her empathy for or understanding of him. Based on this analysis, the therapist can devise a technical strategy. How does understanding this response allow the therapist to make an internal shift that allows her to hear the client more clearly? Would disclosure of the countertransference response or part of it be helpful to the client, the therapeutic relationship, or the therapy process? Does this countertransference response need further processing with a supervisor or consultant? Does it warrant further discussion in the therapist's own psychotherapy or indicate a need for the therapist to return to psychotherapy? Does it indicate areas to explore further with the client, historically, thematically, or interpersonally? Does it inform an interpretation the therapist may offer the client in the future? Throughout the book, we will offer specific examples of this process of countertransference analysis.

Example   A female survivor client came to her first session expressing little hope, but dogged determination to be less isolated and to enjoy life more. She was dressed in stained baggy clothes and seemed unaware of her dishevelled looks. She complained bitterly of other people's unkindness to her and catalogued multiple examples of injuries and wrongs done her. She ignored the end of the session and continued to talk even after repeated

---

*Discussed further in the following chapters.

attempts at closure by the therapist. Over the initial sessions, the therapist found herself feeling revulsion at the client's physical presence and irritation with her apparent entrenched victim identity. She realized she had rarely felt such strong negative reactions to a new client.

She felt uncomfortable and ashamed of these responses and tried to ignore them hoping they would recede. When they did not, she tried to notice the details of her client's physical presence that so repelled her. She recognized the painful absence of self-pride and connection represented by the woman's lack of self-care. She winced at both the historical and current implications of neglect and disrespect. She then shifted her attention to her own experience, realizing the client's martyr stance was similar to her older sister's approach to life. She had often been the object of blame and reproach when her sister felt envious of her belongings, friends, and achievements. She realized she was dreading what she perceived as an inevitable transference of blame, reproach, and thinly disguised envy from this client. At the same time, she saw she was moving ahead of the client by anticipating the relationship that was still forming.

Finally, in consultation (which the therapist sought while deciding whether to refer the client to another therapist), she realized that the client was frustrating all of her attempts to convey hope or to connect empathically with her, just as the therapist's own sister had frustrated her attempts to be accepted and gain her approval. She felt simultaneously defeated and blamed, shut out and devalued, just as she had felt in her family where no one saw her struggle.

After identifying these several sources of her countertransference, the therapist's negative feelings began to recede. She considered how to use the information therapeutically. Eventually, she shared with the client her perception that the client was extremely ambivalent about getting close to people, as reflected by her inattention to her person, her reluctance to hope, and her need to talk over the therapist. The therapist acknowledged that people who have been hurt badly in early relationships protect themselves later on in a variety of ways, some of which may no longer serve their needs in adulthood. She suggested that the client's strong identity as a victim was self-protective, a way to preemptively ward off further disappointment and garner support and sympathy that was missing in childhood. As the discussion continued and the therapist saw she had captured her client's interest, she acknowledged that this victim stance had put her off, thus cutting the client off from the very intimacy she craved as the therapist felt defensive and distant rather than open and curious.

The therapist normalized the client's need for self-protection. By framing the client's behavior as self-protective and positively intended, she invited them both to relate in a nonshaming and nonblaming way. This was curative for both therapist and client as she also worked through her own position of shame in a transmutative interpretation from the countertransference (Kohut, 1971, 1977). Because of this, the client was able to hear these countertransference disclosures nondefensively, and the relationship and the therapy moved forward. The therapist was intrigued to notice that her perception of her client began to shift, She found herself looking forward to sessions because as she felt able to bring herself more fully to the relationship, her interactions with the client became lively and moving.

VICARIOUS TRAUMATIZATION

It is clear that a therapist cannot completely address countertransference in trauma therapy without exploring a phenomenon we have called "vicarious traumatization" (McCann & Pearlman, 1990a). Vicarious traumatization refers to the cumulative transformative effect upon the trauma therapist of working with survivors of traumatic life events. Although we will primarily discuss vicarious traumatization in psychotherapists, the phenomenon is relevant to all trauma workers, including emergency medical technicians, fire fighters, police, criminal defense lawyers, medical personnel, battered women's and homeless shelter staff, sexual assault workers, suicide hotline staff, AIDS volunteers, prison personnel, and trauma researchers, as well as journalists, clergy, and others who engage empathically with victims and survivors.

Definition of Vicarious Traumatization

The construct of vicarious traumatization will be explored in depth in later chapters; at this point, we want to convey a general understanding of the far-reaching effects of trauma therapy on the self of the therapist. Vicarious traumatization was first described by McCann and Pearlman (1990a) who noted the pervasive effects of doing trauma therapy on the identity, world view, psychological needs, beliefs, and memory system of the therapist. As a result of our exposure to the realities of trauma in the world, we are changed. *Vicarious traumatization is the transformation in the inner experience of the therapist that comes about as a result of empathic engagement with clients' trauma material.* This material includes graphic descriptions of violent events, exposure to the realities of people's cruelty to one another, and involvement in trauma related reenactments, either as a participant or as a bystander. It includes being a helpless witness to past events and sometimes present reenactments. We do not assign blame to clients for our experience of vicarious traumatization. Rather, we view it as an occupational hazard, an inevitable effect of trauma work.

Our clients' vivid and sometimes graphic descriptions of their brutal victimizations contribute to our vicarious traumatization. While it is often essential to their healing for clients to share specific traumatic images, we can carry these with us and they may at times appear to us, unbidden, as clear as our own internal images.

Therapy with survivors of childhood abuse confronts us as therapists and members of the human community with the harsh, painful reality of cruelty, selfishness, and evil actions. In order to share with our clients their journeys to reclaim their truth, minds, and bodies, we must be open. Without this commitment, the client cannot commit himself fully to the treatment (Little, 1957). Yet our empathy is a source of our vulnerability to emotional pain and scarring.

We cannot protect ourselves from knowing the atrocities that happened, and we cannot protect our clients from what they have already experienced. This often leaves us in a position of helpless witness to trauma, which is itself traumatic (Herman et al., 1989; Vissing, Straus, Gelles, & Harrop, 1991). Our helplessness is more painful when our clients are locked in repetitive self-destructive reenactments during the therapy. Exposure to and participation in these reenactments is an additional, independent contributor to vicarious traumatization. Reenactments sometimes take the form of witnessing a client's repeated self-destructive behaviors yet being unable to protect him or oneself from the trauma. Reenactments include interactions in which the client unconsciously sets himself up to feel victimized, rejected, or abandoned by the therapist, or in which the therapist unwittingly repeats abusive or neglectful behaviors with the client, or in which the client takes the role of perpetrator, treating the therapist in a sadistic way that is a reflection of his traumatic childhood.

Finally, any trauma inevitably involves traumatic loss of loved others, of dreams, of innocence, of childhood, of undiminished body and mind; after a trauma nothing is ever again the same. This profound loss of the familiar is a hallmark of trauma. As therapists, we confront this reality daily and thus must face daily the potential for such loss in our own lives and in the lives of those we love. Trauma therapy assaults our self-protective beliefs about safety, control, predictability, and attachment.

Vicarious traumatization is a process not an event. It includes our affects and defenses against the affects. That is, it is our strong reactions of grief and rage and outrage which grow over time as we hear repeatedly about the torture, humiliation, and betrayal people perpetrate against others, and also our sorrow, our numbing, and our deep sense of loss which follow those reactions.

If we do not identify and address the risk of vicarious traumatization, we run the danger of not recognizing its effects on our work and therefore our clients. We must understand these normal and predictable responses in order to be free to identify ameliorative strategies and to provide support for our colleagues and students. To protect clients, therapists, and the profession, we have an ethical imperative to acknowledge and address vicarious traumatization.

Vicarious traumatization also carries a social cost. Many people become psychotherapists because they are hopeful about humanity and the possibilities for a better world. Unaddressed vicarious traumatization, manifest in cynicism and despair, results in a loss to society of that hope and the positive actions it fuels. This loss can be experienced by our clients, as we at times join them in their despair; by our friends and families, as we no longer interject optimism, joy, and love into our shared pursuits; and in the larger systems in which we were once active as change agents, and which we may now leave, or withdraw from emotionally in a state of disillusionment and resignation.

THE COUNTERTRANSFERENCE-VICARIOUS TRAUMATIZATION CYCLE

While vicarious traumatization and countertransference are distinct constructs and experiences, *they affect one another*. Countertransference is present in all therapies, representing the therapist's conscious and unconscious responses. It is specific to a given client and the particular therapist-client dyad, and is related to personal conflicts and psychological needs within the therapist. Countertransference provides information about the unique aspects of the therapist and the client in the therapeutic relationship.

Vicarious traumatization is specific to trauma therapy and is the result of an accumulation of experiences across therapies. Its effects are felt beyond a particular therapy relationship, both in other therapy relationships and in the therapist's personal and professional life. A therapist's self-protective responses to vicarious traumatization are evident across all relationships and settings. Vicarious traumatization is permanently transformative, while countertransference is temporally and temporarily linked to a particular period, event, or issue in the therapy or in the therapist's inner or external life as it interacts with the therapy.

Vicarious traumatization and countertransference affect one another in a variety of ways. Vicarious traumatization represents changes in the most intimate psychological workings of the self of the therapist. The self of the therapist is the context for all of her countertransference responses. Thus vicarious traumatization invariably shapes countertransference.

We explore the interaction between countertransference and vicarious traumatization in chapter 15. Here, we want to emphasize that countertransference and vicarious traumatization are highly interrelated experiences. As a therapist experiences increasing levels of vicarious traumatization, her countertransference responses can become stronger and/or less available to conscious awareness. This interaction creates a spiral with potentially disastrous results for the treatment, often resulting in a therapeutic impasse. In addition, it can result in increased vicarious traumatization, with dire consequences for the personal and professional life of the therapist, including loss of personal relationships and preventable job or career changes.

Both countertransference and vicarious traumatization are inevitable processes in psychotherapy with adult survivors of childhood sexual abuse. They are part of the unique contributions of the therapist to the development of the therapeutic relationship. The therapist's attunement to her influence on the therapeutic relationship and the impact of her work on herself is essential to the maintenance of a therapy that is respectful to and safe for both participants.

2

Psychoanalytic Theory and Psychological Trauma: Historical and Critical Review

PSYCHOANALYSIS AND PSYCHOLOGICAL TRAUMA are linked historically and theoretically. From time to time, scholars committed to one or the other of these fields of study have been pitted as adversaries against one another (e.g., asserting that all psychoanalysts interpret trauma material as fantasy); at other times, their differences have been minimized and the fields seen as interchangeable (e.g., asserting that a therapist needs no special training in psychological trauma because one should work with trauma material exactly as one works with any clinical material). Neither position is completely accurate. In fact, historically psychoanalysis has both contributed to and impeded our understanding of the etiological role of trauma in psychopathology and psychological distress, and the psychological treatment of the same.

While psychoanalysis has provided the bedrock for effective psychotherapy with survivors of psychological trauma, it has also set the stage for appalling examples of retraumatizing treatments. How can the same theory both inform and detract from our understanding of traumatogenic factors in psychopathology? How can it both create and impede the development of a therapeutic alliance in these treatments? This chapter explores the historical and developmental context for these paradoxes and, with the following chapter, identifies the contributions of psychoanalysis to an integrative trauma theory, constructivist self development theory (CSDT).

PSYCHOANALYSIS AND TRAUMA THEORIES*

As in the larger society, the recognition within psychoanalysis of traumatic antecedents to psychological symptomatology and distress has emerged, faded, and reemerged across time. The development of many key ideas in both psychoanalysis and trauma theory started in France in the late nineteenth century; the fields of psychoanalysis and trauma then diverged, became parallel, and are now reconverging. As the threads of psychoanalytic and trauma theories separated, psychoanalysis became the realm for understanding the intrapsychic. This move away from the interpersonal is key to understanding the impediments to recovery posed by psychoanalytic theory and practice.

On the other hand, trauma theories have shifted from the individual—with a focus on dissociation and altered states of consciousness—to event-focused work with survivors of combat, natural disasters, and the Nazi Holocaust, and then to population- or victim-centered work with crime victims and victims of sexual assault and domestic violence. Trauma theorists have emphasized cognitive (Epstein, 1994, 1985; Horowitz, 1986; Janoff-Bulman, 1992), behavioral (Keane, Zimering, & Caddell, 1985; Kilpatrick, Veronen, & Resick, 1982), and biological (van der Kolk, 1988) perspectives.† The resulting theories omitted or often underemphasized the interaction between the traumatic event and the particular individual experiencing it.

Psychoanalysis is not a single entity; several schools within psychoanalysis emerged as the field developed and different developmental lines or viewpoints predominated. As these various schools of psychoanalysis evolved, the interpersonal world reasserted itself, theoretically and therapeutically. Yet each school has contributed concepts essential in trauma therapy. For example, the early emphasis on the centrality of the body to

*Thanks to the members of the Western Massachusetts Association of Psychoanalytic Psychologists for their helpful comments.
†For more thorough reviews of this literature, see Herman, 1992 and McCann & Pearlman, 1990b. We refer those interested in the trauma literature to Bard & Sangrey, 1986; Brett & Ostroff, 1985; Burgess & Holmstrom, 1974; Danieli, 1985; Gleser, Green, & Winget, 1981; Kahana, Harel, & Kahana, 1988; Keane, Fairbank, Caddell, Zimering, & Bender, 1985; Lindy, 1988; Roth & Lebowitz, 1988; van der Kolk & van der Hart, 1991; Walker, 1985; and Wilson & Raphael, 1993.

psychological experience outlined in the original drive theory is critical and too often overlooked in trauma work (Attias & Goodwin, 1993; Saakvitne, 1992). The components of the structural model (id, ego, and superego) reintroduce the relationship of the self to the external world (ego) and include precursors of internalized objects (superego). The topographical model (conscious, preconscious, and unconscious) returns to earlier questions of states of consciousness, but with the horizontal framework of repression rather than a vertical framework of dissociation (van der Kolk & van der Hart, 1991). Ego psychologists' emphasis on identity, psychological defenses, adaptation, and child development has contributed significantly to the current recognition of symptoms as adaptations.

Object relations theory elaborated concepts of introjection, internalization, and identification in the context of developmental theory. The concepts of object relationships and object relational paradigms are fundamental to our current understanding of reenactments. Interpersonal psychiatry, the American variant of object relations theory, emphasizes interpersonal relationships and fluidity between the past and the present, and identifies the therapeutic relationship, an intersubjective reality, as a place for exploring the interpersonal experience, including distortions in the present relationship that stem from past relationships. Self psychology emphasizes the concept and integrity of the self and focuses on disorders of self-esteem and self-regulation, and the relation between self and other. The later schools increasingly attend to the person of the therapist and the concept of countertransference.

More recent integrative theories include the self-in-relation, or relational, model (Jordan et al., 1991; Miller, 1976) which emphasizes the psychology of women's development, and constructivist self development theory (McCann & Pearlman, 1990b), a comprehensive personality theory which integrates psychoanalytic and social cognition theories of trauma. These theories integrate psychoanalytic and psychological theories with an understanding of the individual in his or her developmental, social, and cultural context.

FOUR PARALLEL DEVELOPMENTAL LINES*

There are four major overlapping developmental lines central to both psychoanalysis and current trauma theory:

*We borrow the term *developmental line* from Anna Freud's work on developmental lines of childhood, that is parallel and overlapping areas of development (1963).

1. The causal link between childhood sexual trauma and adult symptomatology
2. The elaboration of states of consciousness, specifically the psychological mechanisms of dissociation and repression
3. The recognition that unconscious object relational paradigms reemerge in transference, reenactments, and the repetition compulsion
4. The awareness of the impact of the person of the therapist on the therapeutic process and the concept of countertransference

All four key ideas emerged and were developed or augmented in both the psychoanalytic and trauma literatures and remain central in clinical work with trauma survivor clients.

Childhood Sexual Trauma and Adult Symptomatology

The first developmental line was stated in Freud's (1896) seduction theory. Freud, Breuer, Charcot, and Janet all studied a range of phenomena grouped under the rubric of hysteria, which included dissociation, fugue states, traumatic memories, abreaction, somatization, conversion disorders, constricted affect (sometimes referred to as "la belle indifference"), and flooded affect (all now associated with post-trauma symptomatology). They identified somatic, affective, and cognitive processes of dissociation, repression, and displacement. Out of this work, Freud concluded that the psychoneuroses in general, and hysteria in particular, had their roots in traumatic sexual seductions in childhood; that is, the seduction theory. Although, he later disclaimed the centrality or the *universality* of trauma in the etiology of neuroses, in fact Freud never abandoned (as some have claimed; Masson, 1984) the recognition of actual childhood sexual trauma (Demause, 1991; Levine, 1990), and his work "Studies in Hysteria" (Breuer & Freud, 1893–1895) marked the beginning of the theory of psychoanalysis. Freud's shift away from the seduction theory moved him toward concepts of intrapsychic functioning, psychic reality, fantasy, and compromise formation, creating the psychological theory of psychoanalysis. Theoretically, it was a move inward, away from the interpersonal toward the intrapsychic. For the next eight decades, this move had significant implications for clinicians' understanding of the place of traumatic experiences in individual psychic functioning.

States of Consciousness

The second related developmental line is the elaboration of states of consciousness, focusing on the availability and integration of cognition, affect, memory, and knowledge. This inquiry concentrated initially on hypnosis, repression, and dissociation. At the end of the nineteenth century, hypnosis was in vogue and much effort was extended to understand the parameters of consciousness, mentation, identity, memory, and suggestibility. Freud, Breuer, and Janet each pursued somewhat different topical arenas. Freud elaborated the concept of repression; Breuer, an altered state of consciousness he termed a "hypnoid state"; and Janet, the process of dissociation (1919; van der Hart, Brown, & van der Kolk, 1989; van der Kolk & van der Hart, 1991; Waites, 1993).

While dissociation and repression are key concepts in psychoanalysis and trauma literature, they have evolved in different directions. The terms were used interchangeably by many early psychoanalytic writers, including Freud himself, creating some confusion. Both dissociation and repression are viewed as protective psychological responses employed in the face of intolerable arousal which threatens to overwhelm the individual's ego, sense of self, and psychic integrity. Dissociation is traditionally viewed as a response to external threat (initially) and repression as a response to an internal threat.

Davies and Frawley (1994) discuss several distinctions between the two processes. They conclude that repression is a more cohesive, single-action defense, enacted upon coherent mental contents kept from awareness through signal anxiety and symptom formation, while dissociation represents a failure to process and metabolize events. Dissociation signifies the absence of protective signal functions, and ultimately "foreclosure" of psychic elaboration and developmental processes.

> Repression is an active process through which the ego attains mastery over conflictual material. Dissociation, on the other hand, is the last ditch effort of an overwhelmed ego to salvage some semblance of adequate mental functioning. . . . Repression brings about the forgetting of once familiar mental contents (i.e., events, affects, identifications, etc.). Dissociation on the other hand, leads to severing the connection between one set of mental contents and another. (p. 65)

Current trauma treatment literature emphasizes the necessity that the therapist working with trauma survivors have a conceptual understanding of the process and functions of dissociation (Braun, 1986; Davies & Frawley, 1994; Putnam, 1989; Waites, 1993).*

---

*Dissociative defenses are discussed further in chapter 6.

Transference, Reenactments, and
the Repetition Compulsion

A third developmental line in the parallel history of psychoanalysis and trauma theory is the emergence of the concept of transference, theoretically linked to unconscious object relational paradigms, reenactment, and the repetition compulsion. This line also began in the early work with women "hysterics," many of whom we have reason to believe were adult survivors of childhood sexual abuse (Herman, 1992; Lewis, 1976; Waites, 1993). These ideas flourished especially in the context of object relations theory with its emphasis on the potency of early attachments and object relational paradigms.

Breuer's work with Anna O. and Freud's work with Dora both represent famous cases of transference gone awry (and also probably cases in which the therapist's failure to identify the role of childhood sexual abuse in the treatment and treatment relationship had a profound negative effect on the treatment outcome). Both men were taken aback by the intensity of their female patients' responses to them. Breuer fled the treatment. Freud became entrenched and provoked Dora to flee the treatment. Only later did Freud begin to understand the complex powerful phenomenon of transference, setting the stage for the development of the concept of therapeutic relationship.* Levine (1990) reminds us that Freud developed the seduction theory before he recognized the process of transference, and that his therapeutic technique at that time was "forceful, positive, and determined," including for example the pressure technique in which he pressed on a patient's forehead to stimulate thoughts and memories, as well as verbal insistence or bullying:

> it would not be too far afield to surmise that such forceful intrusions were, in at least some instances, countertransference enactments in which a childhood sexual trauma was symbolically being repeated. (p. 7)

But the complexity of the concept of transference and the blend of conscious (here-and-now relationship) with unconscious (transference, projective identifications) factors did not receive extensive attention until the confluence of several developments with psychology and psychoanalysis.

---

*Therapeutic relationship is not a concept that Freud named or elaborated specifically, but it had its beginnings in the development of the concept of transference (Kahn, 1991).

These converging developments included the emergence of object relations theory (Fairbairn, 1954; Klein, 1975; Mahler, Pine, & Bergman, 1975; Winnicott, 1958) and interpersonal psychiatry (Fromm-Reichmann, 1960; Sullivan, 1953), the elaboration of the concept of countertransference (Benedek, 1953; Heimann, 1950; Little, 1957; Racker, 1957), the evolution of concepts of empathy, genuineness, unconditional positive regard, and nondefensiveness (Gill, 1982, 1983; Rogers, 1951), and the elaboration of self psychology (Kohut, 1971; Stolorow, Brandchaft, & Atwood, 1987).

Increasingly, trauma literature emphasizes the inevitability of unconscious reenactments of traumatic relational paradigms in these treatments (Blank, 1985b; Chu, 1992, Courtois, 1988; Herman, 1992; McCann & Pearlman, 1990b; van der Kolk, 1989; Waites, 1993). One cannot work successfully with trauma survivor clients without an understanding of these inescapable transference and reenactment dynamics.

Countertransference and the Person of the Therapist

A fourth developmental line common within psychoanalysis and trauma theory is the concept of countertransference. This concept is central in the evolution of the concepts of therapeutic alliance and therapeutic relationship. Freud began to bring the person of the therapist into the analysis with the concept of countertransference. The literature on treatment of trauma survivors increasingly recognizes that the therapist's powerful feelings and internal process are critical components of the treatment. Because countertransference is a focus of this book, we will elaborate its history below.

History of Countertransference

Freud first used the term "counter-transference" in his 1910 paper, "The Future Prospects of Psycho-Analytic Therapy," where he emphasized the therapist's need for self-analysis to eradicate countertransference.

> We have become aware of the 'counter-transference', which arises in him [the therapist] as a result of the patient's influence on his unconscious feelings, and we are almost inclined to insist that he shall recognize this counter-transference in himself and overcome it. . . . we have noticed that no psycho-analyst goes further than his own complexes and internal resistances permit; and we consequently require that he shall begin his activity with a self-analysis and continually carry it deeper while he is making his observations on his patients.

Anyone who fails to produce results in a self-analysis of this kind may at once give up any idea of being able to treat patients by analysis. (Freud, 1910, pp. 144–145)

Freud viewed the therapist's response as a hindrance to the analysis and advocated "overcoming" any intrusion of the analyst's self into the analysis. He emphasized a focus on the patient's response (the transference), and thus believed the therapist should maintain a neutral, blank screen presence in order to facilitate the transference process. Therefore the focus of the psychotherapeutic process was to interpret the transference, and the therapist's role was to be a mirror, a blank screen, an uninvolved expert. This belief and emphasis on neutrality continued in the field for several decades (Wachtel, 1982). It is worth noting that this approach, in fact, does not reflect Freud's actual practice, as is clear in his many detailed descriptions of his clinical work (Freud, 1905, 1909a, 1909b; Gay, 1988; Jones, 1953–1957).

In the 1950s there was a surge of interest in the person of the therapist, evident in the increased attention to both the therapeutic relationship and the concept of countertransference. Scholarly discussions of the concept of countertransference exploded, with several groundbreaking papers and multiple conferences on the topic. Interestingly, many key papers were written by prominent female psychoanalysts such as Paula Heimann, Margaret Little, Annie Reich, Frieda Fromm-Reichmann, Mabel Blake Cohen, Theresa Benedek, and Clara Thompson. The William Alanson White Institute, a psychoanalytic institute with a strong interpersonal (Sullivanian) emphasis, sponsored several forums for discussion and elaboration of the concept of countertransference. Margaret Little wrote, "At first, like transference, [countertransference] was regarded as something dangerous and undesirable, but nevertheless unavoidable. Nowadays it is even respectable!" (1957, p. 253)

Benjamin Wolstein, editor of *Essential Papers on Countertransference*, suggested this surge of interest arose from post-Freudian developments in the theory of psychoanalysis.

Ego psychology, object relations, and interpersonal relations rebuilt the structure of psychoanalytic inquiry under the adaptive or consensual point of view. Consistently followed, these perspectives brought countertransference into evidence and made it readily available for exploration in all future psychoanalysis. The change may be epitomized as follows: If adaptive or consensual observation moved psychoanalysts in closer relational proximity to their patients, it also moved patients into closer relational proximity to their psychoanalysts. During the adaptive or consensual study of their external relations, they expanded clinical psychoanalytic inquiry into unexpected internal directions. As psychoanalysts and patients began to experience one another as coparticipants in a shared field of inquiry—both, now capable of participant observation—they found they could do it from both sides of the field. And they became both participant observers and observed participants with one another. (1988, p. 11)

Countertransference literature flourished from the early 1950s to the early 1960s, then diminished markedly. Greenson (1967) suggested that the therapist's fear of his own pathology and primitive affects leads to fear and misuse of countertransference. Similarly, Wolstein posited that the shift away from an awareness of countertransference reflected "unacknowledged yet pressing and unremitting counteranxiety" (1988, p. 11). Framing it positively, Gill (1983) noted that the analyst must feel secure in order to acknowledge countertransference attitudes; this acknowledgment then sets the stage for deeper work. This retreat from the topic of countertransference likely also reflected anxiety and shame stemming from the unrealistic expectation that a good therapist will be "perfectly analyzed" and without conflict or neurosis.

The development of self psychology in the 1970s again led to the awareness of the self of the analyst as a realm for analytic inquiry. Theoretically, self psychology makes room for issues of self-esteem and self-in-relationship in ways that decrease the emphasis on pathology and solely intrapsychic processes. It is perhaps more palatable to include the self of the therapist as we normalize the needs of the self and as we conceptualize human psychology within the larger context of human relationships. As we allow our clients to be more real and complex, we ourselves may also be more real and complex. More recently, as part of the rediscovery of the therapeutic relationship and emphasis on a nonauthoritarian stance by the therapist (Maroda, 1991; Stiver, 1992), the discussion of countertransference includes an emphasis on mutuality and authenticity in the therapeutic relationship (Bollas, 1987; Elkind, 1992; Jacobs, 1991; Jordan et al., 1991; Stolorow et al., 1987).

MAJOR CONTRIBUTIONS TO TRAUMA THERAPY
BY PSYCHOANALYTIC THEORY

Many if not most of our fundamental premises about insight-oriented psychotherapy with trauma survivors—what it is, how it works, and why it works—are originally psychoanalytic in origin. Because the foundation of any insight-oriented psychotherapy is psychoanalytic theory, and because the developmental processes of trauma theory and psychoanalysis are so closely linked, we can identify specific aspects of psychoanalytic theory and technique that inform trauma theory and therapy in general, and CSDT specifically.

The Influence of the Past Upon the Present

The fact that current relationships are influenced by internalized objects and object relationships is a fundamental psychoanalytic concept essential to understanding transference and reenactments in trauma therapies. Present relationships inevitably contain within them attempts to recall, understand, and transform previous important relationships. The therapy relationship will call forth these unconscious organizing principles and provide the context in which they can be made conscious through naming and elaboration. This relatively simple idea elegantly incorporates a developmental perspective and sets the stage for the recognition of the roles that unconscious processes and early relationships play in adult functioning and identity.

Transference

The theoretical concept of transference and the technical issues of interpreting and working through transference in the therapy are topics that have been richly developed in the psychoanalytic literature. Transference reflects an internalized expectation, learned from earlier key relationships, which is seemingly fulfilled in the therapeutic relationship and experienced with intensified affect. The elaboration of object relational paradigms in transference is central to insight-oriented psychotherapy with trauma survivors. Repetition compulsion, a central psychoanalytic concept, plays a role in transference enactments when they represent attempts to master past experiences. Reenactment is a specific repetition of a traumatic event, and can be conceptualized as representing an unconscious way of remembering, knowing, communicating, or integrating through reliving. When interpersonal trauma is part of a client's relational history and intrapsychic object world, the early emergence in the therapy of intense transference dynamics is inevitable.

Developmental Perspective

In order to understand the impact of early childhood events, the therapist and client have to reconstruct not only many of the events, but also the developmental context of the events. Child analysts and developmental psychoanalytic theorists have contributed enormously to our understanding of the complexity and intractability of trauma-related symptoms. The heart of a psychotherapy with a survivor of childhood trauma is the development of the client's empathic understanding of his developmental experience and the integration of the meaning of childhood events with his present identity and interpersonal world.

Individual Differences

The developmental perspective of psychoanalysis implies the importance of individual differences. Each person has different and unique perceptions and experiences influenced at different levels of awareness by internal objects, conflicts, defenses, and identifications. This tenet is essential to current trauma theories. It is integrated into the basic definition of psychological trauma as an event that overwhelms the individual's *perceived* ability to cope (McCann & Pearlman, 1990b). A corollary is that the experience of an event as traumatic is also individual, determined by the unique interaction of the event with the person's perception of the event and his ability to cope with it. The uniqueness of each individual is self-evident given the complexity of conscious, unconscious, biological, interpersonal, and cultural influences on each person.

Unconscious Processes

The second premise of psychoanalytic theory central to both trauma therapy and CSDT is that people are influenced by factors out of their awareness. Unconscious aspects of oneself and one's experience affect actions, feelings, and identity. Unconscious factors influence us both directly and indirectly through psychological defenses, and compromise formations between instincts and prohibitions. The classic goal of psychoanalysis, to make the unconscious conscious, is reflected in the goal of trauma therapy: to allow our clients to reclaim split-off, dissociated, and repressed aspects of themselves and their experiences in order to relinquish their intense suffering for the experience of what Freud termed common misery.

Symptoms as Adaptive

Psychoanalytic theory conceptualized symptoms as compromise formations, that is, responses to intolerable intrapsychic conflict between drives, wishes, or experiences and prohibitions or fears. Symptoms reflected defense mechanisms against intrapsychic conflict and the defenses used were consistent with the personality and history of the individual (A. Freud, 1967). Psychological defenses were mobilized in the service of protecting the psyche. Thus, symptoms were originally viewed as adaptive, not random or simply biological events. A particular symptom was linked to a specific conflict, need, personality style, and experience. This premise leads to the therapeutic question, How does the individual's present experience make sense in the context of his past and intrapsychic dynamics?

A trauma survivor's symptoms reflect the unique manifestations of his psychological needs and resources in the context of his past and current life conditions. Symptoms reflect the *adaptive* response of each individual to the demands of a traumatic experience; thus, in every symptom is a solution, something life affirming and protective of self and relationships. The therapeutic task is then to understand to what problem this symptom is a solution and in what developmental context it emerged. Without this framework, psychotherapy with trauma survivors can become a series of symptom-focused interventions with no recognition of a whole person. Viewing symptoms as adaptations rather than pathologies, as potential strengths rather than inherent weaknesses, sets the tone for a treatment aimed at restoring self-esteem, self-love, and self-confidence.

The Centrality of the Body in Psychological Experience

Freud elaborated the idea of the body as the center of psychological experiences in his original formulations of drive theory, although later schools of psychoanalysis moved away from this idea. The integration of the physical into the psychological is critical to trauma therapy (Attias & Goodwin, 1993; Saakvitne, 1992). This assertion is a major contribution of drive theory to trauma theory. The recognition that the body is the avenue of experience, that affect is experienced in and through the body, that need and desire are experienced in the body leads to the understanding that sexual trauma is experienced and encoded somatically (van der Kolk, 1994). A goal of trauma therapy is to invite the client's awareness of his body in the work, and ultimately for the client to rework his relation with his body and reclaim it as an integrated part of himself rather than a dissociated and despised entity.

The Therapeutic Relationship

The premise that the therapeutic relationship provides the context for healing for trauma survivors in psychotherapy is oft-stated in trauma literature and has origins in psychoanalytic tenets. It is within the relationship and through its conscious and unconscious components that the participants have both the context and material to experience and understand the relationships and relational paradigms from the past.

Our understanding of the development of the therapeutic relationship relies upon psychoanalytic concepts of unconscious reenactments, repetition compulsion, transference and countertransference, and therapeutic frame. This emphasis on the process of the therapeutic relationship and on the events of the therapy rather than simply on the problems or symptoms presented by the client to the therapist has its roots in analytic principles of examined relating.

Therapeutic Frame

The therapeutic frame embodies respect for the complex and powerful meanings of all events in the therapeutic relationship. As Freud came to respect the power of transference, reenactment, and repetition compulsion, and before he had fully grasped the power of countertransference, he recognized the need to examine and maintain clear boundaries around the work. While his theoretical writings outstripped his practice in certain ways, Freud introduced the critical notion that the structure and boundaries of the therapeutic contract define the therapy and determine its task, outcome, and efficacy. The principles of limits and boundaries within the therapeutic or analytic relationship have been tautological with psychoanalytic theories of practice since Freud's technique papers. This work has led to the recognition that the frame of the therapy has profound meaning and is central to the identity and task of the analytic work (Langs, 1973, 1974, 1975). As we discuss in depth in chapter 7, the basic premise of the need for explicit frame, roles, and boundaries in the therapeutic environment is critical to trauma therapy and has its origins in psychoanalytic theory.

Countertransference

While the psychoanalytic ideas about countertransference were slow to be fully articulated, they are perhaps the most important contribution of psychoanalytic theory to trauma therapy. These therapies cannot be successful without attention to and understanding of the therapist's complex conscious and unconscious responses in the work. Psychoanalysis particularly elaborated three aspects of countertransference: the analyst's transference to the patient, the analyst's counterresponse to the patient's transference, and the analyst's need to maintain professional self-esteem and identity. The need to maintain a professional ego ideal is a powerful, though often underaddressed, force that evokes strong dynamics of shame, competition, envy, and pride. Clients play a central role in the development and maintenance of the therapist's identity. Self-conscious evaluation of work and imagined critiques from esteemed teachers, supervisors, and colleagues can profoundly inhibit the therapist's spontaneity and authenticity (Casement, 1991). The specific elaborations of countertransference within trauma theory include therapist responses to particular trauma material, trauma-related symptomatology, and vicarious traumatization.

MAJOR IMPEDIMENTS TO TRAUMA THERAPY BY PSYCHOANALYTIC THEORY

While psychoanalytic theory has contributed enormously to the development of transformative psychotherapy for clients who have suffered trauma, psychoanalytic theory and its interpretation have also created major impediments in such treatments. Many survivors have been neglected and others harmed by the use and misuse of psychoanalytic techniques.

Misinformation

Misinformation about psychoanalytic theory has occurred at three different levels: historical, theoretical, and clinical. Historically, followers of Freud too often rigidified and canonized his work to the detriment of the entire field (Malcolm, 1980). Freud was constantly rethinking and changing his ideas; it is not unusual to identify an idea and find its exact opposite in his later writings. Part of the power and resilience of Freud's ideas lies in his intellectual curiosity and willingness, much of the time, to evaluate his thinking critically and to discard an idea when it did not prove accurate in the context of his clinical experience.* Yet, the fact that psychoanalysis was a theory in development has often been forgotten; his work was and is treated by some as though it were the Bible and psychoanalysts were Fundamentalists with a literalist predilection. This has proven to be a great disservice to the field of psychoanalysis and certainly to many trauma survivors.

Psychoanalytic treatment of trauma survivors has also gone awry through clinical errors that stem from therapists' misinformation about the incidence of trauma, about the reality of trauma, and about post-trauma symptomatology. Posttraumatic stress disorder symptoms have often been misread and misinterpreted in psychoanalytic therapies; one example is dissociation being misread as resistance (Davies & Frawley, 1991).† Brett (1993) discusses two arenas of misinformation within psychoanalysis. The

---

*Freud's struggle to integrate his awareness and understanding of the impact of childhoold sexual abuse is evident throughout his writings, and described by many including Demause (1991), Levine (1990), and Waites (1993).

†In fact, the move away from dissociation toward repression resulted in an abandonment of the original concept of dissociation (different from splitting of the ego), which, it can be argued, created a blind spot in psychoanalytic work with dissociative clients that stymied many treatments.

first is the failure to make clear a distinction between traumatic and non-traumatic phenomenon. She notes that the word trauma was used so broadly within psychoanalysis that it became virtually meaningless. Its misuse reflected the minimization of the existence and importance of traumatic phenomena as well as the misapplication of trauma concepts to nontraumatic domains. Second, Brett stresses the need to integrate models of traumatic and nontraumatic symptom formation in order to understand the complexity of the individual's response to traumatic events. This confusion has led to serious clinical errors, including misinterpretation of transference paradigms that were related to abuse histories, and misinterpretations of directly reported trauma material.

Rejection of the Seduction Theory

Freud's rejection of the seduction theory and his subsequent emphasis on Oedipal dynamics, phallocentric psychology, and intrapsychic fantasy to the exclusion of interpersonal reality clearly have been problematic and have led to serious misdiagnoses and mistreatments. These emphases have received widespread critiques from feminist analysts (Benjamin, 1988; Chodorow, 1989; Lewis, 1976; Miller, 1976; Mitchell, 1974; Schafer, 1983), who identify the limitations of Freud's psychoanalytic theory as applied to the psychology of women, developmental psychology, and survivors of childhood sexual trauma. Freud was of course limited by his own anatomy, culture, neuroses, and ignorance, as we all are. When we do not recognize our limitations and the lenses through which we see and hear our clients' material, we all run the risk of disconnection, failure, and harm to our clients.

Theoretical Authoritarianism

Freud's rejection of the seduction theory contributed to a widespread countertransference fantasy that the analyst knew better than her client the truth of the client's experience. Arrogance may not have been the original intent of psychoanalytic inquiry, but Freud's writings have been used to justify an authoritarian stance and to deny the limitations of the analyst. False confidence is a destructive by-product of this denial. It can lead to an omniscient stance on the part of the therapist that "is subtly infantalizing and consequently undermines and undervalues the patient's own contributions toward understanding his own internal life" (Davies & Frawley, 1994, p. 120). Psychoanalysis became a cloak that gave psychoanalytic therapists confidence, as well as the assurance that as long as they stayed with what their supervisors had taught them, with what the text said, they would not have to be in a place of not knowing—a state not only inevitable, but necessary to trauma therapy. In fact, to deny not knowing is the most dangerous thing a therapist can do. It is certainly dangerous to clients whose quest must be not only for their own truth, but also for the ability to recognize and name it. When psychoanalysis becomes dogma rather than theory, it can be worse than ineffective; it can be harmful.

The Misuse of the Concept of Therapist Neutrality

Over the years, the concept of therapist neutrality became problematic. While originally it was developed to advocate an open-minded, curious stance on the part of the analyst, it evolved into an interpersonal stance. Neutrality came to mean silent, noncommunicative, and nongratifying and was deemed to be good for the client as it allowed the development of a (negative) transference. Stiver (in Miller et al., 1991) writes,

> I was taught that it was both the therapist's neutrality and her/his "non-gratification" of the client, which facilitated the emergence of a "negative transference." That is, these conditions allowed for the release of angry feelings toward significant early figures (mostly mothers) and their projection onto the therapist. But a large part of these angry outbursts toward the therapist may be more an artifact of this therapy model itself, rather than an expression of "negative" transference. The therapist's withholding and "non-gratifying" stance may be enormously frustrating and alienating for the client, who responds with anger, despair, and other negative reactions.

She concludes,

> As long as the therapist remains 'neutral' or relatively noncommunicative, the client does not experience as effectively as she could the significant *differences* between the client's real relationship with the therapist and those relational images from the past which the client re-experiences in the therapy. (p. 9)

At its extreme, the concept of analytic neutrality has been misused to mean disengaged, distant, or simply rude; it has been used punitively, sadistically, and in the service of unanalyzed countertransference. Neutrality has been used as a defense to cover a therapist's interpersonal anxiety,* confusion, anger, lack of understanding, or her experience of not knowing.

*In fact, Freud's technique of sitting behind the couch, outside of his patient's view stemmed not from theory, but originally from his interpersonal anxiety: "I cannot stand being stared at eight hours a day (or longer) by others" (quoted in Gay, 1988, p. 296).

When "neutrality" meant cold, withholding, impersonal behavior, it most certainly affected the client's feelings about the therapist, and about the safety of the therapy (Ferenczi, 1949; Gill, 1982; Jacobs, 1991; Kahn, 1991). Neutrality is necessary but must not be confused with silence, rigidity, or moral neutrality, which Herman (1992) contrasts with therapeutic neutrality. Therapeutic neutrality ideally refers to nonjudgmental attunement, evenly hovering attention, and acceptance of contradictory aspects of the client's self and experience. Jacobs points out that the

> proper use of neutrality . . . requires a considerable degree of inner "neutrality"; that is, a state of mind in which ego functions necessary for analytic work are not impaired by conflict. (p. 146)

The importance of analyzing countertransference and intrapsychic conflict in order to provide a safe, receptive interpersonal space for the therapy is implicit here. Davies and Frawley (1994) define therapeutic neutrality as

> countertransferentially maintaining the capacity to extricate the patient-therapist dyad through interpretation and negotiation from the stalemated and entrenched position and, in so doing, make possible a completely different yet equally problematic interaction. (p. 227)

A silent, "neutral" environment often feels unsafe for adult survivors of childhood trauma, for whom the silence and distance may be familiar, echoing a family which may have used silence punitively or sadistically. Such a climate provides little context for differentiating between past and present relationships. Survivors of malevolent developmental contexts (Gelinas, 1991) may experience neutrality as malevolence, evoking unmanageable terror. Psychotherapy with trauma survivors requires the therapist to be affectively present and genuine. The need for a therapist to be present emotionally and available therapeutically is part of the challenge of these treatments, a challenge that was lost in many psychoanalytic discussions of neutrality. (There are of course notable exceptions, e.g., Fromm-Reichmann, 1960 and Gill, 1982.)

A related issue is the notion of the "blank screen"; it is a fantasy to imagine that two people can be in a room together and one of them convey no information about her person or her emotional, physical, or interpersonal state. The belief that it is possible to be completely blank or utterly neutral reflects the denial of the self of the analyst or therapist as well as the denial of nonverbal communication. Again, this denial relates to the serious legacy within psychoanalysis of failure to understand and utilize the person

and experience of the analyst through her identity, affect, and countertransference.*

Therapist as Authority

The concept of the therapist as an authority with the right to determine the
rules and the truth in the relationship has been a serious impediment to
the development of healing therapeutic relationships. This is illustrated by
the stereotyped analyst who makes an interpretation with which the client
disagrees; the analyst smugly interprets the client's disagreement as denial
or resistance. The underlying assumption is that the analyst cannot be
wrong. This authoritarian role in the therapeutic relationship inevitably
erodes the safety and respect of the therapeutic alliance and leads to a
therapeutic impasse and client-blaming (Maroda, 1991).

Until recently, the psychoanalytic literature has shown one of its greatest
weaknesses in its response to therapeutic impasses. An extension of the
need for the therapist to be certain and correct is a need to locate failure
within the patient or client. Rather than conceptualize a therapeutic impasse as an interpersonal event, theoreticians and clinicians have developed
constructs to support the conclusion that the problem was in the client. One
example is the concept of resistance, which came to be used as a catch-all to
explain a therapy that was not going as the therapist had hoped. Rather
than look at interactive factors or therapist factors, including the therapist's
resistance to painful or conflictual truth or affects, the focus was too often
solely on the client who did not want to get better or who wanted to defeat
the therapist.† This formulation overlooked the possible adaptive aspects
of client resistance: a response to a real psychic terror, fear of the consequences of the therapy, fear of the process of remembering or knowing, or
the developmental achievement of saying "no" (Davies & Frawley, 1994).
Another way of blaming the client is reflected in the creation of diagnostic
categories such as borderline personality disorder, pathological narcissism,
or psychosis, diagnoses that are merely descriptive of a client's current
presentation (divorced from etiology, dynamics, or constructive treatment
implications) and can be client-blaming, cause iatrogenic responses, and
convey despair, hopelessness, and the sentence of chronicity.

Other formulations that can disregard human interaction within the therapeutic relationship include concepts such as the negative therapeutic reaction or the unanalyzable patient. These concepts may be descriptively accu-

---

*For further discussion of therapeutic neutrality and other frame issues see chap-
  ter 7.
†For further discussion see chapter 10.

rate and useful, but when they focus solely on the client and not on the fit between the therapist and client, the possibility of transformative change within the therapy decreases markedly.

Inaccessibility of Psychoanalytic Ideas

Another impediment posed by psychoanalysis or psychoanalytic theory is its inaccessibility. The language of psychoanalysis is often abstruse and imprecise. A related problem is that the language of psychoanalysis is the language of translation (from German) and often awkward, unclear, and impersonal (Gay, 1988). The term "object" is a good example of such shortcomings. Terms such as "infantile sexuality" are misleading and can lead to misinterpretation and adultomorphisms. Moreover, the language itself has become a token of belonging. Psychoanalytic terminology or buzz words, usually multisyllabic, are used to signify membership in an elite intelligentsia. This exclusionary process contradicts the very premises of scientific inquiry. As psychoanalysis became further isolated from the discipline of psychology specifically and from science in general, everyone lost opportunities to learn.

A related impediment lies in the lack of clear operational definitions of such central constructs as transference and repression, as well as certain aspects of psychic structure, such as "the unconscious." While the concepts and process of psychoanalysis and psychoanalytic psychotherapy are necessarily complex, there has been too little attempt to communicate and work with empirical methodology to strengthen the clarity and foundation of the concepts. Many important works (Blatt & Erlich, 1982; Blatt & Ford, 1994; Luborsky, Chandler, Auerback, Cohen, & Bachrach, 1971; Luborsky & Spence, 1978; Mayman, 1967; Shevrin, 1980, 1992; Silverman, 1985) have contributed to this goal, but there is much room for collaboration among psychoanalytic theorists and empirical researchers. The lack of operational constructs limits our ability to explore, develop, and share with others information that might advance the field.

Inattention to the Therapist's Personal
Meaning of Trauma

A serious omission in the psychoanalytic literature is attention to the personal meaning of trauma to the therapist. It is profoundly difficult and personally wrenching to let oneself know that a trauma is real. It is extraordinarily painful to hear and know the truth of the trauma of childhood sexual abuse, of child abuse, of sadistic abuse. There is a universal wish for it not to be true and the effect of that denial has been underestimated in psychoanalytic writings. Brett (1993) suggests that the wish to deny and minimize "both the intensity of the immediate response and the severity of the long-term consequences of trauma" (p. 5) as well as the inevitability of the therapist being traumatized by unmetabolized repetitions of the trauma in the therapy jointly contribute to the historic fluctuations in understanding trauma and the dangerous possibility of knowledge being reversible.

This kind of denial always happens in a context. A significant context for psychoanalysis in America is World War II and the Nazi Holocaust. The fact that so many analysts in America in the 1940s were fleeing the Holocaust and responding to enormous personal, community, and historical trauma is profoundly significant. They were facing both the personal trauma of horror, displacement, and loss, and their own survivor guilt because they were able to leave Europe while those they knew and loved remained and died. This personal context must have had a profound effect on the psychological defenses they needed to manage that horror. It seems plausible that context may have informed their response to trauma material in complicated ways, and may be part of the context of psychoanalytic theory in America that needs to be understood further.

Having reviewed contributions and impediments offered by psychoanalytic theory to trauma treatment, we conclude that the basic tenets of trauma theory and therapy are based in psychoanalytic theory. Yet we must continually examine the strengths and weaknesses of our theories, techniques, and training; both scientific and psychoanalytic traditions require that we continue to augment and refine our knowledge and techniques.

3

Constructivist
Self Development Theory
and Trauma Therapy

THE PREVIOUS CHAPTERS have outlined the central role of theory in trauma therapy, and the contributions and limitations of psychoanalytic theory in its application to treatment with survivors of traumatic life events. This chapter outlines constructivist self development theory (CSDT), a unifying personality theory that integrates the clinical and psychological complexity of psychoanalytic theory with the clarity and contextual emphasis of social learning and other developmental cognitive theories.*

THE THEORY

Any theory relevant to psychotherapy with survivors of childhood interpersonal trauma must speak to the theoretical complexity of the psychotherapeutic process, the interactive nature of psychological and interpersonal

---

*There are many approaches to understanding the adult trauma survivor. The history of other theoretical approaches is reviewed elsewhere (e.g., Herman, 1992; McCann & Pearlman, 1990b). Within the trauma literature, CSDT is consistent with the work of Briere (1989), Courtois (1988), Davies and Frawley (1994), Epstein (1991, 1994), Herman (1992), Horowitz (1986), Janoff-Bulman (1985, 1989a, 1989b, 1992), Parson (1984), and Roth (1989).

processes, and the capacity of the human organism to adapt and survive. Such a theory provides a template for therapists to understand their clients, and the developing therapeutic relationship with them. Ideally, a clinical theory provides a framework that can be applied to the client, the therapist, and the relationship. Any theory of human psychology that is clinically useful should address psychological functioning across the spectrum of health and disorder.

CSDT offers a basis for understanding the psychological, interpersonal, and transpersonal impact of traumatic life events upon the adult survivor. Further, it provides the framework we use for understanding the impact of trauma work upon the therapist (vicarious traumatization). The theory was originally described by McCann and Pearlman (1990b); since then we have continued to develop and revise the theory based on our clinical observations and empirical findings. Thus, while the theory we present here is structurally the same as the original version, some of the specifics differ.

CSDT emphasizes integration, meaning, and adaptation. Rather than identifying a client as a collection of symptoms, it invites the recognition that each individual is an interactive, complex being striving to survive and to manage a particular set of life circumstances. The theory emphasizes the adaptive function of individual behavior and beliefs, and the individual's style of affect management. This approach is fundamentally respectful of the client. Further, it sustains the therapist's hope as it acknowledges the client's strengths and will to survive, and her importance as a collaborative partner in the work of psychotherapy.

The theory integrates psychoanalytic theory with cognitive theories. It draws upon object relations theory (Mahler, Pine, & Bergman, 1975; White & Weiner, 1986), interpersonal psychiatry (Fromm-Reichmann, 1960; Sullivan, 1953), and self psychology (Kohut, 1971, 1977; Stolorow et al., 1987) and is grounded in the basic premises of psychoanalytic treatment. It synthesizes these theories with constructivist thinking (Mahoney, 1981; Mahoney & Lyddon, 1988), social learning theory (Rotter, 1954), and cognitive developmental theory (Piaget, 1971).

Whether single-symptom or multiple-symptom diagnoses (as described in the DSM-IV; APA, 1994), approaches that emphasize symptoms and pathology convey little awareness of a whole person. Their focus is descriptive; such approaches are intentionally behavioral, atheoretical, and do not refer to etiology. These approaches provide no conceptual map for psychotherapy; instead they encourage a finger-in-the-dike approach whose goal is to eradicate or manage symptoms.

Event-focused approaches, on the other hand, give rise to "stage" theories. They may suggest, for example, that traumatized people first go through a period of denial, then a period of feeling overwhelmed, and so forth. Stage theories largely neglect individual differences, implying that all clients go through the same stages, and that clients who do not fit the model are exhibiting pathology; this approach may also encourage the client to move through the stages, rather than to work with and reflect on his own adaptations and pace for recovery. Neither symptom-focused nor event-focused approaches allow for an adequate understanding of individual differences in adaptation, nor do they facilitate the assessment and mobilization of the individual's resources.

CSDT understands the individual's adaptation to trauma as an interaction between his personality and personal history and the traumatic event(s) and its context, within the social and cultural contexts for the event and its aftermath. CSDT has been developed from and applied to our experience with a wide variety of survivor groups (including domestic abuse victims [McCann & Pearlman, 1991], rape victims [Dutton, Burghardt, Perrin, Chrestman, & Halle, 1994; Pearlman & McCann, 1992], childhood sexual abuse survivors, other crime victims, war veterans, and victims of natural and induced disasters, to name a few) and with people presenting with the entire range of symptom patterns (McCann & Pearlman, 1992). Here we present the theory with specific reference to the adult survivor of childhood sexual abuse.

ASSUMPTIONS

Constructivism

The underlying constructivist assumption is that individuals construct and construe their own realities (Epstein, 1985; Mahoney, 1981; Mahoney & Lyddon, 1988). The clinical implication is that *the meaning of the traumatic event is in the survivor's experience of it.* This assumption requires that the therapist listen carefully for the client's experience and interpretation of events. For example, we must not assume that we understand the implications of a survivor's struggle with whether or not he was responsible for his victimization. We must hear each person's story and experience afresh; no matter how many incest survivors we treat, each one will bring a unique perspective on and experience of his own trauma. Each individual is affected in his own unique way. This is not to deny Freud's (1920) assertion that certain events are so overwhelming that they will affect everyone (Scurfield, 1985 reviews these issues), but we cannot assume the same effects or magnitude of effects across persons. Construction of meaning occurs and recurs as new information and experiences are incorporated into an individual's beliefs and systems of meaning. This premise is at the heart of the action of therapeutic change.

Individual Differences

A constructivist perspective implies individual differences in adaptation. Both theoretically and clinically, individual differences in life experience and personal history, in personality and temperament, and in adaptation to and attribution of meaning to trauma are of primary interest. The task of the therapy is for the therapist and client together to come to understand the particular experience, meaning, and adaptation of the client to his life experiences. While the theory proposes psychological arenas vulnerable to the effects of trauma, it merely provides a general guide for the client and therapist as they explore the particular effects of trauma on the self of each client.

Developmental Perspective

As its name implies, the theory emphasizes a developmental perspective. A central premise is that the individual's early development is central to his current way of experiencing and interacting with self and others. In addition, personality continues to develop across the life span. A clinical implication of this perspective is that the developmental period(s) during which sexual abuse occurs provides us with hypotheses about developmental tasks that may be incomplete. With constructivism, it reminds us that experiences of trauma and abuse will be reinterpreted and reconstructed during subsequent developmental stages. A developmental model suggests that earlier trauma will have more pervasive effects on the personality than later trauma (Putnam, 1989). Finally, a developmental theory provides us with a context for the therapy: We view psychotherapy as an interpersonal and developmental experience through which the client can resume some of the developmental processes that were derailed or arrested in childhood because of trauma. This model informs our conceptualization of the therapeutic task, not as reparenting, but as the creation of a facilitating environment (Fromm & Smith, 1989; Winnicott, 1965) for the client's personal growth and development.

Interpersonal Context

Childhood sexual trauma occurs in an interpersonal or relational context, and therefore the context of healing must be interpersonal. Here our work is consistent with that produced by the Stone Center (Jordan et al., 1991; Miller, 1976). The familial developmental context of the sexual abuse and its aftermath, including others' responses to the survivor both then and now, are also an important aspect of the client's interpersonal context. It follows that the healing of psychotherapy occurs in its interpersonal context.

Symptoms as Adaptative Strategies

CSDT views the survivor's symptoms as adaptive strategies that were developed to manage feelings and thoughts that threaten the integrity and safety of the self. Each victim does what he can and must to survive. Adaptation for victims of childhood sexual abuse often includes dissociation, as well as a variety of other behaviors that were essential to survival in childhood, but which may not be in the adult survivor's best interest in a non-trauma context. Yet these behaviors are understandably entrenched and resistant to change; who would readily give up a strategy which had once saved his life?

When the therapist accepts that behaviors such as self-mutilation have a context and an adaptive or protective intent, her therapeutic strategy is defined. In viewing symptoms as adaptive strategies, she can explore together with her client the milieu in which the particular behaviors developed, the purpose they served, their current functions, and ways in which they no longer serve the client well. Of course, such behaviors come to serve additional needs in the survivor's life and his relationships; understanding them is one step toward loosening their tenacity and providing the client greater conscious awareness and control. Conversely, when the therapist assumes these behaviors are solely pathological and destructive, she misses opportunities to learn and to work conjointly with the client toward change.

Familial and Social-Cultural Contexts

In addition to the interpersonal relationship, childhood sexual abuse and recovery occur in larger contexts—familial and social-cultural, for example. First, the family within which the abuse occurs provides a context that allows, supports, or does not prevent the defilement of children. Family contexts can range from overextended, undersupported family systems in which children are neglected and not protected by parents who are themselves vulnerable and overwhelmed, to families where systematic, intentional torture and sadistic abuse of children occurs (Gelinas, 1991, 1994). Further, the family is the context for many survivors' attempts to get help during childhood, sometimes by telling a trusted other. One client told of her wish and belief that a visiting cousin would rescue her from the sadistic abuse she was experiencing at the hands of her father. The cousin was banished from the family home for reasons unknown to the client, and died shortly thereafter. The client transformed this into a belief that hope is dangerous, even deadly.

The social-cultural context in contemporary American society includes traditions of victim-blaming (Ryan, 1971), misogyny (Brownmiller, 1975; MacKinnon, 1987; Roth, 1989; Saakvitne & Pearlman, 1993), homophobia (Blumenfeld, 1992; Brown, 1989; Rich, 1986), ageism, children's lack of rights (Edelman, 1987; Greven, 1991; Holt, 1974), and racism. This context holds both the survivor and his treaters; it informs the victim's perceptions of his abuse (Lebowitz & Roth, 1994) and others' (including mental health professionals') responses to him.

Historical context also shapes responses to childhood sexual abuse. Contemporary American society remains patriarchal, and this patriarchy serves to perpetuate violence against women and children and a lack of support for victims (Herman, 1981, 1992; Mac Ian, 1992; MacKinnon, 1989). Finally, characteristics such as the survivor's age, race, gender, and socioeconomic status form a context which also informs the individual's experiences of victimization and others' responses to him, as well as his access to treatment. For example, being a male incest survivor has different social connotations than being a female survivor in a culture where men are supposed to be powerful and in control. Wealthier and employed individuals continue to have greater access to treatment than those without money or adequate health insurance. These characteristics influence the response of others and thus the context of each survivor's recovery and healing.

DEFINITION OF TRAUMA

While our constructivist perspective implies that each person's experience of childhood sexual abuse is unique, we believe that the power of this particular type of event is such that all who endure it will experience some deleterious aftereffects. Support for this perspective comes from a meta-analysis of 43 empirical studies of the long-term sequelae of childhood sexual abuse; research in both clinical and nonclinical female populations found a significant relationship between a history of childhood sexual abuse and negative long-term sequelae (Neumann, in press). In addition, CSDT-based research with psychiatric patients (Mas, 1992) found that subjects with a history of childhood sexual abuse had qualitatively different psychological presentations than those with histories of physical abuse, other traumas, or no trauma history.

The definition of trauma used within CSDT is a process definition. We define it as the unique individual experience, associated with an event or enduring conditions, in which (1) the individual's ability to integrate affective experience is overwhelmed or (2) the individual experiences a threat to life or bodily integrity. The pathognomonic responses are changes in the individual's (1) frame of reference, or usual way of understanding self and world, including spirituality, (2) capacity to modulate affect and maintain benevolent inner connection with self and others, (3) ability to meet his psychological needs in mature ways, (4) central psychological needs, which are reflected in disrupted cognitive schemas, and (5) memory system, including sensory experience.

ASPECTS OF THE INDIVIDUAL
IMPACTED BY TRAUMA

Frame of Reference

Trauma virtually always affects the individual's frame of reference, which includes world view, identity, and spirituality. Frame of reference refers to the individual's framework for viewing and understanding himself and the world; it incorporates the manner in which an individual relates to and interprets his own experience. It is fundamental to an individual's perception and interpretation of life experiences. Any shift in frame of reference is inherently disorienting and stressful.

World View

World view includes an individual's broadest beliefs about the world, including life philosophy, moral principles, causality, and, as described by Rotter (1966), locus of control. These beliefs frame and inform the individual's experience and interpretation of events in the world, including interpersonal and nonpersonal events. World view incorporates general attitudes about others, including their worth, intentions, and role in the individual's life. It includes overarching beliefs about the benevolence or malevolence of the world, the justice or injustice of life's occurrences, and the randomness or predictability of life events, as discussed by Janoff-Bulman (1992). These beliefs are closely connected with feelings of personal efficacy and spiritual factors such as hope and compassion.

Identity

Identity refers to an individual's sense of self across time, across situations, and across emotional, physiological, and cognitive states. The concept of identity reflects an individual's inner experience of self, including characteristic feeling states, and self in the world. Identity includes one's personal story or narrative and one's sense of oneself as a person, real and ideal, in the past, present, and future. Identity incorporates one's relationship with oneself and one's perception of self in relation to others. It includes but is not limited to racial, maturational, gender, cultural, and vocational identities, as well as the complex internalizations and introjections of, and identifications with, significant others, and roles, projections, and ego ideals experienced within early relationships.

TABLE 3.1

Constructivist Self Development Theory: Aspects of the Self Impacted by Psychological Trauma

Frame of Reference
Framework of beliefs through which the individual interprets experience; includes:

- World view
- Identity
- Spirtuality

Self Capacities
Abilities that enable the individual to maintain a sense of self as consistent and co-herent across time and situations; intrapersonal; includes ability to:

- Tolerate strong affect
- Maintain positive sense of self
- Maintain inner sense of connection with others

Ego Resources
Abilities that enable the individual to meet psychological needs and to relate to oth-ers; interpersonal; includes two types:

- Resources important to the therapy process
  Intelligence, willpower and initiative, awareness of psychological needs, and abilities to be introspective, to strive for personal growth, and to take perspec-tive
- Resources important to protect oneself from future harm
  Abilities to foresee consequences, to establish mature relations with others, to establish boundaries, and to make self-protective judgments

Psychological Needs and Related Cognitive Schemas (in relation to *self* and *others*)

- Safety
  The need to feel secure and reasonably invulnerable to harm by oneself or others
- Trust
  The need to have confidence in one's own perceptions and judgment and to depend on others
- Esteem
  The need to feel valued by oneself and others, and to value others
- Intimacy
  The need to feel connected to oneself and to others
- Control
  The need to feel able to manage one's feelings and behaviors as well as to manage others in interpersonal situations

Memory System

• Verbal	• Somatic
• Affect	• Interpersonal
• Imagery	

Spirituality

Spirituality may be viewed as the meeting place of identity and world view. Spirituality is an inherent human capacity for awareness of an elusive aspect of experience. It refers to the creation of meaning about self in the larger world. It has four components: orientation to the future and sense of meaning in life, awareness of all aspects of life, relation to the nonmaterial aspects of existence, and sense of connection with something beyond oneself. For some, this connection may take the form of a connection with a god or a higher power. For others, the connection may be with nature, with community or humanity, or with some other larger entity or force. The inevitable damage to frame of reference induced by childhood sexual abuse includes damage to one's spirituality. These notions are articulated in more depth elsewhere (Bulman & Wortman 1977; Lifton, 1979; Merwin & Smith-Kurtz, 1988; Neumann & Pearlman, 1994; Sargeant, 1989; Williams, 1988) and are elaborated in chapters 13 and 14.

Therapeutic Work on Frame of Reference

When attuned, a therapist will hear from the first contact with a client information about the client's frame of reference. As they develop their relationship, the therapist and client name and identify the client's core beliefs about self, world, and spirituality, and begin to understand the contexts in which they developed.

Clarification of the client's beliefs about his identity begins early in treatment. The therapist invites her client to notice his relationship to himself as a person, a survivor, a human being. The therapist's responses to the client reflect in various ways her perceptions of who the client is, as a man or woman, as a survivor, as a human being. With individuals with dissociative disorders, one must acknowledge the lost aspects of personal history and time and the partitioning within the personality that has both allowed the person to function and carried such significant costs.

While many survivors view the world as malevolent, it is rarely effective to question these schemas before a client begins to develop a sense of self as worthwhile. Survivors can use therapy early on to explore their own personal philosophies, their understanding of why things happen, and the ways they would like to relate to others. The therapist is a representative of the world, of the "other," and as the client develops trust in the therapist, his world view is often implicitly challenged. One client coped by simply asserting "You don't count" whenever she became aware of contradictions between her beliefs about people in general and her experience of her therapist.

Therapeutic work on spiritual issues often comes into the work at later stages, after the pain of the past has been acknowledged and grieved for some time. As survivor clients look to the future, they may use therapy to explore what will make their lives feel worth living, where they find inspiration and hope. In this work, the role of the therapist is less that of guide and more a witness, and a fellow human who struggles with issues of meaning.

Self Capacities

Self capacities are inner capabilities that allow the individual to maintain a consistent, coherent sense of identity, connection, and positive self-esteem. Self capacities regulate one's inner state. Three specific self capacities are identified in CSDT: (1) the ability to tolerate strong affect and to integrate various affective experiences, (2) the ability to maintain a positive sense of self, and (3) the ability to maintain an inner sense of connection with others.*

The self capacities develop primarily through the process of internalization of early interpersonal experiences of being soothed, held, and recognized as an independent individual worthy of love and esteem. Self capacities develop in the context of a secure base (Bowlby, 1988), that is, a stable attachment to a protective, loving caretaker in the first several years of a child's life. It is obvious that a child raised in a dysfunctional or malevolent family is likely to have underdeveloped self capacities.

> The developmental literature, regardless of the particular psychoanalytic orientation, presupposes that the consolidation of ego development and self integrity begins around a secure attachment to a loving and protective other. This attachment provides the secure base, the backdrop of safety, order, predictability, and control that allows the young child to begin his relationship to our complex, dangerous, and oftentimes, overstimulating world. This secure relationship becomes the haven from which young children draw their confidence in their capacity to control external events. . . . It is also the retreat to which the child withdraws for soothing and comfort when that omnipotence is challenged or thwarted by experiences of failure and frustration. (Davies & Frawley, 1994, p. 46)

*Research in progress is directed toward operationalizing and measuring the self capacities (Pearlman & Deiter, 1995).

Therapeutic Work on Self Capacities

Work on self capacity development occurs within the therapeutic relationship and is the foundation of psychotherapy with survivors of severe childhood sexual, physical, and emotional abuse and neglect. Survivors often experience their emotions as assaultive and disconnected from any context or meaning. They may have only two affective states: flooded or numb. Thus, they often cannot use their feelings to identify their needs or to establish and maintain their safety in the world.

The therapy relationship becomes an important container for affects, and the therapist a benevolent object to be internalized as a resource to help the survivor contain, identify, and utilize his own emotional experience. The progressive internalization of the therapist and the therapeutic relationship forms the basis for the developing capacity to maintain an inner sense of connection with others, related to processes of developing object constancy (Horner, 1986) and evocative memory (Adler & Buie, 1979). A central therapeutic task is for the client to retain a sense of the therapist's presence and existence between sessions (Bowlby, 1988; Mahler et al., 1975); to hold on to the therapist as a consistently benign object, without malevolent transformation (Sullivan, 1953); and to be able to evoke the memory of the therapist when needed. For survivors, this presence addresses earlier absences. As Davies and Frawley (1994) write, "As no parent or loving other appeared to put an end to the nights of terror-filled abuse, the adult survivor becomes unable to call upon internal representations of protective internal objects to help soothe, contain, and ultimately control flashback experiences of panic, disorganization, and physiologically mediated states of intense hyperarousal" (p. 47).

This use of the therapist as a benevolent internal object also serves to modify and detoxify the survivor's relationship with himself. The client begins to develop a sense of "we-ness" that reflects an internalization of the therapist *in relation* to himself. Many survivors experience unremitting self-loathing and castigation. The internalization of the therapist's esteem and gentle strength can serve to intervene in the relentless self-attack. The internalization then, of not just the therapist but of the therapeutic relationship itself, aids the development of an alternative model for interpersonal relating that emphasizes empathy, respect, and protection—rather than disconnection, humiliation, and exploitation.

The therapeutic relationship thus creates the holding environment (Winnicott, 1965) within which therapist and client can address issues of separation anxiety, fear of abandonment, and annihilation anxiety. This holding environment is essential for the development of affect tolerance and integration. Many survivor clients bring to therapy intense fears of flooding, numbness or "deadness," traumatic paralysis, dissociation, and loss of control. At the same time, the experience of a holding environment in psychotherapy can reawaken in the survivor client old yearnings for primary maternal preoccupation, and thus evoke psychological defenses against the expected frustration, anxiety, and grief.

Within the new therapeutic relationship, clients can consider the possibility of a personal identity that incorporates a sense of self in relation to another that is tolerable, touchable, lovable, and nontoxic. This work involves the frequent negotiation of shame; survivor clients are enormously shame-prone and issues of need and expressed affect are powerful triggers for shame and self-loathing. Shame disrupts the therapeutic connection (Beere, 1989; Jordan, 1990; Morrison, 1989; Nathanson, 1987; Wong & Cook, 1992) and therefore the holding environment. Its management both requires and builds self capacities. A therapist will notice what the client finds shaming and find words to approach it with the client. Part of this process is the development of a mutual language in the therapy to communicate needs and feelings and to negotiate dangerous and forbidden territory (e.g., "We can't say the n-word, that is, need"). When a therapist addresses the interpersonal relationship in the therapy from the outset, she lays the groundwork to address the client's relationship with himself. Over time, this process permits therapist and client to decipher internalized object relationships and identify the client's self-parenting style.

Therapeutic work on self capacity development occurs throughout the psychotherapy. It is the foundation for all relationship, memory, and transformative work. As a client internalizes the therapist and the therapeutic relationship, he will have more resources to draw upon on his own behalf and the work of the therapy will be more integrated and productive. This aspect of the work can be very lengthy, often several years, and reoccurs throughout the therapy as new material emerges.

Ego Resources

While self capacities refer to the intrapersonal system, ego resources are inner faculties the individual uses to navigate the interpersonal world and to meet his psychological needs.* Like self capacities, ego resources develop over time through one's early interpersonal experiences—through processes of internalizing significant others and attempts to gain positive reinforcement from others. Ego resources are often used in the service of getting positive interpersonal contact and rewards. Thus, many survivors have

---

*The resources of interest to CSDT come in part from the work of Murray & Kluckhohn (1953).

extremely well-developed ego resources that allow them to identify and meet other people's needs or to excel in certain areas like work, artistic endeavors, or scholarship. Therapists can too easily fail to see the deep pain and struggle of survivor clients who have highly developed ego resources; these clients function in the world in a way that looks competent and successful, and yet, with impaired self capacities, they are filled with self-loathing and terror, and when alone feel overwhelmed with panic and despair.

There are two sets of resources of particular interest to CSDT. The first group of resources are useful to the therapy process and play important roles in achievement, interpersonal relationships, and survival. These include intelligence, willpower and initiative, awareness of one's psychological needs, and the abilities to be introspective, strive for personal growth, and take perspective (which includes empathy, sense of humor, and wisdom).

The second group of resources are important to the individual's ability to protect himself from harm. These include the ability to foresee consequences, the ability to establish mature relations with others (clearly also useful to the therapy process), the ability to establish boundaries between self and others, and the ability to make self-protective judgments.

Therapeutic Work on Ego Resources

The work on ego resources within the therapeutic relationship grows out of noticing, naming, and processing the interpersonal events in the room. One arena for this work is the negotiation of frame and boundaries, the reflection of the structure (or ego) of the therapeutic relationship. Another is the negotiation of conflicts between therapist and client. When the therapist addresses conflict, hurt, and misunderstandings in the context of the therapeutic relationship, she introduces the idea of mutuality and respect for the negotiation of relationships. When a therapist accepts her fallibility and acknowledges the reality of herself and her limitations and mistakes in the relationship, she can explore with the client what is familiar and what is different about the events in the therapeutic relationship compared with events from the past.

Providing an alternative, respectful, and safe interpersonal environment is necessary, but not sufficient for therapeutic change. Therapeutic action also requires the interpretation and understanding of the client's transference, his imposition of object relational paradigms from the past onto the present relationship. Addressing the transference in the therapeutic relationship is essential for transformative change (Davies & Frawley, 1991; Gill, 1979). As a client is invited to notice what is similar and different about his

feelings and situation in the present, he can make connection among patterns in the present and with those of the near and distant past. The patterns
and their connections provide the basis for therapeutic interpretation and
thus make interpretation a tool for either the therapist or the client; that is,
the therapist is teaching the client to make connections for himself, to
understand and change the old patterns in which he is trapped. As he
internalizes the therapist, a client's ego resources allow him increasingly to
understand himself, his needs, and his psychology.

Psychological Needs

An individual's behavior is motivated, and his relationships are shaped, by
his basic psychological needs. These needs develop through early experiences of gratification, frustration, reinforcement, and association. They
both shape and are shaped by one's experience in early caretaking relationships. Needs are not necessarily conscious. They continue to develop over
the life span, but they are less amenable to change over time. Traumatic
events can profoundly impact needs, especially those needs an individual
was attempting to meet in the context of the trauma.

CSDT focuses on five psychological needs: safety, trust/dependency,
esteem, intimacy, and control. Each of these needs is manifest both in
relation to the self and in relation to others. Because of our unique individual histories, each need is more or less salient for each individual. Everyone
has all of these needs (as well as others), and can meet them in more or less
mature ways. These five needs appear to be most sensitive to the effects of
psychological trauma. They were identified through an extensive review of
the trauma literature (McCann, Sakheim, & Abrahamson, 1988), our own
clinical observations, and our continuing research on a measure of psychological needs and cognitive schemas (McCann, Pearlman, Sakheim, Abrahamson, 1988; Pearlman et al., 1992).

Cognitive Schemas

We use the term cognitive schemas to refer to the conscious and unconscious beliefs and expectations individuals have about self and others that
are organized according to central psychological need areas. This portion
of the theory is drawn from the literature on cognitive development (Piaget,
1971) and social cognition (Mahoney, 1981). In CSDT, the schemas of
interest are those that relate to frame of reference and to the five basic
psychological needs. Thus, for example, one's beliefs and expectations
about his safety arise from his experiences related to safety and security and
the ways in which he has understood and made sense of those experiences.
New experiences are filtered through the existing schemas, and will either

be fitted into (assimilated) or reshape (accommodate) existing schemas (Piaget, 1971).

A key point in the theory is that those schemas that are most affected by traumatic experiences are those connected to the individual's most central need areas. Assessment of a client's salient need areas is, then, a primary task of the trauma therapist. Frame of reference is almost invariably impacted by trauma. The other salient needs and schemas are impacted or disrupted selectively, depending upon the situation and the individual.

When we refer to "disrupted" schemas, it is important to note that we believe those schemas reflect the reality of the survivor's childhood experience. Disrupted schemas reflect generalized negative beliefs about self, others, and the possibility of having one's needs met constructively. Outside of a traumatic context, however, these beliefs can impair the individual's relationships with himself and others.

Therapeutic Work on Disrupted Schemas

Addressing a client's psychological needs and related schemas in the context of the therapeutic relationship involves noticing and naming events in the relationship. A therapist can help clients identify their central needs and beliefs or schemas if she listens to their language about themselves, their relationships, values, and viewpoints. Words and phrases such as "unsafe" (safety), "you can't count on anyone" (trust), "humiliate and belittle" (esteem), "get close to" or "connect" (intimacy), and "power" (control) give clear information about someone's salient need areas and disrupted schemas. These themes will emerge consistently in the client's accounts of daily interactions with others, dream material, trauma memories, and transference to the therapist.

Stated or implied beliefs reflect conscious and unconscious schemas. As therapist and client notice these beliefs, over time they can also identify some of their costs and benefits. Where do they serve the client well, protect him, give him information and control? Where do they deprive him of opportunities, relationships, personal gain, or freedom of choice? Schemas often translate to expectations, characteristic ways of relating to others, patterns of managing affect. Therapy creates the opportunity to make connections between current patterns and the past. How were they learned? In what context did these schemas make sense and prove useful, perhaps essential? Do they still fit? Only when the client is conscious of his assumptions can they be questioned or revised.

Therapeutically this process introduces complexity and flexibility to rigidified, often concrete thinking. These beliefs were codified in childhood and often contain aspects of a child's cognition (e.g., concrete operations).

The therapist invites the client to shift from all-or-nothing, dichotomous thinking to more complicated situational, relative thinking. Do these beliefs still hold? Under what circumstances? To what degree?

Over time, by identifying internalized object relational and self paradigms, therapist and client will connect the internal patterns of beliefs and rules to early external relationships. These connections allow for the integration and contextualization of past and present, and thus introduce reflection and conscious choice in the present. Often the individual has come to treat himself, his cognition, body, affect, and psychological needs in a manner that repeats early interpersonal experiences and paradigms. Thus, a client's belief systems and relation to his own psychological needs will often include a reenactment of his early relationships and abuse.

The survivor client who is harshly self-denigrating from the start of therapy often treats himself with utter contempt and scorn. He mocks himself for his feelings, chastises himself for being inarticulate if he doesn't find a word instantly, calls himself stupid when he doesn't know something, and berates himself as a crybaby if he sheds tears. Therapists who work with survivor clients will recognize in this description the familiar presentation of clients whose developmental strivings were met with constant criticism and belittlement, whose feelings were used to humiliate and torment them, and whose needs were identified as shameful and weak. As children they internalized the harsh voices; as adults they repeat them to themselves. These words are codified in beliefs about low self-worth, shameful dependence, and an identity as unlovable.

Self-esteem schemas appear to mediate between an individual's relationship with himself and his relationships with others; preliminary empirical work supports this hypothesis (Black & Pearlman, 1994). Thus, a client whose self-esteem is disrupted will have difficulty, for example, trusting others. The therapeutic work here must focus on the client's self-esteem (and, as indicated by our path analysis, self-intimacy and self-trust) before she can work directly on other-trust. This point was conveyed poignantly in the following interaction between a therapist and client:

Example   In talking about her adolescent relationships, a female survivor client said, "I guess I always felt sort of paranoid, like people would say nice things to me but I couldn't believe them." The therapist noted the disrupted other-trust schema here, and said, "Tell me more." The client said, "I felt so awful about myself that I couldn't imagine other people could really see anything good in me."

As a therapist assesses a client's self capacities, ego resources, and needs and schemas, she can predict central transference paradigms likely to emerge in the therapy. Below we describe the five need/schema areas, give examples of commonly observed disruptions, and present possible manifestations of these conflicts in the transference.

Safety

Safety refers to the individual's need to feel secure and invulnerable to harm. Because childhood sexual abuse impacts upon the physical and emotional integrity of the individual, it is inevitable that survivors will experience disruptions in their beliefs about safety (Pearlman et al., 1992). Disrupted safety schemas can emerge as beliefs about one's self-safety, as an inability to feel safe anywhere; they can also be evident in relation to others, or other-safety. Many survivors fear their own toxicity, a concern that inevitably emerges in the therapy relationship. For example, the client may fear that his presence in the therapist's life will in some way bring harm to the therapist. Another transference manifestation of safety disruptions is fear of the therapist, that she will assault, exploit, or harm the client. A projective transference may result in fears for the therapist's safety, a belief in her vulnerability and fragility.

It is not uncommon for survivors to feel that there is no safe place. Even when invited to imagine or create an inner "safe place" through imagery for self-soothing, some clients cannot conceive of safety. The experience of living in a world in which there is no safety internally or externally is chilling. Some therapists use alternative language to get around this disruption, suggesting a client create a "protected place" (S. Moore, personal communication, 1991).

Trust/dependency

A second central psychological need is trust, which is related to healthy dependency (a concept many survivors believe is an oxymoron). Self-trust is the need to trust one's own perceptions and judgment. Other-trust is the need to count on or depend upon others to meet one's emotional, psychological, or physical needs. Most adult survivors of childhood sexual abuse show both subtle and blatant disruptions in dependency needs. These disruptions are predictable given that childhood sexual abuse often occurs in the context of a trusting, dependent relationship. The experience of abandonment and betrayal is part of the trauma, and is integrated into the adult survivor's expectations of himself and others in the world. Early abandonment experiences can teach the survivor that he cannot trust anyone (other-trust), nor should he trust his own judgment or perceptions about others (self-trust). Alternatively, trust disruptions are sometimes reflected in denial and emerge as indiscriminate misplaced trust in others, leading to revictimization. This pattern reflects an abandonment of one's judgment and oneself; it may appear to be a disruption in other-trust, but really reflects disrupted self-trust. The underlying thought would be, "I can't trust my own judgment, so why bother trying?"

In the transference, disrupted trust schemas can lead to persistent, un-modifiable mistrust of the therapist or the field of mental health. It can emerge in the client's persistent difficulties trusting his therapist to maintain confidentiality, return phone calls, or to return from vacation or maternity leave. Self-trust disruptions can emerge in a client who does not ask any questions of the therapist, or make any requests because he fears he will intrude or take too much and will be unable to judge how much is enough.

Esteem

Self-esteem is the need to hold oneself in positive regard, to value oneself, and to feel valued by others; other-esteem is the need to value others. As survivors struggle to make sense of their abuse experiences, they frequently wish that they had done something differently, and then devalue themselves and their inherent worth. This self-criticism often leads to the conclusion that the survivor deserved the pain and degradation he suffered. Another esteem disruption is the survivor's generalization of his rage and disappoint-ment with the perpetrator and nonprotective caretakers to people in gen-eral. This other-esteem damage is reflected in beliefs that people in general (or all men or all women) are crazy, malevolent, or incompetent.

In the transference, esteem disruptions are evident in the client's inability to imagine the therapist could hold him in esteem and his subsequent expec-tations of criticism. These clients may be unable to tolerate the therapist's benign regard because it contradicts their core beliefs about themselves; they may be unable to value the therapist. Alternatively, they may be espe-cially sensitive to the therapist's failings; they may expect to have to bolster the therapist's esteem by becoming therapeutic self-objects (i.e., making the therapist "look good").

Intimacy

Because childhood sexual abuse involves the violation of intimacy, it is not uncommon for survivors to experience difficulties in both self-intimacy and other-intimacy. Survivors with self-intimacy disruptions have great diffi-culty tolerating time alone, which obviously connects with impaired self capacities. They are often unable to care for and treat themselves lovingly. Individuals with disruptions in other-intimacy often have few friends or intimate connections with others and may believe such connections are not possible for themselves.

In the transference, these disruptions are evident in the client's response to discussions of the therapeutic relationship, a concept that will seem foreign and anxiety-provoking to clients with intimacy disruptions. They may yearn for and despair of connection. They may push for boundary changes (and violations) that promise greater intimacy. Alternatively (and sometimes simultaneously), they may hold tightly to rigid defenses and boundaries to protect themselves from the inevitable disappointment they expect and from the danger they anticipate. A wish to be connected to the therapist can take the form of trying to please the therapist, wishing to know more about her personal life, or identifying with and emulating her.

Control

Self-control is the need to feel in control of one's thoughts, feelings, and behaviors; other-control is the need to control the behaviors of others. Many survivors adapt to experiences of sexual abuse, in which they had little or no control over their bodies, their feelings, or their thoughts, by taking rigid control in adulthood. Dissociation represents a form of attempting to control feelings or thoughts by not allowing them into one's conscious awareness, or attempting to control one's affect by not experiencing certain thoughts (or memories). Disruptions in other-control can manifest themselves either as a strong need to control others or as a sense of helplessness in interpersonal relationships.

In the transference, control needs emerge in themes about power, autonomy, and choice. The client may experience the therapist as controlling or authoritarian, or he may feel the therapist is not sufficiently directive or in control, and fear the consequences. He may strive to control the therapist or the parameters of the treatment in order to quiet his unease about the therapeutic situation. He may project his experience of self as helpless onto the therapist and then strive to control the therapist, punitively or protectively.

Memory System

CSDT's conceptualization of memory is descriptive. It reflects the understanding that traumatic memory commonly involves the fragmentation or dissociation of aspects of the individual's complex experience. We find it useful clinically to identify five aspects of experience (perception), and thus traumatic memory.

1. Verbal memory: the cognitive narrative of the event or sequence of events; what led up to what happened, what happened, and what has happened since

2. Imagery: the pictures and visual images of the event in the survivor's mind
3. Affect: the emotions experienced before, during, and after the trauma
4. Bodily or somatic memory: the physical sensations that represent the trauma
5. Interpersonal memory: the interpersonal sequences that reemerge behaviorally in current relationships that reflect the individual's experience of past abusive relationships.*

All these aspects of memory contain representations of the abuse experience. As a survivor gains access to the different parts, he can understand what happened, externally and internally; identify the central psychological themes; and work it through as a complete, integrated memory. When the memory exists only in fragments (e.g., an image without an accompanying verbal story, or the story with no affect), the fragments can intrude upon the survivor's awareness and result in incomprehensible, intense affect or perhaps a flashback or panic attack.

The clinical implications of the CSDT approach are many. To begin with, it offers a conceptualization of the client and his resources that is nonpathologizing and therefore esteem-enhancing. It also determines that a central task of therapy is to contextualize an individual's experience. In what context do these beliefs and behaviors make sense? What is the context (often interpersonal) for those feelings or fears? Reconnecting an individual's affective, physical, kinesthetic, interpersonal, and assumptive experience to a context lays the foundation for the creation of personal narrative. The creation of narrative allows an individual to locate and experience himself in the continuum of time (Reis, in press), self, and relationships. This process is at the heart of the healing work of trauma therapy.

---

*For further discussion of memory see chapter 6.

Part Two

COUNTERTRANSFERENCE IN PSYCHOTHERAPY WITH INCEST SURVIVORS

4

Countertransference
Responses to Incest

PSYCHOTHERAPY PRESENTS a dangerous and frightening interpersonal dilemma for an incest survivor. Her anguish and need bring her to seek help,
but the tasks of the psychotherapy—the establishment of interpersonal intimacy; the identification and naming of affects; the integration of thoughts,
memories, affects, and bodily sensations; and the clarification of historical
contexts and events—are the very things she has long struggled to avoid in
order to survive.

Because the psychotherapeutic process is often terrifying for survivor
clients and the potential for early negative transferences is high, treatment
failures, impasses, premature termination, negative therapeutic reactions,
and early flight from treatment are great risks in these therapies. Careful,
ongoing examination of transference and countertransference reactions and
tracking of the interpersonal aspects of the therapy are essential to creating
and preserving a protected space or "facilitating environment" (Winnicott,
1965) for the transformative work of the therapy.

All therapists are susceptible to intense and complicated responses both
to incest and to survivors of incest. In order to maintain a therapeutic
stance, the therapist needs to identify, tolerate, and understand her countertransference responses. The therapeutic tasks of building trust, identifying
interpersonal paradigms, and integrating fragmented aspects of the self are

gradual processes. Intensive psychotherapy is a powerful and effective agent of healing and change when grounded in theory with a focus on the therapeutic relationship. This focus requires the therapist's attention to all aspects of the relationship, transferential and real, and continual analysis of her countertransference.

This work is difficult; as therapists, we are asked to hold a range of transferences, affects, and identities that are dystonic at best and toxic at worst. To the extent that we are able to remain attuned to the nuances of our responses to each client, we have a powerful resource to facilitate our connection to, understanding of, empathy and respect for our clients. Countertransference can be used both intrapersonally, for the therapist's own edification and insight, and interpersonally through considered countertransference disclosure, as well as through countertransference-informed exploration of the relationship and the client's experience of the therapist.

A relational approach to psychotherapy in general, and countertransference disclosure in particular, can convey a message to the client that she is neither intolerable nor toxic. Specifically, the client may need to see that she can have an effect on or evoke feelings in the therapist without damaging or depleting her. Many survivors, who took personal responsibility for the their impoverished developmental environments, fear and believe themselves to be untouchable at best and perhaps lethal to others.

In chapter 1, we discussed factors that contribute to countertransference responses to incest survivor clients. In this chapter, we will focus primarily on two of them: the therapist's response to the reality and meaning of incest and child abuse, and her response to the client's particular adaptation to experiences of incest.

Even before seeing a survivor client, a therapist often has countertransference reactions which she then brings into the first session. In response to her knowledge of a client's incest history, a therapist may have a range of intense affective reactions—horror, outrage, anxiety, protectiveness, guilt, identification, disgust, blame, denial, arousal, retaliatory wishes, powerlessness, grief, for example. If she has many survivors among her clients she may feel exhausted, overwhelmed, or full of dread. If she has few, but negative, experiences, she may feel defensive, anxious, or tense.

Countertransference reactions will be modified (or intensified) by a number of therapist and client factors. Therapist factors include: gender, training, years of psychotherapy experience, experience working with incest survivors, awareness of and knowledge about incest, personal experiences of sexual abuse, assault, or incest, personal life circumstances, degree of professional isolation or support, personal psychotherapy experience, and level of comfort with intensive therapy and painful affects. Client factors include: gender, the specific circumstances of the incest (for example, duration, age at onset and discontinuation, level of brutality, relationship to the perpetrator, the role of the other caretakers, other children involved, responses of others to whom the client may have turned for help), and the client's current age, circumstances, symptomatology, and presentation. These specific variables affect the development and intensity of the therapist's countertransference reactions.

Following are several categories of countertransference responses to the meaning of incest. These responses will be modified by the therapist and client factors noted above.

RESPONSE TO TABOO

One area of countertransference is a response to the taboo against incest and to the destruction of our personal and cultural parental imagoes. The feelings elicited in the therapist may include horror, outrage, and disgust, and rage at the parents and society that allow such behaviors to occur. These feelings are often present in the initial phase of disclosure, especially for a new therapist or a therapist relatively new to working with childhood trauma material, or when the nature or maliciousness of the abuse is new to the therapist. While these feelings are often linked to vicarious traumatization, in this chapter, we focus on their countertransference role, that is, their occurrence in a particular therapeutic relationship with a particular client.

Incest is a profoundly disturbing event, and we are all influenced by the cultural taboo against it and concomitant cultural repression and denial of the existence of incestuous relationships. The psychological literature reflects cycles of roughly 30 years in which child abuse is acknowledged and then ignored, a pattern that reflects the power of the wish not to know and the extraordinary difficulty of integrating the reality of childhood trauma into our frame of reference (Brett, 1993). Incest stories are difficult to hear, painful to believe, and hard to absorb in the way one must absorb and metabolize a client's early environment and childhood experience in order to help her reconstruct a comprehensible, affectively accurate understanding of her personal context. It is particularly critical in psychotherapy with an incest survivor that a therapist be consistently alert to personal reactions to the client and her material in order to maintain a therapeutic stance, develop a working alliance, and protect against a potential therapeutic impasse and relational disconnection.

The reality of incest involves exploitation, tyranny, betrayal of trust, crossing of generational boundaries, and violation of deeply held cultural values of maternal and paternal caregiving and protection. At several levels, personal, psychic, and cultural, the therapist's sensibilities are assaulted and her romantic images of childhood are badly shaken. It is difficult to imagine and visualize the details of adult-child sexual intercourse because the images of the actual bodily contact are disturbing and painful. The abusive parent at best exhibits insensitivity or oblivion to, and distortion of, a child's needs and experience, and at worst shows profoundly disturbing levels of sadism, brutality, cruelty, and dominance. This parent may concurrently, however, be the most nurturant person in the family available to this child. These interactions and contradictions fly in the face of our deeply held cultural imagoes of parents as loving caretakers whom we expect to nurture, support, and protect children. We hold strongly to these imagoes because they come from our own real, defensive, and fantasied early experiences and beliefs and our own roles as adults and parents, and they are integral parts of our psychic structures.

Countertransference reactions of outrage, anger, and horror can be useful in the work of psychotherapy; they represent the reality of witnessing, that is, they validate the horror of the violation and demonstrate an appropriate response. Herman (1992) notes the importance of the therapist bearing witness. It is even arguable that these countertransference reactions are necessary and if they are absent a therapist needs to evaluate her potential vicarious traumatization. However, this role must be used cautiously and only in consonance with the client's needs. A therapist's rage for a client and for herself may far exceed the client's subjective experience of rage, and may get in the way of their exploration of more complex, ambivalent feelings of love, loyalty, grief, self-blame, shame, and guilt. When a therapist's feelings lead the therapy and prevent her from hearing the client, the countertransference is obstructing the therapy and the therapist is in danger of reenacting dynamics of earlier relationships in which the child's experience was disregarded and the adult's feelings were projected onto the child.

Survivor guilt is a related countertransference response. For the therapist who herself is not a survivor, the relief and guilt related to not having endured sexual abuse can be very salient. This was the overwhelming experience of nonsurvivor therapists in relation to Nazi Holocaust survivors in Danieli's (1984) seminal research.

A therapist who is a survivor working with clients whose abuse context was more horrific, violent, unrelenting than hers may feel guilt and tempted to diminish her own experience. The therapist may feel guilty if she belongs to a different group from her client but the same group as her perpetrator (a dilemma often experienced by male therapists working with female survivors of father-daughter incest). When the context of a client's abuse includes other factors that stir guilt or survivor guilt, such as membership in an oppressed group to which the therapist does not belong, then the therapist can feel moved to act on the guilt. When working with clients of a different socioeconomic class, religious group, racial or ethnic group, sexual orientation, nationality (including language differences), or generation, a therapist must be alert to countertransference avoidance of issues of identity and difference.

The process of noticing and addressing countertransference feelings about incest allows the therapist to remain affectively present and available to her client. She must attend to her responses so as not to be overwhelmed with her outrage, or stop listening to the client's troubling material, or act impulsively on the client's behalf or press the client to action. Remaining present, connected, and steady in the face of affectively evocative material is an important component of developing a holding relationship. The therapist can achieve this connection through knowing her responses—not pushing them aside, but moving through them to understanding.

A therapist's rage can emerge in many ways, from physical tension, to impulsive or sarcastic retorts about a perpetrator, to detailed fantasies of revenge.

Example   One therapist working with a survivor of childhood sexual abuse by a stepfather who was sadistic, demeaning, and cruel and who used his physical strength to threaten and control his family, found herself having elaborate fantasies of physically and verbally assaulting this man and angrily holding him accountable for his abusive actions. The fantasies became increasingly elaborate and often included her client's participation. Initially, the therapist found the fantasies somewhat enjoyable and a useful release for her rage, but over time she came to question how the fantasies served as a buffer between her and her client. She realized the fantasies denied her experience of her client's true powerlessness and terror as a child, and simultaneously allowed her to collude with her client's denial of her child status, that is, the true limits of her power as a child. As long as the therapist held and elaborated the rage, the client was unable to integrate her rage and terror and sort out real and fantasied levels of power, control, and responsibility. The therapist started listening more carefully for the client's rage, especially as it was manifest when she was expressing or describing terror.

At times, in order to remain open in the therapy, the therapist may need take action outside the therapy relationship. Such actions could be personal, such as weeping for the client, or expressing rage physically by beating pillows, yelling, or engaging in strenuous activity. Sometimes rage for a particular client can also be made more manageable by channeling it into constructive community, social, or legislative action. One therapist started participating annually in her community's "Take Back the Night" march, carrying a sign proclaiming, "No More." Another therapist who was working with a client who had been sexually abused by a prior therapist became more active in working for legislation in her state to address ethical violations by psychotherapists. This action helped her maintain a therapeutic stance with her client who was struggling with intense ambivalent feelings toward the prior therapist, and (unlike her current therapist) was not in a place of outrage or rage much of the time.

PARENTAL COUNTERTRANSFERENCE

A second area of countertransference responses to incest is the wish to repair the damage done, to reparent, to make up for the injuries one's client has suffered. This is a parental countertransference and the feelings may include protectiveness, fear, and anxiety for the client (especially when the client has ongoing destructive contact with parents or other perpetrators), grief, retaliatory wishes, powerlessness, and love. All of these feelings may be appropriate at times and may also be in direct response to the client's presentation and expressed needs. This protective parental stance can also reflect a common countertransference wish to undo the wound of incest, that is, to make up for the deprivation and hurt the client suffered in childhood. The therapist responds to the client as an adult responds to an abandoned, hurt child, that is, to act *in loco parentis* until a parent is located. As the psychotherapy moves forward, this response can be strengthened in response to the therapist and client's developing relationship with memory of being a child held by the adult client, that is, with their deeper understanding of the client's experience as a child whose resources and power were so limited in an adult world. This developmental perspective is critical to understanding the trauma of childhood abuse and is emotionally powerful for both therapist and client.

The concept of the child within the adult can be a very useful metaphor with incest survivors in whom a needful, vulnerable child self or state exists in an encapsulated form, unintegrated into the adult functioning self (Davies & Frawley, 1994; Ferenczi, 1949). Those needs are often an object of the adult survivor's rejection, contempt, and punishment. Unintegrated dependency needs can lead the survivor to reenact repetitively and internally a childhood interpersonal trauma, such as that of the punitive parent abusing the vulnerable child (Montgomery & Greif, 1989). This reenactment takes the form of the client's neglectful, hypercritical, or abusive response to her own feelings, needs, and wishes. It is often the cornerstone of the incest survivor's psychic life and relationship to herself (as well as of her symptomatology or adaptation). A therapist will feel drawn to intervene when repeatedly compelled to witness this internal reenactment of abuse between the dependent child and the neglectful or punitive parent parts of the client. A central goal of psychotherapy with an incest survivor is to redefine these intrapersonal struggles as interpersonal events, in the present with the therapist and in the past with significant others.

How is a Parental
Countertransference Helpful?

The parental countertransference paradigm can be both helpful and problematic. It is helpful for a therapist to note and model appropriate parenting to a client who has lacked that in her life, in order to provide a reality base to help her identify inappropriate parenting from her past and to note inappropriate self-parenting responses in the present. For example, clients often seem surprised and reassured by the explicit naming of the limits in the relationship. When a therapist makes it explicit that the client is not responsible for taking care of or meeting her therapist's needs in the therapeutic relationship, she is making a multilevel intervention: (1) she is clarifying the respectful frame and boundaries of the therapy, (2) she is explicitly differentiating the therapeutic relationship from her client's relationship with her incestuous and narcissistic caretakers from the past, (3) she is modeling the negotiation of responsibilities and boundaries in present relationships, and (4) she is naming the often unspoken parameters of an evolving relationship. This process is one of establishing safety and developing trust and is necessary for the client to express her private feelings and needs in the context of clear boundaries and roles.

Clients who have internalized extraordinarily harsh, punitive parental objects often exhibit surprise when a therapist expresses anger and dismay at their self-destructive or dangerous behavior, or concern for their emotional well-being at times of great pain or stress. One woman noted that it was not until she was in therapy that it occurred to her that the *quality* of her life—not simply whether she was alive or dead—mattered. It is important to note a client's surprise when it occurs and to use it to explore the client's underlying assumptions about parenting, self-care, and what she needs and deserves. The therapist's attitude toward the client as a person of value, who is entitled to care, respect, and tenderness (which she does not have to earn, but deserves because of her existence) is critical to the treatment. Often a survivor does not anticipate or feel she deserves reasonable care, respect, or love from others or herself because she has accepted an identity as bad and unworthy in order to make sense of her painful experience.

How is a Parental
Countertransference Problematic?

Parental countertransference can also be problematic. Reparenting impulses on the part of the therapist can infantilize a client, deny the adult-functioning part of the client, and undermine a client's strengths. Taken

literally, this countertransference implies an unrealistic goal of psychotherapy: to reparent. "It is the therapist's role to enable the child to mourn the
childhood that cannot be, not to live it out in the transference relationship"
(Davies & Frawley, 1994, p. 83).

This countertransference response may parallel the client's primitive
sense of omnipotence, which persists because of developmental tasks that
are incomplete from childhood. It invites a transference to the therapist
as all-powerful, all-knowing, and all-nurturing, which when unanalyzed
ultimately denies the power and self-authority of the client. The therapist
can behave as an authoritarian and directive parent who knows what is best
for the client. This countertransference can encourage overdependence on
the therapist and extreme regression, often replicating the dynamics of an
enmeshed family by giving the message that the therapist needs the client to
be needy, helpless, in pain, and unable to leave.

An insidious sign of this countertransference taken to an extreme is when
a therapist takes as literal a client's question, "Was I abused?" When a
therapist assumes she could have the answer to that question rather than
recognizing the parental transference implied by the client's wish that she
could have the answer, the therapist has moved into a parental countertransference and lost her therapeutic frame. Another problematic manifestation of this countertransference is punitive; under the guise of setting
limits and protecting herself, a therapist can impose rigid boundaries that
always put her needs above those of the client, thus creating a reenactment
of childhood dynamics.

A parental countertransference is not unusual with clients who are vi-
ciously self-destructive or chronically suicidal. These clients often pull for
one of two polarized countertransference responses: rage or pity. A therapist may respond angrily or punitively when she can no longer tolerate the
life or death anxiety she is asked to hold with these clients. When her client
expresses dissociated rage through self-destructive behavior or threats, or
when she feels she needs to be in control of her client's behavior or to
protect her practice from liability threat, a therapist may move to parental
action and try to solve rather than hold her client's conflicting affects and
identities. A therapist can become enraged, consciously or unconsciously,
when a client's chronic destructive behavior belies or defeats the therapist's
sense of being able to help and soothe her clients.

On the other hand, to the extent that a therapist connects with her
client's despair and vulnerability, or with her own affection for the client
and her grief and fear of losing her, the therapist can become protective,
solicitous, and anxious, and neglect to include the client's anger, sadism,
and hate in their mutual understanding of the client's feelings and behavior.
A therapist might then convey, knowingly or inadvertently, the message

that she cannot tolerate the strong, independent, separate, angry parts of the client, and in particular is unable to hear the client's rage, sadism, real guilt, and identification with the aggressor. This countertransference can include an idealization of the client or a view of her as only a passive victim. The client may then feel great guilt and be driven to anger, or moved to betray the therapist to relieve her guilt and prove that her sense of badness is warranted. This betrayal can take the form of keeping secrets from the therapist, engaging in self-destructive behaviors, or sabotaging the therapy. Alternatively, the client may feel rage that the therapist is ignoring her strengths or her vulnerabilities and subsequently withdraw or lash out at the therapist.

In addition, this countertransference, like the response to the taboo of incest, can interfere with a client's freedom to own and explore her profound ambivalence toward her parents, especially her deep love, loyalty, protectiveness, yearning, and feelings of specialness. Parental feelings on the part of the therapist may be connected to or reflect an unrealistic rescue fantasy, a magical wish to undo and erase painful experiences, rather than acknowledge, validate, and think about how to live with their reality and consequences. Incest cannot be erased, but a survivor can own her experience and be less of a victim to its sequelae when they can be acknowledged and addressed.

Acknowledging Parental Countertransference

Another aspect of this parental countertransference is the therapist's conscious wish not to replicate parental failings, which can lead to a catch-22. The therapist may feel guilty or intrusive for asking about details of the abuse or asking probing questions about a client's body or inner life, but on the other hand feel like an absent, neglectful, or unseeing parent if she avoids or does not encourage exploration of these issues. For example, early in the work with bulimic, substance abusing, or self-mutilating clients, a therapist needs to acknowledge the relational dilemma. The client often has strong feelings about the symptom, usually feelings of shame, secrecy, protectiveness, and guilty pleasure coupled with great anxiety, concern, fear, and helplessness. The therapist can acknowledge the potential for interpersonal reenactment, as in the following scenario.

Example   A client opened a session with a veiled allusion to a difficult weekend and then changed the subject. The therapist responded, "While I know it's difficult for us to talk about it when you hurt yourself or struggle with wanting to hurt yourself, I'm also aware that you've struggled with this pain alone for too long. If I ask you about this weekend, I know you may feel ashamed or that I am being intrusive like your father, but if I don't say anything, you may feel abandoned, or that I am being oblivious like your mother. What shall we do here?" Her client sat silent for a moment, and then said, "If you don't ask, I'll never talk about it. I guess I need help."

Naming the transference paradigm up front can modify its toxicity and help prevent a negative therapeutic reaction early in the work. It also serves an educational function about the process of transference in a treatment where the client's experience of transference is likely to be intense, frightening, and overpowering.

It is important to emphasize with clients the essential value of being able to talk about the therapy relationship and the details of what happens between the two people from the outset. This idea of directly naming interpersonal events usually stands in stark contrast to past relationships in an incestuous family, which tend to remain shrouded in secrecy, pathological denial, repression, and lies. It also frees the therapist from countertransference feelings related to secrecy, sadism, and guilt.

Countertransference Love

An important component of a parental countertransference is feelings of love for the client. The literature is surprisingly silent on issues of countertransference love and caring (Roth, 1987; Schwartz, 1988). Therapeutic work with survivors of childhood abuse can be enormously intimate and at times tender. It is not unusual for the therapist and client to feel deep love and caring for one another. This love operates on many levels, developmental as well as psychological. We can love the adult person of our client, who she is and how she has survived. We can love the child she was as well as her contemporary childlike qualities. We can love her strength and will to survive and her sensitivity and vulnerability. We can love her inner beauty and capacity to see and be sensitive to beauty around her. We can love her integrity and sensitivity to others. We can love her courage and her wish to heal and grow. We can love her response to our loving her.

Clinically the effect of the therapist's loving regard is powerful. The developmental context for many clients did not allow the crucial developmental stages of primary maternal or paternal preoccupation—the loving, delighted, complete preoccupation that many parents experience with an infant, or the delight in a toddler and young child's discovery of herself, her body, and her effect on others. The exhibitionism and invitation to be loved and admired that are a natural part of these developmental stages were often met with indifference, humiliation, or exploitation. Clients strive, unconsciously, to rework those experiences and to reclaim that pride and joy in themselves through the therapeutic relationship. The therapist's affection and delight in her client can be a complementary response to these early developmental deficiencies. When a therapist is able to hold a client lovingly in her eyes as the client tentatively explores and becomes acquainted with herself, the client internalizes a benevolent receptive witness to her self-exploration and affirmation. This love takes the form clinically of acceptance and warmth and affirmation of a client's worth.

A therapist may explicitly express caring and respect for her client; however, the power and valence of words need to be considered. Because we do not make distinctions in our language to parallel the classical distinctions among agape and eros (caritas and amor), we need to choose our words carefully and respectfully when disclosing countertransference love. The term "love" is often sexualized and may imply possessiveness or eroticism, and therefore generally is misleading rather than clarifying in the therapeutic relationship. However, the acknowledgment of the therapist's caring, regard, and respect for the client can be genuine, respectful of the frame of the relationship, and valuable to the client.

Both of these areas of countertransference stem from powerful affective responses to the existence of incest, a response that starts with disbelief and horror, then shifts to rage, outrage, and moral indignation, and then to grief. This profound grief underlies much of a therapist's and client's need to flee. Herman (1992) identifies the stage in recovery, after the facts have been recovered and acknowledged, when a client must deal with the intense grief both for the childhood that wasn't and for the pain of living in a world where such hurtful and unfair things happen. She underscores that at this point in treatment a client may decide she cannot go further because the pain and immensity of the grief are too much. We believe this grief is just as painful and difficult for therapists to acknowledge and endure, and yet critical to process if one is to work with incest survivors successfully. A therapist's need to protect herself from the pain of this grief can lead to significant avoidance, denial, and silence in the therapy, which can stymie the therapy. We are asked to sit with our clients in this grief; countertransference denial of or submersion in this grief can render us unavailable to them. On the other hand, sometimes we can acknowledge, share, and together survive "swimming the river of grief." The connection of the therapeutic relationship offsets the painful isolation of grief.

DENIAL: THE WISH NOT TO KNOW

A third general area of countertransference responses relates to the need not to know, not to believe it, to protect oneself from the feelings evoked by the fact of incest. This countertransference reflects the defense against the feelings aroused in the response to the taboo. *Denial of incest and childhood sexual abuse is natural and pervasive.* This denial is not limited to a segment of therapists, but is inherent in all of us in response to powerful cultural and personal taboos and instinctive withdrawal from pain. It can take a variety of forms, from not hearing clues or hints dropped, to doubting the accuracy or veracity of a client's memories, to doubting one's own perceptions or suspicions. It can be intellectualized as a theoretical debate about fact versus fantasy, "true versus false memory," internal versus external reality, or medical-legal evidence. As we become more familiar with certain traumatic stories, our blind spots can shift. Field (1990) persuasively argues that many negative therapeutic reactions are responses to a therapist's denial of or inability to hear about a trauma or abuse history, or a client's perception that the therapist is unwilling or unable to hear this material. This denial can also stem from the therapist's repressed memories of or inability to work through and acknowledge her own history of sexual or other abuse (see also chapter 8).

Pitfalls of Denial

Secrecy

The danger of a therapist's denial is that it reinforces the need for secrecy and the client's belief that she and her experience are unbearable. The burden of secrecy weighs heavily on an incest survivor, who has received repeated messages to keep the secret because the truth is unspeakable, shameful, unbearable to others (often her mother), and, worst of all, will be labeled distorted or untrue. These fears are reinforced by even subtle messages from therapists that they cannot stand or manage the material. Many recommend that therapists ask about sexual abuse history during a consultation if there is any reason to suspect its presence, not because the question is likely to be answered truthfully or completely, but because it lets a client know that the words can be spoken by the therapist and the idea tolerated (Mac Ian & Pearlman, 1992; Pearlman & McCann, 1994).

A therapist's denial of the occurrence of abuse, its significance, or its effect on her client can also reflect an unconscious collusion with her client's and, not infrequently the perpetrator and family's, denial and need not to know. Both participants can collude in denial out of an understandable, conscious or unconscious, wish not to know the true experience of a child in an abusive relationship (Laub & Auerhahn, 1993). When a client reports that she was sexually abused as a child, but has "worked that through" or "processed it" and is "fine now," the therapist may feel tempted to concur with little or no further exploration in order to protect herself from the pain of working it through with her.

Dissociation

Dissociation, a common adaptation to childhood sexual trauma, is related to denial. A client's dissociation is often her response to the internalized mandate not to know, a mandate which requires her to split off parts of her experience and self to avoid — at all costs — the integration of her thoughts, feelings, memories, and bodily sensations. The goal of the psychotherapy is to facilitate this very awareness and integration, and to help make the resulting affects tolerable and comprehensible. The achievement of this goal requires that as therapists, we be able to hear the truth as our clients experience and recover it, including leaving room for later modifications. The wish to deny can lead us to ignore or collude with dissociative processes in the therapy.

Therapists also use dissociation at times to manage the intense affects aroused by these clients and their histories. In fact, it can be useful, even essential, to use dissociative defenses to protect oneself while listening to particularly disturbing or horrific traumatic material in order to remain available to one's client. At times a therapist needs to distance herself and concentrate on remaining calm and overtly receptive, knowing she will need to process her reaction later, alone and with colleagues; by doing so she protects both the client and herself. It is problematic, however, if such defenses become mobilized outside of a therapist's awareness, because that follow-up processing and reconnecting will not occur. If a therapist finds herself dissociating without being aware of it, she needs to explore the issue in supervision, self-analysis, and/or personal psychotherapy to understand the precipitants and personal meaning of her response. Signs of unconscious dissociation include "coming to" in session and realizing one has missed what has been said, being unable to remember parts of the session, and feeling unable to be in the room or in one's body with a particular client.

Rage Displacement

Another pitfall of denial is that the rage, both for the client's pain and for the therapist's discomfort, can be displaced onto the client in the form of blame and censure. This projective process can include labeling the client "hysterical" or "borderline" or "manipulative"; suspecting melodrama, insincerity, deceitfulness, or malingering; or assuming the client had responsibility, significant control or choice about her incestuous relationship (e.g., She could have stopped it, why didn't she just say no or leave the room, the house, the family?). These superego-laden criticisms are particularly dangerous with survivor clients because they are so often feelings shared by the client based on her distorted sense of omnipotence and her need to deny the trauma and her own emotional and physical vulnerability as a child.

SEXUAL AND VOYEURISTIC
COUNTERTRANSFERENCE

A fourth area of countertransference that therapists often find problematic is the sexual and voyeuristic countertransference, a response to one's fascination with the forbidden, and the sadomasochistic fusion of sexuality and aggression represented in sexual abuse. It includes feelings of curiosity, titillation, arousal, and excitement. These feelings are common, yet often the most discomforting because they evoke guilt and shame as well as narcissistic injury to the therapist when they conflict with her identity and ego-ideal, as a therapist, a man or woman, or a human being. As others have noted, therapists commonly feel ashamed of this countertransference with a survivor of sexual abuse (Davies & Frawley, 1994; Gabbard, 1994c). It can seem intolerable to accept feeling like a perpetrator or feeling identified with the client's perpetrator. Without collegial support to name and understand sexual responses, therapists often rely on denial and suppression.

Sexual responses interact with gender issues in the countertransference. Men may feel guilty about their arousal and then angry at the client and perhaps skeptical of her story, or they may see her as seductive, aggressively using her sexuality against him. Women can feel guilty about sexual arousal, then feel shame and confusion, which can be projected onto the client whom they may then see as provoking or wanting the sexual abuse.* Therapists may worry about their sadistic, masochistic, homosexual, or exploitive sexual impulses or feelings. The obvious danger of this countertransference is that the therapist may need to relieve her discomfort by pushing the feelings away, often onto the client, or by pushing the client away. Obviously there are dangers if a therapist does not identify these feelings as countertransference, and instead shows them or acts on them in a way that violates the boundaries, safety, and ethics of the therapeutic relationship.

It is important to note, however, that these feelings, like other types of

---

*There is a whole set of gender countertransference responses to client material about incest and childhood sexual abuse. We have devoted an entire chapter (chapter 9) to the topic because of its complex interaction with the tasks of psychotherapy with adult survivors of childhood sexual abuse.

countertransferences, have an informative and helpful function as well. Specifically, a therapist's awareness of her arousal and concomitant horror provides her with a powerful understanding of an incest survivor's central dilemma as a child. Ehrenberg (1987) notes that one of the prominent and painful sequelae of incest is the disruption of a client's relation to her own desire; because of the intense ambivalence and the great guilt about her physical and emotional arousal in response to the incestuous situation, an incest survivor's experience of sexuality, and of desire more generally, is extremely conflictual. Common solutions to this conflict include chronic dissociation, anhedonia, sexual inhibition, masochistic promiscuity, and sadomasochistic sexuality. A therapist must be able to hear feelings that the client herself believes are unacceptable; this is not possible if the therapist cannot tolerate and examine her own conflictual feelings.

BODY-CENTERED COUNTERTRANSFERENCE

It is easy to assume that countertransference responses will be manifest only in conscious words and feelings. This assumption excludes a whole realm of countertransference experience, one that is key with survivors of physical and sexual abuse whose experiences are often body-centered, as van der Kolk (1994) has also noted. We hold our affects physically and we will respond unconsciously through our bodies to the material and presence of our clients. It is not unusual for a therapist to experience somatic symptoms that parallel her client's body experience.

Example   A therapist described how early in her career as a trauma therapist, she would hold her clients' somatic symptoms. "They would leave the session relieved of a headache. I would have it. They were no longer nauseous. I was. The client would go home relieved, with the illusion of health, and I suffered. This was very painful and it took a long time for me figure out the countertransference at work here. I just thought I wasn't good enough and couldn't take it."

It is common for a therapist to first become aware of a countertransference response through a bodily sensation. Saakvitne (1993c) describes a therapist's experience of nausea in response to a client's childlike seductive behavior (that is, a client who behaves in a manner that is both childlike and sexualized toward the therapist) in the context of an eroticized maternal transference. Others have addressed physical responses such as headaches, sleepiness, numbness, genital pain, throat constriction, sexual arousal, or loss of voice (Armsworth, 1993; Attias & Goodwin, 1993; McDougall, 1989). Many therapists have found themselves involuntarily becoming tearful, weeping, raising their voices, unexpectedly shifting their bodies, or

moving during affectively charged sessions. Bodily countertransference responses can occur in any psychotherapy, but the bodily context of childhood sexual abuse and the omnipresence of dissociative processes in these
therapies make these countertransference responses far more common. The
presence of the therapist's body in the therapy, in the therapeutic relationship and in the therapist's experience is complicated and underexamined.*
We encourage therapists to remain more conscious of their bodies and to
use their physical experience and sensations as part of the relevant clinical
data of the therapeutic relationship.

COUNTERTRANSFERENCE TO COMMON
POST-TRAUMA ADAPTATIONS

Many adult survivors of childhood trauma exhibit symptoms of post-
traumatic stress disorder, dissociative disorders, various eating disorders;
meet criteria for personality disorders; and engage in traumatic reenactments. Their symptoms are severe, anxiety-provoking for both client and
therapist, and difficult to manage clinically. These include relentless suicidal feelings and actions, distressing flashbacks, startle responses, nightmares and night terrors, partial amnesia and fragmented memories,
affective flooding and numbing, self-destructive behaviors (including self-
mutilation, bulimia and anorexia, engagement in abusive relationships,
substance abuse, and other life-threatening behaviors), and intense self-
loathing.

The cumulative effect on the therapist of holding such self-destructive
wishes, impulses, and behaviors is significant. At both an existential and a
clinical level, as therapists, we are asked to hold on to hope in the face of
overwhelming despair. We are asked to witness brutal behavior to someone
we not only care about but also to whom we have made a commitment to
help. We are asked to understand feelings that are abhorrent to us: self-
hatred, the wish to die or to destroy one's body, vicious misogyny, and
complete nihilism. In the face of these feelings, we are left holding the wish
for our client's life, health, and happiness. We hold the life and death
anxiety, the wish for life in the face of (seemingly) certain death. This
painful experience often reflects a split-off memory of the child's experience
of brutal physical and sexual assault and severe emotional and physical
neglect and abandonment. The child who fears for her life (Bloch, 1978)
holds encapsulated the fusion of a wish to live with terror and a belief she
will die. In the countertransference with chronically suicidal and self-
destructive clients, therapists too hold this excruciating paradox.

*For further discussion see chapter 9.

Countertransference responses to this daunting task include intense anxiety, rage, exhaustion, loss of hope and increasing despair, sadism, rescue fantasies, profound self-doubt, and existential crises of faith. This countertransference often dovetails with vicarious traumatization, especially when a therapist has more than one client struggling with these issues or symptoms at a time.

The sensitive disclosure of these countertransference responses is often useful in order to move the dilemma back into the therapeutic relationship and decrease the therapist's feelings of isolation and abandonment by the client. While painful countertransference feelings can evoke impulses to shame or blame the client, the simple acknowledgment of the pain, helplessness, and fear can free the therapist to remain affectively present. This disclosure is not intended to blame the client for the therapist's pain, or to call her names, but rather to express and invite empathy for the role of a helpless witness to heinous assault, a role our clients have often held. For example, it can be a powerful intervention for a therapist to point out to her client that she feels like a helpless witness to the client's self-destruction. When the therapist says she does not wish to participate in such a reenactment because it is painful and hurtful, and it evokes both sorrow and anger in her, she reestablishes the client's self-destructiveness as a relational event. Often a client can connect to her positive feelings for the therapist or the therapeutic relationship even when she is not in touch with any positive feelings for herself or her body. This intervention also opens the door for the analysis of projective identification; therapist and client can consider how the client's role in this enactment enlightens them both about her experience as a helpless witness in the past.

THERAPIST RESPONSES TO VICTIM AS PERPETRATOR

Another difficult aspect of working with incest survivors is the fact that victims can engage in traumatic reenactments in which they play the role of perpetrator, both within and outside the therapy. People who have been abused by those whose role was to protect and care for them can struggle with inappropriate expectations for children and inadequate resources to manage their frustration and needs as parents. As Terr (1990) has also noted, abused children may molest younger children or pets as they struggle to make sense of what is happening to themselves. People who are humiliated can experience rage, which they may turn upon others who are weaker than themselves in an effort to restore some sense of control or esteem. Therapists can be unwilling to hear or believe the client's own experience as perpetrator, which, while far from universal, is not uncommon.

Allowing the potential for a client's abuse of others into the room and the therapeutic relationship requires changes in the therapist's beliefs and affect tolerance. Therapists who have unconsciously needed to see their clients only as victims can feel appalled or betrayed to learn that their clients have also victimized others. When the therapist holds the knowledge that her client may be at risk to harm others, perhaps through child-rearing practices that the therapist views as abusive but which are within the client's normal experience (Greven, 1991), it can lead to conflicts within the therapy and within the therapist. The heightened sense of responsibility to protect children from abuse that a therapist gains from empathic connection to her client can leave her in conflict, torn between empathy for her client and for the client's children. When the therapist struggles with conflicting identities, she is susceptible to shame and guilt, and changes in the realms of identity and world view.

Therapists also have a range of countertransference responses to the client when she is acting as perpetrator against the therapist. Clients who have been abused by persons whom they should have been able to trust may well enact their rage at betrayal against the therapist. When this happens, the therapist may struggle against her own experience of the client as perpetrator, not wishing to see it. She may respond with hurt silence. She may retaliate, using her power to reject and humiliate the client, or create an ultimatum, rather than analyzing the transference enactment or reenactment. She may feel trapped by her empathic connection with the meanings of this enactment, and be unable to hold both empathy and anger. Yet the treatment can only progress when these dynamics are named. Identifying such patterns is the path toward freedom for both therapist and client.

The complexity of our responses to our client's capacity for rage, cruelty, and exploitation toward us can illuminate areas of countertransference dissociation or denial. What aspects of the client or her history are we unwilling to allow into our awareness or into the therapeutic relationship? As we examine our conflicting responses, we ultimately facilitate a more complete and integrated awareness of the person of our client, one that allows for ambivalence, complexity, and contradictions.

PROFESSIONAL IDENTITY AND DISCONNECTION

Another area of countertransference vulnerability has to do with our developing identities as therapists. Professional development has parallels to human development; under stress we return to earlier developmental stages. We carry internalizations of our teachers, supervisors, and mentors, and are susceptible to shame and loss of self-esteem in relation to these internalized, as well as external, colleagues and authorities. Because trauma therapies (and clients with trauma histories) often push us beyond the limits of our training, we must abandon, and be abandoned by, our mentors in some fundamental ways.

This can create a frightening sense of disconnection or isolation, especially for therapists who have not found a collegial support system for the work they do. When a client pushes a therapist in a direction that differs from her training or internal model of a "good therapist" (for example, by asking direct questions, evoking anxiety, pushing her to the edge of her knowledge and experience, questioning or challenging the techniques in which she was trained, asking her to do something she is not accustomed to doing), she is vulnerable to countertransference resentment, shame, guilt, confusion, and insecurity. These feelings can result in a defensive need to return to certainty by making the client wrong or bad, pathologizing the interpersonal process at work, or becoming defensively authoritarian. For example, the therapist may see the client as manipulative or devaluing, and not recognize an opportunity to reconstruct the therapeutic relationship taking into account the needs, limits, and strengths of both participants and their roles.

Keeping this relational perspective requires cognitive flexibility, self-confidence, and nondefensiveness (D. Elliott, personal communication, 1993; Gill, 1982), and no one can maintain those stances all the time. In fact, it can be argued that this relational approach (which we believe is essential with survivors of childhood abuse) is more demanding than a more interpersonally distant stance; the therapist working in this way may be able to see fewer clients before becoming fatigued.

Each therapist constructs a professional ego ideal to which she compares herself automatically and regularly. As a therapist develops skill as a trauma therapist, her ego ideal may well incorporate contradictions: be genuine, but keep therapeutic neutrality; invite a client to notice her interpersonal environment, but do not answer her questions about your feelings; negotiate the therapeutic relationship, but do not be too "gratifying"; invite connection, but do not encourage dependence or regression. These contradictions often mix language and concepts from several different theoretical or assumptive bases, and it can be difficult to sort them out. A therapist will feel discomfort, complicated emotions, and a subtle or strong need for distance as the client evokes these identity conflicts within her.

We believe these professional identity and ego ideal conflicts play a powerful role in a therapist's behavior and countertransference. Bringing the conflicts into conscious awareness and open discussion with colleagues goes a long way toward controlling the potential countertransference enactments of the conflicts. We discuss developmental issues in more depth in chapter 16.

THEORY AS A SOURCE OF
COUNTERTRANSFERENCE

Because theories shape what a therapist perceives and allows to enter the context of her therapies, they also shape countertransference responses. If, for example, a therapist's theory suggests that only whole memories with a narrative, imagery, affect, and bodily sensations are true representations of childhood trauma, she may discount survivor clients' reports of body memories or partial flashbacks (Calof, 1993). If her theory of psychotherapy does not include an awareness of the importance of the therapeutic relationship, she may neglect or become annoyed with clients' attempts to deal with the therapist as a real person rather than as a disengaged expert or transference object. If she does not believe that children are abused sadistically in organized cults, she may overlook or disbelieve clients' reports suggesting such abuse. Stage theories of trauma and recovery can blind a therapist to the individual experience of the client in the room at the moment, or lead to frustration that the client is in stage three without having gone through stage two.

If a client's material forces a therapist to change her assumptions or professional frame of reference, she will be disoriented, resistant, and likely disgruntled. Staying attuned to the internal paradigm clashes can help the therapist accurately sort out the sources of her conscious affective responses.

ORGANIZATIONAL COUNTERTRANSFERENCE

A final important note is that countertransference is not limited as a phenomenon to the client-therapist dyad. Just as clients have transferential responses to clinical organizations (Parson, 1986), the therapist, the client, and the dyad are subject to larger countertransference responses from the institution or organization where the therapy is occurring, from the larger mental health community, and from the society at large. Throughout the book, we stress the valuable role the institution, or organization, and professional collegial relationships have for holding the therapist so that they may do the same for their clients. Organizations, however, not only provide opportunities for therapist support, but also offer countertransference effects on a treatment.

Since it is a rare occurrence to work in private practice only with clients who are never hospitalized, never see colleagues for consultation, and who never need coverage during the therapist's absences, most therapists work in some sort of system that holds them as well as their clients. Traumatized and dissociative clients challenge these systems and can evoke strong system-wide countertransference responses that influence the treatment.

Sometimes, the countertransference effect is obvious: on inpatient units when the team is "split"; when two collaborating clinicians find they have contradictory information from the same client; when an entire clinical staff feels burned out, enraged, or cynical about a particular client; when a therapist finds herself dreading to present a particular client in supervision or when the supervision gets mired in a parallel process. Sometimes the therapist feels the brunt of organizational countertransference to a particular trauma survivor client (or more generally to her work with trauma survivor clients) through her peers' subtle rejection or through their overt challenges of her ways of understanding or working with survivor clients.

Sometimes the signs of countertransference emerge in less obvious ways. Noticing language and communication patterns—or breakdowns in communication—can offer important clues. For example, when a therapist notices that her use of terms is reminiscent of war ("being held hostage," "terrorism," "straight shooter," "point blank," "battle scars"), reflect a need to blame ("manipulative," "resistant," "lazy"), or serve to push away her uncomfortable feelings ("overdramatic," "false memory," "hysterical"), she may realize that she is feeling a need to protect herself from painful feelings. A therapist's feelings of helplessness, anxiety, rage, outrage, fear, powerlessness, and injustice parallel a child's experience; this awareness facilitates the therapist's empathy, allowing her a better understanding of both her client's feelings and the possibilities that were not available to the client (such as speaking or understanding her feelings in context).

In addition, there are larger countertransference issues for trauma therapists. We are always part of a community of therapists, within and across disciplines, and still must contend with those who do not want to believe the pervasiveness of childhood abuse and with those who debate the reality or truth of severe dissociation, dissociative identity disorder, and the existence of organized abuse.

Organizational countertransference issues are powerful and rarely addressed. The opportunities for institutional reenactments, a parallel process between the therapist/client and the institution/therapist are complicated and important to track. One way a therapist can assess these dynamics is to present her work with a trauma survivor client at a staff case conference and to notice the range of responses, the affect tone of the discussion, and the defensive strategies employed to manage the feelings aroused by the case material and the therapeutic relationship. For example, a female therapist presented to a group of predominantly male colleagues her work with an adult female survivor of sadistic child abuse. The clinician's emotional experience of the discussion was of being attacked; simultaneously she felt she had failed to protect her client, a paradox implicit in her parental, protective countertransference. The meeting became a reenactment in which she took the role of her client and her colleagues became the client's family and the larger society. It was critical for her and the therapy that she discuss the experience, explore the complex systemic layers in the work, and examine both therapist and institutional countertransference responses.

Another sign of countertransferential parallel process is the consultation where everyone has an idea, everyone suggests some course of action, and none of it is helpful. Often this is because no one can bear to sit with the therapist's pain, despair, grief, and other intense affects, so they respond with what can be done rather than listening to how the therapist feels. Therapists fall into the same patterns with colleagues that they do with clients.

Another organizational dynamic is the link between discussions of traumatic antecedents to psychopathology in our clients and discussions about gender issues within an organization and society. To begin with, many clients with histories of child sexual abuse are women and they have often been sexually abused and raped by men. In many settings, female therapists are most likely to raise questions of possible child abuse or a PTSD diagnosis. Child sexual abuse happens in a particular social and political gender context that is impossible to ignore as one acknowledges the scope of the problem, as Herman eloquently describes (1981, 1992). For all of these reasons and more, it is clear that working with adult survivors of child abuse raises complex issues within an institution as well as in the specific therapeutic relationship of a therapist-client dyad.

In this chapter, we have described a broad range of often intense, but expectable countertransference responses with clients who are survivors of childhood incest and sexual abuse. Too many of these topics go unspoken and unexplored for a variety of reasons, yet these countertransference issues can potentially undermine an otherwise promising therapy. This work requires courage and humility. When we agree to work with a given survivor client, we are opening ourselves up to an emotional and potentially transforming experience for ourselves as well as our client. This commitment should not be made lightly. We need support for the work and a basis of professional self-esteem and personal self-acceptance to face the complex and at times disturbing aspects of ourselves that will emerge over the course of the work.

5

Countertransference Responses to Common Transference Themes with Incest Survivor Clients

AN INCEST SURVIVOR'S early interpersonal experience of betrayal, fear, excitement, violation, specialness, and abandonment can be expected to be reenacted in the therapeutic relationship. The emergence of these reenactments in the transference is often difficult for the therapist; concomitantly these reenactments are the locus of the therapeutic work.

The trauma of childhood incest profoundly affects an individual's sense of trust and safety in intimate interpersonal relationships. Inevitably, an incest survivor will struggle with powerful, intense, and often frightening transference reactions in a psychotherapy. A critical part of the work is holding a client through these transference storms and surviving the impact of her terror, shame, and self-protective responses on the developing relationship. To provide therapeutic holding in this context requires that the therapist provide explicit education about expectable feelings and process, and be active in naming and exploring transference feelings as they emerge. In this chapter we suggest some variations from traditional psychoanalytic techniques designed to invite a transference neurosis (Fenichel, 1941; Gill, 1954; Greenacre, 1954; Greenson, 1967, 1971).* In psychotherapy with

---

*"Transference neurosis" refers to the reenactment within the therapeutic relationship of all features of the client's past relationships, present conflicts, and her "illness" (Fancher, 1973; Freud, 1905; Greenson, 1967).

survivors of abusive and at times malevolent developmental contexts, the therapist needs to bring the transference process into the conscious work of the therapy sooner than she might using a traditional approach, and the person of the therapist needs to be available for comparison to the object relational expectations of the client.

TRANSFERENCE

Transference refers to the unconscious repetition in a current relationship of patterns of thoughts, feelings, beliefs, expectations, and responses that originated in important early relationships (Freud, 1905; Lane, 1986; Meyers, 1986; Racker, 1957). Stiver (writing in Miller et al., 1991) reminds us that "transference is very much a relational phenomenon; memories of one's past relationships, with their connections and disconnections, are expressed in many ways, in 'a playing out,' often symbolically and without awareness" (p. 8). For survivors of incest, transference responses and reenactments often include dissociated interpersonal aspects of traumatic memories. Many survivors hold on to their history through unconscious recreations of their exploitive early relationships in later relationships. For example, a client might assume that she owes her therapist some favor if the therapist has met her need or wish. A therapist can unwittingly accept such a favor (a gift, a compliment, some caretaking gesture from the client) without noting its context and examining possible underlying assumptions or object relational paradigms, thus perpetuating the client's assumption. In this way, transference can reflect a way of remembering.

At the same time, as Davies and Frawley (1994) remind us, state-dependent traumatic memories are also commonly triggered by aspects of the transference and the experience of the transference-countertransference reenactment. These feelings can evoke anxiety and fear; they may reflect split-off affective memories of trauma or they may evoke traumatic memories and thus further strong feelings in the client.

While transference is an *unconscious* process, the client is *conscious* of her strong feelings toward and about the therapist. As a client is aware of strong feelings, she strives to make sense of them in the present available context, thereby attributing them to the current relationship, and specifically to the therapist. A client's transference reaction is informed from many levels of awareness; she is aware of feelings toward or about the therapist (conscious level), she is unaware of the specific past context (unconscious level), and she is mostly unaware of the associative and assumptive processes linking the present to the past (preconscious level). The therapeutic task is now familiar—to make the unconscious conscious.

How does a therapist assess whether a response is transference-based? A preliminary step is to note the degree of fit between the client's expressed feeling or perception and the therapist's subjective experience.* Making this distinction requires several things: self-attunement, inner clarity about her own feelings and their possible origins, and a combination of humility and robust self-esteem (that is, a solid identity as a "good-enough" therapist), so that the therapeutic process does not threaten her self-worth.

We hypothesize a transference process when our client's affect seems unusually strong or surprisingly mild, when we feel taken by surprise by an assumption our client makes about us or by our client's expectations about our response to her, when we do not recognize ourselves in the descriptions we hear. As we listen for a client's thoughts, feelings, and fantasies about us, we are gathering data about how she fills in the blanks in her knowledge about us (using assumptions based upon her past experiences and information from the current therapy relationship).

Of course, the therapist must identify to which aspects of her actual person, state, and behavior the client may be responding. As Davies and Frawley (1994) point out, an asymmetrical view of transference, one that leaves out the real behavior and person of the therapist as a component of the transference response, can repeat a past traumatic environment for the client where she was endlessly blamed and adults abrogated responsibility for their own actions.

Example   A client became silent midway through her session. When queried, she noted that she had felt very connected to her therapist early in the session, but as she was speaking, she began to feel anxious and wanted to leave. When asked what she noticed as her feelings changed, she commented that the therapist seemed less present than usual, and the client began to fear she was unwanted and a burden to the therapist. The therapist acknowledged that, in fact, she had felt distracted at the outset of the hour for personal reasons, unrelated to the client, but clarified that she did not

---

*Lane (1986) has written an excellent review on transference in which he discusses concurrence in the literature about markers of a transference response. He identifies five markers: (1) distortion of appraisal—the representation of the therapist as the new "object" is distorted and reshaped to fit the earlier mold; (2) affective reactions and emotional postures that seem inappropriate or unexpected and either particularly intense or understated; (3) repetitive or stereotyped responses to the therapist across situations that seem impervious to exploration; (4) widening of the polarities between ambivalent feelings for the therapist (e.g., love-hate; idealization-devaluation), which may indicate old split self and object representations; and (5) unexpected and frequent shifts in attitude in a seemingly random or capricious way (This pattern may also reflect dissociation, altering ego states, or identities).

want the client to leave, nor did she feel angry, burdened, or wish to abandon the client. Together, they were able to reconstruct their interpersonal experience and the inner experience and process of the client as she attached her early experiences of abandonment to the present experience of the therapist's distraction.

The analysis of transference is predicated on the therapist's awareness of herself as an evocative presence in the relationship; without that degree of self-awareness she cannot help clients sort out the present from the past, and risks undermining the very resources she wishes to enhance: reality testing, interpersonal safety, and mutuality.

TRANSFERENCE FROM INCEST SURVIVOR CLIENTS

Transference responses in therapies with survivors will be informed by and reflect the sequelae of childhood sexual trauma, including dissociative phenomena, fluctuating ego states, severely disrupted beliefs about trust, safety, esteem, control, and intimacy, and disruptions in identity, world view, and spirituality. There is agreement in the trauma literature that transference responses of incest survivor clients are powerful and complicated, and must be handled carefully in the therapeutic relationship. Kernberg's description of transference dynamics with "borderline patients" (1975), a group of clients now known to include a very high percentage of adult survivors of child sexual abuse (Herman et al., 1989; Linehan, 1993; Ogata et al., 1990; Westen et al., 1990), emphasizes the role of split object representations and ego states that are dissociated from one another. Ganzarain and Buchele (1988) describe transference reactions for incest survivors as "intense and intractable." Herman (1992) describes traumatic transference as a characteristic response of traumatized clients:

> Their emotional responses to any person of authority have been deformed by the experience of terror. For this reason, traumatic transference reactions have an intense life-or-death quality unparalleled in ordinary therapeutic experience. (p. 136)

Waites (1993) writes, "At some point in an effective intensive therapy, the client almost inevitably experiences the treatment as revictimizing, even though she recognizes that confronting the pain of her past is necessary" (p. 181).

Waites (1993) describes several inherent transference "double binds" with survivors of childhood interpersonal trauma that result from early attachments that were traumatic and "in which the positive aspects of relatedness are viewed as necessarily accompanied by pain" (p. 184). She identifies four classic double bind frameworks in which the transference develops: (1) contact is necessary for survival/contact is dangerous, (2) attachment is desirable/attachment is disappointing, (3) attachment is pleasurable/love means hurting, and (4) attachment is good/love means total surrender. These early templates for attachment and dependence are often at the root of the intense conflicts evoked by the invitation to intimacy in the therapeutic relationship.

Along with others, we have observed the fluid transferences that cycle among victim, perpetrator, and nonprotective bystander which characterize these therapies, again reflecting paradigms learned in the context of early caretaking relationships and applied to the therapeutic relationship (Miller, 1994). Davies and Frawley (1994) identify eight relational positions, within four matrices, alternately enacted in the transference and countertransference by client and therapist: (1) the uninvolved nonabusing parent and the neglected child, (2) the sadistic abuser and the helpless, impotently enraged victim, (3) the idealized, omnipotent rescuer and the entitled child who demands to be rescued, and (4) the seducer and the seduced. They conclude their discussion of these positions by emphasizing the fluidity and dynamic nature of these positions.

The transference and countertransference shifts in this work are rapid and confusing for protracted periods of time. At one moment, the therapist experiences himself as abusing the patient with a premature, penetrating interpretation, only moments later to be cast into the experiential role of victim by the patient who is berating the clinician for his stupidity. Moments later, perhaps when the abused child self has emerged and is curled up weeping on the couch, the therapist becomes a rescuer, fantasizing about tucking the patient under a warm quilt. In the end, it is the clinician's ability to assume, enact, observe, and ultimately, to help make explicit all of the relational stances taken on by each member of the therapeutic dyad without becoming locked into any particular role or relational paradigm, that moves the treatment along, facilitating the patient's identification, working through, and integration of long-fragmented self and object representations. (p. 185)

Below, we identify several categories of transference responses that commonly emerge in therapies with survivors and explore the countertransference responses evoked by them.

COUNTERTRANSFERENCE TO TRANSFERENCE

In response to the client's transference, Racker (1957) proposes two countertransference identification mechanisms, reflecting either a direct identification with the client and her affective or transferential experience (concordant identification), or a responsive identification with the role demands of
a client's affect and transference (complementary identification). The former refers to an empathic, parallel response to the client's present experience. It results in the therapist sharing the client's feelings, attitudes, and
judgments and reflecting them back to the client (anger for anger, hate for
hate, love for love). The latter describes the therapist identifying with the
"other," the transferred object (e.g., the parental object), and having feelings that are complementary to those of the client and consistent with those
of the other. When a client transferentially experiences the therapist as a
derogatory, sadistic parent, the therapist may find herself feeling critical
and contemptuous of her patient.

An additional countertransference process based in identification is an
extension of projective identification; the therapist may assume an (despised) aspect of the identity of the client and the client will identify with
the "other," often an abusive other. Thus, the therapist vividly "knows"
what it is or was like to be the client in her early relational context. The
therapist's affective experience is often intense and intolerable. Without the
framework of projective identification, it is difficult to maintain an empathic connection with one's client.

Example   One client would consistently arrive late for sessions, then
express rage at the therapist for changing the time on the clock in the office.
At the end of these sessions, the client would refuse to leave, claiming that
the therapist was gypping her out of time. The therapist felt increasingly
frustrated and then resentful, and eventually enraged at the client's unfair-
ness and entitlement. She rehearsed incisive and increasingly sarcastic
speeches outlining the client's responsibility for the problem. Before utilizing the diatribe, she noted to the client the next time she was late that they
seemed to have a pattern to their sessions lately that revolved around there
not being enough time or resources for them and it being someone's fault.
She said she had been feeling both blamed and helpless and wondered how
they could do this differently together. As the client listened she recognized
the feelings the therapist was describing as familiar, and noted she felt
blamed and helpless when she arrived late and wanted to make sure it was
her therapist's fault and not hers. Together they recognized that this was
the client's experience in childhood: she was often accused of changing
reality and them blamed for the consequences. For example, her mother

both denied that her father's relatives had abandoned the family when the client was born and blamed the client for the absence of extended family in their lives.

Transference responses have been organized in many ways according to various theoretical constructs (e.g., arrested developmental processes, self psychology needs, object relational paradigms, ego libidinal phases). Using constructivist self development theory* as an organizing template, we propose three major areas in which one can expect transference reactions. The first is in the arena of *self capacities*. These transference responses reflect the client's needs for the therapist to supplement inadequate self capacities, specifically a client's limited capacities for affect tolerance, object constancy, and self-esteem maintenance. The second area of transference responses will emerge from *frame of reference* issues, that is, transferences related to the client's fundamental identity, world view, and spirituality. These transferences will reflect the client's core experiences and related expectations, her wishes and fears about self, other, and the world. Third, transference responses will be informed by an individual's salient *psychological needs and schemas* about safety, esteem, trust and dependency, control, and intimacy for herself and significant others in her life. All three of these areas of transference reflect the repetition of feelings and conflicts from early object relational experiences.

SELF CAPACITY EFFECTS IN THE TRANSFERENCE

The purpose and function of all three self capacities taken together is to maintain a cohesive sense of self. When the client is experiencing extreme alienation from herself, or fear of annihilation of the self, her modes of affect management will infuse the transference.

Ability to Tolerate and
Moderate Strong Affect

Incest involves chronic overstimulation, affective flooding, and the fusion of sexuality, aggression, nurturance, affection, control, and sadism. Many incest survivors rely on dissociative defenses to modulate their affect, including depersonalization, derealization, affective numbing, fragmentation, fugue states, and what has traditionally been identified as hysterical cognition: vague, global, diffuse thinking dominated by denial, repression, and flight of ideas. These mechanisms serve to protect someone from being overwhelmed with feelings and from being too vulnerable to others in rela-

*For further elaboration of CSDT see chapter 3.

tionships. These defenses also help the client retreat and hide from the therapist as a member of a hurtful, untrustworthy world. The client's affects alternate between extreme dissociation or constriction and affective flooding.*

This alternation of dissociation with flooding can make a therapist feel alternately abandoned or assaulted, which may replicate the client's childhood experience in an abusive and neglectful family. Simultaneously, the client's retreat to dissociation and confusion can make the therapist feel responsible or guilty for the client's fear, as though she had been abusive or overstimulating. The therapist may feel abandoned and left alone to guess what the client is experiencing. When a client is flooded with rage, anxiety, or fear, the therapist may feel assaulted, overwhelmed, or helpless and then neglectful or ineffectual for being unable to soothe the client.

At times the therapist is left holding the affect and the client reports feeling little or nothing. In fact, in earlier, often lengthy, stages of the work, it is not uncommon that a therapist learns what her client is feeling through her own affective state, especially when the client is expressing only subjective numbness, confusion, or a bland indifference. The holding of unmanageable affects by the therapist is an important component of the work because it is in the service of a developmental process of the client internalizing a benign object to help her manage painful affects.†

It is therapeutically useful for the therapist explicitly to describe and address her role of holding affects forbidden to the client. When a therapist reminds the client, "You don't have to do this alone," or invites her to leave difficult and painful feelings "here in the office so we can work them through together," and when she notes that she is holding a (disowned) feeling (anxiety, sadness) for the client, she is addressing three therapeutic tasks:

1. She reinforces the therapeutic relationship and clarifies the role of the therapist.
2. She gives permission to the client to have feelings, to need the therapist, and to evoke feelings in the therapist by identifying these processes as part of the work of therapy and not violations or burdens to the therapist.

---

*The psychological pattern of this alternation was initially described by Freud (1939) and later elaborated by Horowitz (1979) and by Roth and Cohen (1986). van der Kolk and Greenberg (1987) describe the pattern of fluctuations between biological states of numbness and hyperarousal, or "biphasic response," in detail.
†Kohut termed this transformative process "transmuting internalization" (1977).

3. She sets the stage for the ongoing process of developmental education that is an important part of trauma therapy.

Many clients have little idea about appropriate developmental needs and processes. When the therapist holds difficult, intolerable affects for the client, she is creates a facilitating environment (Winnicott, 1965) for the developmental tasks of the therapy to occur. To the extent that psychotherapy replicates developmental processes, it provides a forum to demonstrate appropriate steps of development without pathologizing those needs.

When a child is frightened, what does a protective adult do to help the child manage the experience? The adult reassures the child through comforting touch, and she holds the child to let her know she is safe and to help her feel her body. The adult gives words to the experience, naming feelings, context, and reassurance: "You were frightened when that big dog barked at you. It was scary. It's all right. She won't hurt you. I'm here and will keep you safe." This process teaches a child to identify her feelings, to understand the events that evoked the feelings, and to acknowledge resources for safety and support. Over time and many repetitions a child internalizes the adult's words and soothing presence and can reassure and comfort herself in many situations (Bowlby, 1988; Brazelton & Cramer, 1990; Fraiberg, 1959). Discussing how children learn by being soothed is useful for our clients, since generally they did not have these opportunities to internalize a comforting parent figure, and currently need practice at these very skills. Further, naming this holding process with the client makes the developmental work less burdensome, isolating, and confusing for the therapist.

Ability to Maintain an Inner Sense of Connection with Others

Many adult survivor clients bring to any relationship intense fears of abandonment and devastating loss. Their experience of object loss is an experience of utter, existential isolation analogous to a young child left alone in the middle of an endless expanse of space. Thus, separation for these clients can be terrifying, and they are often unable or inadequately able to maintain object constancy, that is, to hold on to important others in their mind and imagination. The therapeutic relationship is made up of repeated separations, connections, and reconnections, at the end of each session as well as during extended separations due to illness, vacations, or missed sessions, and therefore offers endless opportunities to address and work through issues of loss, separation, and connection.

The transference manifestation of this work is in the client's intense anxiety about separation (between sessions, therapist absence, therapist silence in sessions), her fears about the therapist's well-being, and her awareness of and interest in the therapist during separations. This anxiety may be evident in direct expressions of these feelings, in indirect expressions (such as increased anxiety or dissociation toward the end of a session), or in defensive responses to them. Defensive responses can include turning passive into active by psychically banishing the therapist between sessions. A client may express increased suicidal and self-injurious ideation or behavior connected with separations, which may reflect the need to ensure the therapist's active mindfulness by evoking worry, concern, and anxiety in the other. Reis (1993) has suggested that these processes guard against annihilation anxiety following separation. For some clients, evoking worry reflects an unconscious belief that they will be forgotten, psychologically abandoned, unless someone is worried about them (this strategy may reflect an unconscious reenactment of early childhood experiences of life and death anxiety, such as living with a parent who would threaten suicide and leave home). After a therapist's absence a client may become vigilant to empathic failures on the part of the therapist, and critical of the therapist.

For the therapist, this transference can evoke a complementary parental, protective countertransference that impels her to provide the psychic holding and reassurance necessary to facilitate internalization that will ease the client's anxiety. Alternatively, this anxious attachment (Bowlby, 1988) on the part of the client can evoke feelings of being trapped, smothered, or intruded upon, which can lead to reactive distancing and criticalness. When the client is evoking counteranxiety in the therapist through self-injurious impulses or behavior, the therapist can feel tormented and respond with rage, helplessness, self-doubt, and anxiety.

A developmental understanding of the historical and adaptive aspects of the client's transference is key to managing the countertransference. This understanding allows the therapist and client to address constructively the developmental needs being expressed through this transference. For example, when a therapist understands the lack of object constancy in the transference reenactment, she can begin to work with a client by encouraging her to practice "keeping me with you," that is, maintaining an internal image of the therapist and the therapist's voice during separations.

Ability to Maintain a Positive Sense of Self

Another set of transference responses is predicated on the complete absence in many survivor clients of benign self-regard. Adult survivors can experience intense self-loathing and many have formed intractable negative identities to solidify their belief that the hurtful things that were done to them were done because they "deserved it," are "unlovable," "bad," "evil," "cursed," or "stupid." These self-concepts are affectively charged identities. They reflect self capacity deficits and the related feelings are intolerable and emerge as destructive impulses or are dissociated or contained through generalized affective numbing.

The expression of these self-perceptions in the transference takes different forms. Some clients expect, and sometimes require, that the therapist share these views and be intolerant of any different point of view. Other clients live in dread, with the shameful conviction that the therapist will independently arrive at the same conclusions. Yet other clients display defensive hypersensitivity to any evidence that the therapist is being critical or shaming in any way.

These manifestations can invite the therapist to join with the client's perception through concordant identification such that the therapist feels damaged or inadequate, or through complementary identification by participating in shaming or blaming the client. The therapist can feel helpless as she witnesses the client's relentless, often vicious, self-attacks. A therapist may become defensive in the face of relentless vigilant scrutiny or feel depleted and resentful from having to "walk on eggshells" with a particularly shame-prone and vulnerable client.

One easily available countertransference pitfall is for the therapist to engage in repeated (fruitless) arguments with the client about her self-denigration and self-worth. However, countertransference disclosure can be a more valuable use to which to put those feelings. For example, a therapist can tell a client, "It is painful to hear your disrespect and cruelty toward yourself. When you make jokes at your own expense, you invite me to participate in your abusiveness. I want to let you know I decline the invitation." Sometimes one can use humor to point out the interpersonal reenactment emerging. Sometimes it is valuable to name the anger evoked when asked to witness such scathing contempt. Sometimes it is an opportunity to name the unnamed transference, that is, the indirect contempt for the therapist who treats the client and her feelings with respect: "I understand you think it is weak to take those feelings seriously. I want to let you know I do take feelings seriously, I will continue to take them seriously, and I do not intend to feel ashamed about that." When a client is attacking herself in the context of a positive transference, this parallel can interrupt the process as she has to hold the contradictory expectations she has for herself and for the therapist.

Clearly these countertransference responses leave the therapist's self-esteem vulnerable, either through identificatory shame and self-loathing or through secondary shame about countertransference enactments in response to the transference. Again, maintaining a historical and developmental understanding of the psychological processes behind the transference manifestations allows a therapist to identify and try to navigate a therapeutic path through the tangled thicket of negative identity, low self-esteem, and shame present in many survivor clients. This can be an opportunity to educate the client about the process of superego development—both the internalization of parental voices and the self-protective function of those inner warning voices.

For example, many survivors of violent homes have learned out of self-protection to quell any feelings of need, fear, or vulnerability. What may have begun as an internal voice coaching the child to hold back her tears or not show her feelings in order to avoid attack, over time can become a punitive, often sadistic, inner voice. When her therapist suggests that her harsh criticism may have originally had a protective function, a client contextualizes her own inner experience in a new way. Once a client begins to understand that her self-attack starts with fear, she can attend to her safety in a different way. The therapist's recognition of the developmental context and process that leads to the client's persecutory superego frees her from countertransference anger, defensiveness, and pain; this allows the therapist to support the client's need for safety while eschewing her need for self-denigration.

Chronic Suicidality

Chronic suicidality and the wish to be dead are often mechanisms of self-soothing, punishment for feelings, or attempts to exercise control when feeling little control over oneself or others. For some survivor clients, the option of suicide was reassuring during the many years when they were trapped and helpless. For these clients death may have served as a soothing maternal presence: "Then I'll be safe. Then I can rest. I won't feel this pain anymore. Then I'll have control over my body." This solution reflects underdeveloped self capacities, and can be extremely painful and wearing for the therapist. The therapist may be moved to act on the belief that she must protect the client. Alternatively, when talk of death and suicide continues over a long time, the therapist may tune out and miss important changes in the client's level of despair.

It is important for the therapist alone and with the client to distinguish among the client's wish to be dead, her desire to kill herself, and her intent to attempt suicide. Both therapist and client will be able to hold these feelings better if they understand what underlies these wishes and what functions they serve.

Example   A long-term client who was actively engaged in drinking and cutting herself was able to tell the therapist, "You know I'm not really going to kill myself, don't you?" The therapist responded, "No, I don't know that." The client seemed surprised that the therapist took her wish to die and self-mutilation seriously, and that the therapist cared. This realization opened the possibility of talking about the function of suicidal feelings and threats both interpersonally in the therapy and individually for the client.

Moving the intrapersonal process of self-attack and suicide into the relational context of the therapy is a powerful step toward change.

FRAME OF REFERENCE

Therapist as Perpetrator

The client's experience of the therapist as the abuser or perpetrator is a difficult transference paradigm for both parties. For example, in psychotherapy with an adult female survivor of father-daughter incest, the client will often experience the therapist, male or female, as the incestuous father, that is, as seductive, coercive, or dangerous. When the circumstances of the incest or the overall relationship with the abuser has been sadistic and physically and psychologically abusive, the meaning of the expectable transference to the therapist is complex. Sadistic abuse is often predicated on the victim's fear; thus in the transference, the client will expect the therapist to become aroused or receive pleasure from her fear. This expectation can horrify or offend a therapist who is feeling compassion for her client's terror. Two further aspects of the "erotization of fear" (Davies and Frawley, 1994) include the client's subjective experience of the merger of fear and sexual arousal, and the therapist's countertransference experience of arousal and concomitant shame and distress.

A therapist's own outrage at the abuser can prevent her from tolerating or being able to explore the client's experience of her as the abuser. It can be difficult for female therapists to accept the role of a male rapist, particularly if they find themselves identifying with their client as a victim of sexual assault. Male therapists may have a difficult time holding this transference, especially if it interacts with guilt about being the same gender as the client's perpetrator(s). For all therapists, it is difficult to be experienced as a perpetrator of sexual abuse in the context of empathic (often countertransferentially parental) connection with an individual sexually victimized as a child. Typical countertransference responses to a perpetrator transference include being defensive, angry, or hurt that the client doesn't understand that one is trying to be helpful. This transference can also evoke a complementary transference response that is punitive, sadistic, or seductive. When a therapist recognizes this countertransference she can withdraw in shame and abandon the client, thus completing the cycle of the client's transferential expectation of abuse or abandonment. It is important to have support and consultation to remain steady in the face of a transference that can become a malevolent transformation (Sullivan, 1953).

The client may have difficulty naming this transference directly, especially her fear of the therapist's sexual arousal, but it is essential to address the fear and concomitant transference as it emerges. This transference may first emerge in the form of complaints about exploitive aspects of the psychotherapy: how the therapist benefits from the work, for example, by learning at the expense of the client, or the idea that the therapist does not truly care about the client, but is simply listening to painful and humiliating material to earn a fee and will then laugh or marvel at the material with colleagues. Eventually, for many clients it is relieving and helpful for the therapist and client to discuss straightforwardly the client's experience of the therapist as being like her abuser, and her fear of the therapist's sexual arousal. As therapists we may well experience narcissistic injury, denial, and distaste for the comparison. We can then overlook or misperceive the transference itself because it is far from our conscious experience of ourselves and the therapeutic relationship.

It may be more difficult for a therapist who has had entirely different interpersonal experiences and who may be able to develop trust in relationships fairly easily to comprehend the experience of a client who mistrusts and expects disappointment and exploitation. This different developmental context can lead a therapist unwittingly to empathic failures or to shame her client through lack of understanding of the client's automatic mistrust, caution, and fear. For example, early in therapy a survivor client asked the therapist why and how therapy could be helpful. The therapist naively replied, "Just trust me." The client retorted, "If I could do that, I wouldn't be here." Another client reminded her therapist that being told to feel, let alone trusting her feelings, was like being told to step off a 24-story building.

Another component of the perpetrator transference is the client's feeling special to the therapist (which may evoke a parallel experience of specialness and indispensability in the therapist). Incest survivors may invite various modifications of therapeutic boundaries. A therapist's discomfort with the negative transference or comfort with the feeling of specialness can lead her to make special arrangements without careful thought or consultation. (For further discussion of therapeutic boundaries, see chapter 7.) For client and therapist, there may be both gratifications and dangers of feeling special.

In some families, the role of incestuous partner can be both a favored and disadvantaged position. To feel special to a therapist is both exhilarating and validating of the client's worth; yet, it can instantly arouse the specter of exploitation, rape, and loss of control (Ganzarain & Buchele, 1988). Feeling special may also mean being essential; the child may have felt that her role was to sustain, regulate, or make the very existence of the perpetrator possible. The therapeutic task is to discuss both the wish for special status and the fear of its consequences while trying to protect the client from shame or humiliation.

To the extent that the therapist's countertransference wish to make the client special, or the therapist's impulsive and unexamined changes of therapeutic boundaries make the therapist unable to think about these actions and motives, the therapist's guilt and denial will be translated to the client and can set the stage for a client's assumption of danger, revictimization, and corruption. A negative therapeutic reaction can ensue.

Therapist as Collusive Parent

An important corollary to the client's transference to the therapist as an abuser is the transference to the therapist as the collusive or victimized coparent, or passive nonprotective bystander (Miller, 1994). Often the child experienced the other parent, if not also abusive, as allowing the abuse to occur or continue by inaction, passivity, oblivion, weakness, or denial, or because of her own victimization and powerlessness. Sometimes that parent is perceived as getting her needs met or protecting herself at the expense of the child. This transference can emerge explicitly as the client's experience of the therapist as inattentive, inadequately concerned or protective, or disbelieving and entrenched in denial of the client's experience. This transference can also emerge more indirectly when the therapist feels silenced, for example, from fear of shaming or overwhelming the client, and thus fails to address potentially dangerous situations or to ask for elaboration of traumatic memories. At such times, the therapist can participate in a transference reenactment by abandoning the client through inattention and silence.

Participation in transference enactments is inevitable in these therapies. Too often however, therapists can become shame-filled or angry as they recognize the unfolding dynamic. We imagine if we are aware of the potential for reenactments that we can avoid participating in them. This belief sets up an impossible standard; further, these reenactments, in fact, often provide valuable opportunities to rework old patterns in the new therapy relationship. We can be invited into this particular reenactment (of nonprotection or emotional neglect) by a client's unconscious process of dropping a veiled hint we fail to catch, embedding important information in other affect-laden material, bringing up an issue of safety at the very end of a session when there is little or no time to process it, or in a number of other ways. A simple yet powerful way out of the paralysis is for us to have the freedom to name the dilemma without expecting ourselves to solve it singlehandedly.

The therapist can avoid the countertransference trap of feeling like a failure or simply becoming enraged with the client by noting the importance of the material and restating the value of the mutual process of psychotherapy. Reminding a client and oneself that together you can work toward change, while individually you are both more limited, holds the therapeutic relationship as the site of healing without unfairly burdening either participant.

Example   When her client announced at the end of a session that she was feeling suicidal and thinking about quitting therapy because it wasn't helping, the therapist felt defeated and discounted. She felt hurt, and felt a momentary impulse to dismiss her client abruptly. Instead she said, "I can't do this alone, and you are here because you can't do this alone. This is hard work, but we're a good team and I think we can do it together. I hear your fear and your despair. I want you to know I don't feel hopeless. And we can continue to talk about these feelings when we next meet."

A therapist may feel a complementary identification as a depleted mother. She may feel unable to keep track of all the client's needs and therefore want to "tune out" or ignore some troubling data. Alternatively, in response to an identification with the client or in response to her unconscious wishes, the therapist may become overprotective and overresponsible for the client's well-being and safety. Both countertransference responses can lead to exhaustion, resentment, and vicarious traumatization. Further, they can perpetuate a stalemate in the therapy, which then intensifies both countertransference and vicarious traumatization responses. By considering the possible roles being enacted in the transference, both therapist and client can understand and address the current unfolding relational process constructively.

Therapist as Victim or Helpless Witness

Transference organized around the client's identification with the aggressor has two important forms: (1) the client enacts assaults or seductions on the therapist, and (2) the client reenacts the trauma on herself in front of the therapist. The former places the therapist in the role of victim or perpetrator and the latter places her in the role of helpless witness, both of which elicit powerful countertransference responses.

A child who is the recipient of sexually, emotionally, and physically abusive behavior learns firsthand about aggressive seduction, assault, and calculated cruelty. As adults, survivors of abuse are able to mobilize this knowledge in the service of self-protection, unconscious reenactment, and maintenance of a negative identity. The therapist who is the recipient of this treatment is likely to experience many of the feelings of the child victim although modified by her own adult identity, resources, and therapeutic awareness. However, countertransference can both result from this transference and obscure a therapist's recognition of the client's identification with the aggressor.

When any client, but a survivor client in particular, is sexually seductive, it can stir sexual arousal, anxiety, intellectualization, or denial in the therapist. The therapist's awareness of the client's seduction can elicit feelings of discomfort, flattery, anger, confusion, guilt, or combinations of feelings. The arousal of sexual, erotic, or romantic feelings toward a client evokes another overlapping set of feelings, including shame, pleasure, power, and guilt. The issues with same-sex and different-sex therapist-client pairs are both similar and different; we elaborate the details of these issues in chapter 9. A therapist may feel too uncomfortable or embarrassed to discuss the situation with a colleague or supervisor and is then left alone to sort out the complicated personal, interpersonal, and clinical issues at work in the therapeutic relationship. The therapist whose own intimacy needs are not being met is also vulnerable to responding behaviorally to any perceived invitation for sexual or sexualized intimacy with the client, which can lead to a loss of therapeutic frame and corruption of the therapy.

When the reenactment and transference involve aggression and verbal assault, the feelings aroused can include anger, retaliatory wishes, indignation, confusion, shame, paralysis, victimization, and more. The therapist's primary job is to balance appropriate limit-setting, in order to maintain an environment that is safe for both client and therapist, with exploration and interpretation. To do so, the therapist must feel free to protect herself when appropriate and to notice the interpersonal dynamics without becoming mired in the countertransference responses.

These countertransference responses can stem from the current relationship with the client, the therapist's own past experiences of assault, or her internal superego assaults or masochism that may be hooked by the present situation.

Example   One client railed angrily at the therapist each time her treatment had to be reauthorized by her managed care company. She complained bitterly that they were wasting valuable time when the therapist discussed the insurance issues in the therapy sessions, yet she expressed rage at the betrayal when the therapist turned in the report without consulting the client in advance. The therapist felt blocked, frustrated, and angry, and almost missed a report deadline before she caught her passive acting out of this anger. The therapist realized she dreaded every session and emerged tense and furious. She realized the tension in her neck was a familiar response to her relentlessly critical grandmother and saw herself engaging in the kind of passive rebellion that was her only choice in childhood. When the therapist invited a discussion of their interpersonal process around these matters, she spoke of her frustration and noted her silence as a contributing factor to the current impasse. The client agreed that her therapist's passivity and silence frightened and angered her. She added that she had created a no-win situation for both of them in response to her feelings of powerlessness and fear of precipitous loss of the relationship. The therapist's fury shifted to compassion for her client's anxiety in a situation that evoked feelings from earlier traumatic losses.

The work of the therapy is often to redefine the intrapersonal as interpersonal—to help the client see the inner identifications and internalization of hurtful object relations that she endlessly repeats on herself. Thus her internal world has become the locus of reenactment. By relocating those reenactments into the interpersonal realm of the therapeutic relationship, it is possible to begin to identify genetic sources for the relational paradigms. Then it is possible to identify and elaborate the intrapsychic conflicts created by the early interpersonal and developmental context. When a client reenacts her trauma on herself, that is, enacting the roles of both abuser and victim, often through self-destructive behavior (cutting, dangerous promiscuity, taking life-threatening risks, and extraordinarily critical super-ego attacks), the therapist can become a helpless witness. These self-attacks are assaultive to the therapist, but this element is usually out of the client's awareness for quite a while.

These enactments can be difficult for a therapist for several reasons. Her perception of the client as victim of assault can blind her to the rage underlying the client's assaultiveness to herself and the therapist. Concomitantly, her anger at the assault can obscure the therapist's recognition of the client's attempt to master trauma and her subjective experience of helplessness and powerlessness. The shift of these enactments from unconscious to conscious and from intra- to interpersonal allows the client and therapist to name and explore the range of identifications and ambivalent feelings. This arena often includes the need to discuss the masochistic pleasure in pain and sadistic pleasure of fused sexuality, nurturance, and aggression in the incestuous family. These clients often know no way of being held other than to be held painfully. Some clients are skilled at provoking the therapist to reject them, or a group to extrude them. Turning passive into active by evoking attack or rejection is a familiar defense against longing, as well as against the fear that accompanies the anticipation of abuse.

Therapist as Sibling

Somewhat less obvious is the sibling transference in which the therapist is experienced as representing some aspect of a key sibling relationship in the client's family. Siblings are enormously important in abusive families; they are part of the emotional context of the client's childhood experience. Their roles, whether as protectors, rivals, dependents in need of protection, pre-ferred children whose "virtues" were used to shame the client, or compatri-ots in victimization, help determine the client's role in the family. This transference can be overlooked because it may be less compelling to the therapist than her attention to the parents, and because it can often overlap with the therapist's role as a sibling and feelings about her own siblings. The details and the particular valence of the sibling transference or counter-transference may be difficult to hold and notice.

Example   One therapist had an older sister who was more verbal and got more attention from their parents. In working with a very verbal, bright survivor client, the therapist found it difficult to get a word in. Rather than being able to notice and comment on this pattern with the client, the therapist's initial response was helplessness and then rage. In exasperation one day, she interrupted the client with strident tones. When the client expressed discomfort with her anger, the therapist recognized her irritation. She acknowledged her tone, and observed she was feeling shut out by the client and barged in. She suggested that together they could notice their communication patterns; the client then spoke of her fear of the therapist's judgment, and of her subsequent need to fill the air time to prevent the therapist from diagnosing or condemning her.

Therapist as Nurturant Figure

The survivor client may have had one or more significant positive relation-ships in childhood, perhaps with a beloved grandmother, a baby-sitter, a teacher who recognized and encouraged her strengths, a friend's father who took her fishing and treated her like a valued child. The therapist is often the recipient of a positive transference related to this person. This transference can facilitate the development of the therapeutic relationship, and the more the therapist knows about this relationship and its meaning to the client, then and now, the more clues she will have to the client's relational needs. It is too easy to overlook nonfamilial figures; yet maternal and paternal caretaking functions are not limited to mothers and fathers literally.

SCHEMAS AND SALIENT PSYCHOLOGICAL NEEDS

Finally, a whole set of transference responses and the affective tone of the above transference responses are related to the client's psychological needs and the related conscious and unconscious schemas she has developed to make sense of her experience in the world. These transferences will reflect strong needs for and disrupted schemas about safety, trust and dependency, esteem, intimacy, and control. Each transference will interact with the therapist's salient psychological needs and schemas to determine the countertransference.

For example, the client's disruptions in safety will emerge as fears of the therapist, and fears about the therapist's ability to protect the client and herself in the work. In response, a therapist can feel compelled to take full responsibility for creating a sense of safety within the client — an impossible task. If the therapist believes that the therapy can progress only if the client feels safe, she may attempt to provide assurances that are unrealistic, such as telling the client that she will never again be hurt or that the relationship with the therapist will protect her from harm. Disruptions in the client's safety schemas may lead the therapist to argue with the client's fears, or she may become frightened or feel inadequate in response to those fears. She may mistrust her judgment about what is safe or unsafe, or she may underestimate realistic dangers.

Disruptions in trust and dependency are also highly likely for survivors of sexual abuse who were abused in the context of presumably trusting relationships, and the related transference issues will include seeing the therapist as completely trustworthy or utterly untrustworthy and exploitive. Either the counterphobic belief in the therapist's complete trustworthiness or relentless, skeptical testing on the part of the client can put enormous pressure on the therapist to live up to being a perfect caretaker. To the extent that this transference is consistent with a therapist's expectations of herself or her historical role in her family, she is vulnerable to colluding with unrealistic expectations and suffering the emotional, interpersonal, and clinical consequences of the inevitable failure.

When disruptions in self-esteem or esteem for others enter the transference, the therapist can be drawn into being a helpless witness or collusive participant in the client's degradation of herself and others, or can be the recipient of disrespect or scathing contempt and attempts at humiliation. The therapist's own capacity for self-esteem and ability to maintain respect for her client will influence her countertransference response to these transferential dynamics.

When control needs are expressed in the transference, they reflect the client's experience of self as defensively powerful or as vulnerable and powerless. The therapist's countertransference response to the complementary identification of weak or powerful can lead to a variety of feelings including satisfaction, protectiveness, guilt, sadism, fear, or shame. The therapist's recognition of the interaction of her countertransference with the client's transference allows an interactive working-out of issues of control and power. Issues of actual control are important to negotiate clearly in the therapy so that the related transference issues can be sorted out from the real frame and boundaries in the therapeutic relationship.

Throughout the development and elaboration of the therapeutic relationship, needs for and beliefs about the possibility of intimacy with oneself and others will inform the client's transference to the therapist. A client's fear of being alone or wish to be alone and her conviction of her fundamental unlovableness or specialness will inform the transference. The therapist's beliefs about her worthiness of the client's intimate affection and her own beliefs about intimacy will in a like fashion inform her countertransference. A related issue is the therapist's comfort with feelings of fondness, affection, caring, and love, both from and toward the client. Psychotherapy is intimate work; the therapeutic relationship is a uniquely intimate, though bounded, relationship. These relationships challenge the therapist's capacity for intimacy and ways of being in intimate relationships.

Obviously, these examples represent a small sample of possible transference paradigms and related countertransference paradigms. Throughout the book we offer elaborations of many of these patterns and dynamics. In every therapy relationship there is an underlying question of whether and to what extent this relationship will repeat the relational paradigms from the past, and whether and to what extent this relationship will ameliorate and heal the hurts suffered in earlier abusive relationships. These questions are held, consciously and unconsciously, by both therapist and client. Their hoped for and feared answers inform both the transference and the countertransference.

The therapist and client's willingness to notice and name their interpersonal experience allows the transformative work with transference and countertransference dynamics in these therapies. Therapeutic work with and analysis of transference is central and transformative in psychotherapy with adult survivors of childhood sexual abuse. While the provision of an empathic respectful relationship is essential, it is not sufficient to change the deeply entrenched self and object relational paradigms held by survivors of such abuse. A therapist's attunement to her countertransference is an essential tool to her understanding and analyzing the transference.

6

Countertransference Responses to Dissociative Processes in Psychotherapy

DISSOCIATION is an intrapsychic defense, and in psychotherapy it is an interpersonal process. Phenomenologically, it is the separation of mental systems that would ordinarily be integrated. It represents the severing of connections among mental contents and categories that would otherwise elaborate and augment one another. Theoretically, it provides the therapist an invaluable framework for understanding a range of intrapsychic and interpersonal occurrences in psychotherapy with trauma survivors. Awareness of dissociation within the therapeutic relationship will inform the therapist's analysis and use of her countertransference responses.*

For the client, forbidden or threatening affects, memories, and aspects of her self often emerge in the relationship—transferential and real—with the therapist; the client's anxiety is mobilized and then managed with dissociative defenses. As others (Davies & Frawley, 1994; Kluft, 1990a, 1994;

---

*Much has been written elsewhere about dissociation, including excellent recent works on the history of the concept (van der Kolk & van der Hart, 1991), definition (Spiegel & Cardena, 1991), process (Braun, 1988a), social functions (Herman, 1992), and treatment of dissociative disorders (Braun, 1988b; Putnam, 1989; Ross, 1989; Waites, 1993). We refer the reader to these works for in-depth discussion of these issues.

Loewenstein, 1993) have emphasized, countertransference responses to dissociative phenomena are inevitable and essential to track. Because countertransference is often unconscious and therefore not fully available, and dissociation by definition implies a disconnection from awareness, countertransference dynamics in response to dissociation can too easily go unnoticed.

DISSOCIATION: AN OVERVIEW

For over a century, dissociative clients have challenged our core beliefs about personality as a unitary construct. We have been trained and socialized to assume each person has one consistent sense of self. To accommodate a more complex understanding of human experience requires we examine our basic beliefs and consider new constructs. These challenges form the context for the countertransference responses these clients evoke in us.

For trauma survivors, dissociative states are often familiar. Yet, at any given time, a client may experience dissociation as voluntary or involuntary, soothing or terrifying, comforting or isolating, protective or threatening. It is not surprising that these states and their complicated meaning to the client will evoke a myriad of conflicting responses in the therapist.

In parallel, the therapist may use dissociation; at points in the work she may be unaware of aspects of her client, her own inner experience, or her conflicting feelings and beliefs. The therapist may unconsciously collude with the client's dissociation or denial of ambivalence and "forget" for example, that a fear may contain within it a wish (Freud, 1923). The therapist can responsively or independently split her own ambivalence, split certain feelings off from her awareness, or experience a variety of unfamiliar inner states (Loewenstein, 1993).

CSDT Conceptualization of Dissociation*

The need for dissociative defenses reflects developmental and circumstantial limits in an individual's ability to tolerate and manage strong affect, an ability that permits one to maintain a cohesive self and continuous sense of self over time. If the individual began to dissociate in early childhood in response to the overwhelming effects of abuse, she will not have developed these self capacities.

While dissociation protects the self, it does so at a cost. When the individual is threatened with overwhelming affect, dissociation allows her to avoid disintegration by not experiencing the affect. This solution may be

*For additional discussion of this topic see McCann & Pearlman, 1992.

manifest in the client's moving into an altered state of consciousness, into a state of not feeling and not knowing, a state of "not-me" (depersonalization), or a state of unrealness (derealization). In more pronounced dissociative episodes, the client flees the affect by encapsulating it into an altered ego state or an identity (alter) which is experienced as separate from or not under the control of the host personality (Putnam, 1989; Reis, 1993). The paradox here of course is that in the service of preservation of the self and identity, the individual moves into a state whose hallmark is disrupted identity. The price of dissociation, the resulting not-knowing, not-feeling, and not-being, is immense and may prompt the survivor to seek treatment.

Given the client's tenuous or undeveloped self capacities, a dissociative flight from the shared interpersonal space of the therapy is often prompted by the threat of intolerable affect. Flight from affect can be evoked by the threat of remembering or knowing, by interpersonal events, by physiological sensations, or ideational associations.

We suggest that splitting* involves dissociative mechanisms, specifically the dissociation of ambivalently held affects from one another. The ability to tolerate ambivalence requires healthy self capacities. Ambivalence is not only confusing but often intolerable for survivors of childhood sexual trauma; historically, the expression of ambivalence may have made the survivor vulnerable to someone else's distortion of her experience, or led to paralysis. The survivor's inability to tolerate conflicting or contradictory feelings, and her resultant anxiety and fear, can lead to a protective split of ambivalent affects and to a concretization of "either-or" thinking and feeling.

Ambivalence is both an intrapsychic and interpersonal challenge as it includes the ability to hold a positive affect or internalized object in the face of a negative reaction or feeling. Thus clients may dissociate in response to any hint of interpersonal conflict in the therapeutic relationship because they cannot tolerate conflicting feelings about the therapist or conflict in the relationship, fearing violence and object loss.

An individual's frame of reference, reflecting her core beliefs about self and world, is protected by dissociation as well. To the extent that the survivor can keep information about her past abuse out of her awareness, she can hold on to cherished beliefs about other people's (parents, siblings, caretakers) trustworthiness, love for her, value, and capacity for connection. In this way, dissociation can protect the survivor's interpersonal relationships by protecting schemas that form the basis for relationships from

---

*Davies and Frawley (1994) suggest that denial, acting out, projection/introjection, omnipotence, and projective identification are all to some extent variants of splitting.

disconfirming information. This process will be at work in the therapy as well, in ways that both help and impede the developing therapy relationship.

For example, a client may use dissociation in the service of creating and maintaining an idealized transference at a time when she needs to strengthen her alliance with the therapist and develop a sense of safety. If over time the idealization based upon dissociation is not modified, the alliance will become increasingly brittle as the client struggles to preserve the illusion of the absence of conflict, thereby denying each participant's complexity and authenticity. But for some clients in the development of the therapeutic relationship, just as in child development, mutual admiration is necessary for a time for security.

Dissociation also serves to contain traumatic memories. Until they can be remembered or known and processed in a safe place, many survivors encapsulate and keep separate their traumatic imagery, affect, cognitions, and bodily sensations. Dissociation allows for this separation of toxic material until it can be integrated through the therapy process. The therapist's countertransference zeal may tempt her to override these safety precautions without fully respecting the function of the dissociation, especially if she perceives dissociation primarily as a symptom to be purged rather than as an adaptation to be understood, or if she does not respect the importance of the client's controlling the pace of remembering and knowing.

Dissociation in the Therapy Relationship

For those who spent their childhood in an abusive home, the therapeutic situation replicates the most painful dilemma of childhood—the dilemma of yearning accompanied by dread and fear. Dissociation may be a familiar solution to that dilemma.

Dissociation occurs in response to experienced danger, internal or external. The therapeutic relationship will feel dangerous both because of the invitation in the present for connection and trust, and the powerful transferential responses from the past. In response to the therapist and the therapeutic relationship, the client can be "triggered" in a variety of ways and use dissociative defenses to modulate her experience.

As a client moves forward in the relationship toward the therapist, perhaps slowly and tentatively or rapidly and counterphobically or alternating between these two styles, she will experience profound anxiety which she will manage through a range of strategies for modulating interpersonal distance. Early in the therapy, the therapist may primarily represent a dangerous authority figure, someone with the power and credibility that the survivor has been told she lacks. As the relationship progresses and the client reconnects with long-buried, powerful wishes for closeness, nurturance, and connection, her sense of danger and fear will intensify; these are often the very needs associated with abuse in the past. Dissociation is a familiar response to that danger.

Thus, as the therapeutic relationship develops and the therapeutic alliance increases, dissociation in the therapy may also increase, as Davies and Frawley (1991) have also noted. This seeming paradox can be confusing to the therapist if she forgets how dangerous connection and trust are for these clients. For a survivor client caught between the powerful need for interpersonal connection and the inevitable anticipation of danger, hurt, and betrayal, the only solution at the time may be to "leave" via dissociation (Waites, 1993).

Implicit here is the recognition that dissociation occurs in the context of transference. The affects from which a client dissociates are evoked in part by her current transference response to the therapist. In the client's eyes, the therapist may be untrustworthy and dangerous, a perpetrator, seducer, exploiter, yet she wants to trust the therapist and be held and nurtured by her. A client can feel caught in a "double bind" (Bateson, Jackson, Haley, & Weakland, 1956) between a wish and a fear, predicated on compelling and contradictory transferences—a gratifying maternal transference and malevolent abuser transference, for example. As the transferences in the relationship develop and change, so too will the precipitants for dissociation.

A client's dissociation in the therapy relationship serves to protect both the self and the relationship. It is an unconscious, automatic response to an affect that may be only preconscious. Yet the effect of dissociation on the developing relationship can be profound; it disallows the identification of transference and the working-through of conflicts and affects. When dissociation is unconscious, the survivor does not have the choice to remain connected to herself, the present experience, and the therapist. This disconnection prohibits the client from actively assessing danger and repairing a relational rupture. Therefore, the process remains unaltered, a closed loop, because the client cannot bring new experiences to bear on the conscious process of negotiating connection, intimacy, and affect. Thus an important therapeutic task is to begin to make conscious the unconscious mechanisms of dissociation.

DISSOCIATION AS A FRAMEWORK FOR THE THERAPIST

An understanding of dissociative events in the therapy provides a framework for interpreting the client's silences, memory lapses, vague responses, different presentations, and a myriad of interpersonal experiences between the therapist and client. Without this framework, therapists often turn to explanations that rely on concepts such as resistance, passive-aggression, malingering, manipulation, psychosis, acting out, regression, or transference neurosis. When the dynamic is a dissociative one, these explanations by themselves will not lead to successful reconnection and reunification around a common therapeutic goal.

In addition to the *event* of dissociation, we suggest the importance of recognizing the dissociative *process* in the therapy (Saakvitne, 1995). A dissociative event is marked by the occurrence of a moment or episode of dissociation or separation in the psychotherapy session. A dissociative process represents the ongoing separation from consciousness of knowledge, affects, or aspects of the self of the client or therapist, by client and/or therapist.

Our use of the term dissociation may be unfamiliar to some readers. We conceptualize dissociation broadly, to include both dissociative events and processes, for several reasons. First, we see dissociation as the underlying psychological defense for many adult survivors of childhood sexual trauma survivors, who respond to stress by not noticing, not connecting, not knowing. Other defenses commonly used by survivors, such as splitting, projection, projective identification, and denial, can be conceptualized as essentially dissociative to the extent that they are about not knowing or not connecting. Thus, dissociation is a framework within which one can recognize the survivor's consistent defensive need to sever connection—evident across behaviors, symptoms, and psychological defenses. Second, our use of the concept of dissociative process is consistent with our definition of dissociation, a process of separating mental contents. Third, clinically, in understanding our countertransference responses to dissociative clients— including our experiences of not knowing, not noticing, not remembering, and not connecting—we have found a dissociation framework most helpful. Finally, our acknowledgment of these two aspects of dissociation (event and process) is emblematic of our commitment to blend trauma and psychoanalytic theories.

Dissociative Events

Dissociative event refers to the moments in the therapy when a client actively (although not necessarily consciously or intentionally) separates or detaches from some aspect of self and/or the environment (Cardena, in press). A dissociative event can often be recognized by physiological and interpersonal clues. For example, the client's dissociation may become evident in sudden shifts in demeanor, focus of attention, or associational process; in expression of shame or disorientation (which often follows a return from a dissociated state); and in the inability to recall what just happened or what was being discussed. A client's silence, physical movements, absence of eye contact, unseeing stare, distraction, preoccupation, or comments to herself can all reflect an intrapersonal event that is split off from the interpersonal context of the psychotherapy. These events can easily be misinterpreted, leading to confusion or frustration in the therapist.

Example   A single word or phrase can become a clue, as was the case with a client who would say "right" and nod when she was unable to take in something the therapist had said and needed distance from the moment. The word "right" led the therapist to believe the client heard and agreed with her. Yet the client's tone was disengaged, almost dismissive, which left the therapist confused. The therapist initially believed that the ensuing silence indicated that the client was thinking through the therapist's (often painfully accurate) preceding comment. The therapist felt shut out because the client did not share these thoughts with her. Eventually, as she noticed the client's apparent disorientation upon reengaging in conversation, the therapist wondered aloud, "What just happened? Where were you?" and learned of the client's dissociation.

Obvious indicators of age regression or switching identities, ego states, or alters are the most dramatic signs of a dissociative event. These events can evoke complex feelings in the therapist. If it is unfamiliar behavior with this client, or to the therapist in general, she may feel confusion, alarm, disbelief, fear, fascination. When this type of dissociation becomes more familiar to a therapist with a particular client, it can evoke different feelings based upon the particular alters, the previous experiences with age regression, and the timing and context of the dissociation.

When a client dissociates and speaks in a childlike voice, the therapist is particularly vulnerable to powerful countertransference responses, and more vulnerable to vicariously traumatizing effects of the work. It is easy to feel the acute pain of a terrified child who may be reexperiencing abuse through vivid memories which feel like contemporary events. As Loewenstein (1993) reminds us, one countertransference danger with dissociative identity clients is that the therapist will interpret the client's subjective sense of identity as child or adolescent literally, rather than recognizing it as an "enacted representation of the childhood state, not its literal embodiment" (p. 69).

Dissociative Process

Dissociative process refers to the more pervasive and ongoing process of selective awareness and attention. A dissociative process can be more difficult to identify than a dissociative event. Dissociative process refers to the disconnection and removal from awareness of knowledge (information), affect, and aspects of the self of the client and therapist by client and/or therapist. The goal of psychotherapy is to integrate, make the unconscious conscious, and to reclaim the disowned; yet there is enormous conscious and unconscious resistance to this integration and connection.

A dissociative process can be evidenced in a variety of ways. It may take the form of a therapist's not recognizing or remembering material a client has spoken previously. For example, a client may refer to personal information, often quite significant, that amazes the therapist, yet at the same time the information seems vaguely familiar and she thinks she may have heard and known it before. A dissociative process, often countertransference driven, is also likely when a therapist cannot remember the previous session, a phenomenon common with dissociative clients.

A dissociative process is reflected when a therapist responds too literally to a client's transference. In this instance, the therapist actually dissociates or "forgets" the context of the therapeutic process, and thus loses touch with her knowledge about and framework for psychotherapy. For example, when a therapist becomes paralyzed in a session, feeling abusive if she queries a silent client and neglectful if she remains silent, she has accepted as literal a transference reenactment of failed parenting. With her observing therapist self, she could identify other options and move out of the double bind dichotomy in which she and the client are trapped. Similarly when a therapist accepts a particular client's wish for a better childhood as the literal task of the psychotherapy, among other things, she is disconnecting her countertransference wish to reparent from her professional understanding of therapeutic frame and mechanisms of psychotherapy. This dissociation of what one knows as a therapist can thus disinhibit a therapist and allow impulsivity in ways that endanger the therapy.

A dissociative process may occur when a therapist works closely with a client who is in an altered state. A therapist who is normally attuned to the time may lose track of the length of session and be surprised to realize the session is over or past over, or that only ten minutes have passed. Loewenstein (1993) includes "intense imagery, often with a sexual or aggressive content, negative hallucinations, depersonalization, trancelike experiences, countertransferential 'spacing out' and sleepiness, and inability to think" (p. 66) as examples of a therapist's experience of altered perceptions in work with severely dissociative clients. When working with clients on their imagery—traumatic, soothing, or metaphorical—the therapist may enter the client's imaginal and dissociative state, thus creating the potential for connection across modalities. The power of such work is great, but requires the therapist's careful awareness of the frame of the session and her own groundedness.

Some dissociative processes become fixed or stable when over time some aspect of the client or the therapeutic relationship is consistently split off and unacknowledged. The client can "forget," "not know," not incorporate certain material into her thinking.

Example   A client began a session reporting that she was in despair and wanted to die. When the therapist asked what was going on, the client said, "I don't know. I just feel hopeless." Until the therapist wondered if this feeling were connected to a phone call from her father the day before which she had reported in that day's session, the client had no memory of the call, and thus no connection between her mood and the interpersonal event.

The therapist can collude with dissociation and agree not to know, not to query, and not to notice. For example, a therapist may spend an entire session working on the client's anxiety or anger and neglect to connect the mood to the therapist's upcoming vacation, or a recently missed session. The therapist is then agreeing to ignore or disconnect the meaning of the therapeutic relationship from the client's experience. When a therapist focuses on content to the exclusion of process, she may be dissociating meaning and knowledge in a way that parallels the client's family context.

A dissociative process is occurring when a therapist unconsciously agrees to dissociate, split off, and disown aspects of a person, her experience, and feelings to avoid conflicts with her own experience and assumptions. As the therapist becomes aware of this process, often through the subjective experience of surprise, she will realize she has participated in a process of limiting who a client can be.

Example   A client who normally dressed quite professionally, and arrived at every session carefully coifed, made-up, and manicured, stated that she spent weekends in a tattered bathrobe holding her stuffed animals. The therapist was not only surprised, but unable to imagine the client in such a state. She realized she was unwilling to give up her image of the client and had unconsciously agreed not to be aware of any conflicting information, thus repeating a common dynamic for this client in which others saw only her competence and outward appearance and denied or disbelieved the depth of her despair and need.

Every psychotherapy session will reflect both integrative and dissociative processes. Therapists are constantly striving to connect and are unconsciously invited to disconnect conflictual, disturbing, and forbidden information, experiences, affects, and wishes. Attunement to these processes provides key information about conscious and unconscious processes.

COUNTERTRANSFERENCE RESPONSES
TO DISSOCIATION

For heuristic purposes, we discuss the therapist's countertransference to dissociation using a framework based on the motivation or psychic function reflected by the dissociation. These motivations for dissociation are both intrapersonal and interpersonal and share the common thread of serving to protect the client from intolerable affect. The goals of dissociation shape the therapist's experience and responses (Saakvitne, 1995).

Intrapsychic Functions of Dissociation and their Associated Countertransference Responses

The client dissociates in order to protect herself from specific dangers and internal and external sources of intolerable anxiety. We identify three major intrapsychic functions of dissociation below; a fourth, interpersonal, function will be described later in the chapter. These distinctions are hypothetical and overlap with one another, but allow for a clinically based discussion of countertransference responses which can help ground the therapist and guide her interventions. The intrapsychic functions are:

1. To separate oneself from intolerable affects, reflecting the need not to feel
2. To separate oneself from traumatic memories and knowledge, reflecting the need not to know
3. To separate from unacceptable aspects of oneself, reflecting the need not to be oneself

While dissociation is always an interpersonal event in therapeutic relationship, the interpersonal motivation is not necessarily most salient to the client at the time. The therapeutic relationship evokes internal anxiety that can prompt the need to dissociate. Therefore, it is often more fruitful to address and identify the core need reflected in the dissociation. That is, from what is the client aware of needing to separate? a feeling? a memory? an aspect of herself? the therapist?

Separation from Intolerable Affects

Many survivors have learned to fear the experience of affect, which is often accompanied by self-loathing and fears of abandonment or annihilation. Strong feelings are associated with danger, because they can trigger traumatic memories of being flooded with overwhelming feelings and left alone as a child whose mind and body could not hold and make sense of the affective sensations (Krystal, 1978). Strong emotions can also remind a survivor of times when showing feelings made her more vulnerable to harm, torment, or degradation. Particular affects are unbearable or dangerous to certain clients for specific reasons. For one client, fear will be intolerable; for another, longing, desire, or erotic feelings will prompt dissociation; for others, anger, sorrow, or shame will be unacceptable. Yet, inevitably clients will have feelings in therapy, evoked not only by the material, but often by the experience of having a relationship with the therapist.

Countertransference responses to dissociation from affect often start with a therapist's response to being left (often abruptly), either aware or unaware of the client's emerging feelings or their precipitant. The experience of abandonment is always evocative and can stir feelings of loneliness, anxiety, anger, or sometimes relief. A therapist may consciously or unconsciously associate to her own childhood or other experiences of abandonment, and experience related affects. Often the therapist feels simultaneously helpless and anxious to be helpful and back in control. When the therapist cannot tolerate being left or abandoned, she may unwittingly act out her own needs for control or connection, and overlook the protective function of dissociation. This situation can lead to behaviors as subtle as raising one's voice to call the client's name, to crossing the room to touch the client to "bring her back" into the room. While there are times when action from the therapist in response to a client's dissociation can be helpful, it is essential to consider the role of countertransference anger and anxiety as well as the meanings to the client of such action. After such an episode has occurred, the discussion of it can alert the therapist to the client's particular needs. One client told her therapist that she would begin to see the therapist's lips moving but not be able to hear the words, so she wanted a hand signal to alert her to the fact that she had dissociated and the therapist had noticed.

Alternatively, a therapist may become defensively withdrawn or angry, dissociate herself, or abandon the client in response to feeling abandoned.

Example   One client said her former therapist would say to her when she was silent or distant, "Well, if you have nothing to say there is no point in our meeting," thus threatening to end the relationship as punishment for the abandonment. The client reported feeling shamed, punished, and abandoned because she could not overcome her terror, anxiety, or the sense of inner blankness that she did not understand and often interpreted as stupidity. The therapist interpreted her experience, manifest in an anxious silence, as passive aggression, hostility, and resistance.

When we lose sight of the importance of the client's finding a safe way to feel in control, we lose our opportunity to work with her to mobilize her strengths and increase her awareness and control. When we can explore the precipitant for dissociation, while supporting the need for safety and control, we have an opportunity to work together to develop other ways to achieve those goals.

When a client dissociates from feelings, often the feelings themselves are then left with the therapist while the client appears numb or indifferent. The therapist may be left, both in and after the session, feeling profound anxiety, grief, rage, helplessness, arousal, despair, or powerlessness. Those intense feelings are exhausting when felt for two. It is easy to feel burdened and angry at the client's lability and her difficulty putting words to her immediate affective experience.

Example   Over a period of a few months, a therapist found herself feeling exhausted after every session with a highly dissociative client. This was puzzling to her as it did not appear that the client was placing any extraordinary demands upon her. In fact, the client was often quiet in sessions, bringing little compelling material and presenting as passive and somewhat resigned. One day, the therapist said early in a session, "You know I've been noticing something that I don't understand, and maybe you can help me with it. After our sessions lately I've found myself feeling inexplicably weary, as though I had been climbing a steep path for a very long time and carrying something heavy. I can't connect that feeling to what has been happening in here between us, but I wonder if you could help me? Is there anything in what I am describing that is familiar to you?" To the therapist's surprise, the client's eyes instantly filled with tears. She said she spent her entire adolescence feeling that way. She sobbed as she remembered going to bed bone-tired, but unable to sleep because she was so worried and felt so responsible for many things over which she now recognizes she had no possible control. The therapist realized that the client's apparent resignation and placidity reflected her dissociation from these feelings of overwhelming responsibility, loneliness, and fatigue.

When a therapist is left with feelings that are disconnected from context, she may feel the panic, alienation, and "craziness" that this disconnection stimulates (Searles, 1959). As she strives to make sense of her affective experience, the therapist will construct meanings and attribute sources to her feelings. This process of attribution is a central process in transference and countertransference. The context for this meaning-making may be one of disorientation, confusion, or panic for the therapist who feels uncertain about what has happened with the client or why. For example, if a therapist feels the client's dissociated despair, she may conclude that she is despairing in the therapy, and that the therapy, the client, or the therapist herself is hopeless. If the therapist is feeling the client's shame, she may believe that she is an unworthy therapist. Alternatively, the therapist may project that feeling onto the client and feel contempt toward the "manipulative, lazy, or impossible" client. If the therapist is left with strong sexual feelings, she may decide the client was being seductive, and show special attention or tenderness to the client to make her behavior consistent with her feelings, or the therapist may feel ashamed of her sexual feelings. She may try to construct a history for the client in order to make sense of her experience in the relationship. This is a context in which therapists risk jumping to conclusions about clients' histories, rather than exploring both the interpersonal aspects of the therapy and the client's history with therapeutic neutrality.

When the feelings the therapist is holding awaken old conflicts in her, it will influence how she manages the feelings and processes the complex interpersonal and projective context for her current experience. To the extent that our feelings conflict with our identities, personal or professional, or our ego ideal as a therapist, we can struggle with secondary feelings, such as shame, guilt, anger, or confusion.

Example   When one therapist was working with a client who eschewed any dependence on others, she found herself stuck in the therapy, unable to help her client out of her deep shame and self-loathing. Yet the therapist kept putting off calling for a supervision hour, until it dawned on her that she was repeating the client's counterdependent stance out of her own shame and unreasonable expectation that she should be able to figure the dilemma out by herself.

In this struggle to hold difficult feelings, one peril is that the therapist will unconsciously use projection to rid herself of intolerable feelings or unacceptable identities. A therapist can enter a dangerous cycle of unanalyzed projective processes in which the client projects an affect or identity and leaves by dissociation, and then the therapist responds to her countertransference response with projection. At the same time these unconscious processes are also the greatest hope for transformation in psychotherapy. As Davies and Frawley (1991) write,

> the interpretive process within the analytic experience is the only way to end the constant cycle of dissociation, projection, projective identification, and reintrojection that makes the history of abuse not only a painful memory, but an ongoing reality. (p. 30)

A therapist must be able to hold the affect and use it constructively to understand the client's experience and to work together with her toward reconnection.

Separation from Traumatic Memories and Knowledge

Dissociation protects the survivor from traumatic childhood memories and their associated imagery and consequent knowledge. Dissociation is a key process in compliance with the historical edict not to know. This mandate is potent, and becomes an organizing principle of an internal system developed to ensure survival (Laub & Auerhahn, 1993). When not knowing and not remembering are required for psychological and physical survival, the threat of memory or knowledge is intolerable. To understand the effects on the therapist of the client's dissociation from traumatic memory, we need to remember that dissociated memories are stored in a variety of ways. Not all memories are verbally mediated nor necessarily chronological or narrative. Traumatic memories may be experienced as visual imagery memories, as somatic or body memories, as sensory memories (tastes, smells, sounds), and as affective memory (floods of feelings with no apparent context)—any of which may be experienced as separate from knowledge, other affect, or understanding (Braun, 1988a, 1988b).

> To the extent that the traumatic experiences remain unsymbolized, they lie encrusted in a primitive core of unspeakable terror and phenomonologically meaningless panic, intrusive ideation, and somatic sensation. As such, they exist outside the usual domain of recalled experience, unavailable to self-reflective processes and analytic examination. (Davies & Frawley, 1994, p. 45)

In addition, we also include the concept of interpersonal memories, that is, encoded interpersonal sequences that can emerge as automatic behavior in a relational context. This concept reflects an integration of object relations theory concepts of transference with a current understanding of traumatic reenactments in interpersonal realms. It is consistent with Fast's psychoanalytic and developmental event theory (1985) as described by Davies and Frawley (1994):

> [I]t is not only the memory of specific traumatic events that come to be dissociated from other experiences but also the organization of mutually exclusive systems of self and object representations that have been formed in relationship to such traumatic moments. (pp. 45–46)

They continue:

> We believe that events become incorporated and ultimately understood vis a vis the particular matrices of self and object experience

within which they are ensconced and that they are bound together and organized with particular regard to the intense emotional experiences that accompany them. Therefore, it is not the traumatic event alone that becomes significant but of equal importance is the traumatized individual's experience and representation of self within the abusive events and her experience and internalization of the others in his or her world as they are represented at such abusive moments. (p. 64)

These behaviors or interpersonal scenes can feel confusing, dystonic, compulsive, and often shameful to the client. For example, a survivor may find herself responding with panic and rage to the expected departure of a partner, leading to intense self-loathing and the conviction that she will be punished, abandoned, and never loved again. Another survivor is tormented with anxiety when having sex with her partner, leading her to feel terrified, alone, and convinced her partner will reject her. These examples, as well as the reenactment patterns reflected when survivors choose abusive partners, assume demeaning roles in relationships, or engage in hurting themselves or others (Miller, 1994) can reflect the unconscious reenactment of earlier abusive and traumatic relationships, something Laub and Auerhahn (1994) have referred to as the "pantomime of trauma." We view such reenactments as a form of memory, one which often evokes a powerful countertransference response in the therapist.

In addition, clients replay abusive and traumatic interpersonal memories in their relationship with themselves. For example, the internal experience of relentless, harsh, demeaning criticisms can represent split-off memories of interpersonal experiences (that is, internalized objects can reemerge in an unmetabolized form that represent interpersonal memory fragments). One survivor realized that through her obsessive questioning and second-guessing of every decision she made, she was, in effect, doing to herself what her emotionally abusive and relentlessly critical father had done to her in childhood.*

The therapist must be sensitive to the presence of dissociated interpersonal memory fragments in the form of interpersonal reenactments in the therapeutic relationship. Many clients experience these reenactments, sometimes living them out as life themes (Laub & Auerhahn, 1993). Without a framework within which to understand them, the client may feel intensely self-critical and hopeless about the possibility of change (van der Kolk, 1989).

---

*V. Garvin (personal communication, 1994) has suggested that dissociation itself can be a reenactment of an experience of trauma in which the client dissociated; thus, the current dissociation reflects the memory of an earlier dissociation. In addition, she suggests that the client's dissociation may reflect a memory of a perpetrator who was in a dissociated state while abusing the client.

When a client dissociates to avoid a memory and the related affects, the therapist can be left with disturbing fragments of memories: an incomplete idea, an image, a bodily sensation, an affect, or a role in a reenactment, all disconnected from their context and meaning. She may feel confused, "crazy," unsure of what is real or true, reluctant to know more, and fragmented herself. Often the therapist feels the desire to probe for more detail or to ignore the fragment and change the subject to move away from the discomfort of a partial memory. As memories begin to emerge and the client maintains an ambivalent relationship with her memories, the therapist will also hold this ambivalence, which often takes the form of wanting and not wanting to know. The therapist may find herself feeling confused about what she knows to be true, thus simultaneously holding the experiences of knowing and not knowing. The images or fragments of memories may stay with the therapist or appear in her dreams or internal landscape.

A common countertransference response to this discomfort is for the therapist to wish for premature knowing—knowing before the client knows and telling the client her story or history. A therapist must be careful not to ask leading questions or assume to know someone else's truth. Rather, her task is to help hold the affects associated with uncovering and allow (transitional) space and time for the client to be curious and to notice her internal process; her role is to empathize with the agony of not knowing rather than to make suggestions about what might have happened.

This strategy requires the therapist tolerate the experience of "being in the dark," and through that experience better understand her client's subjective experience. When a client starts to remember something and then "disappears," the therapist is often left frustrated and curious. She will often start to imagine what memories the client might have and what might have happened to her. This process itself may reenact an aspect of the abuse; in effect, the client has unconsciously invited the therapist to create sexually perverse fantasies about her.

Separation from Unacceptable Aspects of Oneself

A client's dissociation from self, the need to flee from her identity or aspects of her identity, often begins with the need to rid herself of qualities that she believes made her vulnerable to abuse, including, for example, physical or psychological needs, the wish to be loved, weakness, femaleness, loneliness, or attractiveness. This fragmentation is often linked to profound shame and loathing of the self or those parts of the self. It often reflects the need to separate from aspects of oneself that hold forbidden information, such as the three-year-old who remembers what happened to her; or aspects that behave in certain ways, such as the competent one, the risk-taker, the mother, the protectors, the persecutor. This fragmentation can range from conscious awareness of different parts of oneself (e.g., the child within, the part that goes to work), to co-conscious identities or ego states, to multiple disconnected "personalities" or identities.

This fragmentation challenges our academic and cultural concepts of a unified personality and its functioning. In response, the therapist can feel bewildered, confused, and anxious; she may feel abandoned by the original persona of the client, or manipulated, lied to, or tricked. She may insist there is one true self and any other presentation of the client is untrue, denying the client's subjective experience of split-off parts or selves. This insistence prevents empathic connection with the client, and thus blocks therapeutic action. The therapist risks reenacting childhood traumas of abandonment through disbelief (i.e., when a trusted adult does not believe the child who discloses abuse). Without the framework of dissociation, a therapist can find these changes in ego states impossible to tolerate and may respond by confronting the client, thus becoming adversarial, or by feeling empty, sleepy, bored, or irritated, thus abandoning the client.

A therapist may become aware of split-off aspects of the client through her countertransference complementary maternal protective response. Noticing such a shift in herself allows the therapist to pay attention to what aspects of herself are being magnified and which are being shut out or denied. When a client cannot integrate, for example, her vulnerability and her anger, she invites us likewise to respond selectively to her dissociated parts, and to own the complementary aspect of ourselves as the whole truth. Thus the client who experiences herself as a helpless victim may invite the therapist to assume the identity of protector or bully, and to remain unaware of any contradictory feelings or identities in either party. This process is the heart of the transference-countertransference pairings described in the literature (Davies & Frawley, 1994; Miller, 1994). Remembering the fluidity and contradictions inherent in these identifications helps the therapist stay balanced and able to respond to the rapidly shifting paradigms.

Dissociation from aspects of the self can be manifest in a less dramatic or obvious form, as when a client presents without affect or liveliness. This presentation can take the form of a rather wooden presence, or a social demeanor which is engaging or pleasant but which does not allow a range of affect or any real sense of connection. The client may come across as superficial and the therapist may feel bewildered and eventually bored or annoyed. This presentation can reflect the use of dissociation in the service of becoming invisible, not drawing any attention to oneself. It represents a caricature of a "good girl," a "normal" person, and eradicates all conflict, passion, and unique aspects of an individual. A therapist often becomes aware of this dissociative process through her subjective experience of boredom, apathy, or sleepiness, that is, through the absence of connectedness to and lively interest in the person of her client.

Interpersonal Functions of Dissociation and their Associated Countertransference Responses

The fourth function of dissociation in our model is the need to separate from the interpersonal relationship — to separate from the therapist and the therapeutic relationship. The need for interpersonal distance will arise in the context of particular relational dynamics or transferences and particular points in the development of the therapeutic relationship.

Transference feelings may be experienced as dangerous and prompt dissociation when they represent profound fears, forbidden wishes, or the expectation of traumatic repetitions. In response to the transference, the client dissociates in order to leave the therapist, to hide from the therapist, to protect the therapist, or to render the therapist impotent.

The interpersonal function of dissociation is often not conscious for the client; the intrapsychic dangers to which she is responding may be more readily available. It is easier for her to recognize the intrapersonal context for dissociation for a number of reasons:

1. She is familiar with her experience of dissociation and it predates her relationship with the therapist.
2. Dissociation is an inherently isolating, private experience that many clients assume is unique to them or unique to "crazy" or "disturbed" people.
3. It is only with great caution that a client can allow herself to know that the relationship with the therapist matters to her or that she can feel threatened by or afraid of her therapist or her feelings about her therapist.

Understanding the interpersonal context for dissociation will challenge the client's core defenses, beliefs, and experience of self. For that reason, the work on the interpersonal context for dissociation is often slow.

When a client leaves the connected interpersonal space through dissociation, the therapeutic task is to understand why she felt she had to leave at that moment. There are many possible fears represented by the need to dissociate. For example:

1. The client's feelings toward the therapist, particularly anger, yearning, shame, and sexual attraction, may make the relationship feel unsafe.
2. The client may have felt unsafe because she imagined or assumed that the therapist was feeling angry, disappointed, aroused sexually, or sadistic.
3. The client may have experienced an upsurge of affect that she believed the therapist or the relationship could not handle, or that she could not tolerate feeling in the therapist's presence without humiliation.
4. The client may have imagined she would be placing the therapist in danger if the therapist knew or witnessed what she felt, knew, or remembered.

One goal of psychotherapy is to make the intrapersonal dynamics explicit through the therapeutic relationship, to shift the complex world of introjects, internalizations, and identifications into the relationship between therapist and client where they can be sorted through in safety. During this process the therapist should keep in mind that dissociation provides data about therapeutic technique. At times, fleeing the therapist is an appropriate response to the therapist's behavior. If the therapist is pursuing the client, or urging her to discuss things she is not prepared to talk about, to know things she cannot yet tolerate knowing, or to speak in defiance of internalized edicts or threats from the past, dissociating may be a reasonable response.

The Client's Need to Flee the Therapist

What is an appropriate response to the client's need to dissociate in order to protect herself and the relationship? As with any countertransference response to a transference, a therapist struggles with her experience of the transference identity. When striving to create safety and trust, it is difficult for any therapist to perceive her client's sheer terror, mistrust, and desperate need to flee her presence, and she may feel bewildered at being perceived as threatening. When a therapist realizes she has frightened her client, for example, by expressing anger or annoyance, by raising difficult material, by startling her with words or unexpected movement, by being preoccupied or less available than usual, or by announcing an upcoming absence, she can feel guilty. While it is important to take responsibility for the behaviors to which the client responded, it is equally important not to become mired in guilt. This guilt disempowers the client by giving the therapist complete responsibility, and prevents both therapist and client from understanding the more complicated interaction that occurred between two people and between the past and the present.

Example   A therapist preoccupied with an argument she had the hour
before with her daughter was aware that she was somewhat distracted in a
session with a dissociative client. In the middle of the session, the client
switched to a child alter who cried out, "What have I done? Why are you
angry with me?" The therapist was unable to calm the child alter, and the
client left the session early. She then telephoned the therapist after the
session to ask whether the therapist intended to continue the treatment or
not. The therapist was very puzzled by the question, was concerned, and
felt guilty about letting her personal concerns come into the session. Over
several sessions, the client realized that the therapist's incomplete attention
reminded her of the quiet, seemingly distracted state her stepfather would
go into on the evenings when he later came to her room to sexually abuse
her, after which he would ignore her for days or weeks. This information
previously had been unavailable to both client and therapist, and yet helped
both understand the client's fear responses in other situations.

The Client's Need to Hide from the Therapist

When a client experiences the therapist as an authority or as an intrusive
powerful figure, she may use dissociation to hide from her. The therapist
may then feel she is being toyed with, manipulated, or teased, and become
annoyed and critical. She may respond by becoming scolding or punitive or
acting passively aggressive by "just waiting." Alternatively, the therapist
may give up or pursue the client aggressively. She may feel angry or frustrated about being left trying to do this interpersonal work alone, or self-
critical about her pursuit or abandonment of the client. These dynamics
often contain a powerful and frightening reenactment of hiding and being
pursued.

The therapist's knowing or seeing the client can activate intense shame in
the client, followed by the need to hide. When a client is certain her feelings
are unacceptable, repugnant, or offensive to the therapist, she may hide
in fear and shame. This response reflects an interpersonal (transference)
assumption of the therapist's judgment, and can create a bind for the therapist: She feels she risks shaming the client if she names the hiding behavior,
and abandoning her if she does not.

The Client's Need to Protect the Therapist

When the client fears that her feelings, thoughts, or impulses may be dangerous to the therapist, she may dissociate to protect the person of the
therapist as well as the relationship. This dynamic may emerge when the
client feels angry, vengeful, competitive, powerful, contemptuous, or sadistic. As she becomes aware of this dynamic, the therapist may feel grateful

yet frustrated, perhaps touched by the client's concern for her, perhaps insulted or challenged by the client's underestimation of her abilities. The therapist may invite the client to explore her assumptions and fears about the therapist's strength and weakness, her vulnerabilities and resources. The therapist's understanding of the concepts of transference allows her to listen to this inventory in the context of the client's life experience as well as the context of her therapist-self. This approach also allows the mutual exploration of the client's beliefs about the her own power, destructiveness, and toxicity.

A related dilemma is the client's experience or anticipation of humiliation when experiencing certain feelings in front of the therapist. For many survivors, to be seen needing, wanting, or desiring anything is enormously shaming. For others, to be seen crying or expressing fear is humiliating and potentially dangerous. It can evoke disturbing memories of the abusers' arousal in the face of their fear or pain. The need to block this shame or the potential reenactment is so great that the dissociative defenses are mobilized so rapidly that the therapist may have no idea that a complex event has just occurred in the relationship.

The Client's Need to Disempower the Therapist

Dissociation can render the therapist impotent when it conveys the triumphant message, "You can't get to me. You can't control me or have an effect on me because I can leave." This enactment reflects the client's transferential perception of the therapist as dangerous, persecutory, or sadistic. These transferences may be elicited when the therapist moves the client prematurely toward strong feelings, such as rage, grief, or shame, or toward memories of abuse. Without recognition of the transference, the therapist can easily respond aggressively to the taunt, thus enacting the feared experience.

A malevolent transference can also be elicited by the therapist's invitation to intimacy and connection. While the therapeutic relationship offers appropriate intimacy, acceptance, and understanding of the whole person of the client, this relationship can feel terrifying to individuals to whom intimacy historically has been followed by abuse, abandonment, overstimulation, or rape. One client asked suspiciously, "What do you mean by intimate?" when the therapist mentioned feelings of closeness and intimacy in group psychotherapy. She went on to say that to her, intimacy means sexual intimacy. She was relieved by an explicit discussion of therapeutic relationships and intimacy.

Further, the possibility of intimacy and connection in therapy will stir ancient unmet longings for understanding that are experienced as profoundly dangerous and for some as entrapment or seduction. At such times the client may need to make the therapist powerless, which may feel provocative, taunting, hurtful, or disempowering to the therapist. The therapist may be left feeling defeated and futile, or come to feel like an abusive person. If not carefully untangled, this morass can become a therapeutic impasse.

COUNTERTRANSFERENCE RESPONSES TO PERSONS WITH DISSOCIATIVE IDENTITIES AND RITUAL ABUSE SURVIVORS

When a client maintains distinct, unintegrated identities, ego states, or alter selves, the experience for the therapist is complex. On the one hand, in the immediate moment, when a client speaks out of a different identity, the therapist may instinctively respond in a complementary way. When a client speaks as a young child, one tends to respond as a protective parent; when a client speaks as an angry adolescent, the therapist might respond as a calm, firm, or frustrated adult; and when a client responds as a defensive, protective individual, the therapist may respond cautiously, being respectful of the boundaries being set. However, simultaneously, the therapist may be feeling many different things, including confusion, anxiety, embarrassment, bewilderment, feelings related to her sense of continuity with the client, with herself, with her colleagues, and with her profession and professional identity.

Professional Issues

Therapists who work with severely dissociative clients can feel not only enormous isolation, but also embarrassment or shame, especially if their colleagues, teachers, or mentors do little or no work with such clients, as Davies and Frawley (1994) have also noted. The therapist may fear being seen as unsophisticated, accused of "acting out" with her clients, planting ideas in her clients' minds, or even creating multiple personalities (see Putnam, 1989, and Kluft, 1994, for a discussion of the latter issue). These responses may stem from a sense that one's mentors or colleagues would not conceptualize the client as having dissociative identities. They may stem from the therapist's conceptual difficulty with the clinical presentation of multiplicity or dissociative identities, which require her both to face the existence and aftermath of severe early childhood trauma, and to reconfigure her understanding of human psychology.

When working with a paradigm, theory, or diagnosis that is controversial and new, therapists are vulnerable to an additional set of pressures. It is hard enough to manage the complicated countertransference responses to dissociation without having to face professional disbelief. The therapist can be caught in a larger cultural reenactment of her client's history when her experience of the interpersonal reality of her clinical work is denied by others in the field. It is very important to have consultants and supervisors doing similar work to help work through the cultural and collegial responses. Alternatively, because working with persons with dissociative identities is relatively new for most therapists, the therapist may feel special, as if she were singled out or uniquely qualified to do this groundbreaking work. Such feelings may lead to admiration of or fascination with the client's dissociative abilities, or to exploitation or mistreatment of the client.

Another difficult set of countertransference responses can be stimulated by colleagues who want to be working on the cutting edge and who, through lack of training or experience, are overdiagnosing dissociative identity disorder. This phenomenon is confusing for clients who may be misguided in their healing efforts. It also creates understandable skepticism and disrespect for all mental health professionals, and can produce frustration and anger in trained therapists who are careful in their diagnostic assessments.

Clinical Issues

Countertransference responses to clients with dissociative identities include the therapist's responses to the presence of alter personalities and to particular alters. The client has developed a system of separate ego states to protect herself from intolerable affect, and any threat to that system (including psychotherapy) will raise strong objections from some part of the system. Therapists have strong feelings about being perceived as the enemy when they are trying to help the individual recover and develop an integrated sense of self.

Few transference responses are more difficult to hold than a malevolent perpetrator transference. When this transference is held by a split-off part of the client, by an alter, the therapist may dismiss the feelings as not belonging to the "real client," fear or reject that alter, or feel angry because of the inaccessibility of these feelings to the therapy process. Even when invited to work within the client's dissociation to address split-off parts separately, clinically and conceptually, the therapist must hold on to her integrative conceptualization of the person.

There is a countertransference danger of becoming too literal in the interpretation of dissociative identity disorder, that is, to believe that these identities are reified entities rather than discounted aspects of the self and memory (Chu, 1988; Ross, 1989). The therapist's task, complicated by her countertransference responses, is to understand the client's experience of herself, while holding a conceptualization of multiplicity and dissociative identities as reflecting a self-protective adaptation to early, severe trauma in an individual, a whole person.

The therapist may feel a unique connection with each alter. Often, the therapist forms a strong attachment to the personality that initially enters treatment, and feels less connection and familiarity, and thus less therapeutic alliance, with other alters. In addition, different alters will evoke different countertransference responses from the therapist, thus complicating the already complex business of tracking countertransference within the therapeutic relationship. Therapists commonly connect more readily with aspects of their clients that are familiar; in a client with dissociative identities, this may translate into a differential attachment to the identities most similar or familiar to the therapist. A therapist can feel challenged emotionally and intellectually, and sometimes overwhelmed and inadequate as a professional by the wide range of presentations. Each therapist will have her own responses to different types of alters; her self-knowledge will help her anticipate and understand why she may connect more readily with a strong-willed alter, for example, than with a sweet, compliant one.

Some behaviors or symptoms displayed by clients with dissociative identities are very difficult for the therapist. Severe self-injurious behaviors often put the therapist in the position of helpless witness to current abuse. When these behaviors occur in dissociation, the client may also feel like a helpless witness. At this point, the work is several steps away from a place where the therapist and client can process the interpersonal component of the expressed rage, sadism, and masochism. When dealing with a severely abusive or suicidal alter personality, a therapist can feel invited to participate in the banishment or rejection of certain parts of the self. It is difficult to remain aware that each part of the self represents an attempt to adapt and cope with the original impossible situation. Protecting the more vulnerable parts of the client's self while respecting the fear and anger of the abusive parts is a difficult balance to maintain, especially as the therapist is invited into the client's child-based perceptual world of good and bad. The clinical response includes naming this balance and one's own conflicting countertransference responses.

Example   One client with dissociative identities had a brash adolescent male alter whose job was to keep her from telling the secret of her abuse. As the client began to talk more to the therapist about the abuse by her mother, the young male alter became more enraged, and engaged in more mutilation of the body. A child alter became extremely frightened, and reported to the therapist the angry alter's intent to kill everyone. The therapist felt frightened for the client, concerned about her child-like terror, as represented by the child alter, and impatient with the angry alter. The therapist was able to name her concerns to the host (whom the angry male described as "a wimp") and to the angry alter. At this point, the therapist's fears diminished somewhat, leaving her freer to be helpful. She worked to help the angry alter reframe his task as one of protection and to devise with him a better way of protecting the system.

More generally, severe dissociation can also leave the therapist without a sense of continuity or stability in the work. It can feel confusing and frustrating to encounter different alters within or across sessions. The therapist may engage in a complementary splitting, with a resulting failure to connect the various split-off experiences. For example, the therapist may feel kindly toward and protective of the child alters, angry at alters who harm the client's body, grateful for alters who try to help out. This can lead to a lack of integration within the therapy of the client's fear, rage, and desire to change, as both client and therapist move among the various states and relationships.

These complicated countertransference responses allow the therapist to connect affectively with a client's chronic experiences of herself in the world. These clients often live with a constant sense of shame and alienation. To the extent that the therapist can remain aware of the context of her internal responses, she can feel greater empathy with her clients.

Countertransference Responses to Horrific Material

Hearing a story of sadistic child abuse commonly evokes a need in us to distance (Peck, 1983). It evokes a profound desire not to know and not to believe. It is easier to think of the client as psychotic or manipulative than to believe that people are capable of such behavior toward children and each other. It stirs our own primitive affects and drives and can evoke deep anxiety, shame, and fear of our sadism (Haley, 1974; Scurfield, 1985). We can be appalled at our fascination and interest in the atrocities that clients reveal. We may be frightened and discomfited by our visceral and emotional reactions as we listen. We do not always know what to do with our powerful feelings of horror, rage, sadness, amazement, naivete, and smallness in relation to the enormity of the horror.

It is valuable and self-protective to notice and experience our strong feelings about this work; these responses connect us to our humanity. Our affect will also allow us to connect with our client's process of discovering, knowing, and feeling over time. As the client allows herself to know the abuse was sadistic and intentional, she will experience confusion, great fear, shame, dread, grief, and horror. As we hold the knowledge and the affect, we can help the client pace the work. At times, our awareness of what is coming in the process is part of our countertransference. To the extent that we know how slow and painful this process is, we can find ourselves dreading it for both ourselves and our clients. Such abuse has pervasive destructive effects upon the self of the client. Since we know this and are sometimes aware of it before the client presents those disruptions, this can stir a sense of dread at the enormity of the work ahead.

Therapists often fear material about ritual and cult abuse. They may fear the specific atrocities they may be asked to hear. They may fear the cults themselves, fearing the threat to themselves as the cult struggles to keep secrecy and hold on to its members (i.e., the client). The therapist may come to fear or dread the client's hidden sides, parts of the client that identified with the perpetrators or that committed abuses. The therapist may not want to know parts of the client that can perpetrate abuse on others and have done so in the past. The therapist will have feelings about the possibility or realization that the client may still be involved in a cult.

It is extremely important not to do this work alone. Therapists who work with survivors of ritual or cult abuse can form networks, support, supervision, or study groups, or find another therapist with whom they can discuss the work. First and foremost, we all have to support ourselves; without that we cannot help our clients.

VICARIOUS TRAUMATIZATION IN PSYCHOTHERAPIES WITH DISSOCIATIVE CLIENTS

Working with severely dissociative clients can make therapists especially susceptible to vicarious traumatization which then contributes to their countertransference responses.* When affect or imagery is split off from its context, a therapist is less able to anticipate and protect herself. We use affect, just as the body uses sensation and pain, as part of a protective warning system that allows us to know of approaching danger and potential harm or pleasure.

When a client's childhood experience includes abuse whose intent was to inflict harm, the affects aroused in the therapist are more intense and distressing. This includes abuse that took place in malevolent developmental contexts (Gelinas, 1994), physical or sexual abuse where the arousal of the perpetrator was heightened by the pain and terror of the child (Goodwin, 1993), and abuse that occurred as part of an organized event,

*For further discussion of the relation between countertransference and vicarious traumatization see chapter 15.

religion, or organization of people, such as ritual or cult abuse (Sakheim & Devine, 1992b).

These malevolent, sadistic, ritualistic, and cult contexts are not uncommon in the history of clients with severe dissociation and multiple personality (Putnam, 1989; Sakheim & Devine, 1992b). Hearing these memories and witnessing the clinical sequelae and reenactments evoke powerful countertransference responses as well as vicarious traumatization. Our world view is altered as we witness so closely the reality of the intentional, cruel, sadistic behaviors of one human being toward another.

The less we are able to process the events in the therapeutic relationship and the connection of our feelings to those events, the less we will be able to protect ourselves and to remain connected to ourselves and our clients in a respectful way. We need to be particularly attuned to our capacity to relate to ourselves in dissociated ways, particularly to our ability to develop split identities which include only parts of ourselves (e.g., warm nurturant therapist, social comic, competent administrator). Indeed we may enter our own dissociative process in response to this work, unconsciously allowing only certain parts of ourselves to enter into the therapeutic relationship. While obviously the therapist makes choices about which aspects of herself to bring into a therapeutic relationship, the role can invite compartmentalization. We must balance the demands of our work and role with conscious attention to our physical, emotional, intellectual, psychological, spiritual, and interpersonal needs in a way that allows for recognition and integration of different aspects of ourselves.

7

The Influence of
Countertransference on
Therapeutic Frame and Boundaries

THE THERAPEUTIC RELATIONSHIP is contained by the therapeutic frame; this frame creates the uniquely bounded intimate relationship that defines psychotherapy. While most clinicians would agree on this premise, there are significant variations in practice both across clinicians and across clients for the same clinician. Experienced trauma therapists agree that the establishment and maintenance of a therapeutic frame can be extremely difficult with survivor clients (Chu, 1988; Kauffman, 1993), and many clinicians who feel quite clear about their beliefs and practices have found themselves in boundary quagmires with their survivor clients.

The process of establishing and negotiating the boundaries of the therapeutic frame is crucial in any psychotherapy (Langs, 1975), but is particularly critical in psychotherapy with survivors of childhood sexual abuse (Herman, 1992; McCann & Pearlman, 1990b). Because their trauma was predicated on violations of physical and psychological boundaries, these clients are both sensitive and extremely vulnerable to boundary blurring or violation in subsequent relationships (Armsworth, 1989; Kluft, 1990b). Whether a client is vigilant and attuned to all potential violations, or dissociative and driven to unconscious reenactments of earlier violations, boundaries will be a key therapeutic issue and metaphor.

In the negotiation of boundary issues, the therapist strives to remain aware of the complex dynamics among wishes, fears, competing needs, ethics, and power. Some aspects of the frame are fixed and will not change, based upon the theoretical premise of the work, basic ethical principles, or the therapist's consistent needs or limitations. Other aspects of the frame are subject to negotiation between the client and therapist over time, which is an important part of the therapy. Clinicians often have little formal training or education about therapeutic frame, yet must negotiate boundary issues in every therapy. It is challenging to remain conscious of the complex levels of meaning and potential pitfalls in the maintenance of therapeutic frame and boundaries in these psychotherapies. We find five strategies are helpful to keep in mind:

1. Having a clear theoretical framework for the therapeutic relationship and specifically for the boundaries and frame of this relationship with sexual abuse survivors
2. Setting a clear therapy framework with each client
3. Knowing ourselves and our own histories, weaknesses, and vulnerabilities through personal therapy and reflection during and between sessions
4. Receiving consultation and supervision on a regular basis
5. Discussing frame issues with clients openly and over time, especially when the client requests a change

Countertransference plays a major role in the therapist's response to boundary challenges and in the decisions that result, as Davies and Frawley (1994) have also noted. Unrecognized or unanalyzed countertransference contributes both to boundaries that are unclear, inconsistent, or diffuse and to boundaries that are harmful because of their rigidity and nonmutuality. The therapist's clear understanding of her conceptual framework for psychotherapy provides a touchstone that allows her to notice variations from her normal or common practices. These changes give clues to countertransference, transference, and reenactment issues in the therapy (Langs, 1975).

At the same time, the negotiation of these issues provides fertile ground for exploring and understanding object relational paradigms, identity issues, and schema disruptions. Discussing frame issues provides an opportunity for the conscious negotiation of basic components of interpersonal relationships in the context of the transformative therapeutic relationship. For clients whose needs have historically been used as a means of exploitation or humiliation, the interpersonal process of acknowledging different needs and developing boundaries that take those needs into account is revelatory and healing.

THE THERAPEUTIC FRAME

The frame of the therapy is the interpersonal manifestation of the theoretical model of the psychotherapy. It defines the tasks, roles, structure, and boundaries of both the therapy and the therapeutic relationship. While it incorporates the administrative and financial considerations of the psychotherapeutic contract, it is more than rules or a contract. The frame of therapy reflects expectations for each participant that arise from the theoretical conceptualization of both the goal and process of psychotherapy. The boundaries of therapy are the specific manifestations of the frame, the guidelines that govern the behavior of client and therapist in the therapeutic relationship and create the safe, predictable holding environment necessary for the work.

The therapeutic frame includes such issues as appointment times and length of sessions, fees, forms of address, shared information, therapist availability, physical space, touch, social manner, language, confidentiality, and so forth. Further, the therapeutic frame includes the expectations that boundaries will be named and interpersonal events noticed and discussed. When an initial contact includes this necessary information, the stage is set for a relationship in which predictability and mutual respect will be maintained.

The therapist's countertransference responses to the incest survivor's poignant fear and mistrust commonly affect the frame of the therapy. One therapist may impose firm boundaries in response to a complementary identification as a powerful authority figure, or assume a paternalistic role as protector in response to the client's fears. Another therapist may modify boundaries to dispel the client's perception of her as an abusive authority. She may deny or abdicate the power she does have rather than provide a healing interpersonal experience of respectful power and mutual negotiation.

The therapeutic frame is the frame of reference for the therapy, including concepts of self and other, and values that create meaning and predictability.* Alterations to or disregard for the frame will have a significant impact just as any assault to one's frame of reference is disruptive. The resulting loss of bearings leads to crises of faith, trust, identity, meaning, hope, and safety. The opposite is also true; the proper establishment and maintenance of a shared frame for the therapy provides a context within which a client's disrupted personal frame of reference can begin to be restored.

The creation of a therapeutic frame includes the acknowledgment of

---

*See chapter 3 for further elaboration of frame of reference.

issues of power, authority, trust, and dependence. As a professional, the therapist is imbued with power both because of the societal attribution of authority to healers and because of the client's personal experience of pain, need, and dependence (Peterson, 1992). The client's perception of the therapist's power is directly related to her vulnerability, distress, pain, and need; survivors of childhood abuse often experience themselves as vulnerable to a powerful therapist.

In the transference, the client may experience the therapist's power as authoritative knowledge, control, the power to reject or abandon, the power to hurt and humiliate, or the power to define the truth, as well as the power to help or heal. Each client's specific self and object relational beliefs lead to particular experiences of the therapist's power. For example, a client's low self-esteem increases her experience of her therapist's power to devalue her. Her experience of dependency needs increases her perception of her therapist's power to abandon or betray her. A client vulnerable to shame will see her therapist as a mighty judge with the ability to disconnect from and devalue her. The strategies a client may employ to protect herself from her therapist's perceived power can be confusing and burdensome to the therapist, especially if she does not recognize the protective function of such maneuvers. For example, when a client requests that a therapist remain in her chair while the client leaves the office at the end of a session (or prefers to enter the office behind the therapist rather than go in first), the therapist might feel controlled or misunderstood if she does not recognize her client's attempt to create conditions that protect her from fear, thus facilitating the development of trust in the relationship. Without this understanding, negative countertransference responses are stronger and play a larger role in boundary negotiations.

ESTABLISHING AND MAINTAINING BOUNDARIES

Ideally, a therapist addresses the framework and the meanings of boundaries with the client from the beginning. This openness often contrasts starkly with a client's experience of her own family rules as fixed, arbitrary, and nonnegotiable. A therapist's countertransference-driven reluctance to name boundaries will impede the healing power of the therapy. For example, if the therapist accepts the client's projected expectation of deprivation or harshness from her, she may forego naming boundaries out of a wish to be gratifying. If the therapist is uncomfortable with the power imbued in her as therapist, she may avoid setting limits. If she fears shaming a client, she may avoid naming a conflict. If a therapist is conflicted about charging for her services, she may neglect to address fees. If a therapist believes she should be everything to her client, she may fail to set limits on her availability. Each of these examples reflects the therapist's failure to include her own needs and limitations in the therapeutic relationship, creating a therapeutic climate ripe for distortion and exploitive reenactments that will be harmful to both participants.

Discussions of boundaries define the therapeutic relationship as mutual, a process in which all interactions, including the therapist's behavior and decisions, are open for review. For example, when a therapist asks a client by what name she wishes to be called, she invites the client to notice that her name matters and that she has choices within the therapeutic relationship. How the client addresses the therapist has meanings to the client and implications for the power dynamics of the relationship. However, countertransference can interfere with this discussion if the therapist feels unsure of herself and is not sure she is willing or able to tolerate the client's scrutiny or observations.

The process of negotiation may feel unfamiliar or uncomfortable to some therapists. If a therapist is accustomed to a more authoritative role as expert, she will assume that boundaries are simply rules created by the therapist for both members of the relationship. This approach eliminates a crucial arena for therapeutic work; by recreating an authoritarian, nonmutual context for the relationship, the therapist loses the opportunity to help the client learn new ways of relating and develop negotiation and assertiveness skills.

Gratification and Deprivation

Gratification and power are central in the negotiation of boundaries. The issue of therapeutic abstinence has a long history in psychoanalytic theory. In his paper, "Observations on Transference-Love," Freud states,

> analytic technique requires of the physician that he should deny to the patient who is craving for love the satisfaction she demands. The treatment must be carried out in abstinence. By this I do not mean physical abstinence alone, nor yet the deprivation of everything that the patient desires, for perhaps no sick person could tolerate this. Instead, I shall state it as a fundamental principle that the patient's need and longing should be allowed to persist in her, in order that they may serve as forces impelling her to do work and to make changes, and that we must beware of appeasing those forces by means of surrogates. (1915, pp. 164–165)

In explicit reference to psychotherapeutic work with survivors of incest, Davies and Frawley define the function of therapeutic abstinence as follows:

The notion of abstinence rests, we believe, on the therapist's ability to protect the illusory quality of the transitional space in which transference and countertransference play themselves out, to guard against becoming entrenched in actual, behavioral confirmations of the patient's transference experience, unconsciously reenacted outside the province of therapeutic interpretation and negotiation. Such actualization of what should remain symbolic in therapy could bring about a dangerous collapse of the transitional arena and seriously impede further therapeutic progress. (1994, p. 227)

One plane in which these issues are negotiated with some clients is that of touch in therapy. Particularly for clients whose abusive context was one of enormous emotional deprivation and whose early maternal environment was neglectful or cold, the desire for physical touch can feel compelling to the therapist (Carlson, 1990). For some therapists touch is never a part of clinical work; others may incorporate physical touch into the framework of the therapy in carefully considered ways. In the latter case, it is important that touch be initiated by the client and that it never be sexual in nature. This distinction is not always straightforward, of course, with clients whose childhood experiences fused nonsexual and sexual touch. Thus, the distinction in the therapy must be discussed explicitly.

The discussion of touch can open up important themes in the therapy, including experiences of early maternal deprivation, reenactments of the fusion of the yearning for maternal connection with erotic arousal, reenactments of sexual seduction, countertransference wishes to reparent, and the therapist's wish to give more than she has to give.* The elaboration of these themes is essential, and separate from the need to arrive at a decision about therapist-client touch. The meaning of touch is unique with each client and can change over time as the relationship and its vicissitudes unfold (Sakheim & Devine, 1992b). It is essential that the therapist be comfortable personally and ethically with any decision. Thus, one therapist may only feel comfortable with a touch of hands, while another may feel comfortable, after discussion, with a client-initiated hug.

Example   One client expressed a desire for a hug at the end of each session. Before deciding, the therapist and client spent several sessions exploring what the hug represented to the client (in this case, a wish for touch that she initiated), what it might be like to hug the therapist (comforting and scary), and what it felt like to ask (frightening and exciting). After the

*See Maroda (1991) for further discussion of countertransference issues in the negotiation of touch.

discussion, the client's press for action diminished and she decided not to change their accustomed way of doing things, and noted that she felt closer to the therapist and safer in the relationship.

The boundaries of a therapeutic relationship protect the client and therapist from inappropriate expectations and the damage caused by unprocessed miscommunication. Further, they model self-respect in relationships as a component of trust and safety. The therapist models this attitude when she invites discussion of such questions as: Why is the request occurring now? What would it mean to you (the client) to change this boundary? How might it be helpful? harmful? problematic? What would it mean in the relationship if we did/did not make this change? Does the therapist feel comfortable, theoretically and personally, with the change? Some of these answers will not be knowable in advance. Following a decision on whether to modify a boundary, the therapist and client can continue to discuss the effects of the process over time—not with a model of right or wrong, but with a curiosity about the range of meanings and effects this decision might have had.

THERAPEUTIC BOUNDARIES WITH INCEST SURVIVORS

Boundaries represent protection for and definition of the self and the therapeutic relationship. Survivor clients will struggle with intense wishes for and fears of boundary changes. Certain boundary changes, such as extended sessions, communication with other treaters, and certain types of therapist disclosure, can sometimes be helpful. On the one hand, a changed or breached boundary can represent to the client being special to and valued by the therapist; on the other hand, any change can evoke a sense of danger, anxiety, and the assumption that the therapist will expect something (often sexual) in return, and often pleasure and fear are felt simultaneously.

Clinically, open discussion and negotiation of boundaries are therapeutic. Yet naming and noticing the client's wishes for or fears of moving closer to the therapist can evoke enormous shame in survivor clients; shame can in turn prompt powerful defensive responses (e.g., dissociation, projection, withdrawal, rage). A client whose childhood wishes for attention and nurturance were taken as invitations or rationales for violation may feel anxious and threatened when the therapist invites discussion of a boundary (e.g., a question about the therapist's personal life, a request for touch, a gift to the therapist) or comments on her wish for closeness.

A relational, developmental approach to these dilemmas emphasizes that a client can learn from current behaviors about past behaviors that were adaptive or representative of the rules of childhood. This framework invites a client to notice and understand her previously forbidden wishes, fears, and beliefs in a nonpunitive, nonshaming, nonblaming way.

Example   When a client shamefacedly insisted that her phone call to her therapist was not made to "get attention," her therapist noted that the client seemed to think that wanting attention was a bad thing. The therapist normalized the need and universal wish to be attended to, that is, listened to and held. She speculated that if someone were not allowed simply to want attention, she would have to be in enormous distress to justify interpersonal contact.

COUNTERTRANSFERENCE IN THE
NEGOTIATION OF BOUNDARIES

Countertransference influences both the establishment and maintenance of therapeutic frame. Many boundary negotiations hinge on assumptions about the roles of client and therapist. These beliefs tap into identity issues, both professional and personal, for the therapist, and are thus susceptible to countertransference influences. If either party views the therapist as protector, nurturant parent, or friend, the relationship will take a very different course than if the therapist is viewed as a guide and companion on a healing journey. If therapist or client views the client as a supplicant, a patient, or a child, the boundaries and the course of treatment will differ from those that reflect the view of the client as someone attempting to understand her past and shape her future. Therapies with survivor clients can evoke fantasies on the part of both participants that the therapist will be the perfect, all-giving mother or father to make up for deprivation and harm in the past.

The therapist's fantasies and affect inform countertransference responses to boundary issues. When a therapist identifies with a client, she can wish to provide for her something that has been helpful to her or something for which she yearns.* When a therapist is angry at her client, she can wish to distance from her, to send her away, to hide behind rigid boundaries. When feeling betrayed, a therapist can become careless about the boundary of confidentiality, especially when collaborative therapists or treatment team members invite her to criticize her client. When a therapist is feeling despair with her client, she can become more passive and stop noticing and naming the interpersonal process. When a therapist feels shame about her work with a client, she can blame herself or the client, and then act punitively toward either party.

---

*See chapter 8 for discussion of specific countertransference issues for therapists who are survivors of childhood sexual abuse.

Therapist identity factors influence boundary decisions. When a therapist believes that supporting or changing a particular boundary is inconsistent with her theoretical perspectives on the nature of psychotherapy or her professional identity, she will feel conflicted in the face of a client's request or a colleague's recommendation to do so. A therapist can feel enormous pressure to adapt her behavior to alleviate the painful conflict. When a client experiences the therapist's reluctance or refusal to answer a question or give a hug as withholding, rigid, cold, cruel, or shaming, the therapist may struggle with her need to be and be seen as a compassionate therapist.

Alternatively, when the therapist has negotiated with a client an alteration in the frame (for example, to have phone contact outside of a session or to extend a session beyond 50 minutes), she may feel a disconnection with her ego ideal, and thus feel shame.* This disconnection may reflect anxiety about discrepancies she perceives between her clinical decisions and her training; differences from important teachers or supervisors from the past; conflicts with her fantasies about practices of idealized teachers, supervisors, or therapists; fantasies about her model of an ideal therapist; or discrepancies with her understanding of what is curative in psychotherapy with sexual abuse survivors.

Shame inhibits many therapists from discussing boundary issues in supervision or with colleagues. The ensuing silence often reenacts the dynamics of an abuse survivor's life and poses a dangerous potential for the therapist to become isolated in the work.

Example   One therapist felt conflicted about a client's request for a hug at the end of every session. The client, a survivor of emotional neglect as well as extensive sexual abuse, posed the initial request with some shyness at the very end of a difficult session. The therapist spontaneously hugged her, but later felt unclear about why she had done so. In the next session, the client opened with great distress about a crisis in her marriage, which filled the hour. At the end of that session, she got up to leave, hugged the therapist, and left. The therapist felt frustrated with herself for not discussing the hug in the session, and then felt uncomfortable about bringing it up in supervision because she felt she had mismanaged the situation. Over time, as the hug became an integral part of the session endings, the therapist felt increasingly helpless and paralyzed with both her client and her supervisor. Thus, rather than opening up the therapy by providing an opportunity

---

*These ego ideals reflect the therapist's ideals and goals for herself as a healer, interpreter, and facilitator of her clients' journeys and process, her feelings about her theoretical orientation and discipline, as well as internalizations of her teachers, and therapist(s) or analyst(s).

to discuss connection and separation, touch, and wishes for nurturance, the hug became a symbol of nonmutuality and silence.

It is through our open curiosity about the process, ourselves, and our clients, and through our willingness to observe the developing relationship, that we protect ourselves, our clients, and the work. We learn as much, if not more, from decisions we later revise or regret as we do from decisions we later repeat and laud. The situation described above eventually provided the therapist and client with the opportunity not only to discuss the meaning of a hug between them, but the meaning of their silence and abdication of voluntary choice. We must allow ourselves to make and examine mistakes in order to be open to the mutual learning necessary to our clients' growth.

THERAPIST DISCLOSURE AND THERAPEUTIC FRAME

Disclosure of Countertransference

Countertransference disclosure reflects a specific boundary negotiation and therefore aspect of the frame, and provides us with a model for negotiating other boundary and frame issues.*

Tansey and Burke (1989) have categorized three schools of thought about countertransference disclosure, varying according to their openness to the use of countertransference disclosure in analytic psychotherapy. The "conservatives" discourage any disclosure of countertransference to the client, believing it to be burdensome to the client and self-indulgent for the therapist. The "moderate" school advocates occasional disclosure with certain clients. The "radicals" support more extensive disclosure of countertransference, viewing it as an integral part of the interpersonal analytic process. Countertransference disclosure can often further the interpersonal process of the therapy because the countertransference arises in the context of the therapeutic relationship. It is important to consider the goal or purpose of a countertransference disclosure, and to make sure it is in the service of the client's treatment and forward movement, and not in the service of the therapist's needs.

The disclosure of countertransference is different from factual disclosure in that it is interpersonal and specific to the relationship with the client. It can also be very personal to the therapist (Jacobs, 1991). How does one

---

*We refer the reader to Maroda (1991) for an excellent discussion of the history and specifics of countertransference disclosure.

figure out when it is useful to bring countertransference into the active relationship?

Gorkin (1987) writes that there are five general reasons for countertransference disclosure cited in the literature:

1. To confirm the patient's sense of reality
2. To establish the therapist's honesty or genuineness
3. To establish the therapist's humanness
4. To clarify both the fact and the nature of the patient's impact on the therapist and on people in general
5. To resolve a treatment impasse

Maroda (1991), who identifies herself as part of the radical school, concludes,

> the underlying principle that should guide disclosure is as follows: The therapist must disclose whatever is necessary to facilitate the patient's awareness and acceptance of the truth. . . . The timing, nature, and extent of the countertransference disclosure can only be determined by the therapist in consultation with the patient. This second principle addresses the longstanding problem of how to determine what will be helpful and what will be "burdensome." The answer to the question, "How will you know what to say and when to say it?," is "Ask the patient." (p. 87)

Basescu (1990) presents a thoughtful and respectful approach to the use of the self in psychotherapy. He encourages the disclosure of relevant information, suggesting, "The mutuality of relevant self-revelation works against the mystification of experience in the relationship and allows for the development of intimacy and trust" (p. 162).

Thoughtful countertransference disclosure is a useful tool in psychotherapy with adult survivors of childhood sexual abuse. Because these clients come to any new relationship with assumptions based upon their experiences in earlier exploitive, abusive, and nonmutual relationships, the use of the new therapeutic relationship to undo old patterns and create new ways of relating is a critical component of the psychotherapy. The therapist's attunement to and expression of her countertransference not only allows her to remain connected to herself, but also provides a possible avenue for remaining connected to the interpersonal situation and to the client.

Example   A therapist would find tears coming to her eyes when listening to one client whose language was factual and unemotional but whose

bare-bones descriptions of childhood events were poignant in their omis-
sions. At one such time, the client stated angrily, "I don't like it when you
cry. I'm not feeling anything so it doesn't seem authentic to me. It's con-
trived." The therapist said, "I'm feeling a lot of pain for the little girl who
was trying so hard to get her needs met, to feel noticed and loved." The
client sat back with a look of surprise and said, "I've never allowed myself
to see it that way, to feel the pain. I think it would be overwhelming for
me." She quietly began to weep, and the therapy moved to a new level of
intimacy.

Davies and Frawley (1994) make the point that with certain clients for
whom the process of symbolizing and naming their experience is severely
compromised, it is only through the therapist's willingness to notice and
name her inner experience that the therapeutic pair can develop a shared
language to elaborate the client's experience. This process is often central in
the transformation of behavioral enactment to symbolic representation.

Disclosure of Associations

The therapist's associative process in psychotherapy is a rich source of
information. It can provide her with access to the full range of her creative,
nonlinear cognitive abilities. She can use her associative process to identify
emerging countertransference and unspoken themes in the client's material.
At times a therapist can share her associations to communicate with her
client in a simple yet powerful way.

Example   A client started a session describing a disturbing sense of
being frozen, yet feeling painful, lurching moves toward change. The therapist had a vivid image of ice breaking on a river, with loud tormenting
groans, and then the emergence of the pressing river beneath to move the
ice floes along the river. The client elaborated a metaphor of a body encased
in ice, and spoke of psychotherapy as a thawing process. She then fell silent
and seemed stuck. The therapist said she had a somewhat different ice
image as the woman spoke and asked if she might share it. She described
her vision of the river, and noted that the river was alive, moving, and
always present under the ice. The client then spoke of her fear of her strong
feelings, especially anger and desire. The session began to flow again. By
offering her own image, the therapist joined the client in the realm of
metaphor, but offered an image infused with hope and movement to augment the original static image.

Sometimes the therapist has associations to her own experience. While
caution is warranted in sharing these associations lest the therapy become a
forum for the therapist's needs, on occasion it can be useful.

Example   One client spent much of her session discussing her dread of an upcoming dentist visit. Toward the end of the session, the therapist focused on self-care strategies the client could employ to support herself. After discussing many strategies to use before, during, and after the appointment, the therapist added, "You know, when I was a child and went to the dentist, my dentist had a toy box in the waiting room. After the appointment, each child could choose a toy from the box. Maybe you need something fun to look forward to." The client, who often worked with her child self, brightened and said, "My little girl [self] would like that." The therapist responded to the unspoken awareness of an inconsolable frightened child and offered a model for helping a child manage anxiety. By bringing herself into the process, she normalized the fear and joined with her client in delight at being comforted.

Countertransference Influences on Interpretation

Interpretations serve to identify themes in the client's material, explicate interpersonal and transference paradigms in the therapeutic relationship, and connect a contemporary interaction with something from the client's past. Ideally, interpretations move the therapy forward by helping a client understand and make connections that free her from rigidified patterns from the past.

There are two notable countertransference-related issues involved with interpretations with trauma survivors. The first is the tone of the interpretation. The tone of delivery reflects the therapist's frame for her role; at times it also reflects her countertransference. Survivors of child abuse have too often had their reality defined for them and too often been blamed for events that were outside their control. These historical relational events contribute to clients' often acute sensitivity to the imposition of someone else's perception and to the experience of being blamed or criticized. Too often therapists use interpretation in the service of managing their own anxiety about not knowing. These interpretations can be didactic, effectively imposing the therapist's constructions on the client's experiences, rather than inviting curiosity and opening up additional possibilities. Thus when the client reports an interaction with another person, her therapist might ask, "Is that familiar to you?" or "That sounds like interactions you have described with your sister." It is valuable early in the relationship to invite the client to let the therapist know whether her interpretations seem correct. When a client responds compliantly, "I guess so" or "You must be right," a therapist can address her seeming willingness to accept someone else's perception as her truth, and encourage her to wait until she knows what is true for herself. After offering an interpretation, a therapist can ask, "Does that feel right or true for you?"

Second, the timing of interpretations is critical. The therapist should name these connections as she thinks the client is ready and open to hearing them. However, countertransference can influence her decisions to offer an interpretation. She may be tempted to push the client along because of her own impatience with the process or because of external demands to speed up therapy. She may refrain from making a connection out of her fear of evoking shame, anger, or a traumatic memory. The therapist's ongoing attunement to her inner state, her countertransference, and her observation of her client's feedback help her evaluate the timing of clinical interpretations.

Self-disclosure and Responses to Client Questions

It is a myth that a therapist is "incognito" (Maroda, 1991) or a blank screen. Given that a client naturally observes quite a lot about her therapist, including her office, dress, body language and facial expressions, and interpersonal style, the therapist should consider what information is available, what information is helpful, and how the exchange of that information is negotiated. When the client notices and asks about the therapist, the content of her question may focus on the person or history of the therapist, but its emergence at this precise instant may arise from an awareness of the therapist's manner in the moment. Thus the distinction between personal information and here-and-now information is not always clear.

What does it mean and how does it feel for both parties to ask, to be asked, and to tell or not? There are few hard and fast rules concerning therapist self-disclosure. A client's curiosity about the person of the therapist is natural and expectable. In fact, if a client never asks any questions, it is worth noticing and wondering about the internal rules or safety precautions at work. An open, noncritical invitation to discuss the meaning of the question and the impact of its answer on the relationship sets the stage for a respectful, clinically useful approach. The essential considerations are the therapist's personal comfort and the client's best interest from a theoretical perspective. The goal is always to keep in mind the frame, and its relation to the underlying theory of treatment.

We have found that decisions about self-disclosure in trauma therapies reflect three factors.

1. *The fact that the client is a trauma survivor.* In addition to their sensitivity to boundary issues, many trauma survivors need the therapist to be more genuine in the therapy relationship. Issues of trust and intimacy are

salient for many survivors, and the experience of a distant other is not one that is curative for childhood abuse survivors (Herman, 1992; McCann & Pearlman, 1990b).

2. *The length of time a particular client is in treatment.* As the relationship between therapist and client deepens, the therapist may bring more of herself into the room. With a foundation of experience of the therapist, the client will be better able to integrate what the therapist says and does, and may feel more comfortable questioning the therapist. The therapist, for her part, will have a deepening sense of what works for this client and how the client may perceive things the therapist says.

3. *The extent of the therapist's psychotherapy experience.* Finally, as the therapist becomes more experienced, she generally feels better able to trust her experience and instincts and less compelled to work by rules. Therapists often use rules when they are feeling lost, and at times this is appropriate. Yet, as the therapist's confidence grows, she increasingly trusts her instincts, and knows how to sort out her countertransference issues.

The most common therapist disclosures will concern the therapist's here-and-now experiences, that is, within the therapy relationship and hour. Simply verifying or confirming a client's sense of interpersonal reality is an important therapeutic intervention when it is accurate and nonharmful to do so. One arena is the client's perception of the therapist in the room. Yet even this seemingly straightforward task is complicated by the possible unspoken transference context for all questions.

Example   A therapist and her client came to recognize that whenever the client started a session with the question "How are you?" they needed to examine the therapeutic relationship. After several experiences of the client querying about the therapist and the therapist responding, "I wonder why you are asking that today, in particular," they learned that the client asked when either she noticed something troubling in the therapist's manner or presentation (e.g., looking tired or ill), or she worried that she had harmed, angered, or depleted the therapist in the previous session.

Therapists may be nonplused by clients' direct questions. Clients may ask about the therapist's experience in the therapy relationship (Are you angry? Am I boring? Am I too intense for you?), about the therapist's professional training and experience (Where did you go to school? How long have you been doing therapy? What is your theoretical orientation?), about the therapist's current personal life circumstances (Are you married? Do you have children? Are you gay/lesbian/bisexual?), and about the therapist's personal history (Where did you grow up? Were your parents' divorced? Are you an incest survivor?). It is not unusual for these questions about the therapist to come up in therapy with survivor clients.

Surrey writes in Miller et al. (1991),

> Mutuality in therapy would suggest engaging with the client around
> such decisions, giving clear and honest explanations about why one
> may not be disclosing. Opening to an interchange around the decision
> may lead us to more possibilities for productive change. . . . the
> criteria I use to decide about verbal or conscious disclosure . . . center
> around the potential impact on the client, myself, and the relation-
> ship. Will this help move the relationship toward expanded connec-
> tion? Will it enhance the possibilities of empathic joining, either
> through my reaching out to join with the client or, sometimes, by
> asking the client to stretch to encompass something difficult to hear
> from me? Also important are: my assessment of how well I know the
> person, how strong or fragile the relationship is, how much might the
> material effect the client's freedom to be spontaneous without fear of
> burdening me; or how much will *not* sharing something have a nega-
> tive impact on my being present and responsive in the relationship.
> (p. 11)

The meaning of information and secrets is central for survivors of child
abuse for whom secrecy meant danger. Survivors may experience fear and
fascination about secrets and have little understanding or inadequate guidelines for privacy and personal boundaries. The distinction between secret
(imposed silence) and private (chosen silence) is important for self-
protection and self-respect. The therapist's response to these questions and
style of talking about the questions and their meaning can have a profound
effect on the work. At times, answering information questions is useful, for
example, when it aids in the development of object constancy.

Example   One client who had experienced multiple childhood aban-
donments always wanted to know where the therapist was going while on
vacation. In the ensuing discussion, it was clear that it was very important
to her to visualize the therapist in the vacation environment; it helped her
sustain her sense of connection with the therapist.

In some instances, answering the question reveals an underlying dynamic
not previously evident. Not surprisingly, the process is usually more significant than the content.

Example   One client whose mother had been very blaming and shaming refused to discuss with the therapist her reasons for wanting to know
where the therapist was going on vacation, and was enraged with the therapist for not telling her. Finally the therapist decided to answer the question

to see whether answering was indeed as helpful as the client insisted it would be. When the therapist responded that she was taking a trip to the Caribbean, the client became further enraged, demanding, "Why won't you answer my question?" The therapist was taken aback and said, "I don't understand." The client replied, "The Caribbean! That's so vague! It could be any one of those islands." She went on to berate the therapist for her life of ease and to complain that the therapist was lording her happiness over the client whom she was abandoning. The therapist pointed out the client's anger and pain, but also noted that by asking the question, the client had invited the therapist to participate in a destructive interaction. The client then used the therapist's response as ammunition against herself, the therapist, and the therapy relationship. This experience can inform later responses to questions in this therapy.

In a much later interaction, this same client continuously persisted in asking the therapist what she thought of her. The therapist attempted to understand the question with the client and was consistently met with rage at these efforts. Eventually, the therapist responded that she saw the client as both resilient and troubled. In the next session, the client came back saying she was extremely upset at the word "troubled." The therapist squirmed and felt she had made a mistake in answering the question, finding confirmation in the client's response. Seeing the therapist's discomfort, the client said, "Now don't take that to mean you shouldn't have answered. It's okay that you answered, because even though I'm upset, we can talk about it."

It is not unusual to find oneself handling the same question posed by two clients differently. The theoretical reasons for such differences will ideally be based in a conceptualization of what is helpful with each client rather than on our different countertransference responses.

The therapist's physical and mental state can play a role in how she handles a question. If the therapist is tired or frustrated, for reasons related or unrelated to the client, she may be less likely to explore the meaning and more likely either simply to answer or refuse to answer. If she feels vulnerable about a topic, she may prefer not to answer. When the question taps into conflictual identity areas (survivor status,* sexual orientation, religious affiliation), the therapist may feel her privacy invaded, and need to set limits to protect her privacy.

The meaning of the gay or lesbian therapist's choice to be out with clients can be complicated with survivors of sexual abuse. Any disclosure is a personal decision, informed by the therapeutic frame and clinical need.

---

*For discussion of therapist disclosure of personal history of childhood sexual abuse, see chapter 8.

Disclosing the therapist's sexual preference can unintentionally eroticize the transference, or frighten the client by introducing the therapist's sexual behavior into the relationship and her fantasy prematurely. The disclosure may evoke parallels to inappropriate parental disclosures; in many families where there is incest, parents have often inappropriately talked about their sexual lives and fantasies with their children. Survivors often recall feeling overstimulated, confused, and anxious. On the other hand, gay, lesbian, bisexual, or undecided clients can feel enormously alone and ashamed of their confusion. This isolation parallels and may be interwoven with the secrecy and isolation of childhood sexual abuse. A therapist's comfortable and direct openness about his or her sexual orientation is affirming and may counteract the client's shame and unconscious confusion between sexual abuse and sexual orientation. In many therapies it is possible to be affirming and informative about the client's sexuality with or without the therapist altering the frame of the therapy relationship by disclosing personal information.

The issue of therapist self-disclosure can be especially difficult with survivor clients because of the enormous shame many clients feel when they believe or fear they have transgressed a boundary. Therapists may struggle to sort out how to respond, act impulsively, respond defensively or rigidly, or feel bullied into disclosing information they consider private. Therapists may feel intruded upon and helpless, or fear that they have crossed a boundary by being too personal with a client, thus burdening or exploiting the client. Either of these scenarios may reflect a projective identification or reenactment of the client's experience.

The meanings of the questions and the answers differ for each client. What a therapist is comfortable sharing is a matter of her comfort in sharing personal information with others in general and with clients in particular. Many countertransference dynamics can interfere with this process. If a therapist does not feel she has the right to have needs in the relationship, or is afraid of being a perpetrator by denying the client something the client says she needs, the therapist risks violating her own boundaries by answering a question or saying something that does not feel comfortable. The outcome may well be resentment, which the therapist may act out in punitive or withholding ways in the therapy. Consultation or supervision is an invaluable tool for sorting out how to respond to specific questions with a with a particular client at a particular point in the therapeutic process.

Impact of the Therapist's Personal Distress

There are times when every therapist is in personal distress for reasons unrelated to the client or to her work. At such times, it may be useful for the therapist to share some information with the client, to validate the client's perception that the therapist is distressed and to clarify that it is unrelated to the client (Basescu, 1990; Fromm-Reichmann, 1960). For childhood abuse survivors in particular, it can be frightening to sense distress that is unnamed. An incest survivor client may quickly assume that the therapist is upset with her, and may fear an explosion like that experienced with angry parents. It is especially important for therapists who are experiencing chronic distress as a result of external life stressors (e.g., a relationship ending, a chronically ill or dying loved one; bereavement, a life-threatening illness) to seek regular consultation with a colleague with whom they can discuss the impact of their own life experiences on their work, and find ways of validating clients' perceptions without frightening or burdening their clients.

Example   A therapist whose sister was pregnant found herself distracted during a week when her sister went into premature labor. One day between sessions, she received a distressing phone call from her family saying that her sister might lose the pregnancy. Her next client was a highly sensitive woman whose mother had been explosive and unpredictable. Shortly after the client entered the room, she fell silent. The therapist noted the client's withdrawal and asked her what was happening. The client expressed a desire to leave immediately. The therapist asked whether she was sensing something that felt unsafe. The client responded that the therapist seemed changed. The therapist then let the client know that something painful was happening in her personal life and that she was indeed somewhat distracted, but that she felt she could be available to the client, especially having told her that she was distracted. They agreed to go on with the session and to touch base again shortly to see how it was going and whether or not to continue that day. Both client and therapist were relieved to have named the obvious and to have together created a plan for staying aware of their feelings.

ALTERATIONS IN THE THERAPEUTIC FRAME AND BOUNDARIES

It is not inherently good or bad to alter or modify the therapeutic frame; it is grist for the therapeutic mill — and another relational event in the psychotherapy for therapist and client to observe and understand. Some psychoanalytic practitioners have suggested that an alteration of frame (e.g., the therapist becoming more responsive) diminishes the therapy (i.e., it becomes "supportive" rather than uncovering therapy) and infantalizes and undermines the client. They hold that traditional neutrality is good technique and good for the client (Jacobs, 1994). On the other hand, there are therapists who define genuineness as spontaneity, believing that if the therapist feels an urge to act, she should do so in the service of "authenticity" without considering countertransference or therapeutic effect. We espouse neither position; the former negates the valid need of the client to have the person of the therapist available and the latter results in the needs of the therapist overruling those of the client. Rather, we recommend a thoughtful assessment of the relational needs and therapeutic process in the context of a theory-based therapeutic framework.

We propose four guidelines for considering frame changes:

1. Consider whether there is a theoretical basis for making or not making the change.
2. Discuss the proposed change in depth with the client.
3. Observe and discuss with the client the effects of the proposed change (whether or not it was ultimately made) over time.
4. Make use of supervision or consultation to assess the potential for unconscious identifications or reenactments on the part of the therapist.

Essentially, the question is: How can the therapist best facilitate this individual's therapeutic work in a way that is respectful to both parties? To do so requires that the therapist understand the meaning of the frame alteration and note her countertransference. This goal is not always achieved before making an alteration, but the process continues before and after such decisions.

The therapeutic frame is challenged when therapist and client have unexpected contact outside of the therapy or when there is a change in payment plan. It is challenged when therapist or client requests a change in the time frame (e.g., extend or shorten session time) or includes others (family members, consulting professionals, letters of advocacy) in their communication. Requests to modify or change boundaries can evoke anxiety and therefore need discussion. We cannot assume we know the meaning a frame change has to the client (e.g., When is a request a test to check the limits or safety, to see if the therapist recognizes the boundary being crossed?). A therapist and client need time to consider the relevant issues, often overlooked when either feels compelled to decide immediately. Discussing the meaning of a changed boundary models the importance of respect for personal boundaries and the regulation of distance and disclosure in a relationship.

Therapy is a relationship that is focused upon the needs of the client; the therapist addresses her needs in part through setting a frame for therapy that is appropriate to both the client and to her own therapeutic style and personal needs. For example, by setting a fee and scheduling the sessions at times that are convenient, the therapist lessens the potential for resentment toward the client. When the therapist responds to a client's request with the recognition that those needs are valid and reasonable, *and* that she may not be able to meet them, she separates the client's needs from her limitations and her own needs; this is something her early caretakers may not have done. Therapists charge for missed sessions and take vacations to care for themselves; they do not go to work when they are sick because their needs must take priority if they are to care for others. The open acknowledgment that these decisions are for the therapist and not primarily for the client is useful. It not only provides a powerful model of self-care and self-respect, but also reassures the client that the therapist will be honest with her and that she will take care of herself and not be harmed or depleted by work.

The interaction of the client's real needs, the therapist's real limitations, and the countertransference makes the assessment of these situations challenging. Therapists work hard with clients to encourage their development of a healthy sense of entitlement; thus, it may be a major achievement for a client to ask for something from the therapist and she may then feel unable or unwilling to say no. At that juncture, the therapist can confuse the client's right to want and ask for something with her ability and responsibility to provide it. As the therapist works with both her importance to the client and the client's disappointment in the therapists and others, together they face the client's grief about needs that have not been or cannot be met. Coming up against the limits of the therapist and therapy is as important as being able to make use of the rich resources in the therapeutic relationship.

Alterations Requested by Clients in Crisis

Sometimes clients ask for boundary or frame changes in times of crisis or acute distress. For example, a client may request phone contact between sessions, extra sessions, or therapist contact with family members or other treating professionals. A therapist's countertransference (e.g., her feeling of responsibility, her wish to be helpful, her annoyance at or delight in being asked) can shape her responses to such requests.

When the current life circumstances of a client are crisis-filled or particularly compelling, the therapist often wants to do more to help the client suffer less. When a therapist is feeling anxious (or holding the client's profound annihilation anxiety), the therapist may feel compelled to act to relieve the unbearable tension of her own anxiety. This anxiety can fuel rescue fantasies and wishes to create safety or a perfect holding environment for a tormented client. The therapist may find herself considering recommending medication, hospitalization, a referral to a therapy group, more frequent or longer sessions, phone contact between sessions, or contact with the client's family or support network. Her compassion can stir a wish to extend herself beyond the established boundaries of the therapeutic relationship. Some changes in frame may indeed be indicated at times of crisis, but the therapist must be clear about why she is considering them now, and whether she is responding in the way likely to be in the best long-term interest of the client and the therapeutic relationship.

There are two particular pitfalls to these responses in the face of crisis. One is the danger that the therapist will become overactive and unwittingly preclude the symbolic internalization of therapeutic relationship in favor of a literal dependence that undermines rather than facilitates the client's autonomous functioning. The second danger is that she can overlook the multiple meanings of the client's demands for care. Davies and Frawley (1994) give a detailed example of the client's wish for rescue that represents an unconscious identification with her abuser and conclude:

> Requests that are contextually embedded in a history of abuse and neglect, plaintively echoed by the very child who endured such maltreatment, can move the most resolute believer in the powers of abstinence and neutrality to inappropriate acts of heroic salvation. However, no sooner does the idealized savior-therapist make contact with the abused child persona than the operative relational matrix shifts and we are simultaneously dealing with enactments of the omnipotent, counterabusive child, that aspect of the child that is identified with her abusive parent or other. (p. 82)

When the client's crisis includes severe post-traumatic stress symptoms, nightmares, flashbacks, or intrusive imagery or other sensory experiences, the therapist often feels compelled to be more active in the face of the client's distress, fear, and pain. The amount of psychic pain survivor clients can experience in the course of the work of psychotherapy is excruciating to witness, and a client's deep wish that her therapist could alleviate or soothe her pain leads one to consider ways to intervene that may include changes in boundaries. Davies and Frawley (1991) remind us that this work, "challenges the analyst's capacity to withstand his patient's despair and the limitations of his own abilities to alleviate suffering" (p. 26).

A specific instance familiar to trauma therapists is the dilemma of responding when a client moves into a traumatic memory or dissociative state toward the end of a session. This can raise a variety of feelings in the therapist, including concern about ending the session at the agreed time and annoyance with herself or the client for not being able to manage the time differently. If the therapist ends the session on time, she may feel guilty and/or worried about the client. If she extends the session, she may feel resentful and/or concerned about the implicit message to the client about an unplanned and unprocessed boundary shift.

Technically, it is important to address the very real psychological need for containment and reconnection with the present and with safety. In part, this event may reflect a need to incorporate a different structure into the frame of the session. In recognition of the often difficult task of separation, and the need to move back to connection with the adult self and present context, it is often useful to mark the last 10 to 15 minutes of a session as a transition period. This allows therapist and client to make conscious the process in which they are engaged and to address the psychological tasks involved.

Some trauma therapists subscribe to a "rule of thirds" for the structure of a session for intensive work with a highly dissociative or distressed client: In the first part, therapist and client identify an issue; in the second, they process the issue; and in the third they work on grounding the client (Herman, 1992). We think of our structure less in terms of issues and more in terms of the therapeutic relationship. Early in the session, we address the process of reconnection, encouraging the client to make a transition to the therapy and the relationship before she moves into conflictual material. We also create transition time at the end of the session. This structure is concretized in our survivor groups where we start with a check-in, work on themes that emerge, and end with a wrap-up.* The emphasis on the process of transition, and specifically on connection, separation, and reconnection, recognizes these as areas of vulnerability and developmental need for survivors.

The existence of the therapeutic frame creates multiple opportunities to rework developmental challenges, including separation and object constancy. The frame of the hour creates the repetition of reconnecting, connecting, and separating in every session. These are not incidental psychological tasks, but in fact essential and difficult for survivor clients, who have experienced traumatic separation, abandonment, and loss. When a client struggles with a traumatic memory at the end of a session, it is valuable to explore in the next session why the memory arose at that point in the session. A client may note an affective connection between her feelings about leaving the session and the feelings evoked in the memory, or she may have been unable to gain access to or speak the memory until the prospect of leaving was imminent.

Feelings of frustration, guilt, anxiety, or overprotectiveness on the part of the therapist can block the essential exploration of the rhythm of the

*For more elaboration of this model, see chapter 11.

session and the emergence of particular responses on the part of the client such as dissociation or flashbacks. Without such discussions, the therapist may leave her clients caught in the web of their habitual post-traumatic adaptations. Without an understanding of the developmental processes at work, she can become easily exasperated and simply blame the client. If she recognizes the difficulty with separation, but does not respect the limitations in self-capacities inherent in it, it is easy to see the client or her behavior as "manipulative" and, by shaming her, abandon the therapeutic task and the client.

Example   One survivor client made the not uncommon request for longer sessions on a regular basis. As she and her therapist discussed this wish, they learned that it took the client 15 to 20 minutes each week to assess whether the therapist had changed significantly. Her fear related to the client's experience of her mother as unpredictable: at times loving and available, at other times suddenly violent, and at still other times announcing that she was leaving (and disappearing for days). As they understood this transference together, they agreed to try the session-and-a-half format (75 minutes) for two months. The client felt deeply moved that the therapist would both explore and respond to her request.

The client may at times express the wish for the therapist to change her interpersonal style — to demonstrate more spontaneity or warmth, less reactivity, or more or less formality. The negotiation of the therapist's way of being and of her role is often compelling and complicated for the therapist. It can be difficult to sort out the extent to which the request should be understood in terms of unmet needs and/or transferences from the client's past or should be managed through a change on the part of the therapist.

Example   One client asked her therapist not to react when she related trauma memories. When the therapist asked for clarification, the client said, "I want you to listen but not move, not move a muscle. I can't stand it if you show a reaction, because no matter what it is, I will react to it and then I won't be able to talk." The therapist initially accepted this need as valid and thought the client was appropriately asking for a neutral therapeutic environment. Yet she continued to feel uneasy and self-conscious in subsequent sessions. She brought to supervision the question of whether she was too reactive with this client, and as she described her feelings she recognized her fury at being asked to behave like a passive victim. In the next session, she and the client revisited the topic and the therapist was able to be clear about her experience. Together they explored the client's fear that she would have to shift her focus from herself to the therapist if she saw an emotional response on the therapist's part. The therapist spoke not only of her own need to be emotionally present and not shut down or physically paralyzed, but also of her confidence that she would take care of herself and respect the client's need to be sure of that. This reworking of their mutual needs then set the stage for the examination of the transference reenactment in which the client unwittingly repeated with the therapist her own traumatic experience of being forced to stay completely still and not show any emotion when being sexually abused. She had not remembered this aspect of her abuse experience previously.

The Meaning of Mutuality

There has been much discussion about the meaning of mutuality and genuineness in psychotherapy (Heyward, 1993; Jordan et al., 1991; Miller et al., 1991). It is a valuable and complex discussion. It occurs in the context of a theoretical paradigm shift toward a more relational model of psychotherapy that reframes the conceptualization of the therapist's role. For the purposes of therapeutic technique, this discussion must be placed in the context of a thorough understanding of the complexity of the therapeutic process and the therapeutic relationship. We do not believe that mutuality in a therapeutic relationship negates the real power differential inherent in the roles of therapist and client. The Stone Center research group addresses this distinction:

> For the therapist, mutuality refers to this way of being in relationship: empathically attuned, emotionally responsive, authentically present, and open to change. . . . It is essential to emphasize what we do *not* mean. We certainly do not mean disclosing anything and everything with no sense of purpose, impact, or timing, or responsibility, nor do we suggest inattention to the complex power dynamics of this relationship. . . . Mutuality does not mean equality, sameness, or a simplistic notion of mutual personal disclosure. (Miller et al., 1991, p. 11)

Transference is a powerful and necessary component of the therapeutic relationship; it creates a unique dynamic that does not end with the end of a therapeutic contract. Thus, we do not believe that therapists and clients are or should become friends (Heyward, 1993). The relationship is structured according to the roles and behaviors that create the conditions for therapeutic understanding and change and define it as psychotherapy. The therapeutic frame itself structures the relationship in a particular way that precludes an equal friendship.

Influences from Outside
the Therapeutic Dyad

Alterations Requested by Third Parties

We are often pressed by outside forces to modify our boundaries. Insurance and managed care companies invite us to modify confidentiality boundaries, participate in a process that may be intrusive, and to act in a paternalistic role vis-a-vis our clients (Saakvitne & Abrahamson, 1994). Concerned, threatened, or angry family members may pressure us for contact and information. Legal issues can arise with survivor clients that result in our being contacted by lawyers for information or opinions. Collaborating therapists may call to discuss the work without the consent or awareness of the client. Any of these requests may feel either supportive or intrusive to the therapist, often depending on the approach taken by the third party.

All these presses require the therapist maintain a conceptual and ethical clarity about the therapeutic frame. It is important to remember that while the therapist has clear responsibility, the commitment to the frame must be mutual (Davies & Frawley, 1994). A therapist should consult with the client about any outside contact and clarify the frame of the relationship. Specific written authorization to release information to each and every person who requests it serves therapeutic and relational as well as legal purposes; it reinforces to both therapist and client the importance and consistency of the frame, and of the relationship.

Alterations Originating in Supervision

Consultation or supervision can lead a therapist to desire or suggest changes in boundaries. While these may be helpful shifts, they require the same thoughtful consideration and discussion between client and therapist. In our roles as trauma therapy supervisors, we often find ourselves suggesting to therapists that they pay more attention to boundaries, both in the interest of client trust and safety and therapist self-care.

Example   One therapist noted in a supervision session that her clients had her home telephone number and that she accepted calls on a 24-hour basis. She reported feeling burned out and resentful of her clients' calls. The supervisor explored the meanings of this with the therapist, who came to realize that she was compensating for her own parents' unavailability to her in childhood by being endlessly available. Through these discussions, the therapist eventually decided to contract with an answering service, to ask her clients not to call her at home, and to share weekend coverage with a colleague so she could have some weekends off. These major frame changes had to be processed with clients, who had a variety of responses to them. One of the unexpected responses from some clients was, "You must think I'm doing better!"

Any shift in boundaries can be an important clue to our countertransference. Especially when a boundary changes without prior discussion in the therapy and in its supervision, it is important to examine the range of precipitants for the change, and then to discuss the change after the fact both with the client and with a supervisor. All changes in frame provide important clues to countertransference.

8

Countertransference Themes for Survivor Therapists

RECENT RESEARCH on the personal experiences of psychotherapists has found therapists reporting childhood sexual abuse in a range from 13 percent for male psychologists (Pope & Feldman-Summers, 1992) to 26 to 43 percent for female therapists (Elliott & Guy, 1993; Schauben & Frazier, in press). Briere (1989) estimates that at least 33 percent of female and 10 to 15 percent of male therapists have sexual abuse histories and that a much larger percentage has been victimized physically and emotionally in childhood.

Briere notes that his personal impression is that psychotherapists are considerably more likely than professionals in other fields to have been maltreated as children. Kluft (1994) draws upon epidemiological research showing that 38 percent of women have had unwanted sexual experiences before age 18 (Russell, 1986) and that 38 out of 100 women with documented childhood sexual trauma did not report it ("or appeared to have forgotten it") on 17-year follow-up (Williams, 1992) to conclude that, given the greater proportion of women in mental health fields, "our colleagues will include a higher percentage of female mental health professionals who were molested in some way during childhood" (p. 5). These suppositions are supported by recent studies that have found higher rates of all childhood abuse in mental health professionals than in other professionals, the former ranging from 30 to 66 percent (Elliott & Guy, 1993; Follette et al., 1994; Pope & Feldman-Summers, 1992), the latter from 20 to 49 percent (Elliott & Guy, 1993; Follette et al., 1994; Schauben & Frazier, in press).

The therapist's attunement to others is part of what leads her to commit herself to a series of intense, intimate relationships with her clients. In these relationships, she focuses intently on another person, opening herself to knowing and being with this person, empathizing with her affective, associative, and cognitive experience, identifying aspects of the person that are unknown or unspoken to herself, while remaining acutely aware of her own affective and associative responses to the client. This capacity for relatedness is an extension of interpersonal styles learned in the therapist's childhood and modified through her later experiences.

Many survivors of childhood sexual abuse have developed heightened capacities to be attentive to the needs of others, to be excellent caretakers, and simultaneously to know and not know. It is not surprising that children who have organized their lives around such functions might become psychotherapists, a role in which they can continue patterns begun in their families of origin, and which allows a therapist to receive recognition that may have been missing. It can be gratifying to use these skills on behalf of others.

Their personal history can make survivors well-suited to the role of therapist in a number ways, including their acute sensitivity to the affects, needs, and unspoken defenses of another, and their highly developed capacity for empathy (Courtois, 1988; Davies & Frawley, 1994). They often bring to the work an unsurpassed commitment and an understanding of the depth of the effects of childhood sexual abuse and its nuances. Survivor therapists who have worked to understand the impact of their histories on their development and themselves in the present may have a special appreciation of the arduous healing journey faced by their survivor clients. However, for some, the role of therapist can become an extension of a self-defeating pattern of overextending oneself in relationships at one's own expense. In addition, survivor therapists face particular countertransference dilemmas.

Although this chapter focuses on countertransference themes for survivor therapists, many of the issues we address are relevant for all therapists who work with adult survivors of childhood trauma; all therapists bring a range of personal experiences from their own histories and developmental contexts to their therapeutic relationships.

PROFESSIONAL RESPONSE

Countertransference issues for therapists who are themselves adult survivors of childhood sexual abuse and incest are underaddressed in the literature. In fact, the existence of these therapists is treated as a shameful secret in the profession. The professional neglect of this group is an abandonment with significant personal and professional consequences. For therapists, the dangers of this silence include isolation, vicarious traumatization, and unchecked countertransference reenactments. The failure of our field to acknowledge the unique gifts of and challenges for these therapists has deprived them of a professional literature and learning opportunities to aid in their training and ongoing professional development.

The absence of this topic from the psychological and psychotherapeutic literature parallels the slow progress of the profession toward recognition of the prevalence of child sexual abuse in the lives of our clients, which as recently as 10 to 15 years ago was widely discounted. Kluft (1994) describes the difficulty he had publishing a paper on survivor therapists who might suffer from dissociative disorders; he attributed his failure to the disbelief in the profession regarding dissociative disorders. The gap in the literature reflects our reluctance to acknowledge our vulnerability and fallibility as therapists, as well as the historical tradition of discounting the effect on the client of the person of the therapist.

This neglect leaves survivor therapists on their own to struggle with their feelings and to work out delicate countertransference issues. Without a literature or other professional acknowledgment of their existence and special issues, the fear of making mistakes common to all therapists can be greater for survivor therapists. Many feelings, including shame about their survivor status, confusion about boundaries, and conflict about disclosing, parallel the difficulties faced by survivors in their relationships outside of therapy.

However, we need a cautionary note: When we discuss this particular group of therapists we run the risk of overgeneralization, sensationalism, pathologizing survivors of childhood sexual abuse, or contributing to the myth that therapists are and are supposed to be invulnerable. Either pathologizing or ignoring survivor therapists contributes to their shame and disenfranchisement. In their workshops for survivor therapists, E. Schatzow and J. Yassen (personal communication, 1991) invite participants to "list some of the issues" for a therapist who is a survivor of childhood sexual abuse; workshop participants virtually always emphasize the need for silence and secrecy in their workplaces and professional lives because of the danger of stigmatization. The message in the profession has been that to be known as a survivor is to be seen as damaged, devalued, and inadequate as a therapist. The mentality described by one therapist as "once damaged, always broken" conveys a disturbing message in a field that purports to offer treatment and hope.

An alternative overgeneralization is that a survivor therapist is a spokesperson for survivors or is a one-theme therapist. An extension of this stereo-type is the notion that a therapist must have experienced child sexual abuse to work effectively with survivor clients; this conclusion is both reductionis-tic and inaccurate. All therapists will have life experiences that are relevant and irrelevant to their clients' lives and experiences. Similarities are fre-quently both a help and a hindrance.

While they may have some common experiences, survivor therapists and their experiences differ from one another. Each will have her own unique experience of her abuse, the family dynamics around her abuse, and subse-quent history, and thus a unique frame of reference and pattern of psycho-logical needs, cognitive schemas, self capacities, and ego resources. The effects of a therapist's abuse history on her therapeutic relationships are complicated and complex.

SPECIAL COUNTERTRANSFERENCE ISSUES FOR SURVIVOR THERAPISTS

Some survivor therapists remember the abuse, at least partially, and others do not, having completely dissociated or repressed the memories. Thera-pists in the former group are in a position to evaluate the impact of their histories on their countertransference with survivor clients; those in the latter group are likely to find themselves having strong reactions to their survivor clients that they may not understand. They may find themselves feeling especially anxious, angry, rejecting, judgmental, or especially pro-tective, identified with, fond of, aroused by, or fascinated by survivor cli-ents. An unaware survivor therapist may be unusually rigid or permissive about boundaries, do things she has never done or usually would not do with a client, or be especially preoccupied with or very private about certain clients.

These patterns reflect important countertransference responses which may (or may not) suggest the existence of an abuse history in the therapist. When any therapist is unable to discover anything in her conscious aware-ness that helps her understand particularly strong feelings about a client, she needs to make use of avenues to unconscious issues, including fantasies, free associations, dreams, and imagery. A trusting supervisory relationship and personal psychotherapy are invaluable in helping the therapist under-stand her most perplexing countertransference responses. Davies and Fraw-ley (1994) make the point that if a therapist does recover memories of her own abuse through exposure in her clinical work to trauma material, she may have "strong countertransference feelings about the patient(s) who 'caused' the memories to emerge" (p. 166).

A therapist who does remember and know her childhood experiences will be better able to track the influence of her history within particular therapeutic relationships. Yet countertransference reflects both conscious and unconscious processes, and no therapist can maintain full awareness and clarity on her own.

In many ways, countertransference patterns for therapists who are survivors of childhood abuse resemble those for nonsurvivor therapists. However, the aftermath of childhood sexual trauma can be particularly problematic for a therapist for three reasons.

First, childhood sexual abuse affects every aspect of a person's being. The effects are pervasive and the interconnected issues that emerge relate to fundamental aspects of self, object relations, and world view. A survivor's experience of affect, of his or her body, memories, knowledge, and identity are profoundly altered and affect every aspect of his or her life. All relate to the self, which is the therapist's primary therapeutic tool. When these sequelae to abuse exist outside of the therapist's awareness or understanding, her work can be compromised. A therapist creates safety in part by knowing, noticing, and understanding what she brings into the therapeutic relationship. Thus, dissociated or unconscious conflicts and defenses can sabotage a therapy relationship.

For example, many survivors struggle with suicidal wishes, fantasies, impulses, and actions. A survivor therapist may have a particularly difficult time with these themes in her psychotherapies with survivor clients.

Example   One survivor therapist found herself intensely anxious about a client who had expressed a wish to die. She felt a strong urge to call her client and other people in her client's life, something she had never done as a therapist. She recognized that her client's passive suicidal wishes were reminding her of a level of despair she had felt in the past and still feared. Her press for action reflected her terror of her own pain.

Example   Another survivor therapist found herself enraged with a client who called to tell her she had made a suicidal gesture. As the therapist explored in her therapy the intensity of her rage, she connected it to her anger, fear, and sadness for her father who had attempted suicide in her childhood. She realized she felt burdened with responsibility for something over which she had virtually no control and left all alone to manage it.
Suicidal clients can be especially difficult because they challenge a survivor therapist's often familiar sense of complete overresponsibility, and the "risk management" policies of the profession often collude to heighten the therapist's anxiety and sense of helpless fear.

A second reason the aftermath of childhood trauma can be problematic for the survivor therapist involves affect. The affects aroused by and associated with sexual abuse are particularly intense, whether in conscious awareness or in the strength of the defenses necessary to keep them out of awareness. The therapist's experience of powerful feelings of anxiety, fear, shame, rage, and grief or the defenses she employs to ward off these feelings can be intensified in response to her client's material. Alternatively her affects or defenses can intrude into the clinical space and override or subsume her client's experience.

Third and finally, the defenses that a survivor develops are strong, deeply entrenched, and generalized rather than specific because of the nature of the trauma. The trauma and betrayal occur in the context of an early trusting interpersonal relationship and therefore profoundly affect not only the individual's sense of self and other, but also the characteristic modes of managing affects and utilizing ego resources. The defenses are global, not focused, and include dissociation, denial, projection, projective identification, and repression. A therapist's defensive style is a key agent of countertransference.

Therapist Self-Protection

Countertransference is primarily organized around affects evoked in the therapist that are intolerable and give rise to unconscious defenses and potential behavioral ("acting out") responses. A given client's clinical material, transference, and interpersonal style may stir intense feelings, dystonic identities, or painful memories in the survivor therapist.* At that point, the therapist's focus shifts away from the client toward meeting her own needs. To protect herself, the therapist may turn to old defenses which developed to maintain an acceptable sense of self.

For example, a therapist who feels fear may respond by asserting her power in the therapeutic relationship. A therapist who needs to be seen as a good person to protect herself from shame or guilt may promote or maintain an idealized transference and be unable to tolerate any negative or critical feelings from her client. Either therapist may need to be needed to feel powerful or worthwhile and may then encourage a client's exclusive dependence on her and block moves toward autonomy, independence, or connection with others.

A shame-filled therapist may feel she must be whatever the client wants and thus allow abusive treatment by a client (e.g., denigration or unrelenting criticism), agree to any request or demand from a client, or engage in inappropriate behaviors because of her inability to set necessary protective

---

*For a discussion of vicarious traumatization issues for survivor therapists, see chapter 14, pp. 309–311.

limits. A therapist in despair can feel paralyzed and become emotionally absent, sleepy, or passive in the face of a client's pain and need.

In general, defensive reactions to the potent affective responses of fear, anger, shame, anxiety, and grief will be mobilized to protect the therapist's self, in much the same way that she as a child protected herself in the face of overwhelming affect. For example, a therapist who has repressed memories about childhood sexual abuse has the need not to know which may be manifest in the therapy as the inability to hear her client, or the need to deny the client's truth. The deepening of the therapeutic relationship can evoke anxiety, leading the therapist to pull away and provoke a rupture in the relationship, including premature termination.

Specific topics may be difficult for certain survivor therapists to hear or address. Sometimes it is difficult for a survivor therapist to hear historical material that too closely resembles her experience. Sometimes it is difficult to hear thematic material that is too close to unresolved or painful issues for her. For example, gender issues can be particularly difficult. One outcome of childhood sexual abuse is profound disturbances in establishing and maintaining a positive gender identity (Saakvitne & Pearlman, 1993). It is critical to address these issues with survivor clients, but this work may be difficult for a therapist who feels deep shame about her gender. For women survivors, an important piece of therapeutic work centers around addressing issues of feminine identity: what it means to be female, the ways early sexual exploitation affected one's sense of herself as female, and her relationship with her body (Saakvitne, 1992). A female therapist is a role model and must be able to hold and tolerate her client's strong feelings of shame, loathing, anxiety, and desire. In the same way, male survivor therapists struggle with issues of masculine identity. Survivor therapists for whom gender identity issues are unresolved will have difficulty helping their survivor clients through this terrain.

Self-esteem is often maintained by holding on to an identity historically associated with rewards, usually acceptance or attention. A survivor therapist who has not worked through the contradictory and conflictual identities related to her abusive experiences may maintain a defensive "good-girl" identity, which may be organized around reaction formation and denial. The therapist cannot tolerate either her aggression or her potential to identify with her aggressor (Davies & Frawley, 1994). This limited identity can be played out in the therapy relationship through a need for an idealized transference, a need to deny aggression in one's survivor client, and failure to address ambivalence in the therapy.

Davies and Frawley (1994) identify another danger for survivor therapists who assume a "persistently masochistic position" with clients and thus provoke or perpetuate their clients' sadistic acting out behaviors. They suggest this reenactment allows the therapist to maintain an unconscious attachment to her own abuser by remaining a victim while simultaneously preserving an attachment to her nonprotective parent or other who was blind to the abuse just as she is blind to her client's abuse of her. At the same time, this pattern also allows the therapist to continue to disavow her own sadism by unconsciously allowing her client to enact it. Again this enactment serves to maintain a good object identity.

> Keeping the relationship with patients primarily loving and "nice" may also represent survivor/therapist attempts to compensate patients and themselves for the wonderful childhood neither ever had. (Davies & Frawley, p. 166)

Overall, the danger here is that the therapist will not hear what the client needs to say because of her conscious and unconscious preoccupation with her own needs. This unconscious myopia renders a therapist unable to analyze positive or negative transference, unable to see the client as a separate person with unique individual needs, and thus at risk for retraumatizing or reenacting early destructive interpersonal patterns with the client.

Projection in Countertransference

Interpersonal interactions in abusive families are often based upon unchecked projection. The child is rarely seen as a separate individual, but instead is used as a vessel for the adult's projections. A therapist raised in this context may be unaware of her projection and potential to project. She may also have difficulty recognizing when she is the object of a client's projections for two reasons: (1) being the object of projection is familiar and not dystonic and therefore can go unnoticed; and (2) her need to see the client as an idealized victim requires she not see negative, aggressive aspects of her client. Projection is a central factor in problematic countertransferences. The therapist's projections onto the client can lead to the unraveling of a therapy.

Projection occurs in two ways. One is the projection of the whole self, that is, the use of the client as a self-object, a mirror of the therapist's self. Thus, the survivor therapist may assume the client's experiences are just like her own, that the client felt the same way, had the same conflicts, and coped in the same ways. This pattern is often a reenactment of a common dynamic in an incestuous family in which parents experience children as extensions of themselves, as feeling, believing, and thinking exactly the same way. These parents would fly into a narcissistic rage at any assertion of their child's independence, separateness, or autonomy. The child learns that love is predicated on being the same. A therapist who grew up with such a belief may unconsciously reenact it with her clients, especially those who elicit a conscious or unconscious identification. As Wilson et al. (1994) point out, this process interferes with the therapist's empathic understanding of the client's experience.

Example   A client told of her father's habit of taking her on business trips as his "date." Her therapist, a survivor of paternal incest, responded immediately that his behavior was inappropriate, and focused on the client's anger. The more she spoke of the client's violation and inevitable rage, the more silent the client became. At first the therapist didn't notice her silence. Then she thought the client was listening. Then she assumed the client was denying her anger. Only in the next session when the client firmly expressed her frustration did the therapist realize that her client's experience was entirely different; she had felt validated and cherished on these trips. This is not to say the therapist's response was inaccurate, but it was not empathic to her client's current experience.

The second way projection occurs is as a vehicle for ridding the therapist of uncomfortable affects by attributing them to the client. An angry, shameful, overwhelmed therapist may experience the client as rageful, shameful, or bad, or as a helpless victim. The survivor therapist can find herself feeling extremely critical of her clients, reflecting a need to emphasize the difference between her and them.

Example   A therapist working with a client struggling with long-term depression, hopelessness, and self-destructive impulses found her tolerance running low. Her interventions no longer seemed helpful, but she could not tolerate self-doubt in her professional work as her work was her major source of self-esteem. She began to see her client as resistant and mired in a self-pity. She became increasingly annoyed and critical with the client and about the client in supervision. She did not notice her countertransference until her supervisor commented on her unusually critical tone with this client. The therapist recognized in her tone an inner voice she had often used against herself in the past. She recognized her despair about the therapy and familiar feelings of failure and self-criticism, which she was then able to discuss with her supervisor.

In these difficult, often long-term therapies, the survivor therapist's self-criticality and harsh superego can be particular liabilities.

These two projective processes for managing affect—one of identification and one of differentiation—determine the countertransference enactments in response to affect. For example, a therapist who feels rage and is engaged in an identification with her client may require the client to feel anger (toward a perpetrator or partner, for example), regardless of the appropriateness for the client. Or, if rage is intolerable or unacceptable to the therapist, she may be unable to hear her client's anger. Similarly, a therapist who feels shame may not be able to tolerate her client's need to idealize and value her. Or if the therapist is unconsciously distancing herself from her own shame by differentiating herself from the client, she may require an idealized transference and be intolerant of any negative feelings the client may have about her.

These countertransference issues are complex and will change over time as the survivor therapist grows in professional and personal experience. Grellert (1992) categorizes survivor therapists' countertransferences as homogenous—those experienced by many or most therapists—and idiosyncratic—those unique to an individual's experience and self. She writes of the tracking of "idiosyncratic responses":

> the therapist is aware of an empathic identification with the patient's suffering, but simultaneously must differentiate "Like me, but not me" distinctions. . . . Although there may be no such thing as objectivity, the term is designed to address the clarity one has when there is an absence of contamination by other subjective experiences. (p. 8)

BOUNDARY ISSUES FOR SURVIVOR THERAPISTS

While all therapists struggle with boundary issues in trauma therapies, a therapist whose personal history is characterized by boundary violations may not have the signal anxiety necessary to assess appropriate boundaries, as Kluft (1994) also notes. For this reason, therapists who are survivors of childhood sexual abuse may also be at risk for violating therapeutic boundaries, for being psychologically inappropriate and abusive, and for being involved sexually with clients. These violations and abuses can occur in a context that a survivor therapist believes is therapeutic, but in reality is organized by her own needs, defenses, and distortions of interpersonal relationships. The therapist must attempt to remain aware of these issues at all times. The consequences of these blind spots or clinical reenactments are profound. Clients are severely retraumatized by involvement with a therapist who reenacts (not symbolically, in the transference, but actually) the client's childhood trauma and family dynamics. These events can also destroy the therapist's professional esteem and identity. These dangers underscore the critical importance of adequate, responsible training, individual treatment for therapists, ongoing supervision for clinicians, and enforceable monitoring of the professions to protect against reenactments of unresolved traumas with clients.

Self-Disclosure of Survivor Status

It is not uncommon for incest survivors to ask whether their therapist has a history of childhood sexual abuse. While there are many points of view on the disclosure of a therapist's personal history of childhood sexual abuse, we suggest great caution for any therapist considering making this disclosure to her client. The information will be meaningful to a client in many, often contradictory ways, too often in ways that are far from the therapist's intent and that impede the work. The therapist's disclosure of childhood sexual abuse can too easily invite the client to take care of the therapist, particularly when the client has a core identity as a caretaker. She can be burdened with fantasies about the therapist's pain, fragility, or superior strength and character, all of which inhibit a client's sense of safety and openness. Self-disclosure can also invite the fantasy that the therapist has resolved her own issues in the correct, complete, and perfect way (Marvasti, 1992; Saakvitne, 1991), a fantasy that the client often uses in the service of self-loathing: "So how come you ended up a doctor and I'm a psych patient in a hospital? I knew it was just me over-reacting like my family always said."

Certainly such issues can be addressed in the therapy, but they are not ordinary or necessary "grist for the mill." There is a serious potential to breach a critical boundary of the therapeutic frame and compromise the safety of the therapeutic relationship. It is too easy to disclose out of countertransference needs such as a wish for admiration, connection, avoidance of transference, support, or self-reassurance. The decision should not be made impulsively, but in light of the client's dynamics and clinical needs. One should discuss the decision ahead of time in supervision or consultation with a respected colleague and address the particular context of a given client's request for this information.

In some circumstances, it may feel difficult for a survivor therapist not to disclose her abuse history. Marvasti (1992) suggests that a therapist may feel she is again keeping the incest secret, a reenactment which can lead to problematic countertransference feelings such as guilt, resentment, or blame.

Therapists may feel compelled by the client's (sometimes expressed) need for a positive role model as a symbol of hope for healing. The therapist may feel a political wish for solidarity and "speaking out." A therapist may be moved by her empathy and concordant experience and wish to share her sense of connection with a client who experiences existential isolation. Another therapist may wish to tell a particular client about her personal experiences to reassure the client that her responses are normal or adaptive. While these considerations are valid, the meanings of the disclosure are complex. It is easy for a therapist to be mistaken in her assumptions about these meanings. The client may be experiencing a fear that needs exploration, not confirmation; for example, she may fear she will not be understood by a nonsurvivor therapist or that she will have to protect or rescue a survivor therapist.

When a client asks a therapist if she is a survivor, the therapist needs to affirm her right to ask and her understandable curiosity. She can wonder with her client about the meaning of the question, why it comes up when it does, and what ideas and fantasies come to mind about the subject and the meaning of the therapist giving an answer or not. However, it is respectful to let a client know ahead of time if the therapist does not plan to answer the question. We tell our clients that we do not generally answer this question, and explain why. In our experience, clients to whom this information is essential ask it in the initial phone contact or consultation (and we usually tell clients that we choose not to answer that question); at this point, clients sometimes decide they prefer to work with a therapist who is an acknowledged survivor. The question has different meanings when asked later in the therapy, and often after exploration, clients have found the answer is no longer important.

Occasionally, the question arises in the termination process, often at the very end of the treatment; the decision at that point is a very individual one based upon the therapist's assessment of the client's best interest and her own personal comfort level. It is important for a therapist who does disclose her personal history to remember that a client can never be asked to keep information secret, so the therapist must be willing to have the information be known more widely.

Clients' ambivalence about knowing the therapist's survivor status is best illustrated in group therapy. When someone asks the question in group, another group member almost invariably says, "I don't want to know!" This leads to a spirited discussion of why some people want to know and others do not. Whatever the decision, it will have transference implications (Courtois, 1988). It is important the therapist handle this and all personal questions in a way that both respects the client's right to ask and the therapist's right to choose whether or not to answer.

PERSONAL PSYCHOTHERAPY

A critical step for survivor therapists is to engage in their own personal psychotherapy. Personal psychotherapy, ongoing supervision, and consultation all support the therapist and acknowledge the enormous complexity of the work and of the human psyche. We are the tools of our trade: We use ourselves, our perceptions, affect, intelligence, insight, and intuition to understand, connect with, and help our clients.

A therapist who is a survivor of child sexual abuse needs to address the impact of her childhood experiences on her self and relationships. This includes addressing particular memories; the impact of the abuse on her sense of self, safety, sexuality, and trust; and its impact on interpersonal relationships, including intimacy with and expectations of others. Issues of trust, control, boundaries, and self-esteem are central in psychotherapeutic work with survivors of incest. We must know our own issues and limits in these arenas in order as therapists to be confident and consistent in the face of our clients' needs. The client's and therapist's experiences will often overlap (Courtois, 1988; Grellert, 1992), and a therapist's awareness of her areas of vulnerability will protect her and her client. External supports (supervision, personal therapy, colleagues, and friends) create a context that contains the work and contextualizes her therapist self as one aspect of her personhood.

In addition, personal experience as a client in the therapeutic process is essential to any therapist's full understanding of the complexities of the process. Survivor therapists who have not had their own intensive therapy will be ill-prepared for the intensity of the feelings and intimacy in the therapies they conduct. There is no substitute for personal experience in developing respect for the vulnerability and fear inherent in allowing another person, one's therapist, into one's most private and personal psychological space. It is uncomfortable to have strong transference feelings, and often embarrassing to acknowledge and discuss them. It is difficult to again experience feelings associated with a painful childhood. The therapist's personal struggle with these feelings and with the comforting and uncomfortable intimacy of a therapeutic relationship allows her to maintain empathy for her clients' struggles and respect for their courage.

It is imperative that a survivor therapist herself receive the kind of respectful attention she is giving her clients; it is easy for a therapist to become resentful and feel envious of clients who are receiving better care than she.

COUNTERTRANSFERENCE IN PSYCHOTHERAPY WITH SURVIVOR THERAPISTS

There are particular countertransference challenges for the therapist treating a survivor therapist. There are two major, conflicting sources of countertransference: countertransference responses to an incest survivor and countertransference responses to another therapist.

What do trauma therapists need to be aware of when working with survivor therapist clients? A therapist client needs the space, safety, and respect to be a client, not a colleague. That means not being treated as if she were special, with the attendant meanings and expectations that can be frightening to any childhood abuse survivor. It also means not being devalued, in a one-down position because she is a survivor.

One potential reenactment is to treat the client like a parentified child. When the client is also a therapist, it is very important to keep roles clear in the therapeutic relationship while respecting the therapist-client's professional identity and work. Responding to her as a colleague first deprives her of her right to depend on the therapist in order to explore her conflicts about and need for dependence and trust. In the therapy office, she needs to be a client, not a colleague as Kluft, 1994, has also noted. The therapist's temptation to discuss professional issues or do other business in a therapy hour with a therapist-client may reflect the therapist's discomfort with the power dynamics of the therapy relationship. It is useful for the therapist to notice if she is using a different language with her therapist clients, perhaps using more clinical jargon. These retreats from therapist-client roles abandon the survivor therapist client and often reenact childhood experiences.

It is important to address explicitly the meaning of professional identity issues in the therapeutic relationship. Failing to do so can raise both parties' anxiety, while open discussion of the boundary questions establishes safety and respect. What does it mean that one's therapist is in the same field (same or different discipline)? What about professional contacts the therapist and client have in common? How will boundaries be handled when the professional and clinical roles overlap, for example, when they meet at a conference? How will confidentiality be managed? How will they work with discovering they have colleagues or clients in common?

In psychotherapies with survivor therapists, it is imperative not to assume that they can do for themselves what they do for their own clients. Just as with other survivors, their clients may be used as examples or metaphors; similarly, other adults and children in their lives may be a means to develop greater empathy for themselves. However, in her own therapy, a survivor therapist is struggling with her own difficulties caring for herself.

When a survivor therapist client brings case material into a session and invites her therapist to offer supervision, the therapist needs to maintain role clarity. Her task is to listen to the material with her therapist client foremost in mind, and not accept the invitation to make the client's client her main concern. When tempted to do so, a therapist should examine her countertransference. This temptation may reflect her greater comfort or self-esteem as a supervisor and retreat from her therapist role. It may reflect performance anxiety about being a therapist to a therapist, or avoidance of competitive issues with a potential colleague. The therapeutic work requires that the therapist explore the meaning and motivation of the invitation for her to change roles taking into account the context of the survivor therapist's life and conflicts, and the unfolding therapeutic relationship.

The treating therapist must also be alert to dynamics of competition and envy in therapies with survivor therapists. How does the therapist feel when she admires her client's clinical work? Can she delight in her successes and triumphs without feeling diminished? To identify related transference themes she should understand the client's childhood experience of her parents' ability to support her competence, autonomy, and continued need for support and caretaking, which of course tend to be limited in abusive and dysfunctional families. The therapist's ability to accept her client's strengths without acting out envy or the need to be needed, and to accept her client's abilities without then assuming that the client doesn't need her can counteract a therapist-survivor client's experience of no-win situations at every developmental stage.

Different countertransference responses will be evoked in situations in which the treating therapist fears that the therapist client may be reenacting her own childhood dynamics with her survivor clients. The therapist may feel protective, horrified, fearful, anxious, or cautious, fearing for the safety of her client's clients (a parallel response to therapists' concern for some clients' children). One route the therapist may be tempted to take is to move into a supervisory stance because it may feel safer than addressing the issue through an exploration of the client's dynamics, fantasies, and projections. Kluft (1994) reports he requires his therapist clients be in regular clinical supervision in order to protect the therapy from his countertransference anxiety for their clients (p. 7).

It is important to examine the transference implications of the therapist's professional misconduct and to look for reenactments occurring in the therapeutic relationship, for example, expression of anger at the therapist; self- (and other-) defeating behavior to punish the therapist; shame enactment, to show herself as unworthy to the therapist; inviting rescue; making the therapist a helpless witness to abuse. Any of these dynamics may occur with any survivor client. However, the willingness and ability to address them with a therapist client may be less because of strong feelings of identification or misplaced feelings of protectiveness toward a survivor therapist client.

Incest survivors can be outstanding therapists for incest survivor clients. Their own experiences and personal healing can make them deeply empathic and strong advocates for their clients. However, empathy without technique and good intentions without training are especially dangerous to clients with seriously disturbed family histories. There are many survivors of child sexual abuse across the many disciplines of psychotherapists and mental health workers. These therapists need treatment, training, and supervision in order to be sensitive and responsive to the complicated issues of technique and countertransference in their clinical work. We as a field need to make this possible, to be able to learn from and support one another in our work.

9

The Role of Gender
in Transference
and Countertransference

SEXUAL ABUSE is a gendered issue; gender-related transference and counter-transference themes are inescapable in psychotherapy with incest survivors. A therapist's awareness of gender dynamics in the therapy with incest survivors is essential and opens multiple avenues for working through identity, esteem, and body issues.

To begin with, childhood sexual abuse has a profound impact on the survivor's sense of feminine or masculine identity. The realities of the bodily contact and assault, and their interpersonal context, inform the development of the individual's beliefs and emotions about his or her body, sense of self and other as female or male, sexuality, gender, and worth (Maltz & Holman, 1987; Saakvitne, 1992). A client will weave her beliefs and conflicts about her gender throughout the therapy in a variety of direct and indirect ways and these will interact with the therapist's own gender identity, conflicts, and beliefs.*

---

*We are two female therapists who work with more female than male survivors of childhood sexual abuse. Therefore we have more knowledge about and experience with women's gender issues. Many of the issues we identify will be true for male therapists and survivors. We are indebted to colleagues who have discussed the chapter and shared their experiences with us, especially Paul Adler, Ph.D.

The Creation of Meaning

In the face of traumatic events, an individual strives to create meaning. Gender identity is one component of the meaning system constructed in the aftermath of childhood trauma. Without resources to process and integrate affect, the child's construction of meaning will be based upon damaged, wounded aspects of the self and destructive malevolent object relational paradigms. This negative influence is often evident in gender identity. Thus, at times, the construction of meaning ensures the survival of the organism, but at the expense of the self. The therapeutic goal is to reconsider meaning, contextualize and symbolize experience, and reclaim disavowed aspects of the self.

Gender — femaleness and maleness, femininity and masculinity, or femininities and masculinities (Chodorow, 1989) — is a social and personal construction; yet it starts with biology. While the attributes "feminine" and "masculine" are constructed and often subjective, the fact of gender is not. Males and females have different bodies; the experience of childhood sexual abuse occurs in the context of the child's gendered body. Gender is a crucial component of identity; in gender identity the individual integrates her physical being with her psychological and spiritual self. Attention to the client's relation to her or his body and the need for resolution and healing of feminine and masculine identity are central in the treatment of adult survivors of childhood sexual abuse.

While the importance of gender in the experience of childhood sexual abuse seems self-evident, in many therapies with incest survivors issues of gender identity and esteem are barely addressed. There are several reasons for this avoidance, many of them originating with the therapist. In the current climate, therapists are sometimes silenced out of a misguided "political correctness," as though the words feminine and masculine were mutually exclusive and inherently sexist. Additionally, therapists are influenced by their conflicts about gender identity and role, their resultant anxiety, denial, and lack of awareness, as well as by their ignorance and the effects of cultural misinformation and silencing. As a society and a field, therapists are too often undereducated and misinformed about issues of gender and sexuality. Biases and assumptions masquerade as knowledge and can lead to countertransference morasses.

Gender-Based Countertransference

Countertransference responses to gender issues are influenced by the therapist's own gender identity conflicts, socialization, beliefs, and politics. Gender is a deeply personal construct informed in a social context. As mental health professionals we can too easily assume we are enlightened and free from gender role stereotypes. It is important to respect the force of these deep and powerful stereotypes; the social gender context in which our clients develop and through which they examine and come to understand their early experiences of sexual abuse is the same social gender context in which we developed (Saakvitne & Pearlman, 1993).* The patriarchal (often femiphobic) cultural mores lead all of us to deny women power and esteem and to deny men emotional and interpersonal connectedness. When therapist and client are exposed to the same media, cultural, and political messages, they will internalize similar valued and devalued images. These internalized values influence the therapy and emerge in the therapist's countertransference. The organization that forms the context for the therapist's work will also hold and reflect gender assumptions and values that will in turn influence her psychotherapies.

Gender Issues in Organizations

Complicated gender issues are always present within organizations that work with victims of sexual violence. These organizations often function as microcosms of the larger society that is struggling to assimilate previously banished knowledge about childhood sexual abuse. When only one or a few staff members are knowledgeable about sexual abuse issues, they become spokespeople for abuse issues and can also be targets for conflict about and denial of incest. When those staff members are women and their challengers are men, gender conflicts can emerge in the organization as polarized battles that are destructive (and usually reductionistic). When the organization has a traditional structure of male administrators and female front line staff, the situation is ripe for the reenactment of abuse dynamics and cultural patriarchy within the power structure of the organization. This scenario stirs strong feelings in all participants and without analysis leads to countertransference enactments in and about therapies.

One enactment of this dynamic occurs in the organizational countertransference to the therapeutic dyad, the client-therapist pair. In response to organizational pressures and responses to a female survivor client, the therapist may feel identified with and protective of her client. This response

---

*Clearly, there will be cultural, familial, and individual differences between therapist and client that are relevant to gender identity and role. Yet the pervasive impact of the "dominant culture," through instruments of mass media, the legal and justice system, and the financial and educational system of the country, provide a common context within which there are cultural, familial, and individual variations.

can lead her to feel and behave like a champion of the client in and outside therapy sessions. She and/or the organization can make her responsible for her client's behavior; she then abdicates her role as observer to her client's experience. She and the client may join together against an abusive, persecutory other and become embroiled in a reenactment rather than able to interpret and work through the experience. Both the therapist and organization have the responsibility to protect against such a dynamic. The organization's mechanisms for noticing and monitoring its countertransference create a holding environment for therapists and clients that protects against these countertherapeutic reenactments.

These issues are best understood and addressed constructively through active naming and discussing. When the organizational climate is one that addresses conflict, stereotypes, and culturally based gender dynamics, the therapists within the organization will be more attuned to and freer to address these issues in their clinical work.

An organizational aspect of each psychotherapy is its supervision or consultation. The gender of the supervisor adds another level and opportunity for gender-related countertransference to influence the treatment. The supervisor can offer a different perspective to help the therapist sort out her own, often automatic or unconscious, presuppositions and gender-dominated assumptions. When a therapy seems mired down in gender issues, consulting with a supervisor of a different gender can be helpful. Because gender-based countertransference responses are often quite personal and difficult to address, the supervisory relationship needs to model trust, respect, and freedom to speak of confusion, uncertainty, and other feelings.

Problematic gender-based countertransference responses emerge in three clinical arenas. The first is therapeutic work on gender identity and gender roles. The second is gender-dominated responses to childhood sexual abuse and incest material. The third is erotic and sexual responses in the therapeutic relationship.

GENDER IDENTITY

Therapeutic work on gender identity issues is complex for many reasons. Gender includes many components: the body, sexuality, self-esteem, gender roles, identifications, introjects, and meaning. This material emerges in a variety of disguised ways in the treatment: in fantasy, imagery, dream, and transference material. In psychotherapy with survivors of sexual abuse, gender issues are particularly conflictual and emotion-laden. In order to set

the stage for a discussion of the strong, often unconscious, countertransference responses, we will summarize some of the clinical issues likely to
emerge.

Developmental Context for Gender Identity

Gender identity is a key component of identity, and both are profoundly
impacted by childhood sexual trauma. The physical realities of childhood
sexual abuse inform and define a girl's (and then a woman's) and boy's
(and then a man's) sense of self as female or male in bodily, sexual, interpersonal, and social realms. The child's experience of sexual overstimulation, the frequently painful, sometimes violent nature of the physical violation by penetration, the relative sense of smallness and powerlessness, the
confusing experience of body parts that often have no names (Lerner,
1988), are not fully visible, and whose sensations are confusing and mixed
up with elimination functions, and the experience of terror as a context for
a child's discovery of her emerging sexuality, all indelibly affect the child's
relation with her body.

Further, the unconscious association of the vulnerability of childhood
with one's gender can lead to shame and despair for both male and female
victims. Clinically and theoretically, gender identity and shame are inextri-
cably linked for incest and other childhood sexual abuse survivors.* For
women, the connection of femaleness to victimization and weakness is reinforced by both societal disempowerment and individual psychological defenses, including dissociation and repression, that reinforce not knowing
and not heeding experienced affect. For male survivors, the connection of
maleness to shame is reinforced by both societal denial of men's vulnerability and victimization and individual defenses, including denial and projection, that reinforce externalization and rejection of one's experienced affect.
Thus, the development of gender identity for sexual abuse survivors takes
place in the context of the sexual abuse of their bodies and the larger
context of a society that is misogynist and victim-blaming.

Consequently, a central arena of harm for a survivor of childhood sexual
abuse is that of positive gender identity. For some women survivors, to be
female means to be abused, to be deserving of or entitled only to abuse, to
be vulnerable to betrayal, violation, exploitation, humiliation, and pain.
For some male survivors, the contrast between their experience of relative
powerlessness and vulnerability and the cultural imago of invulnerable,
powerful males leads to shame and silence.

---

*Several gender-related dynamics described in this chapter are true for many clients
who are not survivors of sexual abuse. The shared cultural context informs gender
identity for all men and women.

The valence of gender issues for the survivor intensifies when her abuse has become a salient organizing component of her identity, as a victim or a survivor. This intensity can catch the therapist off guard, for example, when a client moves into rage, or terror, or humiliation when the therapist explicitly acknowledges her gender (what one client, who spoke only of "the body," referred to scathingly as "that word," i.e., woman).

Shame about gender is common for all survivors, and they express their shame in gender-determined ways. Shame may emerge in the context of rigid, gender-role stereotypes, in passivity, masochism, hyperfemininity, and self-attack for women, and in hypermasculinity and aggressive, competitive denial of vulnerability for men. It may emerge in defensive rejections of gender role stereotypes, in counterphobic hypersexuality, identification with the aggressor, or rejection of femininity for women, and in passive aggression, angry dependency, and rejection of masculinity in men. In response, a therapist can move to a complementary gender role, or challenge the gender role assumptions of the client without recognizing the underlying shame dynamic. Male and female survivors may strive to desex themselves, that is, to become asexual, neuter, or nongendered, in order to protect themselves from the external threat of abuse and the internal threat of shame.

Countertransference responses that are rooted in the therapist's gender role stereotypes prevent the therapeutic exploration of gender assumptions. If the therapist accepts a gender role as "appropriate," she can collude with her client's foreclosure of other aspects of herself. Challenges to gender roles are inherently anxiety-provoking; struggling with a client's gender role will press us to examine our own choices and beliefs. For example, when a woman client assumes she should have a child, or a man assumes he should want a promotion, we may fail to hear their ambivalence if we have agreed with (and conformed to) the "shoulds" ourselves. If we have not given ourselves permission to question our choices, we may be unable to hear or support our clients' endeavors.

Incest survivors learn from their childhood exploitative sexual experiences about relationships and about themselves as female or male in relation to others. Clients bring these beliefs, about themselves and others, into the therapeutic relationship. Thus, a survivor may deduce from her experience that she can only get her affectional needs met by being sexual, or by being hurt. Another may come to believe that the only way to connect is through violence and victimization, thus mimicking and identifying with the powerful and abusive figures from his past. When a child is humiliated, hurt, and denigrated as part of the abuse, she or he may come to believe that she deserves such treatment because she is female.

Another may believe that her gender made her vulnerable to abuse and come to hate her gender and the body that incorporates that gender. One may try to eradicate the gender of one's body by starving oneself to destroy physical evidence, by body building to exaggerate physical characteristics of strength, or by covering one's body in a layer of disguising fat or baggy, nondescript clothes. A woman may attack those parts of her body that make her female, or attack her whole body as a representation of weakness when she feels needy or vulnerable. Survivors may behave in ways that deny vulnerability or allow them to forget that they have a gender. Some survivors live in a constant state of dissociation (as either child alters or intellectualized, efficient workers, for example), avoid sexual contact, or engage only in friendships that do not include intimacy or the possibility for feelings that would prompt bodily sensations.

Abusive relationships in childhood shape beliefs about others; survivors may experience all men or all women as sexualized, or idealized, or devalued. They will assume a complementary role in relation to their expectation: as the object of desire or a victim, and similarly or dissimilarly idealized or devalued themselves. These expectations will be elaborated in the therapeutic relationship.

Countertransference Responses to Gender Identity*

Therapists should name and notice gender assumptions a female client brings directly and transferentially into the therapeutic relationship. By trying to make conscious and open to observation assumptions that are unconscious and automatic, the therapist breaks the cycle of silence and collusion and invites the client to join her in rethinking gender stereotypes. When the therapist feels invited to reinforce messages received from key people in the client's past, together they can explore what the client learned about herself as a female in these significant early relationships.

Therapists' responses to a client's beliefs about what it means to be a woman will be informed by their own experiences as men or women in this culture. Countertransference will reflect each therapist's beliefs about women's roles, her internalization and awareness of cultural misogyny, and her personal work on identity, intimate relationships, family and parental relationships, and personal histories. Therapists and clients can experience a deep sense of loss, interwoven with rage, about living in a culture, and

---

*This section will focus on work with women clients on issues of feminine identity. However, because our culture automatically feminizes victimhood, male survivors of childhood sexual victimization struggle with fear and contempt for the feminine within themselves. Therefore, many of the themes of reclaiming the power and acceptance of the feminine also pertain to male survivors.

perhaps in relationships, which so limit women and men from connecting with their authentic selves. For other therapists and clients, gender issues, personal and cultural, remain largely out of awareness. They may question the relevance or importance of feminine and masculine identity and its context, or may defensively reject the premise that gender is an affectively charged construction that influences one's perception of identity and interpersonal relationships. Thus, they overlook key connections between shame and gender, anger and gender, and identity and gender.

Survivors bring issues of gender into therapy directly and indirectly, in words, through their treatment of their bodies, and through their interpersonal behavior and roles in intimate relationships, including the therapeutic relationship. The therapist's challenge is to understand and explore the client's experience, noting the familial, social, cultural, and political context, but leaving space for the client to find her own way. It is sometimes difficult to hold the balance, naming social context without politicizing the therapy in a way that meets the therapist's rather than the client's needs.

Example   One therapist felt filled with outrage as she witnessed her client's struggle within her marriage to speak her own needs. The client's childhood sexual victimizations and religious upbringing had resulted in her belief that being a woman meant being silent or silenced and serving others. The therapist was most helpful when she could question the client's beliefs gently, or wonder with the client what would be different for her if she spoke. The therapist was least helpful when she challenged or argued with the client, or got angry on her client's behalf. The former intervention allowed the client to explore her fears of losing her husband and her connection to his family, her primary source of support. The latter evoked shame and silence in her.

Gender and the Body in Psychotherapy

A client's relationship with her body is a rich source of material for gender-related themes. Inviting a client to attend to her body counteracts dissociation and provides an important resource for identity consolidation and interpersonal safety. When a child needs to disconnect from her bodily experience and awareness, the maturational process of developing an integrated identity as female is derailed. Remaining in touch with one's bodily experience is central to developing a sense of oneself in space and relation to others, differentiating self from other, establishing interpersonal boundaries, maintaining affective attunement, identifying danger, and enjoying one's body, sensuality, and sexuality; Attias and Goodwin (1993) have noted many of these issues as well. Attention to the client's relationship with her body also facilitates resolution and healing of damaged feminine identity.

Three related arenas of countertransference are evoked by clinical work on a client's relationship to her body: (1) the therapist's awareness of her own body and (2) of the client's body, and (3) the client's awareness of the therapist's body.

The Therapist's Awareness of Her Own Body

The therapist's relationship with her own body will affect her understanding and openness to the client's work. A therapist who is unable to be "in her body," or to notice, respect, and love her body may have difficulty working with her clients' hatred and estrangement from their bodies. A female therapist who has struggled with conflicts about her weight or eating may feel fascination and admiration for an anorexic client's thinness and "control," and fail to see the intense pain and grave danger of her illusory control. The therapist's ability to hear and address a client's experience of her body often determines whether or not the client's feelings about her body are discussed in the therapy process because survivor clients will often keep their bodies dissociated from themselves and the therapy indefinitely. In particular, clients rarely move spontaneously into the realm of meaning; for example, while they may criticize their weight or breast or hip size without invitation, they rarely discuss their experience of being female.

The Therapist's Awareness of the Client's Body

The therapist's response to her client's body informs her countertransference; we have all been trained to judge women's bodies by certain cultural standards. The client's physical presence and demeanor in relation to the therapist can evoke strong feelings. These unconscious, automatic assumptions, or conscious, but uncomfortable feelings of criticism, attraction, admiration, distaste, envy, or curiosity can inhibit the therapist from exploration or lead her to erroneous conclusions that precipitate empathic failures.

Example   One strikingly beautiful survivor client came to therapy with painfully low self-esteem and unhappy with her romantic relationships. In initial sessions, the therapist was aware of feeling envious and then less compassionate. She had to remind herself that the client's self-esteem was deeply damaged and that the client had suffered deeply, despite (and in the client's view, because of) her beauty. The cultural assumption that happiness accompanies beauty is powerful and pervasive and, combined with the therapist's strong personal attraction to and envy of the client, set the stage for powerful reenactments for the client. Only after grappling with her "untherapeutic" feelings and understanding their sources, could the therapist consider the client's subjective experience. Then she could also recognize her unconscious identification with the client's experience of her mother as deeply envious and resentful of her attractive daughter.

The Client's Awareness of the Therapist's Body

As a client struggles with feelings about her body, she will notice her therapist's body. As we invite clients to name and notice their experience in the room with us, we must include our physical presence as part of our therapeutic selves; this is often an unfamiliar and uncomfortable prospect. Frequently, as clients work on feminine and masculine identity, the person and physical presence of the therapist becomes very important. This can be evident in the client's looking, gazing, or glancing, looking away or down, or self-consciousness about being seen, wishes for touch, and curiosity about the person of the therapist. The therapist can respond to her client's curiosity, interest, admiration, denigration, yearning, and fantasies in a variety of ways. The therapist's ability to integrate and understand the client's context, the therapeutic process, and her own issues will enrich the unfolding work.

Example   At one point in a long therapy, a survivor frequently gazed at her therapist's face for long moments without speaking. Initially the therapist believed the client was dissociating during such extended silences. But when they discussed the interaction, the client was able eventually to articulate how soothing she found the therapist's face. The therapist then felt more discomfort during the client's gazing, realizing she was more comfortable with the possibility of dissociation than with the client's maternal longings. The next time it happened, the therapist looked away and changed the subject. The client responded with shame. The therapist realized her response. In her therapy she could connect her discomfort to her own disavowed feelings of maternal longing, and in supervision she gained a better understanding of her client's developmental needs. She returned to the therapy better able to accept her client's admiration and longing.

Gender-Dominated Transference Themes

The working through of gender identity issues entails complex transference dynamics involving both maternal and paternal transferences with powerful childhood feelings and wishes. Exploration and analysis of these transferences provide a crucial opportunity for the client to know and begin to integrate split-off and devalued aspects of herself.

As a female client examines her feelings about being a woman, she will look to her therapist to represent both her wishes and fears about who she can be. She will both expect a familiar rejection of herself and wish for a validation of her self-worth. As a male client examines his feelings about being a man, he will expect his therapist to respond to him in familiar ways, reinforcing his limited repertoire of feelings, while simultaneously fearing that he will be challenged to enter new realms of experience. The fluidity between the wish and the fear, between hope and despair, is a hallmark of these therapies.

A survivor may expect the therapist to despise her and see her as damaged, weak, greedy, or entitled. She may despise the therapist, especially when the therapist is gentle, nonretaliatory, or understanding. She may idealize the therapist and devalue herself by comparison. Or she may idealize the therapist in order to protect her from her rage or love, either of which she may believe to be toxic. She may be certain that the therapist is waiting to humiliate, exploit, or violate her as soon as the therapist earns her trust. She may crave the therapist's attention and gaze, but simultaneously feel invaded and violated by that attention. She may dread naming her body for fear that doing so would invite the therapist to claim, possess, fantasize about, or violate her body. Yet, she may wish to feel held by speaking her fears and fantasies about her body, wishing for information, reassurance, and help with her confusion. She may wish for a nurturant, respectful relationship in which she can get her affectional needs met without having to be sexual, and yet simultaneously despair of that possibility, or believe that being sexual would allow her to be in control and deny her dependent feelings.

In the face of these complicated, contradictory wishes, a therapist can feel confused or stymied. She may respond to only one message of an ambivalent wish and disregard the possibility that its opposite is also true, and then be surprised by the client's distress, or experience of being misunderstood. She may feel paralyzed or resentful of the bind she feels she is in, between wishes and fears. Once she is aware of the contradictions and their context, a therapist can name the dilemma with the client and begin to unravel the conflicting wishes and fears.

Eroticized Maternal Transference

One manifestation of this dynamic is an eroticized maternal transference in which longing for maternal holding and primary maternal preoccupation merges with erotic feelings (Saakvitne, 1993c).* This transference is likely

---

*This section emphasizes the primary maternal component of erotic transference; we discuss other types of erotic and sexual responses later in the chapter.

to emerge with both male and female therapists although the countertransference responses may vary somewhat.

An eroticized maternal transference has its foundation in childhood sexual abuse; it reflects the fusion and confusion of the maternal and the erotic, of wishes for nurturance with arousal and fear of violation (Ferenczi, 1949). When in the course of striving to get normal affectional needs met, a child receives a sexualized response, over time she will experience confusion between affectionate and sexual, maternal and erotic, and dependent and aggressive feelings. As she becomes aware of erotic arousal, however vaguely, a client is often then frightened, ashamed, and afraid of the therapist's abandonment and revulsion or, through projection, of the therapist's sexual advances. Female clients are often frightened of these feelings toward a female therapist and expect a rejecting, abandoning, or violating response. This expectation is informed by their projection of self-contempt, revulsion for their sexuality, and homophobia, as well as by self-loathing and scorn for needy, infantile feelings, and fear learned from their early experience of violation which occurred in response to their needs. A male client may feel shame and anger in response to these feelings toward a female therapist, but humiliation, confusion, and rage when they emerge in relation to a male therapist.

Gender socialization and identity will influence a therapist's countertransference responses to both maternal and erotic transferences and so certainly to a transference that blends the two. A female therapist may see only the maternal aspect of the transference. She may then become more strongly maternal, overprotective, or resentful of increased demands. She may deny the sensuality, out of her need to desexualize a victim of childhood sexual abuse, her fear of female sexuality, or homophobia. She can invite increased dependence without examining the erotic context, or express greater tenderness without acknowledging the potential seductive effect or taking seriously the client's heightened anxiety and self-loathing. Male therapists may more readily see the erotic component of the transference with female clients and the competitive, aggressive aspects of the transference with male clients. They may then overfocus on Oedipal interpretations. They may respond flirtatiously, or defensively with more rigid boundaries and firm limits, or distance from the client to remove themselves from uncomfortable countertransference responses.

GENDER-RELATED COUNTERTRANSFERENCE TO INCEST

A client's experience of childhood sexual abuse intensifies gender factors in the transference and countertransference. This work will challenge therapists' identities and deeply ingrained beliefs about themselves in relation to women and men. This section elaborates countertransference patterns within particular therapist-client gender pairs in trauma therapies. These sections obviously entail generalizations, and there is much overlap among the themes; we encourage readers to read all four sections.*

Female Therapist-Female Client

Given the incidence rates for women of childhood sexual abuse (20% to 38%: Herman, 1981; Russell, 1984), attempted sexual assault (17% to 46%: Schauben & Frazier, in press; Russell, 1984), sexual harassment (45% to 69%: Salisbury, Ginorio, Remick, & Stringer, 1986; Schauben & Frazier), and rape (19% to 26%: Schauben & Frazier; Russell), it is easy for female therapists to identify with female clients' experiences of victimization and vulnerability to victimization. Each therapist has her own psychological ways of managing the reality of her vulnerability, such as denial, intellectualization, and projection. These defensive styles will shape countertransference responses, and in particular, her tolerance of and empathy for clients' experiences of terror, vulnerability, rage, and reenactments of being unprotected.

While identification with a survivor client can facilitate empathy, it can also lead a therapist to assume that she knows or understands more of her client's experience than she does. One incest survivor who clearly understood this preceded her description of a brutal assault she had suffered, with the warning, "What gets to you the most is probably not what got to me the most."

A focus on the client as victim can blind the therapist to the client's other identifications and feelings including rage, sadism, power, and sexuality. Female therapists may have particular difficulty with their female clients' aggression and sexuality. Particularly if the therapist is conflicted about her own aggression and sexuality, or the fusion of sexuality with aggression that can occur with victims of sexual abuse, she may minimize, deny, or condemn these aspects of her female clients. She may be unable to tolerate the complementary countertransference responses to an angry or erotic transference; specifically, if her own anger or arousal is dystonic, she may project her conflictual feelings onto her client and condemn them.†

---

*Both maternal and paternal, and perpetrator and protector transferences will emerge over time with either gender therapist and can be explored and worked through productively. Thus, unless a client expresses a clear preference, we do not assume a preferred gender pairing for survivors of childhood sexual abuse.
†For further discussion of the dynamics for therapists who are themselves survivors of childhood sexual abuse, see chapter 8.

A female therapist is, among other things, a role model for a female client. It is important that she treat herself and her clients with respect and gentle strength. This means protecting herself by maintaining appropriate boundaries and limits, and valuing her femaleness and that of her female clients. A female therapist is inevitably called upon to rework some of the client's historical interactions with maternal figures. This role includes giving permission and valuing a female client's feminine qualities, including her liveliness, intuitiveness, sensitivity, capacity for connection, and uniqueness. At times, this work asks a therapist to give permission to her clients that may well have been denied her in her own childhood. Therefore, a female therapist must examine these issues in her life or she risks unconsciously repeating to her clients the negative messages she received.

Alternatively, a client entrenched in hatred of her femaleness may devalue her therapist because she is a woman. The client may see her therapist as powerless, denigrated, and worthless, and despair of getting help from her. She will focus on real or perceived qualities in the therapist that she despises in herself. The therapist's ability to remain steadfast in her own self-esteem without retaliation toward the client creates space for the client to examine her contempt and observe a woman who is neither a victim nor an abuser.

Internalized Misogyny

Internalized misogyny is the internalization of cultural misogyny, "the pervasive devaluation of feminine traits and the hatred of women" (Saakvitne & Pearlman, 1993, p. 247). As we explore our clients' internalized misogyny, we must examine our own internalized negative beliefs about women and femaleness. Clues to these beliefs include distancing ourselves from the client, colluding with her denigration, imposing our different values, dissociating or ignoring her self-debasement, or joining with her self-ridicule. It is painful and sometimes enraging to hear the learned contempt unconsciously parroted by our clients toward themselves. Our responses will be informed by our own conscious and unconscious beliefs about women, and by our response to this particular woman client. As we invite each of our female clients to notice and know what she believes about women, we must have the courage to examine our own beliefs and feelings. When we ask her about her feminine ego ideal, what kind of a woman she wants to be, we must examine our own ego ideals and their sources.

It can be extraordinarily difficult to witness the intense self-loathing and hatred of their own femininity expressed by many adult female incest survivors. Their often bitter recriminations, scathing devaluation, and physical and psychological self-attacks place the therapist as a helpless witness to a brutal misogynist assault. When we comment and invite the client's observation on this process, we interrupt the unspoken reenactment. When we say, "I see it differently," we introduce an alternative viewpoint and force the unconscious, automatic assumptions to be noticed and named. By bringing the misogyny into awareness, we can also work with our client to understand the function of this contempt and self-hatred. What are the alternatives? What does she fear even more? How did her femaleness become the target, and is another part of her being protected by this strategy? When "femaleness" represents childhood, sexuality, emotional dependence, or the experience of having a feeling, then hating or denying femaleness may be safer than facing the knowledge of trauma and loss.

Female Therapist-Male Client

The socialized balance of power is reversed in the female therapist-male client pairing. When the male client is also a survivor, this reversal is compounded. If unconscious of these dynamics, the female therapist may attempt to restore the balance by deferring to the client around issues of frame, by not exploring the sexual abuse material adequately for fear of shaming him, by treating him more as a friend or colleague than as a client, or by becoming flirtatious with him. Male clients whose perpetrators were women will hold complicated feelings about the female therapist, who in turn may withdraw, feel confused or angry at the client, or act punitively or seductively toward him as part of an unconscious reenactment of the abuse.

Gender-dominated countertransferences between female therapists and male survivor clients are complicated and easy to overlook. Male clients may feel enormous shame in telling a female therapist about the occurrence and the details of sexual abuse, and the therapist can respond in a complementary way in her wish to protect the male from shame. This protection can take the form of conscious or unconscious deferments to reaffirm his power and status in the therapy relationship or to deny the inherent power of the therapist because she is female and fears emasculating the client. She may respond aggressively or contemptuously to his shame. Alternatively, the therapist may respond to the client's defensive aggression or sexuality in a stereotypical way by flirting or feeling flattered or intimidated.

When a male survivor client experiences shame and rage at himself for being vulnerable to victimization, he may become enraged at the therapist because she elicits his feelings of need and yearning for caretaking. She may react with fear and have difficulty assessing real and fantasied threats expressed by male clients. If the therapist is frightened, intimidated, or shamed by his rage and contempt, she loses the opportunity to work through with him his defensive patterns and disavowed longings. To the extent that the female therapist holds stereotypes and wishes for male strength and protectiveness, she may be intolerant or judgmental of her male client's dependence and vulnerability, and thus unconsciously collude with his own punitive superego. As a culture, we are more tolerant of a woman's experience of herself as a child than we are of a man's. Women therapists may be uninformed about men's bodies and not know how to help a male client struggle with questions about his body, his genitals, or sexuality.

Female therapists often have difficulty with a male client's romantic or erotic transference. Geller's (1990) research suggests that female therapists feel "de-skilled" by male client's sexualized response. Alternatively, a therapist may feel flattered and empowered by her male client's expressed attraction. They may have difficulty correctly identifying the maternal wish in an eroticized maternal transference, or alternatively deny the erotic and experience their client only as a young child.

Male Therapist-Female Client

For male therapists, the task is complicated in different ways. A female client may look to the male therapist for familiar negative or mixed messages about her worth and loveability as a woman. She may assume the male therapist will require her to sacrifice herself or parts of herself to protect his esteem and power — as her perpetrator(s) and the culture at large has taught her. When a male therapist is unconflictedly supportive of a female client's move toward self-acceptance, she may struggle with confusion or anger as her familiar beliefs are challenged. The therapist's capacity to take delight in his client developing a positive sense of self as a woman is a powerful component in the therapeutic holding environment. His support for a female client's quest for knowledge and personal power inherently mitigates against a culture that denies both.

In addition to patterns we have already discussed, there are additional pitfalls in trauma therapies with male therapists and female clients. Men who become therapists and work with trauma survivors are often exquisitely attuned to issues of gender socialization and inequalities. Because many survivor clients are women who were sexually abused in childhood by men (Herman, 1981), male therapists may feel guilty and ashamed by association and struggle with feelings of culpability and defensive anger at the same time. This response can reflect "guilt by association" or a countertransference pressure to accept empathically the client's displacement of anger toward her perpetrator(s) onto all men (Adler, 1993). These feelings can interfere with the therapist's openness to hear his client's anger or fear, or it can make him cautious and apologetic. In the latter case, the therapist can mistakenly treat transference anger and blame as fact, and fail to explore and analyze the transferential context.

Male therapists may feel guilty for their own manliness. In the face of a negative transference to himself as a man, a male therapist may feel he has two choices: to abandon his strength and assertiveness and stop being "a man," or abandon his nurturant therapist self and become aggressive and invulnerable. Male therapists may feel compassionate, maternal, or care-taking paternal feelings, but continue to receive a negative paternal-perpetrator transference and feel frustrated in their ability to soothe and care for a vulnerable client. Female clients who have been sexually abused by men often experience immediate and strong transferences to the male therapist as a perpetrator, or counterphobically, as a conquest to be wooed, seduced, and thus controlled in order to ensure safety.

Female clients may hold a dual expectation in therapy with a male thera-pist; one the one hand, they expect him to reenact abuse and boundary violations experienced in the original abuse and perhaps in other power relationships with previous therapists, teachers, bosses, or medical person-nel. On the other hand, they may expect and hope that this time it will be different. The latter wish will lead to numerous tests. The therapist will be asked to prove that he is indeed a good therapist and a trustworthy person, who is also male (Adler, 1993).

Early in the therapy, the male therapist may receive conflicting messages from the client and at the same time be preoccupied with having to prove that he is not a perpetrator, but a "good guy," and "an innocent man." In the service of boundary clarity, male therapists may unwittingly be rejecting and shaming in response to maternal transferences or the client's infantile longings. The client may hold an authority transference and expect the therapist to be in control and know what is going on, an impossible task in the midst of these complicated unfolding dynamics. Male therapists may feel at a loss to understand certain aspects of their female clients' experience (for example, women's bodies, their interpersonal or sexual experiences). Requiring himself to know inhibits the therapist's freedom to ask without feeling voyeuristic, to learn from his woman client what he needs to know in order to be helpful to her. If a therapist expects himself to be an expert, this inevitable dilemma can evoke shame and feelings of inadequacy, which lead to difficult countertransference responses.

Male Therapist-Male Client

There are unique countertransference issues in this pairing as well as those that are common to other pairings (Meth et al., 1990). Male clients often expect contempt from male therapists for their current feelings and past victimization (Mac Ian, 1992). The male therapist may unwittingly minimize the child victim's vulnerability in his need to deny the realities of the sexual abuse of boys. For the nonsurvivor male therapist, feelings of survivor guilt and fear may be transformed into oversolicitous behavior or pity or contempt for the male victim. An overuse of psychoeducation in a therapy may reflect the therapist's defensive move to more intellectualized interventions in avoidance of conflictual affective or instinctual gender related material (likewise the client's repeated request for information or education can reflect the same dynamic).

Male therapists often have difficulty with the imagery of the sexual abuse, specifically anal rape, of young boys. In addition, the therapist may fear both vicarious traumatization through empathic listening to details of abuse, and direct traumatization when his client turns passive into active and literally or symbolically attacks and tries to dominate the therapist. The aggression and violence of male rape stirs deep and primitive fears and feelings in the therapist. If these feelings are conscious, the therapist can use them to identify his needs for protection and to recognize interpersonal dynamics in the relationship. If the fears and defenses against them remain unconscious, neither therapist nor client has protection, and the therapeutic relationship loses the resource of his countertransference analysis.

Male therapists bring the same gender role stereotypes into the therapy with male survivor clients as female therapists do. These can be further complicated by the therapist's identification with or need to distance from the client's experienced vulnerability. Alternatively, a male therapist may be frustrated with his client's need to deny vulnerability to the male therapist, the repeated reenactment of gender role stereotypes of male bonding through aggression that relies on denial of feelings of dependence and vulnerability. Men who are drawn to the profession because they value their capacity for connection and compassion may identify with a client's vulnerability or be uncomfortable with his aggression and socialization into traditional male roles.

The deeply inbred homophobia of the culture can lead both male clients and therapists to fear and reject feelings of warmth and closeness to one another. Jacobs (1991) and Gabbard (1994a) have described the countertransference denial and distancing from male clients' maternal transference and yearning that result from the therapist's conflicts about his own yearning and feelings of vulnerability.

Whether the client expresses the transference directly or indirectly, whether infused with aggression and/or erotic material, the therapist's anxiety and discomfort can lead him to empathic failure and unconscious reenactments of emotional abandonment and rejection if he has not examined his conflicts. When men are taught to idealize power and control, the inevitable power structure of the therapy situation can evoke masochistic and sadistic dynamics in either or both participants. Male stereotypes emphasize that physical strength and achievement, restricted affect (except anger), avoidance of intimacy with same sex peers, and action-oriented models of aid (Pleck, 1981) work against the psychotherapeutic process. The therapy may need to begin with the unlearning of these assumptions.

Gender of Perpetrator

Another factor in gender-related countertransference is the therapist's response to the gender of the perpetrator. Same-gender therapists may be sensitive to perpetrator transferences earlier in the therapy and may become defensive or overanticipate the transference. Different-gender therapists may assume they will not be experienced as dangerous and may feel taken aback or injured when the client exhibits fear of them.

While sex role stereotypes have led us to downplay or to accept as inevitable men's abuse of children, as a society and as a field we tend to deny sexual abuse of children by women. We often experience complicated countertransference responses to female perpetrators of sexual abuse against children, responses informed by our powerful and early beliefs about mothers and mothering. It is more disturbing to face the capacity for cruelty and exploitation in the gender that is identified as responsible for child-rearing. Biological and psychological theories asserting women's inherent capacity for caretaking and nurturance have been further romanticized and elaborated culturally and hold central positions in our collective psyches. Our horror at maternal caretaking gone awry can have a powerful impact on our responses to survivors of maternal abuse.

Finally, although the literature is growing (Banning, 1989; Elliott, 1994; Finkelhor & Russell, 1984), there is less written about female (or maternal) than male perpetrators of child sexual abuse. There are many possible explanations for this silence. It may reflect the possibilities that women are less likely to abuse children sexually than are men, that female sexual abuse of children may be more covert, and that our cultural reluctance to acknowledge this abuse is even greater than our reluctance to acknowledge incest in general.

EROTIC OR SEXUAL RESPONSES IN THE THERAPEUTIC RELATIONSHIP

Therapists often are particularly uncomfortable with erotic and voyeuristic countertransference responses in these therapies. Yet the content of trauma material often arouses fascination both because of the power of the cultural taboo against incest and the sadomasochistic fusion of sexuality and aggression. This fascination can feel ego-dystonic to the therapist. In addition, clients' affective material can include unmodulated instincts and strong "primitive" desires for gratification, possession, and entitlement that connect with the therapist's unacknowledged or disavowed feelings. While the research of Pope and his colleagues (Pope & Bouhoutsos, 1986; Pope, Keith-Spiegel, & Tabachnick, 1986) normalizes sexual countertransference feelings in therapists, many therapists feel confused and ashamed of these feelings. In particular, with incest survivor clients, feelings of sexual arousal can stir guilt, shame, confusion, or horror, especially when the arousal occurs in response to stories of abuse. Davies and Frawley (1994) emphasize the inevitable yet discomforting responses of arousal therapists have to clients' erotization of fear, learned in childhood experiences of sexual abuse.

Another realm of countertransference is the therapist's response to overtly or covertly erotic material and transference dynamics. This erotic material includes clinical material or interpersonal behavior that elicits sexual or romantic feelings in the therapist. One task is to understand the source of the therapist's feelings to distinguish the therapist's needs and projections from the client's needs, fantasies, and transference. The therapeutic relationship is an intimate relationship in which many strong feelings of attachment, love, attraction, and infatuation are likely to emerge. The therapeutic goal is to create a safe, bounded relationship in which the client's feelings can be named and understood without shame or danger of enactment. This can be a difficult task for the therapist for a variety of reasons. Therapists are rarely prepared for the intensity of these feelings and often feel embarrassed, awkward, or anxious about their responses and consequently are reluctant to discuss them in supervision or with colleagues. Being the recipient of such strong feelings can bring up the therapist's own longings, relationship needs, or romantic ideals.

Therapists need to be respectful of various forms of love, sexuality, and connection and make the therapeutic space safe for all feelings and fantasies, with a clear understanding that feelings can be spoken but not acted upon and that fantasy is a thought, not an action. A major goal of psychotherapy with survivors of childhood sexual abuse is the opportunity to claim and reclaim split-off and denigrated aspects of themselves, including their desire (Ehrenberg, 1987), passion, sexuality, and their own complex capacity to love and connect with another person.

Hearing clients' tender feelings in the context of their early betrayals and violations strengthens the therapist's wish to respond differently and supportively. When these strong feelings are toward a same-sex therapist, both client and therapist may struggle with their homophobia, arousal, confusion, and fears. Therapists can deny their affectionate and erotic responses, move to a cognitive intervention, shore up a boundary, or strive to "cure" the client's dependence. Some therapists will pathologize a homoerotic transference, or precipitously assume and interpret a causal relation to childhood sexual abuse. Gabbard (1994c) describes his analytic work with a young man who spoke at length of his aggressive sexual fantasies about the therapist. However, when they explored the maternal longings represented by the wish to suck his therapist's penis, and the client broke into painful sobs, Gabbard noted his own intense anxiety and embarrassment and impulse to redirect the client. He could more easily accept nonloving aggressive sexuality, than his client's (and his own) painful yearning and wish for love.

When a client's erotic wishes are sadistic and hurtful, when a client's self-destruction or aggression is eroticized, or when the client's attachment is through conflict and hurt, the therapist's countertransference response is often significant. The fusion of sexuality and aggression is inevitable when a child learns about his or her sexuality through exploitation and pain. For the therapist, the reemergence of this fusion can be personally painful, historically familiar or unfamiliar, and anxiety-provoking because it inevitably evokes primitive and forbidden fantasies and powerful feelings. Again, this material and the therapist's responses can be particularly difficult to bring to consultation or supervision and yet cannot be sorted out alone because the potential for confusion of the client's and therapist's unconscious material is too great. The therapist's anxiety and arousal serve as a marker for the need to talk about the particular therapeutic relationship.

Same-Sex Erotic and Affectional Attachment

Whether or not either therapist or client is lesbian, gay, or bisexual, the cultural taboos against same-sex erotic and affectional attachments invade the therapeutic relationship. These prohibitions can emerge in countertransference denial or discomfort with affectionate or erotic feelings in the therapy. The cultural taboo and requirement of silence and secrecy about homosexuality create a parallel between sexuality and incest dynamics, noted by many gay and lesbian clients. As one client mused, "Being secret about my sex life is familiar. It has always been secret, but sometimes it is confusing. Is my love now wrong the way the incest was wrong? Is it hurting me? Can I trust my experience?"

While psychological and biological literature is clear that humans are inherently bisexual (Blumenfeld, 1992; Boston Lesbian Psychologies Collective, 1987; Kus, 1990; Masters & Johnson 1966; Money, 1987), that fact is neither taught nor accepted in most therapists' training, and therapists often have few if any ways of understanding and managing either their own or their clients' anxiety and confusion.

We believe that a therapist who is not familiar and comfortable with her or his bisexuality will be limited clinically and subject to problematic countertransference in therapeutic work with survivors, as well as with any gay, lesbian, or bisexual client.

Issues for Gay and Lesbian Therapists with Survivor Clients

Gay, lesbian, or bisexual therapists may struggle with another level of anxiety with erotic or eroticized material from same-sex clients. They may be listening for coming out themes or worried that their client is responding to clues from them.* This anxiety can emerge in countertransference responses that shut down the exploration of the complicated affectional and erotic longings.

Because sexual abuse is a gendered event and because clients and therapists alike carry into the therapy conscious and unconscious conflicts about gender and sexuality, special attention to gender-related countertransference responses is important. With awareness, these dynamics can inform and enrich the therapeutic process. We believe that psychotherapy provides an invaluable opportunity for a survivor to heal and reclaim her or his right to a positive identity as a woman or man. The therapist's greater awareness of personal and social gender dynamics will enhance her clinical work on gender identity.

*For discussion of therapist decisions about disclosure of sexual orientation, see chapter 7.

10

Therapeutic Impasses
with Survivor Clients

IT IS CLEAR from the chapters thus far that psychotherapy with survivor clients is complex and emotionally charged work. These psychotherapies require therapist and client to experience intense and difficult emotions, to remain connected through complicated transference and countertransference reactions, enactments, and interactions, and to move forward through memories and knowledge that stir deep fears and wishes. Managing the evolving demands of these therapies requires flexibility and responsiveness from the therapist which are difficult to sustain without serious lapses. At times, these lapses can cause the therapy to become stuck or reach an impasse. This experience is painful, frustrating, and potentially shaming for both therapist and client.

Therapeutic impasses by definition indicate a feeling of being stuck, of being unable to progress or move forward on the part of therapist, client, or both. Feeling stuck often challenges the identity and esteem of a therapist; it is understandable that impasses consistently evoke strong countertransference responses. Therapeutic impasses are difficult and can last for a prolonged period of time. Their resolution demands our most intuitive and creative work at a time when we may be feeling most ineffective and depleted. Yet the successful resolution of a therapeutic impasse can be the nexus of a transformative experience for both client and therapist (Ehrenberg, 1992; Elkind, 1992). For a survivor, the experience of working through a relational impasse can begin to alter her automatic and deep despair and hopelessness in the face of interpersonal disappointment.

WHAT IS A THERAPEUTIC IMPASSE?

In her excellent book on resolving therapeutic impasses, Elkind (1992) identifies three categories of therapeutic impasse that can lead to ruptured therapies or terminations. The first emerges when there is a mismatch between therapist and client on any of several relevant dimensions, including gender, theoretical orientation, age, personalities, empathic capacities, or core vulnerabilities. The second two are particularly relevant in psychotherapy with adult survivors of childhood sexual abuse. The second category she dubs a stalemate, when the therapist and client become entrenched in a repetitive pattern of relating that ultimately precludes therapeutic movement and working through. Elkind's third category of impasse is that in which the client or therapist is wounded by one another in an area of "primary vulnerability."

> When patients are wounded in an area of primary vulnerability by their therapist, or when therapists are wounded in an area of primary vulnerability by their patients, painful impasses can ensue. Therapists, thrown off by the intense and seemingly extreme responses of their wounded patients, are in danger of responding to the patients in a manner that creates an additional level of wounding and places the therapeutic relationship in jeopardy. . . . When therapists feel devalued and discounted, their capacity to empathize with their patients is thwarted because their psychological energy is directed toward the preservation of their sense of therapist-self, and their need for empathic understanding and appreciation is heightened. (p. 11)

Schwaber (1993) emphasizes that therapeutic impasses can take several forms, some dramatic and some quiet. She asks, "How is it experienced and by whom?" Sometimes only the therapist or only the client feels at an impasse. Sometimes both feel stuck, and sometimes neither is aware that they are participating in a therapeutic dance in which a core theme persists, unnoticed and unattended, between them. Jacobs (1991) stresses that therapeutic impasses can come about when the therapist is unable to notice her own conflicts and defenses and the ways they affect the therapeutic relationship. He emphasizes the necessity of humility and ongoing self-analysis for the therapist and maintains that if therapists are willing to learn, their clients will teach them to become the therapist they need them to be.

Stiver (1992) has defined therapeutic impasse as an experience, held by therapist and client over a protracted period of time, in which client and therapist feel disconnected from one another and do not know how to reconnect. An impasse can be reflected in a period of unmitigated despair, anger, or frustration on the part of either client or therapist. At times, a client can seem to remain in the same psychological place over a long period of time, repeating complaints and hopeless predictions about the future, voicing pessimism about therapy and the possibility of change.

Therapeutic impasses often reflect denied or dissociated aspects of the client, therapist, or therapeutic relationship. Some impasses occur when client and therapist remain connected, but core conflicts are omitted in conscious and unconscious ways by both participants. Thus, they maintain a safe distance but refrain from deepening the connection. This pattern often reflects the dissociation of conflict, negative feelings such as envy or rage, or feelings of longing, love, or sexual attraction. It can reflect an interactive stalemate organized around internalized and projective identities of perpetrator, child victim, and nonprotective bystander (Loris, 1994; Miller, 1994).

An impasse may be evident when a client consistently and constantly feels disappointed in and uncared about by her therapist. The client may become and remain enraged with the therapist, repeatedly pointing out the therapist's mistakes, slights, inattentiveness, and repetitions of the client's painful past experiences. Over time the therapy feels aversive for both participants; the therapist comes to feel beleaguered, defensive, and resentful while the client feels increasingly misunderstood, unheard, angry, guilty, and despairing. Greenson writes, "the insufficiently analyzed negative transference is the most frequent cause of stalemated analysis" (1967, p. 233). In therapy with trauma survivors, negative transferences are often to the therapist as a perpetrator and abuser. Therapists are often uncomfortable exploring this type of negative transferences.

A therapeutic impasse can also be manifest as intractable negative transference, or malevolent transformation. When the client's experience of the therapist as sadistic, exploitive, neglectful, or narcissistic is unmodifiable over time and interpersonal experience, an impasse can ensue. This type of impasse often interacts with the therapist's countertransference to her client's past victimization, leading to attempts to placate or reassure the client. She may try to appease the client, but do so at her own expense, thus behaving in a masochistic manner which can evoke more punitiveness from the client. This pattern creates a reenactment in which the client becomes the perpetrator and the therapist the victim, leaving both in untenable identities. This cycle of aggression, guilt, and masochism is not uncommon (Davies & Frawley, 1991; Kauffman, 1993), but is painful to both participants and destructive to the therapy.

With survivors, an impasse may be evident in repeated reenactments outside the therapy or in client behaviors that undermine the treatment, such as unremitting substance abuse, repeated suicide attempts and rehospitalizations, recurrent medical crises, or invited physical interventions (e.g., invasive medical procedures, plastic surgery, tattooing, or body piercing). Other times, the client or therapist moves into extreme passivity, withdrawal, or distance. This may be obvious or disguised by a pseudoengagement, with sessions filled with repetitive unmutative material and interactions. This phenomenon resembles what Winnicott (1965) describes as "analyses of the false self." Sometimes these therapies seem to teeter eternally on the brink of an impasse, neither reaching a crisis, nor moving into truly productive relational work.

Empirical data support clinical experience on the hardship impasses pose for the therapist. It is well-documented that psychotherapists suffer when clients fail to show observable progress (Deutsch, 1984; Farber & Heifetz, 1982). In response to this distress, therapists have a range of responses — some helpful and others defensive or reactive. When the responsive exacerbate the impasse, both client and therapist can become mired in a swamp of hopelessness and impotence. The 117 psychologists surveyed by Gamble et al. (1994) reported that their trauma clients are more likely than nontrauma clients to engage in a variety of stressful behaviors, and that the therapists generally find these same behaviors more distressing with their survivor clients than non-survivors.

A Framework for Understanding
Therapeutic Impasse

Traditional approaches to failed therapies or therapeutic impasses have emphasized deficits, despair, and intractability.* For the most part they have underemphasized or ignored the interactive, relational process of the therapy, and therefore did not give rise to constructive interactive solutions. Thus, they provide a way out, but no way through.

These approaches have relied on two underlying assumptions: (1) some clients are completely untreatable and (2) if someone is treatable, then any therapist can work effectively with her. The former assumption blames the

*See Finelli (1987) for a review of the literature on negative therapeutic reaction; Wachtel (1982), on resistance; Greenson (1967), on the unanalyzable patient; and Racker (1957), Schafer (1983), and Searles (1979) on underanalyzed countertransference.

client. The latter assumption ignores not only the multifaceted interactions of therapist and client's psychological needs and personality styles, but also the interpersonal complexities inherent in an intensive psychotherapy relationship. We cannot reduce therapeutic impasses to pathology; they must be understood as an interaction of the complicated needs, feelings, beliefs, and psychological and interpersonal styles of two people engaged in a complex, intimate process together.

Alternatively, if we understand therapeutic impasses and resistance in a relational context, we open up the possibility for understanding without blame and processing without shame. This understanding inherently mitigates against the reenactments often at the root of interpersonal impasses, as it is premised on mutual responsibility and a shared goal of therapeutic connection and understanding. Thus, it reconnects us with the essential task of the therapeutic relationship.

Impasses are a result of the developing interactive dynamic of the therapeutic relationship. The working through of the impasse requires mutual examination of the feelings, fantasies, and fears stirred by the present relationship. A relational, constructivist model assumes psychotherapy is a process of connection in which *both* parties are open to insight and change.

Often the resolution of therapeutic impasses turns on the therapist's ability to continue her self-exploration. Clients' material and personhood will awaken in the therapist personal insight, pain, memories, old feelings, and unresolved conflicts. Jacobs (1994) reminds us how difficult change is and how natural resistance is and invites us to consider the inevitable impact of our own resistance on the psychotherapies we conduct.

EFFECTS OF A THERAPEUTIC IMPASSE

While an impasse may arise from various sources and take different forms, the effects of the impasse on the therapist and client are fairly consistent. Both parties can experience feelings of personal failure and a sense of impending loss and disconnection. A therapeutic impasse can evoke despair, in the context of a psychotherapy that represents hope for both the client and the therapist. Not uncommonly, each person wishes to assign blame and to escape the painful dilemma through precipitous action, such as referral, ultimatum, or confrontation. When acted upon, these responses often deepen both the impasse and the individual's shame. Both client and therapist may use the impasse against themselves through self-criticism and self-loathing. The paralysis that ensues as each struggles with her individual pain and frustration can prevent both participants from looking at the relational interaction that is contributing to the impasse.

Frequently both parties enter into the therapeutic relationship with the wish and an illusion that it is possible not to repeat the client's early hurtful relationships. A reenactment leads to an impasse when it remains unrecognized or unanalyzed, or when both parties move into rigid, polarized positions. As the therapeutic relationship inevitably reenacts aspects of early painful relationships, each person may feel a sense of failure, horror, and hurt. These feelings can block a therapeutic examination of both the reenactment, and of the rescue fantasy embedded in the belief that they could avoid such a reenactment. As these dynamics emerge in the therapy, both client and therapist may wish to deny them and their participation in them. This denial may reflect the need to deny certain aspects of the client or the therapist. For some therapists it is especially uncomfortable to hold the dual truth of the client's victimization and sadistic rage. This denial can result in the therapist's failure to set limits on clients' aggression toward her (Davies & Frawley, 1994).

COUNTERTRANSFERENCE FACTORS IN
THERAPEUTIC IMPASSES

Therapeutic impasses that develop in psychotherapy with clients who are survivors of incest and childhood sexual abuse reflect specific interpersonal patterns. For childhood survivors of abuse whose early environment was often one of emotional neglect and insufficient mirroring and holding, the interpersonal situation of the psychotherapy can stir deep, often forbidden, feelings of yearning.

Stiver (1992) describes a pattern in which some clients begin treatment relying on a familiar conciliatory role, with a compliant, other-pleasing interpersonal style. They are cooperative and appreciative and emphasize their respect for and gratitude to the therapist. The therapist is then taken aback when some years into the treatment, she finds herself bogged down in a stalemate in which therapy feels stuck, lifeless, and disconnected. As the relationship develops, the client grows more aware of forbidden yearnings for connection with her real self, her true self. These yearnings may evoke dread in the client, who then becomes more vigilant and withdrawn. The client cannot return to the pseudo-connection of the false self, but neither can she yet move forward to expose her authentic self and the deep yearning and neediness she feels. It is easy to misjudge the interpersonal skills of a client who initially seems to negotiate a relationship effortlessly.

Survivor clients in therapy often connect with or realize their desire for maternal holding, for unconditional love, for soothing touch, for a loving gaze. These feelings, long ago banished, associated with danger and shame, and thus forbidden, emerge into awareness and can be expressed and struggled with in a variety of ways. Some clients become more dependent, and at times demanding; others become more counterdependent and self-hating; and others push the therapist away, angrily feeling exposed and sadistically tormented by their growing attachment and need. The yearning can be experienced as sexualized by survivor clients for whom affectional needs were met in the past with sexual exploitation. A therapist may react with alarm or misinterpret maternal longing, while the client may experience increased levels of terror and rage which neither she nor her therapist may understand.

Because these dependent feelings are conflictual for many survivor clients and therapists, they are often masked by defenses. The therapist's conflicts and defenses can blind her to the client's defensive process. For example, the therapist can too easily accept a client's counterdependent stance without recognizing the dependency needs it serves to deny. She may see only the erotic in an eroticized maternal transference (Saakvitne, 1993c) or alternatively see only the maternal longing without recognizing the eroticized energy. When a client is angry and critical, the therapist can fail to see the underlying fear. Strong emotions in psychotherapy often reflect defenses against painful ambivalence. If the therapist overlooks ambivalence, she colludes with a dissociative process and simply holds the complementary feelings. The closer the client's dependency conflicts are to the therapist's, the more likely the therapist will be to miss the complexity of her client's feelings and defenses against feelings.

Example   One survivor client presented initially as fiercely independent. She had a physical disability, which made routine activities such as walking, driving, and lifting extremely painful, yet she insisted upon a degree of self-reliance that clearly exceeded her physical capacities. The therapist, himself a very independent and self-reliant individual, would only half-heartedly question the client's resistance to asking for or accepting help. His main response to this behavior was one of admiration of the client's determination and willpower. Well into the therapy, the therapist became aware that the treatment was no longer progressing. Through consultation, the therapist understood that the relatively unexplored counterdependency, including the client's shame about her dependency needs, was an impediment to the client's acknowledgment of all of her strong feelings for the therapist, and thus to further progress in the therapy. He realized how closely his own psychological needs and defenses in this realm resembled the client's and was then able to acknowledge with the client why he thought they were stuck: Their similarities had blinded him to something important.

Therapists have several countertransference reactions to the emergence of these feelings. No therapist is immune to yearning for love, soothing, and nurturance, and their clients' wishes will interact with their own wishes, fears, and defenses. To the extent that they deny their own yearning, they can become anxious, resentful, or judgmental in response to their clients' yearning. Male therapists have been socialized to deny maternal cravings and may be particularly uncomfortable accepting and holding these feelings (Gabbard, 1994a; Saakvitne, 1993c).

A therapist may envy her clients for getting what she craves (as she provides it for them) and express that envy through subtle rejection or contempt. The (common) designation of dependent yearnings as "regressive" reflects the discomfort in the field with normal developmental needs. Dependence is a part of connection and a prerequisite for independence. The therapist's conflicts will inform her reaction to clients who comfortably express the needs she denies herself. The therapist may feel greater annoyance, resentment, or self-righteous judgment toward clients whom she experiences as demanding or entitled if their demands reflect those she forbids herself.

As clients reclaim aspects of themselves that have been denied, they bring more complex needs and feelings to the therapy relationship. And as they become more authentic, they ask the same of their therapists. Yet, the therapist may instead withdraw in the face of the invitation to bring herself more fully into the relationship. To the extent that the therapist uses her role to hide or distance herself, the affective immediacy of certain clients will evoke anxiety and retreat. This retreat can in turn evoke in the client fears of abandonment or repetition of old messages that her feelings are too dangerous or intolerable to the therapist, which elicits shame, anger, and despair in the client. When this dynamic is unspoken, it can lead to an impasse in the therapeutic relationship.

Finally, sometimes a therapeutic impasse emerges based on a client's unspoken assumptions or fears about the therapist. Survivor clients hold powerful fantasies about their power, toxicity, and capacity to deplete their therapist. A client may pull back to protect the therapist without telling her she thinks the therapist is in danger. A client may be angry about her feelings of attachment or about the emergence of hope or of needs she has yet to express. Often after a vacation or separation this anger is elicited as much by the attachment the therapist has evoked as the abandonment of her absence.

Cooperman (1969) notes that a therapeutic impasse can come about when a client responds to the therapist's real distraction or preoccupation. She may feel tricked into caring for or needing the therapist. At other times there can be complex interactions going on within a client's mind between herself and her therapist, unbeknownst to the therapist.

Example   When a therapist asked a client if she were angry at the therapist, the client replied, "No, why would I be angry at you?" In the following session, however, she said, "You were right that I was angry, but you couldn't know why. I was angry because of a conversation I had about you that I haven't told you about and I'm angry because I'm making you a gift that you don't know about." The therapist accurately identified the client's anger but did not have the context for the anger because the interpersonal events had not yet left the intrapersonal space of the client's mind.

Sometimes clients hold specific fears that a therapist will be hurt if they share certain information (e.g., about the actions of a still-threatening abuser or group, such as a cult). They fear they will be hurt if they share their feelings or fantasies or curiosity about the therapist. They may fear they are being perpetrators if they intrude in any way by asking a question or even noticing something about the therapist.

Example   One client became silent and withdrawn for several sessions. After many invitations to notice what had changed in the relationship, she anxiously shared that she had seen her therapist at an event where she assumed her therapist would not want to be seen. The client felt guilty and afraid she had done something wrong and expected to be summarily dismissed from therapy. Her therapist, who had not known her client had seen her outside of session, explored the client's assumptions that she would not want to be seen and the client's fear of becoming intrusive like her abuser.

When the client's strong feelings toward her therapist remain unspoken, it can lead to confusion in the therapist and, in time, to therapeutic impasse.

Example   One therapy felt stuck to client and therapist for many months, although they discussed many concerns in the client's current family and work situation. Eventually the client referred to a "familiar" feeling of fear as she described overhearing an argument at her workplace. At the end of her account, her therapist queried, "Fear is familiar? What are you thinking of?" The client began to disclose previously unmentioned memories of violence in her family of origin. She struggled with shame for betraying a family secret and fear that the therapist would judge her negatively. Subsequently, the treatment moved forward.

It is important that the therapist allow herself to trust her instincts that something is not being spoken, and name this with the client without pushing her. The simple acknowledgment of something not yet spoken can forestall therapist confusion or frustration, client fear and shame, and a therapeutic impasse.

THERAPIST CONTRIBUTIONS TO
THERAPEUTIC IMPASSES

Some countertransference responses to transference can serve to maintain rather than dispel the transference. Unconscious participation in the client's object relational scripts or frameworks can lead to an impasse in which the client feels validated in her belief that all relationships are untrustworthy, and the therapist feels guilty and simultaneously wronged. The therapist's intrapsychic defensive style, resources for interpersonal relationships, and salient needs for esteem, intimacy, trust, control, and safety can contribute to the development of a therapeutic impasse or create blindspots to her own self-analysis as she tries to unravel an impasse.

The client's manner of expressing affect will interact with the therapist's style of managing affect. If the client's affects and their intensity are anxiety-provoking or intolerable to the therapist, she will automatically turn to her repertoire of defenses to cope. When strong primitive affects are disturbing or disorganizing to the therapist, she will have difficulty hearing her client's murderous rage, oral incorporative fantasies, primitive envy, and sadistic retaliatory wishes. She may interpret, pathologize, silence, or refer the client or use projection, denial, dissociation, intellectualization, or any of a range of other psychological defenses as self-protection. For example, when a client's envious rage toward a sibling stirs a therapist's unresolved forbidden childhood wishes, she may act psychologically to rid herself of the conflict, potentially at the client's expense.

Another factor with survivor clients is that the therapist is often one of many, the most recent in a long succession of treatments. Many of these clients have been failed repeatedly by the mental health system. While some have been helped, others have been labeled, pathologized, restrained, medicated inappropriately, misunderstood, contradicted, blamed, and abused. The therapist's motivation to be helpful is increased by her perception of the client's prior experiences. In that context, a therapeutic impasse can evoke greater anger, cynicism, and despair from the client and perhaps guilt, pain, or a wish to blame the client from the therapist.

Therapist-Client Fit

The fit between a given client and therapist is determined by certain fundamental psychological and interpersonal characteristics, including each individual's tolerance for affect, defensive style, salient psychological needs, world view, and basic ways of relating to self and others. Elkind (1992) provides an excellent overview of issues of fit between therapist and client. Here we explore aspects of fit that are especially relevant to therapeutic impasse with survivor clients.

Elkind (1992) proposes that the interaction of a client's and therapist's particular areas of personal vulnerability can lead to a therapeutic impasse, as each person scrambles to protect herself from the interpersonal danger represented by the relationship at a given time. A common version of this dilemma occurs with a client who fears and expects disappointment or rejection from the therapist. When the client experiences or suspects a betrayal, she may try to cover her hurt with anger and attack the therapist. To the extent that the therapist may struggle with esteem issues, she may fear to acknowledge her imperfections and consequently become increasingly defensive and then critical of the client. The two parties then become entrenched in their self-protective positions and repeatedly reenact each other's worse fear. Elkind writes,

> I emphasize the importance of recognizing the therapist-in-the-patient and the patient-in-the-therapist because . . . predicaments in therapeutic relationships have the best chance of being worked with constructively when the strengths and vulnerabilities of both participants . . . are acknowledged and explored. A major challenge facing the profession consists of finding constructive ways of including the vulnerabilities of psychotherapists, without discrediting their capacity to help patients, as well as those of patients in understanding the experiences that occur within the therapeutic relationship. The most problematic impasses, woundings, and ruptures occur when patients' and therapists' vulnerabilities intersect in problematic ways. (p. 3)

Elkind's concept of primary vulnerabilities is rooted in developmental theory. She posits that these vulnerabilities stem from our earliest relationships and attachment experiences; these vulnerabilities then provide a lens through which the individual perceives herself and her relationships.

Elkind argues that the popular notion that therapists are bastions of good psychological health, "'good object' healers," has proved to be a serious disservice to patients and therapists alike. As long as we operate under the illusion that therapists are inherently healthy and interpersonally and intrapsychically unconflicted, we fail to equip ourselves to examine the reality of the psychotherapeutic process. It is important to look at real points of disconnection. We cannot always understand our clients perfectly. Of course, our own blind spots, conflicts, perspective, and experiences will affect how we hear and understand our clients' experiences. In fact, a therapist does not know when she meets a new client how this client will touch her, how the relationship will elicit her vulnerabilities, or how their connection will change her.

The therapist cannot become someone else for her clients. She must acknowledge, to herself and at times to the client, who she is and how that affects her response to this client. This both validates a client's experience of differences and models a self-respectful way of acknowledging limitations and differences without having to shame or blame either party.

Example   One long-term survivor client asked her therapist to be "more real" with her. Over time, it became clear that the client wanted the therapist to hug her, to share more personal anecdotes in the therapy, and in other ways to do things that were not comfortable, theoretically or personally, for this therapist. Initially the therapist attempted to resolve this issue by exploring the meanings and history of the client's expressed needs, discussions which perplexed and annoyed the client. This led to much discussion about whether they could continue to work together, much frustration on the part of the client, and a good deal of self-examination and feelings of inadequacy on the part of the therapist. Eventually, during one of these discussions, the therapist told the client, "I'm a fairly reserved person, and it feels like you're asking me to behave in a way that isn't really comfortable for me." This acknowledgment settled the client's anxiety related to these discussions, and in fact gave the client what she was asking for at a deeper level: a more "real" therapist.

COUNTERTRANSFERENCE RESPONSES TO THERAPEUTIC IMPASSES

Therapeutic impasses are particularly painful in psychotherapy with childhood sexual abuse survivors. The wishes to provide a context for healing and to avoid repeating painful betrayals and hurts from the past can make a therapist feel greater guilt and pain during a therapeutic impasse. Impasses with survivor clients are more often accompanied by a malevolent transference, which can be deeply distressing to the therapist. If the therapist does not see the impasse as part of the therapeutic process, she can lose the hope and belief that she and her client will work it through together, and will then be most vulnerable to despair.

The therapist caught with a client in a prolonged period of impasse may feel like a failure or a perpetrator, become bored or angry with the client, or resent the client for wanting something the therapist feels she cannot give. She may dread sessions with the client, and feel guilt, shame, and intense self-doubt or self-loathing. These feelings can lead to changes in the therapist's behavior, including emotional withdrawal or sleepiness in sessions, missing or being late for appointments, failing to return phone calls, and making mistakes in billing. If the therapist feels primarily guilty, the billing errors will tend to favor the client, or she may become apologetic with the client, fail to hold time boundaries adequately, agree to meet with the client outside of sessions, and so forth. When resentful, a therapist may find herself making billing errors in her own favor or charging for missed sessions or phone calls when she had not done so previously or doing so with insufficient processing. When frustration and anger are primary, the therapist may use sarcasm, be harshly critical or judgmental, yell at the client, terminate the treatment inappropriately or prematurely, blame the client, or harm the client in other significant ways with impulsive or inappropriate actions.

A therapist who is a partner in a blocked therapy may become overactive. Anxiety and a wish to change the current stalemate can result in overuse of adjunctive approaches including hypnosis, medication referrals, group therapy, creative arts therapies, hospitalization, or referral to self-help groups, all locating the problem in the client. Adjunctive treatments must be chosen because of their specific value for the client, not as an antidote to a therapeutic impasse.

ADDRESSING THERAPEUTIC IMPASSES WITH SURVIVOR CLIENTS

As a therapist recognizes a potential or existent impasse, she needs to contextualize it within the events of the therapeutic relationship, and add to that understanding her own self-analysis to understand her contributions to the unfolding process. She can then bring this process back into the therapeutic relationship and suggest that together she and her client try to sort out the personal and interpersonal contexts for their current dilemma. There are two grounding principles for working through the impasse:

1. The therapist must remain genuine, authentic, and honest without shaming, blaming, or being condescending to the client.
2. The therapist must stay within the frame of therapy.

Example   A therapist noticed her client seemed to be significantly more withdrawn, quiet, and unresponsive in several sessions. The therapist had been away on several occasions over the previous months and felt guilty about the unusually high number of absences. She neglected to address the client's withdrawal until a supervisor explored her inattention. She then realized she was afraid she would invite the client's expression of hurt and anger about her abandonment, and thought that hearing these feelings from her client would remind her of her own mother's manner toward her as she separated and left home: critical, guilt-inducing, and pathetic. When she raised both the client's withdrawal and her absences with the client, she felt able to hear the client's anger and sadness without personalizing it and could then acknowledge the hardship imposed by her frequent absences on the client and on the therapy.

COUNTERTRANSFERENCE DISCLOSURE IN THE FACE OF THERAPEUTIC IMPASSE

The emphasis on noticing and using countertransference throughout this volume underscores the psychotherapeutic endeavor as a mutual process. It may involve risk for the therapist who relinquishes the role of expert, and is left to sit with what she does not know and with her human fallibility. The therapist's choice to speak her affective and associative experiences acknowledges that both parties are in the process of understanding the client's experience in its full context. In that work, both can be bewildered and uncertain and have a range of feelings. This humility, while freeing the therapist from the burdens of unrealistic expectations, also opens the door to greater anxiety and confusion. It does not mean she deprives herself of her real knowledge and skills, but that she simply recognizes their limits and acknowledges the client's wisdom about herself. Because countertransference disclosure, the process of sharing one's associations and feelings in a considered way with the client, reaffirms the mutual goal and the relationship, it can increase the likelihood a therapist and client can work through a therapeutic impasse.

The therapist's choice to bring her countertransference response back into the relationship is a powerful relational action. It models for the client the interpersonal frame and context of the therapy and can mitigate against historically familiar dichotomous models of conflict negotiation. For therapists, the experience of being caught in a therapeutic impasse can deepen their respect for and appreciation of the importance of the therapeutic relationship.

The expression of affect can allow a therapist to connect empathically with the client and reconnect with her own humanity which can be powerful for both therapist and client. The therapist's expression of feelings also serves to normalize strong feelings and to model appropriate affective responses to painful events. Often the therapist's acknowledgment of the pain of the impasse, the feelings of loss of connection, can begin to bridge the chasm of indifference the client may fear, assume, or experience.

Example   A client asked a therapist a question about her personal life that the therapist decided not to answer. The client felt deeply hurt. Although the therapist had discussed her reasons for not answering the question, both personal and theoretical, the client focused on her experience of being treated as "less than." After many sessions spent processing the interaction, the client started a session expressing her ongoing anger and hurt. The therapist felt angry and unappreciated because she had struggled to decide how to respond to the question and spent several sessions processing it with the client. Yet, as she responded to her client she found herself unexpectedly moved to tears as she said, "It's painful to hear that you feel I treated you disrespectfully. It's very important to me to treat you with the respect you deserve." The client noted her strong feelings and struggled to make sense of the evidence that her therapist cared about the relationship and the quality of the relationship.

Countertransference disclosure occurs within the frame of the therapy where the mutual goal is the client's healing. However, disclosure is not without hazards. Maintaining the frame includes not only observing boundaries and roles, but also keeping in mind the task of the therapy. A therapeutic impasse can cause either member of the therapy dyad to lose sight of the goal or task of the therapy. It is particularly important to remain focused on the purpose of the relationship and the work, that is, to examine and understand together the client's experience in the world with the hope of expanding the client's inner and external resources and ability to pursue her dreams. In an impasse, both client and therapist can lose sight of the need for reflection and feel a press toward action, or agree to redefine the therapeutic task as reparenting, avoiding reenactments, solving problems, or supporting the client in her daily life, without examining her experience. Too often with survivor clients this enactment takes the form of both parties implicitly agreeing that the therapist should compensate for the client's earlier losses (Davies & Frawley, 1994). If the frame is lost, the work becomes stalemated, caught in the convergence of contradictory goals and roles. Maintaining the frame at these times requires not rules, but rather attending to the meaning of the relationship structure and the assumptions underlying the negotiations of the relationship. It is also essential that the therapist be aware of the potential to punish or neglect her client in the service of "being genuine." She should not express anger in sadistic or punitive ways under the guise of authenticity.

Example   A therapist realized she had been stuck in a particular therapy. She entered the next session determined to do things differently. She opened the session by stating that she was angry and frustrated. She listed all the signs of a therapeutic impasse, pointed out the client's self- and therapy-defeating behaviors, and concluded with an ultimatum. She conceptualized this intervention as countertransference disclosure and felt she was being real. Immediately after she finished, the therapist felt assertive and relieved to have spoken her feelings, but gradually she became aware of a profound disconnection from her client, who had shrunk into her chair and grown silent. The therapist invited her client to speak what she was feeling. The client expressed fear, confusion, hurt, and shame. She said she felt like the therapist had said that everything in the therapy was the client's fault and that it was up to her to fix it or leave. She felt blamed and overwhelmed. The therapist realized she had abandoned the relationship to dump her frustration and shame about the impasse. She responded, "You're right. I did blame you and it's not that simple. I'm sorry. I want to be helpful to you and I am frustrated and worried because I don't think I'm doing that very well. I guess I wanted an easy answer to make the problem go away, but it's our problem to look at together. Let's try again."

CONSULTATION

Consultation is a powerful tool for working through a therapeutic impasse. Stiver (1992) notes that one function of consultation is the introduction of a third person whom both members of the therapy can trust. When the therapist has lost sight of her hope and her confidence in the process, she will need help through consultation in order not to repeat the abandonment of the client and to renew her trust in the work of psychotherapy. This may require work and consultation on these feelings before the therapist shares them with the client.

Elkind (1992) notes that the ongoing availability of a consultant may serve as an anchor for a survivor client who may periodically need outside assistance in checking out whether the therapist is trustworthy and whether the client is unknowingly allowing herself to be abused. The therapist's suggestion that a consultation with a third party may be useful reminds the survivor client that this relationship is not secret, and that the therapist is interested in working with the client to find help. A consultation can also serve to dilute the transference or countertransference when they have become intractable at a given point in the work. The experience of a compassionate, nonblaming listener can begin to heal both members' experiences of disconnection. The therapist's openness to consultation provides a model for the client of the possibility of availing oneself of multiple resources for getting help. Working through an impasse generally takes time. The therapist, the client, or the pair may meet with the consultant a few times over the course of some weeks or months.

TRANSFERENCE AND COUNTERTRANSFERENCE IMPEDIMENTS TO WORKING THROUGH A THERAPEUTIC IMPASSE

Potential transference impediments to the resolution of a therapeutic impasse include terror and despair. Therapist contributions to difficulties in resolution include feeling shame, losing perspective, and sharing in the client's despair.

The quality of a client's acute distress, especially her terror, makes the therapeutic task of examining the transferential feelings at times enormously difficult. With survivor clients the therapist must be explicit about safety. That often includes being very direct about what she is not going to do: blame the client, hit, yell, leave abruptly, throw the client out, terminate the therapy precipitously, or give up hope. A consultant or third party may be necessary for the client to examine her terror when it becomes activated in relation to the therapist as perpetrator.

A client's capacity for despair in the face of conflict or interpersonal disappointment is also a significant factor that can impede the resolution of a therapeutic impasse. The therapist holds the concept of healing over time, as well as faith in the process of psychotherapy, in the face of the client's feeling that her despair has no conceivable end. The negotiation of hope and despair is fundamental. Part of the spiritual damage of childhood sexual abuse is the assault on hope. The choice to enter therapy is a defiant act for a person who, as a child, had to give up her hope for protection and nurturance. The therapist's ability to maintain her hope for the client, for the process of psychotherapy, and for the relationship will shift with various personal and countertransference responses.

When the therapist can acknowledge but not share the client's despair, she protects the hope on which the work is built. Kauffman (1993) makes the important point that a therapist can acknowledge her helplessness in the face of an impasse and not also become hopeless. The honest appraisal of the limits of the therapist's control and the belief in the mutual ability of the therapist and client together to work through an impasse is the foundation of this therapeutic work. When a therapist tells her client, "I know this work is difficult, but I have faith in us. We have worked through a lot of difficult things together and we'll figure this one out too," she does not deny the client's distress, but affirms the resilience of the relationship to survive painful feelings.

The therapist's shame for her feelings, actions, or inability to prevent the impasse can lead her to become paralyzed in her thinking, and isolated from sources of help. Her shame can interact with the client's anger or guilt or the client's fears about her toxicity and then crystallize rather than ameliorate the impasse.

When negotiating a conflict that is or may become an impasse, a common pitfall is to become immersed in the content to the exclusion of the process. When caught up in the particulars of the struggle within the impasse, the therapist may fail to see the forest for the trees. The client may have a litany of particular complaints or a focal issue that sets the stage for the impasse; if we remain concretely tied to negotiating the details, we can lose sight of the larger issues and patterns in the current situation. Sometimes, the way out of an impasse is to change the subject; that is, to step back from the immediate conflict to discuss the relational process at work.

Example   One therapist came to realize that it was a warning or a "red flag" whenever she felt overwhelmed with a particular client's many pressing needs, and found herself thinking, "How can we possibly get to all these issues in fifty minutes. Therefore, how can I possibly be of help to this client? But she is in such distress. Maybe therapy isn't what she needs." She and the client came to identify that pattern as a clue that they needed to tend to the relationship. By absorbing the transference of an overwhelmed depleted caretaker, the therapist was picking up on the underlying relational dynamic at work. She would note to her client, "Here we are again. I wonder what is going on in our relationship right now?" She and her client came to realize that these sessions often occurred close to upcoming absences of the therapist, and they were able to discuss the client's fear of being left without her therapist's support.

WHEN SHOULD A THERAPY END
BECAUSE OF AN IMPASSE?

There are times when, in spite of our best efforts, a therapeutic impasse leads to the end of a therapy. There are circumstances in which a therapy should end and a client may need to continue her work with another therapist, perhaps building on work that was done in the current therapy. While consultation is always helpful in assessing this question, there are some general guidelines to follow in considering whether ending the therapy might be the best decision.

1. *A therapy should end when it has become abusive or exploitative.* Any time a therapist is behaving in an abusive manner (e.g., engaging in any sexual contact, being physically inappropriate or harmful, intentionally or unconsciously hurting a client, or using the client to meet her own needs at the client's expense), the therapy relationship should end. If a client is

being physically or emotionally abusive to the therapist and the therapist is unable to set limits to maintain safety, or the client is unable or unwilling to abide by the limits, the therapy should end.

2. *Some countertransference issues can become irresolvable.* When a therapist feels a powerful, unchanging countertransference response to a client that is not modified with examination and analysis, her ability to be open to the client is severely compromised. If the countertransference is sexual, sadistic, or hateful, immediate consultation is indicated, and if the countertransference is unchangeable, the therapy may need to end. If a therapist's identification with a client is too strong, her ability to hear the client's unique truth is compromised and the therapy needs to be assessed for workability.

3. *When there is a problematic fit between the therapist's personality or defensive style and the client or the client's abusive family members, the reworking of old object relational paradigms in the new therapy relationship may not be possible.* When a conflictual transference response is too close to the actual person or circumstances of the therapist, the work of the therapy may be compromised.

Example   A therapist struggling with an addiction felt paralyzed in response to a client's transference to her as an alcoholic father. She recognized the rich and important clinical material, but did not feel comfortable, personally or clinically, sharing her personal circumstances and yet they were present in every session. The therapist acknowledged to the client that because of her own personal issues, she found the herself unable to help the client through some very important processes. Over time she and her client decided that the client needed to work with a different therapist to do the next part of her work. It was a painful decision, but both participants remained connected and able to acknowledge what the relationship could and could not be.

4. *Sometimes a therapist's interpersonal style and a client's needs constantly clash.* It may be that the client cannot tolerate the therapist's authentic self, or vice versa. One of the best general strategies for the therapist attempting to respond to a therapeutic impasse is to become more authentic. As this shift occurs, the client may find herself unable to feel safe or comfortable with a more real, more human therapist. If this conflict is part of an impasse or is magnified as a therapist responds to an impasse and cannot be addressed successfully, it may be a reason to end a treatment. The therapist should discuss this both in consultation and with the client.

Even if a therapy ends in an impasse, it does not have to be a negative ending and it does not have to negate the productive and useful work done nor the importance of the relationship. It can be useful to a client to work on different issues at different times with different therapists. It is not unusual for the process of remembering childhood abuse to occur in stages, or at different times in someone's development. In addition, it is helpful and hopeful for someone who has trusted almost no one to develop multiple trusting relationships. Clients get different things from different therapeutic relationships. It is a new idea for many survivors that a separation does not have to mean that someone was bad and is being punished. Having multiple therapy relationships over time may provide a way for a survivor to establish safety by modulating distance, intimacy, and disclosure in her relationships. At the same time the survivor is enlarging her field of interpersonal resources and the number of safe objects in the world.

THERAPEUTIC IMPASSE AS THERAPEUTIC OPPORTUNITY

A number of authors (Atwood, Stolorow, & Trop, 1989; Ehrenberg, 1992; Elkind, 1992; Maroda, 1991) have noted that a therapeutic impasse is a therapeutic opportunity. It is in these struggles that we often do the central work of the therapy. Our willingness to take part in the struggle in a genuine, personal way also communicates the mutuality of the therapeutic process. In struggling with and surviving a therapeutic impasse, whatever its resolution, client and therapist may experience a strengthening of the therapeutic bond. It is often in this aspect of the work that the concept of therapeutic relationship becomes most relevant and real.

Psychotherapy with survivor clients is often difficult and profoundly moving work and therapeutic impasses are inevitable in most of these therapies. The process of working these through and mutually surviving, growing, and gaining in self-knowledge and safe intimacy is a truly moving experience for both members of the therapeutic relationship.

11

Cotherapists' Countertransference in Group Therapy with Incest Survivors

GROUP PSYCHOTHERAPY with cotherapists creates a unique context for countertransference "a deux." Each therapist's countertransference responses integrate responses to particular clients, to the group as a whole, and to the cotherapist. This chapter emphasizes the unique countertransference dynamics that emerge in the context of incest survivor group psychotherapy with a cotherapist.

THE UNIQUE CONTEXT OF GROUP THERAPY

The healing power of group psychotherapy stems from not only the therapeutic relationship with the therapists, but also from the relationships that develop among group members and within the group itself. Courtois (1988) identifies the development of a therapeutic alliance with other group members as a central component of a positive group therapy experience. This multirelational context is at the heart of the transformative effect of group therapy for survivors.

In group psychotherapy, context, process, and the therapist's role differ from those in individual psychotherapy. The therapy occurs in the *context* of a group of women, two of whom are therapists.* The *process* focuses on noticing interpersonal events in the group, with other members and with the therapists. The *role* of the therapists is to facilitate the connection among the group members and witness those relationships, and to interpret historical themes and group process. In survivor groups, therapists and members serve as witnesses to truths being spoken, to interpersonal risks being taken, and to the members' courage to change and their capacity for compassion and connection.

The therapists listen to each individual member and cull the central group themes and areas for therapeutic work. Group therapists serve as guides and facilitators as often as they engage directly in interpersonal negotiations or transference explorations. Courtois (1988) recommends the therapists function as "content and process observers." They make connections within, between, and among clients and themselves. They connect the clients' experience in the present to events and feelings from the past.

They make connections both within the group and beyond the group to emphasize a societal context for women's experience. Their shared experience as women within the culture connects the therapists to the group in a profoundly meaningful way and influences their countertransference. In addition, each therapist's countertransference will be influenced by her particular relationship with her cotherapist and by the various relationships among group members and between group members and each therapist.

LONG-TERM GROUP PSYCHOTHERAPY FOR INCEST SURVIVORS†

The goal of group treatment for survivors is the enhancement of each member's capacity for positive, respectful relationships with herself and with others. The group provides an opportunity for members to use their relationships with the therapists and one another to understand how their abuse histories have shaped their beliefs about themselves and others, and how these beliefs in turn shape their relationships.

The groups we co-lead are long-term process-oriented groups. We have

---

*Obviously, there are survivor groups for male survivors and male cotherapists. However, both the groups we do and the vast majority of survivor groups are groups for women run by one or two female therapists.
†Our center also offers short-term, theory-based, theme-focused survivor groups, but our experience is with long-term groups. Some (e.g., Herman, 1992) have advised against the use of long-term open-ended groups for uncovering work with trauma survivors. Our experience is different; we have found that the in-depth work on relationships and self that can occur in long-term, process-focused groups is invaluable and not possible in short-term, task-focused groups.

a structural framework,* but the bulk of the group is unstructured and the pace, topics, and themes emerge from the clients' material and the group process. Group process themes include frame issues, boundaries, transitions of membership, communication, connection, and conscious and unconscious processes within the group. Some of the themes that commonly emerge include:

1. When the past is repeated in the present: what is the same and what is different (this includes the impact of prior abusive relationships and their context)
2. The management of anger: what it is and isn't, what its power and limitations are; how each member can use her anger to facilitate relationships, personal safety, and respect
3. Trauma and remembering and not remembering: ways of knowing and holding truth, the nature of traumatic memories, living with doubt and denial
4. Negotiation of relationships, with particular reference to power, control, empowerment, choice, and respect
5. Repetition and reenactments: fears of identification with aggressors, of victimization, of being made a helpless witness, of compulsion, and other forms of helplessness
6. Symptoms and behavior as adaptations to life circumstances in particular developmental contexts: understanding and honoring one's attempts to survive
7. One's relationship to one's own needs, yearning, dependence, and independence

Like many others, we recommend strongly that survivor group therapy be conducted by cotherapists. The interactions among the group members are complex, the affects expressed are intense, and the needs of the individual members and the group as a whole are extensive. The transferences and related countertransference responses are complicated. A cotherapist is a

---

*We start each group with a "check-in" in which we ask each member to speak any thoughts or feelings from last session and to say briefly where she is today. We then identify central themes evident in the check-in process and the group progresses in an unstructured way. During the last 15 minutes of group, we invite each member to say what the group has been like for her that day and what she knows about what she will be needing for herself. This can be something concrete, like a walk in the woods, a bubble bath, or contact with supportive friends, or something more abstract, like being gentle with herself. This model addresses the developmental processes of attachment, connection, and separation inherent in every session.

resource for managing the group's many (and sometimes conflicting) needs, strong affects, complicated dynamics, and concurrent events. This interdependence requires that the cotherapists develop a mutually respectful relationship. Communication is key and their work is enhanced by processing each group before and after sessions. This format allows the cotherapists to notice and understand both individual and shared countertransference responses.

Other Formats

Survivor groups that use other formats will undoubtedly raise some different countertransference and vicarious traumatization issues. Therapists who work in hospital-based groups must deal with a very different set of concerns related to frequently changing membership, boundaries, safety, confidentiality, and the treatment team context. Therapists who do not have the option of working with a cotherapist will face alone the sometimes difficult tasks of holding hope and managing the multiple agendas of the group. Where cotherapists are assigned to a group and to one another, issues of therapist compatibility can create very difficult countertransference responses to the group and its transferences.

Short-term survivor groups also raise different issues for therapists that can be both easier and more difficult to negotiate. On the one hand, because the work is time-limited, it will not become mired in repetition or despair. The work can be focused, intense, and feel satisfying to client and therapist. On the other hand, there is not time to follow up on some issues or to examine in depth the connections within and among group members. It can be difficult to hold an individual's pain without the more intensive relational and historical context available in individual and long-term work. While we do not address all the specific issues of different settings and models of group treatment, many of the clinical and therapist issues discussed below are relevant.

COUNTERTRANSFERENCE IN
THE SURVIVOR GROUP

"Clearly there is no more important phenomenon in group treatment than the leader's countertransference, and there is nothing more deadly than the therapist's failure to recognize and use it" (Ormont, 1992, pp. 11–12). Working as a cotherapist in a group setting can activate particular needs, desires, and fears for the therapists in a way that differs from individual therapies. The shifting identifications and complex associative process to group material, spoken and unspoken, are potent contributors to countertransference responses within and between the cotherapists. In survivor group therapy, countertransference is influenced by three factors:

1. The cotherapy relationship
2. The three levels of group process (the group as a whole, interpersonal relationships within the group, and individual members and their dynamics)
3. The meanings of being a part of a group (of women) as well as therapist to the group

The Cotherapy Relationship

Cotherapy provides one of the few professional opportunities to practice psychotherapy with and in front of a colleague. Most therapists do not work in view of others and many feel reluctant, self-conscious, or anxious about the prospect of being observed in their work. Further, many therapists have more extensive training in individual than group therapy, or in group work but not survivor groups and therefore group therapy for survivors often requires new skills and sensibilities. A therapist for whom group work is new may feel additionally exposed by her cotherapist's presence. A less experienced therapist may feel ashamed or inadequate in front of a more experienced therapist. These anxieties can interact with group dynamics and intensify countertransference responses.

Example   A new therapist joined an ongoing group after a cotherapist left. This therapist had less experience in group psychotherapy than her cotherapist and felt very anxious that she would not measure up or would make mistakes. The group members were predictably angry at her as a new leader and the replacement for the former therapist, whom they valued. She took much of their criticism and seeming indifference to heart and felt that her worst fears about her inadequacy as a therapist were being confirmed. She worked with her cotherapist in consultation to separate the issues of professional development and her understandable anxiety about developing a new working relationship with her cotherapist from the important group dynamics that had far more to do with her role in the group and with the group's history than with her particular style or skill as a therapist. As she separated the various issues, she was better able to withstand the countertransference feelings of incompetence and inadequacy, described by Epstein (1987) as "bad-analyst" or "no-good-analyst" identifications.

Issues of competition, self-doubt, pride, and envy between cotherapists are expectable at times. The therapist's professional identity is often an important source of self-esteem. The literature on cotherapy relationships (e.g., Dick, Lessler, & Whiteside, 1980; Nicholas & Collins, 1992; Winter, 1976) suggests that cotherapists commonly go through predictable stages in the development of their relationship. The first stage revolves around issues of individual self-esteem, shame, and self-consciousness. The second stage resembles the early phase of a marriage, the development of communication and negotiation skills and increased intimacy. The third stage is the establishment of coparenting skills and techniques. These stages parallel the development of the group as well, moving from an individual focus to a cohesive working body. This final stage is the most stable for group members.

Theoretical Compatibility

Experts on cotherapy find that the single most significant factor in cotherapists' compatibility is the consonance of their theoretical styles (Nicholas & Collins, 1992; Paulson, Burroughs, & Gelb, 1976). Courtois (1988) writes,

> Whatever their preferred style, both therapists must coordinate their approach to the treatment so that they are relatively compatible and support one another. They must function as a team to guard against being split into good and bad parents, but their individuality should come through as they engage with the group and its members. (p. 266)

Negotiation of the Cotherapy Relationship

Cotherapy provides a wonderful experience of sharing profoundly difficult yet rewarding work with a colleague. It is a relief to have a collaborator in the task of thinking through and understanding individual and group dynamics. It is helpful and validating to share emotional responses and perceptions of events in a group session. It is a comfort to share responsibility and a joy to share successes. The opportunity for reality testing, hypothesis testing, and collaborative meaning-making is stimulating and educative. We make a point of noting what we liked about each other's interventions after every group. By doing so, we affirm our respect and appreciation for one another's work and can then address problems in the group as a team. This approach has provided us with a secure base for our work as cotherapists.

The cotherapy relationship adds a layer of complexity to the awareness of interpersonal dynamics among group members and of relational and transference dynamics between clients and therapists. Specifically, therapists' ways of managing their relationship with each other influence the clients' sense of safety and trust in the group (McGee & Schuman, 1970). Group members will be sensitive to conflicts between the therapists, and the therapists must address their differences with one another.

Shared and Split Countertransference

At times cotherapists share countertransference; they may share a rejecting countertransference to a challenging client, or a depleted countertransference toward a needy client. They may consciously or unconsciously create a shared defense or identification. For example, to reassure themselves in the face of the clients' pain, anger, grief, and severe symptomatology, cotherapists may unite and create an us-them split. Therapists also join forces to coparent, for example, to feel mutual fascination, protectiveness, or tenderness toward a certain client or the group as a whole. When group clients are particularly angry at one therapist, her cotherapist may feel compelled to rescue her "from the clients," thereby creating an us-them split.

The cotherapists' relationship can rouse protective feelings toward one another. While the cotherapists' connection helps them to hold their clients' pain, as Belle (1982) has pointed out, there are also stresses associated with caring. One may know about specific events or feelings, current or historical, in the life of her cotherapist which are touched by clients' stories or dynamics. If the cotherapists consult about other cases together, they may be aware of other clients outside the group whose stories are echoed by group members' stories. If one knows her cotherapist well enough, she may see strains of a hard day in her face and feel her pain as she is doing a difficult piece of work in the group.

A split countertransference is not uncommon and can be extremely useful; however this phenomenon can also stress a cotherapy relationship. For a variety of reasons, one therapist may feel more connected, protective, or sympathetic toward a particular client. Her cotherapist may feel angry or judgmental toward the same client. The cotherapists' different perspectives can help each therapist sort out aspects of her own countertransference response and identify split-off aspects of the client that may be represented in the partial countertransference. It is enormously helpful when one's cotherapist is *not* having the same response because it allows the therapist some distance to observe herself in relation to this client while allowing the client's needs to be met by the other therapist. When both therapists have the same strong negative countertransference response to a client or a group, consultation can be useful and may be essential.

Therapist Self-Disclosure in Group

Another arena for cotherapist dynamics is that of therapist self-disclosure. Members will pose questions to the therapists at different times in the group. The negotiation of these questions may bring to the fore differences in the cotherapists' clinical, theoretical, or interpersonal styles. They may set a policy with one another regarding certain questions before they arise, but address others as they come up.

Example   One group member, who was repeatedly abandoned in childhood, became very anxious every time either therapist went away. She wanted to know where the therapist was going, whether she was coming back, and what connections the therapist had to ensure her return. The first time the question arose, toward the end of the session before one therapist was to be away, the therapist simply answered, "vacationing in Maine." Later she and her cotherapist agreed that the decision to respond needed further processing with other group members. However, when the other therapist was to be away, she felt uncomfortable because she preferred not to share more information, regardless of the group opinion. Ultimately she decided to reply that she would be away on personal business, which both responded to the group's request for information and set a boundary that the group members respected.

Group members wonder and often ask whether the therapists are survivors. When therapists differ in both their survivor status and in their feelings about self-disclosure, negotiation of this question can be complicated.* We recommend that therapists be consistent within a group about this disclosure; to do so requires that the cotherapists discuss and agree upon an approach ahead of time. It is important for a survivor therapist to feel comfortable sharing this with her cotherapist in order to have the support to acknowledge any particular areas of countertransference vulnerability. In general, cotherapy is intimate work and over the course of discussing the group and processing countertransference responses cotherapists come to know each other in very personal ways. Cotherapists need to negotiate differences in style in a way that is respectful of their individual differences as well as respectful of the group's needs for consistency and partnership between the cotherapists.

Interventions

Balancing the complex and sometimes competing needs of individuals and the group as a whole will highlight differences in the two therapists' styles.

*For further discussion of this question, see chapter 8.

In any moment in group therapy, there are several possible interventions and levels of intervention (Bion, 1961; Fried, 1971). Each therapist's usual style of working may at times conflict with and at times complement her cotherapist's style. A therapist can feel frustrated if she is trying to do a piece of individual work while her cotherapist is moving the focus to the group as a whole. Processing these differences after the session builds colleagueship and strengthens both the cotherapy relationship and each therapist's flexibility in clinical thinking. There are rarely right or wrong technical decisions, but different interventions elicit different group dynamics.

The Three Levels of Group Process

There are three relational levels that determine both clinical interpretations and countertransference responses. The first level is the group as a whole, that is, the shared themes, identity, and unconscious process of the entire group. The second level is the interpersonal relationships that develop within the group, both among group members and between group members and the therapists. The third level includes the individual members' unique intrapsychic processes, needs, and conflicts that will elicit complex responses from the therapists. The needs and circumstances of the group members can be compelling and therapists often feel pulled to address these individual issues. Yet the power of survivor group therapy is in the work on interpersonal relationship and group-as-a-whole themes. These factors are influenced by the developmental stage of the group.

Therapists' Responses to the Group as a Whole

Group formation and identity. The issues related to the formation of a new group and adding members to an existing group relate to the group as a whole. As a group is forming there are common themes of trust, safety, belonging, and the creation of a group identity. In the countertransference, therapists may feel impatient or anxious, and, like the clients, focus on the often compelling content and ignore the necessary and inevitable process of group formation. The most common initial response of new members is "I don't belong here." One client feels her abuse history is not as severe as or is more severe than or in some way very different from others'. Another client worries that she is too old or too young, or the only heterosexual or lesbian member, the only married or single person, the only mother, and so forth. Another member feels she is in a different stage of the work, more or less advanced than other members. Yet another woman is ashamed that she has more or fewer memories than other group members. The perceptions of differences are especially salient as new members struggle to come to terms with their identities as incest survivors, which they often feel they broadcast as they enter the room. As one woman said, "Walking in the door is telling."*

Starting a new survivor group is a very slow and time-consuming process. The therapists feel eager to engage in the work for which they formed the group. They may feel frustrated at the necessary slow pace of the work and the clients' enormous anxiety, caution, and seeming inability to recognize the symbolic meaning of their fears of not belonging. Yet, struggling with the meaning of belonging, that is, issues of inclusion and exclusion, connection and separation, sameness and difference, safety and trust, is the ongoing work of the group.

As a group evolves, it develops an identity or character in the eyes of each therapist. Therapists have general responses to a group as a whole, based in part upon the identity the group currently has for them. The character of the group may be playful, tough, competitive, warm, depleted, cohesive, fragmented, tormented, angry. These identities, as well as the therapist's responses to them, shift across time.

Membership changes. The negotiation of membership changes evokes intense feelings in group members and complicated countertransference responses in therapists. Any group struggles with change and the therapists will feel the group process pull to create stasis. Group members react strongly and in the context of their life experiences to transitions and change in the group, especially those over which they feel little or no control. These changes provide opportunities for deep work on life transitions and issues of attachment, separation, and working through.

Cotherapists may feel ambivalent about membership changes. The therapists may feel guilty about evoking members' anxiety and fear, yet irritated when the group does not want new members who ensure the continuity and viability of the group. They may feel torn between financial need and clinical comfort. It is comfortable to work with a familiar group and difficult to process the group conflict and transference in response to a new member. Either or both can collude with the group's complaint that group business is a "distraction" and forget that group process is the work of group therapy. The cotherapists may split this ambivalence and find themselves disagreeing about whether, how, and when to add members, or taking different stands on whether a prospective member is a good fit with the group or a leaving member has given enough notice of her intent to leave. Our

---

*In our groups, no group member is in individual therapy with either cotherapist. In groups where some group members are also individual clients of one of the therapists, however, another issue of difference arises: the different roles of those members who are and those who are not in individual therapy with the group therapists.

experience with our own ambivalence (individual and shared) and with the group's is that it has never been a mistake to take the extra time needed to process the addition of a group member or a group member's leaving.

When a new client joins an ongoing group, therapists' wishes to protect the group and the new member may conflict. They may feel angry with "old members" for extruding a new member, embarrassed for or impatient with a new member, wanting her to be perfect and fit immediately into the group.* In survivor groups, a new member can spark issues related to memories of mother leaving to have a baby and the onset of abuse in her absence. A new member's arrival may raise memories of the birth and subsequent abuse of younger siblings in relation to which the client may have felt responsible and helpless. The potency of the perpetrator-victim projections, and the blame and shame dynamics common in survivor groups intensify the normal group dynamics. For survivors, normal hostility and sibling rivalry evoke fears of violence and murderous rage. For new members, normal feelings of anxiety and fears of rejection feel like victimization and annihilation. The cotherapists are called upon to hold these intense feelings within a conceptual framework of normal group development.

Creation of safety. The work to identify the conditions and prerequisites for safety is the foundation of the group. It requires that the therapists understand multiple aspects of safety, real and perceived, and maintain clarity about the limits of the "safety" that they can provide and clients can expect. For example, clients in group will not be safe from having hurt feelings or uncomfortable feelings; they will not be safe from experiencing new memories or intrusive symptoms. The therapists can provide rules and thus some safety with respect to physical touch, verbal abuse, intentional harm, and loss of boundaries.

The recurrent need to address issues of safety and trust in a survivor group can fatigue therapists and elicit impatience. Therapists juggle conflicting tasks; naming group dynamics and inviting the airing of conflicts can feel at odds with supporting self-protection for clients and respecting their fears. Survivors have been deeply betrayed and badly harmed, and many have developed a sensitivity to the potential to be hurt, and sometimes respond as if threatened before they have become fully aware of a new situation. Clients recurrently experience fear, anxiety, and hurt feelings in group therapy; these experiences will often evoke terror and the need to reestablish interpersonal safety. The task of the group, however, is to separate the past from the present. The experience of a similar feeling from the past does *not* mean the current event *is the same* as the past event. The

---

*Yalom (1975) provides helpful guidelines for adding new members.

group provides the opportunity for clients to respond differently to their feelings and the interpersonal relationships. In group, doing it differently often starts with speaking their experience.

Therapists have relatively less control over the therapeutic environment in group therapy than in individual therapy. A countertransference feeling of responsibility or wish for control can interact with clients' transferential wishes for protection and security, leaving a therapist anxious, angry, or confused and vulnerable to becoming overactive or controlling.

Example   When struggling about group boundary issues, a group member angrily told the therapists she wished they would just make clear and strict rules. The therapists were aware of their ambivalence, both believing that the group processing of certain boundaries was important therapeutic work and yet feeling a wish to respond to the client's clear anxiety. In addition, the client's request was couched in terms of their competence as therapists: "Any good therapist would be very clear and strict about these rules." The therapists were aware of their defensive response, both wanting to justify their position theoretically while wishing to create rules to prove their competence and assertiveness as therapists.

Collusion with group defenses. These conflicts can lead therapists to participate unwittingly in the avoidance of certain key issues or conflicts. There may be an unconscious and hence unspoken agreement to avoid conflict, either with a group member or with the therapists.

Example   One group member dominated a group for many sessions with her rage at the therapists. The therapists worked with the client to understand the rage. Meanwhile, other group members were very angry at the client, but did not speak this because they were afraid of having her rage turned on them. The therapists assumed their silence and brief comments reflected involvement in the process, and missed the underlying conflict.

This issues takes on special meaning in a survivor group where people's anger in the family in childhood was often expressed through violence and abuse. The therapists strive to make it possible for the group to express anger while acknowledging their fears in the context of historical dangers and their current fantasies. Because anger is associated with abuse, clients often need to practice, and in response the therapists must be resilient, honest, and nonretaliatory. When there is much inter-member conflict, the therapists need to address the possibility that anger at them is being displaced within the group. The therapists must be prepared to withstand and in fact invite the clients' anger at them. Using anger constructively in the service of strengthening connection is a new concept for many survivor clients who have lived in terror of anger. A group forum is a powerful context for demonstrating and modeling the constructive negotiation of anger and conflict.

Negative transference. Transference responses held by the group as a whole are powerful. A therapy group provides a strong pull for reenactments of family dynamics (Abney, Yang, & Paulson, 1992; Courtois, 1988; Ganzarain & Buchele, 1986). The therapists are inevitably perceived as parents, and for incest survivors this transference often means perpetrator, nonprotective witness, helpless bystander, preoccupied narcissist, and absent other. Because the group is often experienced as a new or surrogate family (Courtois), the therapists will draw transferences based on each member's own experiences of her parents and caretakers. These projective identities raise strong feelings in the therapists, including frustration and anger at being perceived as neglectful or abusive. When the group criticizes one or both therapists, the therapists can feel defensive or shamed or protective of one another. Therapist's roles in their own families of origin will inevitably affect their levels of attunement to certain group dynamics and clients.

Sometimes a stable transference split can evolve in which one therapist is perceived as protective or nurturing while the other is seen as cold or abusive. Therapists can contribute to this split if one therapist consistently has the role of handling "group business" (i.e., fees, missed appointments, insurance matters, frame issues such as starting or ending the session); if one therapist manages all between-session contact with clients; or if one therapist routinely works at the individual level while the other works at the group-as-a-whole level. One therapist may unconsciously wish to flee certain transferences and act out the role of good parent in contrast to her cotherapist who is left in the role of bad parent. If unaddressed, this split can lead to problematic countertransference issues, reflecting responses to the clients' stable transference and to the cotherapist who shares an alter ego, the other half of the ambivalent attachment. This dynamic creates a stalemate because the integration of ambivalent feelings and recognition of complexity in human relationships is blocked by a dichotomous split that precludes the fullness of each therapist self.

The therapists' self-esteem and identity as "good-enough" therapists will be challenged when group members voice their ambivalence about the effectiveness of group therapy ("This isn't helping; this isn't what I need"), their anger about fees ("We've already paid"), their fears and anger about new members entering the group, their anger or envy about the therapists' behaviors or about their perceptions of the therapists (such as taking vacations, not answering personal questions, having an easy life, benefitting from their pain—i.e., making a living from survivors' need for treatment, not being a survivor, being a survivor). Under assault, therapists can feel defensive, frustrated that these issues never seem to be resolved, and guilty or ashamed about their therapeutic or personal style. The therapists may feel as if they are endlessly fighting fires, or feel unseen except as a projective or transferential object.

The transference to the therapist as perpetrator or bystander takes on an added nuance in relation to individual members. As the therapist is working with an individual on an issue, the group is watching. If the client moves into intense pain, perhaps through making a connection between current experiences and her abuse, the other group members may view the therapist as perpetrator, and themselves as helpless bystanders. If so, they may respond aggressively to rework their own history which they are projecting onto the current group event. On the other hand, if a client angrily accuses the therapist of being hurtful or malicious, other group members may be able to see it differently. The presence of witnesses and comembers provides clients with a unique opportunity to sort out projective from reactive processes and these interactions are often the heart of group therapy. Education about transference and projection is especially helpful to survivor clients who have so often been recipients of projection and whose perceptions of interpersonal reality were so often called into question.

Cotherapist absence. Therapist absences are meaningful to members and cotherapists. Survivors' abandonment fears, arising from disrupted or absent caretaking and thus unmet dependency needs, can be expressed as anger at the absent therapist. Group members may instinctively protect the remaining therapist when her cotherapist is away. The "good" therapist can feel guilty about holding the good role and worried about her own upcoming vacation and resulting fall from grace. The "bad" therapist can feel guilty, angry, resentful, or confused. If unnamed, the group may treat this dynamic as fact rather than a transference that emerges in the context of a real interpersonal event.

Individual countertransference vulnerabilities. Each therapist's conflicts will influence her awareness of and responses to certain group dynamics. To the extent that she brings to the group a fear of conflict in groups (families), she may fail to address or name conflict either in the group or with her cotherapist and respond with silence, passive aggression, victimization, or smoldering resentment. Over time, this failure significantly decreases the potential for safety in the group. Group safety requires the structure for safe respectful naming and negotiation of anger, different needs and opinions, and conflict.

A therapist who fears feelings of envy may overlook or ignore evidence of envy dynamics in the group or between herself and her cotherapist. A therapist who does not allow herself to wish to be noticed or special may respond to these wishes from group members with shaming or criticism.

Many therapists come from family contexts in which they took care of others' needs at the expense of their own; group contexts can support clients' asserting their needs and this concentrated expression of needs can stir old conflicts for the therapist.

Projection. The group members can fuel one another's projections. Projection of anger results in a perpetrator transference and victim identity. Projection of shame can result in contempt, humiliation, or disgust in the therapist. Projection of a harsh superego introject can manifest itself in guilt or judgmental condemnation. Exploring such projections without shaming the client and educating the group about projection and transference in interpersonal relationships is an essential part of group therapy. Clients may share a projection or transference to a therapist and use this shared experience to validate their perceptions of the therapist's lack of caring or remoteness, for example. It is extremely important for the therapist to reflect honestly on her own feelings and behavior. As Ormont (1991) points out, if therapists are open to hearing, they will learn a great deal about themselves from their clients' observations (Kaiser, 1965). A strong cotherapy relationship can be invaluable in helping therapists discover the kernel of truth in the projections and transferences.

Therapists' Responses to the Interpersonal Process in the Group

As the group develops, group members will begin to relate to one another and the work of the group can in part focus on interpersonal process. With this shift comes another set of countertransference issues.

Therapists are not in control of group members' responses to one another, either helpful and hurtful. They do not have the degree of control over the therapeutic environment that one has in individual therapy.

Example   After a particularly difficult but effective piece of work with a newer client's despair, self-loathing, and self-punitive impulses, another client quickly spoke, discounting the therapist's words of hope and elaborating her own pain in support of the first client's despair. The first client who had only begun tentatively to move away from her entrenched, injured stance looked confused, then joined with the second client in listing evidence for hopeless despair. The therapist felt angry because her work with one group member seemed undone by another, and both therapists' irritation and disappointment prevented them from noticing the more obvious sibling rivalry and competition evident in the process.

The intensity of the intergroup transferences that develop in survivor groups can pose particular challenges. Over time, clients will experience one another as siblings, sometimes valued and sometimes hated. Clients' intense feelings of rage and envy can elicit protective feelings in the therapists and discomfort at the intensity of the affect directed toward other group members.

When anxious, clients from families dominated by cruelty, blame, and shame will respond to any intervention as if they were being blamed or shamed. This dynamic can emerge with a client whose characteristic life experience is as a victim of blame and shame with whom other group members may unconsciously identify. In particular, they see a hated aspect of themselves, a victim, someone who can only express anger indirectly through self-defeating behaviors. Group members often then project their victimhood and passive aggression onto this client and, through projective identification, blame and shame her for it. Simultaneously, the experience of a group member as victim mobilizes aggression and identification with aggressors, which can be quite disturbing for group members who can feel enormous shame and guilt for their hostility. They will strive to exaggerate the provocation to rid themselves of the sense of badness and the cycle resumes. This cycle is the core of scapegoating; therapists are susceptible to getting caught in the projective identification which renders them unable to address the group dynamic and work with the complicated shame and blame, and the complex identifications as victim, abuser, and bystander.

There are many competing needs in a survivor group. Therapists often feel conflicted, protective of those who are reluctant to speak, yet concerned about silencing those who want to express strong feelings. Some individuals want to tell their stories, while others may not want to hear graphic or familiar trauma material. Some cannot tolerate others' silence, while those who are silent may be struggling simply to sit in the room. Those who cannot yet speak may feel envious of those who can, while those who do speak may feel envious of the apparent equanimity of those who are silent. Some people with a strong need to control others will stir strong feelings in those who have an equally strong need to not be controlled. Feelings of competition, envy, and fear arise among members. One of the therapists' major tasks is to name these conflicting needs and styles and to help clients learn that there is room for a variety of styles and for conflicting needs in the group. This requires that the therapists manage their own desires to rescue or protect, to interfere with or take control of the process, to avoid conflict.

Example   In the context of one client sharing a particularly painful abuse memory, one therapist invited other group members to notice what was happening for them as they listened. The woman who had been speaking, who had naturally been in a state of considerable shame as she recounted her abuse experience, felt slighted by the therapist's return to the group as a whole and the other group members' feelings. Her shame about what she had shared was then transformed into rage at the therapist. In addition, her awareness that others were witnessing her rage at the therapist in response to her intolerable shame, led her to feel humiliated and hopeless. The therapist felt remorse for having hurt the first group member, concern about neglecting the others, inadequate to meet all of the competing needs, paralyzed as she considered how to intervene with a particularly shame-prone client, and embarrassed about all of this happening in the presence of her cotherapist. For her part, the cotherapist felt critical, helpless, and guilty, having seen where things went awry but not having intervened.

Clients who have been abused or humiliated in a group by multiple perpetrators (as in cult abuse or gang rape) often have strong reactions to group therapy. The therapists may be aware of this history, which may be slow to emerge in the group itself. Simply telling about their abuse experiences can be retraumatizing for many clients (Beere, 1989; Wong & Cook, 1992). Sitting in a circle and opening up strong affect can stimulate flashbacks or dissociation for some group abuse survivors. One step in managing this common therapeutic dilemma is to name it in the group, acknowledging this possibility (or reality, once it has happened). Another is to create a norm that ensures that the sharing of trauma material will be done in a context that allows the therapists to check in frequently with both the person speaking and those listening. Therapists can feel empathy for their clients' fear, anger for their hurt, and sensitivity to their shame. Yet, if the therapists are afraid of eliciting shame (inevitable in group therapy), they can become avoidant or overprotective and participate in the dissociative process of avoiding trauma material or certain subjects (such as anger, sexuality, or envy). Their empathy for the clients' shame frees them to name the dilemma and invite group work on the silencing power of shame. Alternatively, a therapist's countertransference wish to protect clients from difficult feelings inevitably evoked in group, serves to shut down group process.

Therapists' Responses to Individuals in the Group

As a group gels, it can feel like there is never enough time for everyone's concerns to be addressed. Often our 1-1/2 hour group sessions fly by without an opportunity to address many of the important issues individuals have raised at check-in. Group invites a transferential reenactment of inadequate supplies of attention and care; there is never enough to go around, both for clients from abusive families and for therapists whose job in their own families of origin may have been to try to meet everyone's needs. The therapists may feel beleaguered by the group's demands and either succumb to guilt or feel resentful of the wish that they each have "five breasts." Therapists may feel critical of a member who dominates with concerns that don't deepen the group work; worried about or frustrated with the member who rarely talks; irritated with the member who brings up an important issue such as suicide, intergroup conflict, or ending therapy at the end of a session; grateful to the client who does a contained, effective piece of work that invites other group members to participate; and appreciative of a client who points out a dynamic the therapists may have missed.

Example   One group therapist struggled with her cotherapist to understand her strong feelings of outrage toward a particular group client who frequently expressed dissatisfaction with the therapists' activity level in the group. In consultation, the therapist complained, "Nothing we do is enough. No matter what we say it won't be enough for her. She seems to think she deserves to have all the work done for her." She and her cotherapist noted the strong feelings evident behind her words, and she reflected that her current feelings reminded her of familiar feelings from her past. She was a parentified child who had silenced her needs to protect her often overwhelmed mother, but she had always resented her younger sister who seemed able to assert her needs and wishes with impunity. As she considered what the client was requesting from the therapists, she acknowledged that the wishes were reasonable, but they were things for which she had always been unable to ask: help, support, recognition of her hard work, and validation of her needs.

Again, therapists' feelings are intensified because of the group setting, decreased control, increased observation of their work, and increased needs from multiple clients. The therapists' clear vision of what group has to offer and the curative power of group will help protect them from a literal response to the metaphoric issue. Much of the work of any group therapy is not about content, but about the process, in this case the process of negotiating one's needs in the world and in relationships.

The tension for group members between individual needs and group needs often emerges as a debate about the topic of group process and frame discussions. Group process discussions are often seen as "diversions" or detours from the work of the group. It is essential that the therapists hold a clear theoretical framework for group therapy that helps them recognize the false dichotomy and appreciate the transformative work of analyzing group process. The negotiation of conflict and frame issues within group is one of the most important opportunities in group therapy.

Both speaking and not speaking that which the therapists observe have extensive ramifications. The processes of scapegoating and of assuming a "victim" role are potent forces in many survivor groups. Therapists can easily be drawn into rigid scripts with only three parts: victim, perpetrator, and nonprotective bystander. Commenting on a survivor's ways of protecting herself can evoke tremendous shame in a group setting. Yet silence reenacts a painfully familiar scenario from the group members' childhoods: A difficult reality is not being acknowledged, and needed help is not being given. The solution is to speak to the process and remind the group that there are more options. This work occurs and reoccurs throughout the life of the group. In the moment, the familiar scripts are compelling to all involved. Cotherapists rely on one another and on consultation to remain free from the powerful projective process.

Dissociation in Group

As in individual therapy, dissociation occurs in group therapy as both dissociative events and dissociative processes (see chapter 6). The majority of clients in a survivor group are familiar with dissociation (although not necessarily its name and function). Thus, dissociation is both a topic of discussion in groups, and a significant factor in group process.

Dissociative events occur when certain clients clearly dissociate during a group session. A client's dissociation may take the form of an almost imperceptible move into silence or it may be something as dramatic as a person with dissociative identities switching from one ego state to another while speaking. The impact of this behavior on the group will depend upon the context. To the extent that the therapists work with the group to normalize dissociation as a self-protective response to sensed threat, group members can come to accept and discuss dissociation as an understandable response to the anxiety of the moment. This example also reflects the value of the use of psychoeducation in groups in response to the group's needs. Shared information and resources are some of the benefits of groups for survivors. Managing a highly dissociative client in group can be complicated, and it is certainly one of many aspects of group work with childhood abuse survivors that supports our belief that such groups are best led by two therapists.

One client's dissociation may remind others of their own. Because dissociation can be frightening, both to observe and to experience, the group leaders may feel protective of the other clients when someone visibly dissociates. Responses to overt dissociation will be developed in response to the group's and client's needs. Bringing a client back from a dissociated state needs to be done gently, and this work clearly puts a momentary halt to all other group processing. Often a client who has dissociated is initially shame-filled and confused. She does not remember what happened, is initially disoriented, and wonders what she did that everyone else in the room knows about. The therapists must manage their concerns about the member who has dissociated, the other clients' needs, and their own feelings about this interruption in group process. The function of dissociation is manifold and includes its function in the group. For example, the group member may have needed the group process to stop at that time, or she may have served a group-as-a-whole need to move away from conflict or secrets. The therapists' task is to integrate the client's dissociation into its context, individual, interpersonal, and group. Clearly this requires that the therapists be familiar with dissociation both clinically and conceptually.

Dissociative process in groups can be evident as therapists realize that they and the group have unwittingly colluded or agreed to avoid certain material, to remain silent about certain group behaviors, or to consistently leave out a certain member or topic. It is not unusual for a long-term survivor group to neglect to mention incest for long periods of time, often reflecting a dissociative process. A group can "agree" to avoid conflict unless the therapists are alert to opportunities to notice and invite discussion of differences. If clients have contact outside the group that is not mentioned in the group, there is potential for a dissociative process. A powerful antidote to the dissociative process is for the therapists to invite clients to say what is happening in the moment; therapists also need to monitor themselves and each other for consistent patterns of avoidance.

WITNESSING AND VICARIOUS TRAUMATIZATION

While witnessing is part of the curative action of group psychotherapy (as others, e.g., Herman, 1992, have noted), it can be very painful to witness someone's pain with others. Therapists may want to look away, a human response to expressions of strong affect in this culture. At these times, therapists are indeed bystanders, and will feel the paralysis, shame, curiosity, and concern that bystanders experience. Yet in this context they have the opportunity to be active, rather than passive, bystanders (Staub, 1989, 1992). When immersed in the experience of the group, therapists may temporarily lose sight of the opportunity to help the client do it differently this time. Yet, their very presence as active listeners and their willingness to feel in response to clients' stories is a reworking of the passive bystandership clients experienced in childhood. When therapists can speak their inner experience of the hearing, they begin to transform their clients' experience and expectation of indifference, denial, and hostility from the world.

The undeniable reality of the extent of child sexual abuse and its tragic aftermath is a constant presence in a survivor group (and, indeed, it is the therapists' job to continue to bring the group back to "and how does that relate to sexual abuse?"). This reality impacts upon the therapists' frames of reference. When therapists think of the group members as a cross section of society, they can feel despair for society and the world. In contrast to individual therapy, where there is more opportunity to explore and develop the context, therapists often hear about group clients' acute symptoms without a full knowledge of the developmental history and contexts that help them hold trauma material.

There are particular aspects of the therapists' relationships with the group that fuel vicarious traumatization. Exposure to trauma material can be greater in group than in individual therapy. Sitting in a room with seven survivors, knowing their histories and their pain, is deeply painful although it also contains the evidence of the power of connection as a healing force. Therapists are exposed to the cumulative effect of hearing and holding awareness of multiple trauma stories within a given group. When a client describes a painful symptom and several group members say they have experienced the same thing, the therapist can feel great sadness, helpless rage, and horror. In one group, all the members reported wanting to die in childhood. The therapists were aware of another level of feeling the enormous pain and cost of childhood sexual abuse.

When clients move into their hopelessness about ever recovering, leading normal lives, being happy, not living in fear, therapists can find it more difficult to be the "container" of hope (Bion, 1961). The group can spiral downward at times, and the despair of seven people is far more powerful than that of one person. This can be one of the more difficult affects for the therapists to hold. After all, is it not our hope for our clients' healing that keeps us in the work? Without that hope, it is very difficult to do this demanding work. When the group moves into collective despair, the presence of a cotherapist can help us hold the hope.

To the extent that a deeper relationship protects against vicarious traumatization by providing a context for the work, therapists are that much more susceptible to vicarious traumatization in group work. At times, a client will tell a horrific memory, during which she is filled with pain. As the therapists work with the client to process her experience, there are six other group members who are reacting in various ways to the work, individuals whose needs must also be considered. In addition to the conflicting demands upon the therapists, it is very difficult to enter into a very challenging and painful piece of work with someone and not be able to complete that piece. Yet the therapists and other group members are often left with unfinished feelings related to the memory. In part because of the many needs in the group, in part because an intense piece of memory work stirs memories for other members which will need to be processed, and in part because the group often wants to move away from the intense pain, the focus may not return next time to the member who was working on a memory last session. This can leave the cotherapists wondering or worrying about that group member, while feeling concerned about the impact and needs of others.

On the other side, it is sometimes easier to hold hope when there are people in the room at different points in their recovery. In addition to validating one another's pain, survivors can also provide models of healing for one another. It is very moving to see a group of women heal together, providing the therapist with both hope and satisfaction. Therapists can feel great fondness, pride, and connection with the group of women with whom they work; we have often noted our deep admiration for our group clients as we observe their courage, honesty, and determination. The gift of humor is often present in groups, and group sessions can be filled with great warmth. This experience can impact positively upon the therapists' frames of reference.

Participation in a Group of Women

A unique aspect of these groups is that they are made up of women. This makeup has significance for group process and countertransference in several realms. Some themes related to gender that emerge in group include:

1. Women's socialization, the influence of culture, specifically sexism and gender role stereotypes, on group members
2. The importance of connection in women's lives
3. The role of motherhood for women, that is, chosen, unchosen, without choice, and women's relationships to their mothers
4. Women's loss of voice, self-doubt in a social and developmental context
5. The feminization of victimization, that is, the role of pervasive violence against women, blaming the victim, and women living with fear
6. For survivors, the formation of a negative feminine identity, conflicts with one's female body and gender identity
7. Prohibitions against women's anger, assertiveness, selfishness, and sadism

There are also unique experiences of connection, intimacy, poignancy, and warmth in these groups. At times a special feeling of tenderness can emerge over the course of a group session. At these times, the group may include the therapists in the warmth and caring in the room. This warmth can evoke a countertransference wish to belong to the group, to join with group members as a member. When witnessing the close relationships among women in the group, each therapist may feel a wish to be known as herself and not "just" a projective object. Working as cotherapists provides some protection against the sense of exclusion.

Particularly when the group is addressing issues that invite solidarity— issues of cultural misogyny, social discrimination, gender role stereotyping, or hope for transformation—therapists may resonate and feel their own pain, rage, and sadness. There is important healing for group members here, and these sessions are meaningful and restorative for the therapists as well.

As therapists, we have been profoundly moved by our group clients and their process. We have felt privileged to be part of the power of group support, validation, and speech. In group, survivors have the opportunity to speak, be heard, and be connected in a new and empowering way. The cotherapists experience this connection and interpersonal process in the context of their own relationship as well. This relationship provides a unique opportunity for the identification and processing of countertransference responses.

12

Double Jeopardy: Countertransference with Clients Sexually Abused by Previous Therapists

SEVERAL STUDIES have found that incest survivor clients as a group are particularly vulnerable to experiencing sexual boundary violations in psychotherapy (Armsworth, 1989; Kluft, 1990b; Pope, 1994; Pope & Vetter, 1991). Clients who have been sexually abused by a therapist evoke complicated and powerful responses from later therapists and the subsequent psychotherapy is often uniquely challenging. Establishing trust and safety is particularly complex and delicate in these subsequent therapeutic relationships. In addition to the manifold countertransference responses described in earlier chapters, these therapies call into question the therapist's professional identity, professional affiliations and loyalties, and her ideals about psychotherapy and therapists.

As we have emphasized, a key therapeutic goal in psychotherapy with survivors is to use the new interpersonal environment of the therapeutic relationship to rework and heal the damage done in the developmental context of violations in early, trusting relationships. There are often enormous pressures in trauma therapy to respond to the client's intense affect, vulnerability, and deep yearning for love. The therapist is asked to bring herself to the therapy in a genuine and warm, yet clearly bounded and respectful, way. Sexual actions by a therapist undermine the fundamental principles of what is curative about psychotherapy: the safety to separate

255

thoughts, feelings, and fantasies from action and the creation of a respectful, compassionate, safe holding environment in which interpersonal events
can be examined and understood in both their present and historical context. Sexual contact between therapist and client destroys the fabric of the
therapeutic endeavor.

We believe that sexual or sexualized contact between therapist and client, whether in the course of or after the ending of the therapeutic relationship, is never in the best interest of the client (Gabbard, 1994b). One of the
major tasks of therapy for a survivor is to learn or relearn how to manage
intimacy and boundaries. It must be safe for the client to experience intimacy in the therapeutic relationship without the possibility of sexual behavior. When this boundary is breached, and the survivor goes to another
therapist, that breach creates the context for the subsequent therapy for
both client and therapist.

Recent literature indicates that as many as one-third of female incest
survivors who seek therapy become sexually involved in therapist-client
sexual relations (Armsworth, 1989). This rate is two to three times the
incidence of therapist-client sexual involvement in general (Armsworth),
and some authors (Kluft, 1990b; Pope & Bouhoutsos, 1986; Pope & Vetter, 1991) have observed that women with histories of incest are the highest
risk group for therapist sexual exploitation. Female clients are at highest
risk, with both male and female therapists. According to the extant research, the highest rate of violation is by male therapists with female clients
(from 83 to 88 percent of cases). Reported ranges for other gender pairings
are as follows: male/male, 6 to 8 percent; female/female, 1 to 10 percent;
and female perpetrator/male victim, 2 to 4 percent (Kuchan, in Schoener,
Milgrom, Gonsiorek, Luepker, & Conroe, 1989).

Sexual abuse of clients crosses all mental health disciplines and theoretical orientations. While some studies (Borys & Pope, 1989) suggest that
psychodynamic therapists are more sensitive to and aware of boundary and
frame issues, these therapists tend also to be less well-trained in trauma
theory and therapy, and too often psychoanalytic therapists work in isolation with insufficient support and consultation. On the other hand, non-
psychodynamic therapists whose clinical focus is problem solving or symptom focused are often undertrained in issues of frame and boundaries and
unaware of the complex transference dynamics and reenactments likely in
these therapies. This unfamiliarity can leave a therapist ill-equipped for
some of the conscious and unconscious interpersonal process and boundary
challenges in these therapies. Subsequent psychotherapies always involve
complex negotiations of interpersonal and psychic boundaries. Most therapists have little formal training in understanding and negotiating boundaries in a psychotherapy in a clinically informed, ethically consistent, and

personally respectful way. This training lacuna results in dangerous ethical quandaries.

OVERARCHING COUNTERTRANSFERENCE THEMES

There are several reasons why these therapies are especially difficult for subsequent therapists (Saakvitne, 1993b). The work we do as therapists is intimately part of who we are. As therapists who work with clients who have suffered severe deprivation and abuse in childhood, we must hold on to our faith in the process of psychotherapy and in humanity, and rely on our hope and idealism in the face of clients' painful, oppressive despair.

When we first face the reality of therapist sexual abuse of clients, this idealism is assaulted. Our internal world is shaken; our ego ideal, internal mentors and role models, and belief in our own safety from boundary violations is no longer unassailable. We can begin to question ourselves relentlessly, or zealously and self-righteously affirm our ethical purity. We may behave as many incestuous family members do; in order to protect our view of reality and of ourselves and our profession, we can deny the validity of what we are hearing, and instead blame and shame the victim, overtly with denials and anger, or covertly with disbelief, labels, diagnoses, interpretations, and silence (Pope, 1994).

Some therapists are survivors of childhood sexual abuse and have been sexually exploited by their own therapists. For these therapists, the shock of discovering that therapists can abuse clients may be less, and thus they may be able to be more present with their therapist abuse survivor clients. They may however struggle to be able to hear the client's unique experience and not assume they know from their experience what the client felt and wanted. They may carry a "soul sadness" (Chessick, 1978) or feelings of futile rage as they see their experience repeated with others who sought help. They may feel isolated, worried lest they enact abuse upon their own clients, but afraid to talk to their colleagues about their experiences. They may struggle with familiar questions about boundaries and about what is normal that are then compounded by their personal experience of an abusive therapy relationship.

Shame and Denial

When faced with a client who is telling us about a sexual relationship with a former therapist, the subsequent therapist may struggle with shame. Because one's identity as a therapist is such an important aspect of oneself, a therapist will want to make the other therapist as different from herself as possible; thus she may be more comfortable if the person is of a different discipline, is not licensed, does not share her theoretical orientation, or gender. When a therapist is ashamed for the profession she may be at risk to project her discomfort, and disbelieve or blame the client.

The resultant wish not to know can prompt a therapist to accept too readily a client's vague reasons for changing therapists or not returning to a prior therapist. Sensing, yet fending off knowing, that a client has been involved sexually with a prior therapist, a therapist may not explore fully a former therapy relationship and its ending.

Example   A client was referred to a psychologist by her former therapist when she moved out of state. The client spoke freely about her previous therapy and mentioned another earlier therapy relationship. The therapist asked why the client had decided not to return to her first therapist. The client was vague and changed the subject. Gradually, the therapist gleaned that the first therapist had an extensive social relationship with the client while seeing her for therapy. Subsequently, the therapist became quite focused on the client's feelings of loss and abandonment by the most recent therapist. When her supervisor wondered why she seemed to be belaboring a well-explored issue, the therapist realized she was avoiding exploration of the earlier therapy relationship because she feared it was also sexual and did not trust herself not to speak her outrage. Once she recognized her resistance, a few open-ended questions created space for the client to discuss the earlier therapy relationship, its boundary violations, and her feelings and confusion about it.

Anger

When a therapist accepts and believes that her client was sexually exploited by a therapist, she may struggle not only with shame, but also with horror, fury, or outrage. If she accepts the premise of an inviolable therapeutic and ethical frame, her basic beliefs and values are challenged by the breach of that frame and its boundaries. She can be consumed with anger at the abusive therapist for violating professional ethics and thus sullying the collective trustworthiness of the profession, as well as for the specific harm her client has suffered. This rage may fuel a wish to act or to press the client to act—which leads the therapist to abandon the client in the service of her own needs, thus repeating the dynamic of the previous, abusive, therapy, and perhaps the client's childhood experience as well.

There can be a place for a therapist's anger, outrage, and guilt in social, political, and legislative action and in our professional and licensing organizations; in her therapy office, though, she needs to be with her clients' experience and needs. It is important to examine the role of guilt or zeal in decisions to encourage a client to pursue legal or ethical actions against the previous therapist (Pope, 1994). As in all frame decisions, the therapist must have a clear understanding of her countertransference responses, the theoretical rationale, and the implications for the treatment of a decision to support or encourage a decision to pursue action.

This anger can precipitate a loss of faith in the profession and a crisis of trust in the therapist; a therapist can feel isolated and suspicious of any therapist she does not know well. This isolation can put her at risk to underexamine her own work. Her anger can lead her to overprotect and infantilize the client, and underanalyze the complex dynamics of the abusive therapy. As with incest, a client often has deeply conflicted feelings, including love, hurt, betrayal, and feeling special in relation to her former therapist.

Guilt

Another general countertransference response is guilt; the subsequent therapist is a member of the field that harmed the client. This countertransference may parallel the response of the nonperpetrating parent in an incest family. A therapist can respond with a wish to compensate the client for this betrayal and to redeem the field. The therapist must be wary of a countertransference wish to be perfect and infallible in order to protect the client from further hurt and to protect herself from the client's anger and her own guilt. Infallibility is an unattainable goal and therefore a dangerous countertransference wish.

The therapist's guilt can motivate her to respond to transference mistrust as if it were her betrayal; she may feel paralyzed, fear being abusive, or become apologetic. She may need to see her client as a helpless victim in order to feel like a rescuer, a good therapist and parent, and start to vary the frame or boundaries in an unexamined way. She may feel guilty about her own therapeutic mistakes or perceived transgressions. If a therapist becomes consumed with self-doubt, she may retreat to rigidity and distance that can feel cold or punitive to the client. The therapist can become paralyzed and fear to make even thoughtful modifications in the structure of the therapeutic relationship; in effect, she moves out of the relationship and into an authoritarian mode, in part, rigidifying her behavior to contain her anxiety about her own impulses.

Example   A client who had been in an abusive therapy relationship requested that she and her subsequent therapist have a longer-than-usual session. Initially, the therapist said that would not be possible because therapy sessions were set at 50 minutes, and then invited the client to say more about her thoughts. The client looked embarrassed and apologized for asking. After consultation the therapist realized she had hidden behind a rule, rather than explore the wishes and feelings both she and her client had about spending more time together. She acknowledged that she liked the client very much and the idea of an extended session felt intriguing and special. On the other hand, she was often quite tired after 50-minute sessions with this client because of the affective intensity of the material and the complexities of the relational dynamics, so she also felt some dread about doing an extended session. When she recognized her mixed feelings, she went back to the client and said she was disappointed in the way she herself had responded and suggested they reopen the discussion to understand more about the range of feelings and meanings to the client and the relationship.

Loss of Therapeutic Frame

A central danger is that any or all of these strong responses can lead the therapist to shift the frame and overlook the task of psychotherapy. While the therapist's behavior is always her own responsibility, it is helpful to the client to understand her role and to understand what factors prevented her from acting in her own best interest. This approach does not and should not blame the client, but examines the role and function of traumatic reenactment and works to empower a client to be able to make self-protective judgments and decisions. The work to identify and elaborate connections between the childhood and adult abusive relationships should unfold gradually. Moving too quickly to a genetic interpretation can lead a client to perceive the therapist as not hearing, minimizing her pain, deflecting attention from a colleague, or blaming her for what happened. On the other hand, helping the client recognize her childhood sexual abuse as a context in which she learned to evaluate boundaries provides a context for her difficulty with self-protection.

In creating meaning, one identifies choices and the possibility of control of future events. The interpersonal event of a therapist's sexual misconduct has enormous meaning and significance to a client with a history of childhood incest. It is likely not the first reenactment of her childhood betrayal, nor will it necessarily be the last. But for her, the therapeutic space, an environment that was to create a safe holding for the impulses, wishes, and compulsive reenactment that is often part of remembering, knowing, and creating personal meaning, was annihilated by the therapist's action and violation of role, boundaries, and ethics. In the subsequent therapy, as the new therapist works to reestablish the integrity of this therapeutic space, part of her task is to listen and develop with the client the narrative and its meaning, not to impose on it her needs and press for action.

The therapist's countertransference is particularly intense when a client continues to be involved sexually with a former therapist and either does not perceive the sexual involvement as problematic, or is unable to disentangle herself from the relationship. The subsequent therapist may have strong feelings of rage, frustration, or protectiveness toward the client. Just as in therapy with adult survivors who continue to be involved with their perpetrators, it is most helpful when the therapist can invite the client to notice the ways the relationship may be meeting certain psychological needs and creating or perpetuating difficulties for her, without shaming or blaming her or issuing an ultimatum to end the relationship. If the client could simply leave, she would. The therapist's job is to manage this countertransference and remain consistent and available to the client to help her consider her needs and choices in the context of her present and past relational experiences.

When a therapist dreads that her client will perceive her as also abusive, she will not be open to the likely fears and transferences of the client. A therapist who is afraid of her client, or fears offending or hurting the feelings of her client, will be inhibited in her manner, and compromised as a therapist. The therapist may become so preoccupied with her fantasies about this client, and her feelings of vulnerability in relation to the client that she loses sight of both the client and the therapeutic task. With this frame, the therapist may become cautious about offering interpretations, commenting on interpersonal dynamics, or posing any questions about, for example, the possibility or experience of childhood sexual abuse out of fear of rebuke, criticism, or legal action.

When this countertransference develops to a specific fear that the client will charge her with unethical or illegal conduct, this paralysis creates an impossible treatment relationship. When a therapist categorizes her client as litigious, her fear often drowns clinical awareness of her client's dynamics, vulnerabilities, and fears. The therapist too often distances from and objectifies the client. These fears and fantasies must be considered within the context of the client's dynamics and perception of her previous therapy relationship; they must be addressed in an open discussion between client and therapist about what might lead to a repetition of the previous therapy relationship. Again, consultation with a third party is invaluable in understanding and managing these feelings.

The Client's Fears

Another common countertransference issue relates to the client's fears and expectations (and sometimes ambivalent wishes) that the subsequent therapist will exploit her sexually. The therapist may feel insulted or apologetic and defensive or oversolicitous. Too often a therapist moves defensively to interpret the client's unconscious wishes for boundary violations inaccurately or prematurely. When narcissistically wounded, we often become impatient with these clients' chronic mistrust.

Example   One woman who had been sexually involved with a former female therapist questioned her new therapist incessantly about whether or not she was a lesbian. The client believed that if she knew her new therapist was straight, there would be no danger of sexual involvement. Her therapist felt irritated about the implicit assumptions in this belief and became fatigued with the client's difficulty trusting her. After consultation, the therapist focused on her client's need to establish safety, and felt less distracted by the specific content. She was able to stay with the process and allow the client the many months necessary for her to develop the trust necessary to feeling safe in the new therapy relationship.

Therapists' Vulnerability to Boundary Violations

Each therapist has to examine and acknowledge her vulnerability to participating in the type of reenactment represented by therapist sexual contact with a survivor client. It is countertransference denial to believe a therapist is invulnerable to violations and the context of those violations. Any therapist can unwittingly move into the comfortable experience of superiority in which she feels smug and invulnerable to errors or ethical violations. But, in fact, we all have the capacity to lose sight of the client's needs as we pursue our own needs, to enact the narcissistic dynamics of an incestuous family in which those with power create a world in which they are the ultimate authority or the only one whose needs matter. As soon as we believe that we are inherently safe from becoming a perpetrator or violating a boundary, we are in grave danger.

COUNTERTRANSFERENCE RESPONSES TO COMMON TRANSFERENCE THEMES

There are four common transference paradigms for clients sexually abused in prior therapies and several possible countertransference responses to them. These transferences parallel the transference themes experienced by many incest survivors as they recreate their family contexts in the therapeutic relationship.

Therapist as Perpetrator

The subsequent therapist will inevitably be perceived as untrustworthy, as a potential perpetrator. Although the potency of this mistrust may fluctuate at different times in the work, the therapist is always suspect. These fears often intensify around breaks or disruptions in the work, such as vacations and unexpected absences, and with any changes in therapeutic frame, especially those in which the therapist is or is seen as making a request or wanting something from the client. After one therapist cancelled a session unexpectedly due to a family illness, a client with whom she had worked for two years had a return of her earlier fears and began noticing mannerisms (e.g., the therapist resting her chin on her hand) that reminded the client of her prior, abusive, therapist.

Countertransference Responses

No one likes to be experienced as a perpetrator. While a therapist may be used to this transference from childhood abuse survivors, it is much more uncomfortable when it is specific to her role as a therapist and stems from violations committed by colleagues. It conflicts with her identity both as a trustworthy person and a helpful, ethical therapist. It is unsettling, frustrating, and sometimes painful to work hard to be consistent and respectful and strive to gain someone's trust, only to make a mistake and then learn that, despite months of work, there is no credit in the trust bank.

In response a therapist may lose her spontaneity. She may disconnect from herself and come to mistrust her intuition, leaving her resentful, paralyzed, and depressed. She may also become exasperated, defensive, or indignant. She may have difficulty tolerating her real failures out of fear of being "bad" like the former therapist or she may require her clients to notice her virtues. When a therapist needs her clients to reflect her self-esteem to her, she is in danger of recreating dynamics of narcissistic parents who treated their child as a self-object. It is important to differentiate treating one's client as a mirroring self-object from taking satisfaction in a client's expression of thanks, or sharing with pride in a client's growth. When a therapist loses the ability to experience the client as a separate person with her own needs, feelings, and experience, her potential to abuse the client increases significantly.

Example   When discussing her therapist's upcoming absence and their missed sessions, a client asked where she was going to be. Her therapist told her it was a working week and that she would be at home doing some writing. The client was outraged and demanded to know how her therapist could justify abandoning her clients in that way. The therapist replied that it was primarily for herself; it was not for her clients and in fact was not necessarily in their best interests. The client continued to express her indignation. Toward the end of the session, when the therapist again ac-

knowledged how difficult this absence was for the client, the client ex-
claimed triumphantly, "Oh, then you do feel guilty." In a subsequent session, the client was ridden with guilt, remorse, and fear; she felt she had
been abusive by wishing to evoke guilt in the therapist. The therapist suggested that the wish was an understandable response to feeling hurt and
disregarded, and added, "It is true I feel bad when something I do is hurtful
to you. However, I'm not beating myself up, nor do I feel like a bad person.
It's my job to take care of my self-esteem." In a later session, the client
asked more about the therapist's writings. She was interested in the therapist's work to train other therapists in trauma therapy. The therapist acknowledged that her work incorporated things she had learned with this
client, and noted that training therapists was a way to channel her feelings
about the kinds of abusive therapy experiences this client had experienced
previously. The client was pleased that her experience contributed to the
prevention of abusive therapies.

Therapist as Guild Member

A second common transference is the experience of the subsequent therapist
as one of "Them," the fraternity of therapists. The client will expect the
subsequent therapist to cover for her colleagues in the profession, and thus
to blame and shame the client, either by not believing her or by blaming
her for the therapist's behavior. This transference often reflects the client's
experience of telling an adult about the abuse in childhood. Early experiences of disclosure set the stage for later trust, shame, and identity schemas,
just as the aftermath of disclosure can be a critical factor in the trauma of
the abuse. The original trauma becomes embedded in the larger traumatic
context of neglect, denial, and blame. Similarly, many therapeutic failures
become more traumatic when the therapist denies or fails to own her mistakes and behaviors. Clients often assume a therapist will be unwilling to
hear about their negative experiences in therapy and unable to say anything
critical about another professional.

Countertransference Responses

The countertransference response to being seen as a guild member starts
with discomfort because it is, in part true. However, it also feels insulting
to a subsequent therapist who wishes to differentiate herself from the re-
nounced other. As a woman, she may be shocked or offended when compared to a male therapist who seduced and violated a client. Her homophobia or feminism can blind her to her own seductiveness and the client's
experience of her power. This transference is narcissistically wounding
when it conflicts with treasured aspects of her identity (ethics, values, and

commitment to stand up for what is right). When the therapist becomes overactive in her attempts to disprove this transference, she may be responding to a deeper fear that the transference is true—that she does feel loyalty to her colleagues or the field, and that she does have the potential to misuse her power as a therapist. It can be helpful to remember that a therapist's natural identification is with her colleagues and pride in our work does not turn us into perpetrators.

A therapist offsets the malevolence of this transference by her willingness to discuss her behaviors and openness to acknowledging her fallibility. Processing the therapist's mistakes provides the most powerful context for interpersonal healing in the therapy. When a therapist acknowledges her potential for error and invites discussion of her mistakes, she invites mutuality in the therapeutic relationship and weakens the client's transference to her as authority. Without being self-denigrating she can clarify that she will make mistakes, and will inadvertently hurt her client's feelings, but that anger and hurt can be spoken and repairs made in the relationship. When a therapist expresses her willingness to learn from her client how to be most helpful within the frame and ethics of therapy and the limits of her abilities, the stage is set for a respectful, nonabusive therapy.

This transference will be particularly evocative when the previous, abusive, therapist is someone known to the subsequent therapist. Here particularly she may struggle with her wish to know what really happened, and it can be difficult to stay with the client rather than pursuing information about the situation. Of course situations that involve a direct conflict of interest (when the prior therapist is an employer or close personal friend) compromise the therapeutic process and relationship too severely, and such cases should not be accepted. Not uncommonly, however, the information that the client has been abused by a therapist or the name of the therapist will not be revealed until the subsequent therapy is well underway, after the client has had an opportunity to assess for herself how comfortable she is talking about the situation with the new therapist.

Example   A client told her therapist about a sexual relationship she had with a teacher when in prep school. In the following session, she said, "You know, I said that I'd never told anybody. That isn't completely true. I told a therapist I saw when I was in college. He asked me a lot of details about the sex, and as I was leaving the session he patted my behind. At our next session he asked me to go to lunch with him. I never went back—and I never said anything to anybody about him or my teacher." The therapist responded with some animation, "It isn't surprising that you haven't told again. To be met with such a violation in the face of telling about a violation of trust and boundaries is inexcusable." The client looked surprised.

She remarked, "I thought you guys—therapists—couldn't say anything about each other's work. Even though I trust you, I never mentioned this here because I thought you would just have to stay silent—or you'd think it was my fault."

In most therapies with survivors of therapist abuse, it is useful to consult with colleagues to stay clear about one's own countertransference responses, yet both transference and countertransference dynamics can inhibit such a consultation. Issues of confidentiality and secrecy become potent in these therapies. In cases which are complicated by the therapist's relationship with the former therapist, consultation is imperative and the conflict needs to be named and explored in the therapy, including an assessment of whether the current therapist will be able to be effective and emotionally present for the client.

Therapist as Saviour

The third common transference to the subsequent therapist is that she is all good, the complete opposite of the "bad" former therapist, an omnipotent perfect parent, and perhaps the one who will "make it up" to the client and renew her faith in people. This transference, if unexamined, precludes the recognition and working through of the inevitable ambivalence toward the former therapist and avoids (or postpones) the negative transference in the present therapy. This idealizing transference is often brittle in its intensity and ferocity.

Countertransference Responses

The transference to the therapist as saviour is particularly insidious because it feels gratifying and ego-syntonic. Each of us wants to be a good therapist and to provide a curative experience. This transference flows comfortably with our own internal therapist ego ideal and our professional goals—to be experienced as helpful and well-intentioned. Further, with a survivor of incest and therapist abuse, this transference may feel like a relief from malevolent perpetrator transferences. Thus, we may fail to notice it *is* transference.

This transference is precarious because empathic failure is sure to follow, and in fact, must occur in order for the therapeutic work to progress. Knowing from experience how unstable this transference is, the therapist may feel uneasy, yet reluctant to end the "honeymoon." Here is a place where the vicarious traumatization-countertransference cycle (described in chapter 15) can emerge. If the therapist is feeling depleted or despairing from too much trauma work with too little support (common effects of vicarious traumatization), she may fail to notice that the idealization is a transference response, or she may have difficulty naming it because it can serve as a temporary antidote to the fatigue and despair.

However, the therapist needs to explore this transference rather than instantly attempt to debunk it. When idealization serves the development of trust and a therapeutic alliance, it can be important, but we can allow it without colluding with it.

The wish to be a perfect therapist is also consistent with a countertransference wish to be a perfect mother or parent. This wish can lead to extending oneself and one's boundaries in a way that unconsciously recreates boundary violations or mixed messages which can then contribute to the client's confusion about her power, her power to corrupt, her irresistibility, and the general lack of safety in the world. It leads to fatigue and dread in the therapist who knows she will ultimately fail. For some therapists, this unrealistic standard repeats childhood issues of trying to be perfect to win a parent's love or approval.

Example   A client who had worked with her therapist for 1 1/2 years held firmly to an idealized view of the therapist. She denied ever feeling angry or disappointed in the therapist. She was highly self-critical and often compared herself disfavorably to the therapist, but was always grateful to her for her understanding and for her clear boundaries and reliability. On one occasion, the therapist needed to reschedule an appointment, which she subsequently forgot. The client was very hurt, and knowing how consistent her therapist was, correctly surmised that it reflected the therapist's feelings about her. She took it to confirm the message she felt in a previous abusive therapy that she was unlovable and only good for exploitation. In processing her countertransference in supervision and with the client, the therapist acknowledged that she was angry with the client, in part because she felt that she had been put on a pedestal and could not get down. First, she felt at a distance from the client and unable to be real because she had to be perfect. Second, she knew it was just a matter of time before she fell off, but the fall was getting longer and longer. She brought these insights back to the therapy. "So perhaps I screwed up to get it over with and bring who I really am, a human who makes mistakes, into our relationship. I did not intend to hurt you. I apologize for forgetting our session, but perhaps we can gain something from this that will make our relationship stronger."

Alternatively, the therapist can feel competitive with the former therapist in a way that recreates sibling dynamics from her past. This dynamic is particularly available when the client idealizes the former therapist, often for her or his willingness to cross boundaries, and then complains bitterly about her current therapist's rigidity and (emotional) stinginess. The client may then play the part of a parent choosing between siblings. For both client and therapist, this triangle can stir old loyalty conflicts (V. Garvin, personal communication, 1994).

Therapist as Victim

A fourth transference emerges from the client's identification with the aggressor. This is a sadistic transference in which the client expresses her outrage and defends against her experienced powerlessness by trying to torment and control the therapist. This transference is manifest in various behaviors on the part of the client: nothing the therapist does is right; she may scrutinize every word for evidence of disrespect, incompetence, or abuse; she may constantly ask the therapist to modify her style, her office, herself to accommodate her needs and fears. Through this process, the therapist becomes the victim and the client, the tormenter. If the therapist is unable to set limits and fails to treat herself with respect, she allows the client to become a perpetrator and the client often then spirals downward into self-loathing, depression, shame, and despair.

Countertransference Responses

The therapist's response to the sadistic transference can be either masochistic or sadistic or alternate between the two. Her guilt and compassion for the client can lead her to overlook the client's aggression and reenactment, but her defensiveness and narcissism can lead her to overlook the client's fear and hurt. The therapist needs to keep the client's ambivalence and contradictory experiences of self in mind, and to modulate her response to her assaults while remaining respectful and protective of herself and the therapeutic relationship.

Example   A male therapist working with a female incest survivor and survivor of sexual abuse by a former male therapist found himself in a masochistic reenactment that caught him by surprise. His client was the first survivor of therapist abuse with whom he had worked and he had very strong feelings of outrage and anger about her experiences. He felt flattered that after "shopping," she chose him as a therapist and self-consciously strove to live up to her trust. They focused extensively on issues of safety in the first months, and he often invited her to tell him what she needed from him in order to feel safe (falling into a countertransference assumption that he alone could create a sense of safety for her by his behavior). Whenever she expressed a concern, he modified his behavior, demeanor, dress, and office to alleviate her anxiety. She continued to express fear and to experiment with her newfound control. After several months, the therapist realized in consultation that he was dressing specially for her, moving office furniture just for her sessions, and was virtually silenced, neutered, and made into a nonperson in the relationship. He was furious, and ashamed of his fury because he realized he had a hand in the unfolding process. As he started to reassert himself into the therapy, his client became more frightened, controlling, and strident in her demands. She experienced his presence as threatening and accused him of being intrusive and authoritarian. The therapist felt alternately enraged and self-effacing. Neither position allowed a resolution. After sessions in which she berated him, the client was filled with shame and self-loathing. After several attempts to discuss the pattern, they decided together to get a consultation to help them rework their therapy relationship.

COUNTERTRANSFERENCE WITH CLIENTS SEXUALLY ABUSED BY NON-MENTAL HEALTH PROFESSIONALS

Sexual misconduct and abuse occur in a variety of professional relationships (Peterson, 1992). We hear of sexual exploitation in the context of clients' childhood and adult relationships with clergy, teachers, physicians, chiropractors, emergency services personnel, lawyers, nurses, massage therapists, and all sorts of professionals, healers, and advisors. Inherent in all these relationships is a power differential based on the client's experience of a need for the knowledge and service offered by the provider. This relationship paradigm inevitably mimics early childhood dynamics. The greater the distress and need of the client, the greater the dependence on and vulnerability to the provider. Thus, it is not surprising that clients are particularly vulnerable at times of great personal change (divorce, diagnosis of life-threatening illness, bereavement and loss). Also not surprisingly, when professionals are going through such transitions, they are at greater risk to violate boundaries, as they project their unmet needs onto the client and act on them (Schoener et al., 1989).

The range of reactions felt by the subsequent psychotherapist will be informed by her identification with the general category of professionals and her own experiences with these professionals (e.g., a deeply religious Catholic therapist may suffer more conflict and pain hearing about a priest sexually abusing a parishioner), as well as the specific details of the client's particular experiences.

EMOTIONAL ABUSE BY A PRIOR THERAPIST

An interaction is abusive when a therapist is seeking to meet her needs at the expense of the client. Abusive interactions are those which exploit or degrade the client (even if the manifest intent is to reassure, satisfy, or provide a "corrective emotional experience"), are denied by the therapist or acknowledged but defined as therapeutic (i.e., for the client's own good), or take place outside the necessary, appropriate, or usual therapeutic frame. When the therapist uses her position of relative power to shape the interaction and define the shared reality in ways that serve her own personal needs but harm the client, the therapy has become injurious. These behaviors can include:

- Disclosing personal problems in detail and seeking emotional support from a client
- Socializing or seeking contact with clients outside of the office and therapeutic relationship frame, such as soliciting professional or business advice, services, or financial arrangements
- Using the authority of the therapist role to be insulting, critical, or intentionally shaming or degrading to clients
- Holding the client responsible for everything that occurs in the therapy and refusing to consider or acknowledge the therapist's role in therapeutic dilemmas or impasses
- Terminating abruptly without adequate communication or provisions for transfer and closure

Certainly there are incidents that are clearly abusive and incidents that are less clear and need to be discussed and understood. A key differentiating factor is a therapist's willingness to discuss a conflict, to take responsibility for her actions and behavior, to be respectful of both the client and herself, and to seek outside consultation and encourage the client to do likewise when there is an irreconcilable conflict. Allowing a therapy to be open to examination by others goes a long way toward safeguarding both parties.

A number of particular circumstances can contribute to therapies becoming emotionally abusive or injurious. One is a therapist's lack of training in trauma therapy combined with unrealistic expectations for herself and the client. Many therapists use a little knowledge of therapy technique and hide behind it to manage their own confusion, fear, and insecurity. A common example is that of the therapist who often remains silent in the belief that she is providing a "blank screen," and then interprets her client's frustration as resistance. Over time this pattern erodes the relationship and the client's sense of self.

The misuse of psychoanalytic principles to blame clients for therapeutic impasses has happened too frequently with therapists undertrained in therapeutic techniques, or undertrained in work with trauma survivors, and can be emotionally abusive (see chapter 2). Likewise, a therapist who sees her role as authoritarian may try to impose her perceptions, beliefs, and need for control on a client who may be struggling to free herself from such control from the past. When a therapist asserts a personal bias disguised as clinical expertise (e.g., homophobia, sexism), she degrades and diminishes her clients and the profession.

Therapists can become injurious in the context of frustrated rescue fantasies, when they believe they have or should have more power over a client's process or progress than they can possibly have. When a rescue fantasy is fueled by a need for control, by a narcissistic need to be revered as a competent, powerful therapist, or by a need to be seen by one's colleagues as effective, a therapist can get into a power struggle with the client that centers more on the therapist's needs than the client's.

When a therapist struggles with shame or a sense of diminishment (internally or in front of her colleagues), she can take a therapeutic impasse personally and blame or become enraged at the client. A therapist can become enamored or attracted to the client's power, abilities, attractiveness, money, or knowledge and want it for herself. Some therapists enter the field for reasons that have to do with power and esteem needs that are counter to productive therapy. Individuals and training professionals need to be more attuned to screening issues (Adler, 1992; Benson, Apfel, Grossman, Benjamin, & Howe, 1992; Rice, 1992). The role of therapist brings with it enormous ethical and interpersonal responsibility.

Countertransference Responses

While a therapist may comfort herself with a false sense of security that she could never be sexual with her clients, she usually cannot successfully convince herself that she could never be insensitive or hurtful. Because the details of emotional abuse are closer to ordinary failures of empathy, understanding, or thoughtlessness, a therapist will feel more guilty and at risk. Guilt can make a therapist want to minimize or deny another therapist's actions. Issues of professional etiquette and loyalty also emerge and cause a therapist to feel caught in a bind, as though being asked to pass judgment. The therapist must remain focused on the client's experience; while she may hear about events out of their context, her job is to recognize and explore the client's experience of irreconcilable differences and deep hurt.

We need to face our own potential for such behavior and discuss with our client how we want to address experiences of hurt or failure in the present relationship. Failure is not abuse; if we remember that therapeutic or empathic failure is both inevitable and necessary to psychotherapy, we will be free to use and work with our failures by admitting, exploring, and learning from them.

The transformative effect of the therapy occurs in the negotiation of the therapeutic relationship, specifically the negotiation of conflict, needs, and hurt in ways that are different from the past. Reminding clients early in the therapy that the therapist will make mistakes, misunderstand the client, and miss the boat, and actively inviting the client to point out these occurrences conveys two messages: *that the therapist is neither going to expect nor collude with the client's expectation that the therapist be perfect, and that mistakes and hurts can be addressed and repaired in a relationship.*

Example   A client told her therapist in an initial session about an error made by her former therapist, and added challengingly that she expected therapists to walk on water. The therapist retorted, "I assure you, you'll have a pretty soggy therapist here," a response which not only proved prophetic, but for which the therapist has remained grateful ever since both as a reminder to herself and a reflection for the client of truth in advertising.

The exploration of a client's reports of emotional abuse in a prior therapy includes the identification of what was hurtful in the interaction, an exploration of how it could have been different, and a clarification of the client's needs, recognizing both the current and past contexts of those needs. It is important to remind oneself and one's client that the therapist is simply human, undeniably fallible, and that the best that therapist and client can do together is to keep communication open and respectful and recognize the inevitability of misunderstanding and disconnection. Repair and reconnection are the goals of the new therapeutic relationship. They are skills that will need — and will get — much practice.

Example   A consultant sat in on a session with a survivor of severe sadistic abuse and her therapist at the request of the pair who were having difficulty moving through an interaction in which the client felt the therapist had hurt her. After some discussion between the consultant and the client, the client said, "I guess you're saying all relationships have problems. And the problem isn't the problem. The problem is what happens next; that's when you see if you can figure it out together. If not, then *that's* the problem."

FALSE ALLEGATIONS OF THERAPIST ABUSE

Of course there are occurrences of and opportunities for false accusations of therapist sexual or emotional abuse or exploitation. A therapist must remember that her job is to be the therapist, not judge or jury. The task is to hear the client's experience and to help her make sense of her personal narrative and related experience of herself and others in the world. As the therapist comes to know the client and her way of being in the world, she will understand the clinical material in a developing context of the client's history, her characteristic ways of experiencing affect and relationships, and her own interpersonal relationship with her. This process and way of knowing unfold over time; at any given time, a therapist has only partial information and will respond to what she hears in the context of that partial information. Her task is not to ascertain historical truth, but to examine and elaborate the narrative truth as her client reports an event and elaborates its meaning to her.

However, as a therapist comes to know her client more completely, including her rage, aggression, capacity to identify with aggressors, and retaliatory impulses, she may suspect or recognize an accusation to be part of a process of acting out, reenactment, punishment, projective identification, or murderous rage. A therapist's language needs to incorporate aggression and anger as well as pain and compassion into the therapeutic work in order to invite the client to explore all aspects of self, motivation, and truth. The therapist's willingness to name and explore both constructive and destructive aspects of interpersonal events, present and past, allows her client to integrate contradictory and conflictual experiences of self and other. Whenever a therapist feels compelled to identify an interpersonal event as all-good or all-bad, she should be cautious. The original abuse inevitably involves complicated ambivalent feelings, and the same is true of subsequent relationships.

When a therapist feels that she or a colleague is being unfairly accused, she can raise her confusion and dilemma with the client. She can invite the client to explore the various ways of understanding her experience, and be willing to do the same herself. The goal is for the therapist to hold onto her sense of truth while remaining empathically connected to the client's experience in her given context. Over time, as a client moves out of a particularly vulnerable state, she may be able to expand her ways of understanding an earlier event. Sometimes, a client presents rage at other treaters as a way of testing her therapist's ability to hear her anger, or as a way of expressing indirect disappointment. For example, the on-call clinician may be criticized harshly by a client whose own therapist is unavailable when the client feels she cannot afford to risk anger at her own therapist whom she needs. Sometimes a client wants to make sure her therapist recognizes that therapists can and do make mistakes for which they are responsible. A therapist's desire to remain in the client's good graces may blind her to the indirect meanings of the anger or criticism expressed about another provider.

The therapist's ability to stay in a neutral place of not knowing can be challenged when the client files or plans to file ethical or legal charges against the previous therapist. This situation is further complicated when the client asks the subsequent therapist to testify or to provide her notes or a deposition. Our belief is that one clinician cannot effectively evaluate, treat, and testify for a client. When accepting new psychotherapy cases in which legal action is a possibility, we are clear with the client in advance that the role of therapist is separate from the role of legal advocate or assessor. This serves the client's best interests as it allows the treating clinician to accept all of the client's feelings without needing to weigh and judge. However, as noted above, the client may not introduce the possibility of legal or ethical action until the therapy is well underway. At this point, it is essential for the therapist to obtain ongoing consultation to remain clear about her role with the client and to have a place to discuss her concerns and questions. If she finds herself unable to remain neutral, the client is best served by an honest discussion of the dilemma and possibly a referral.

IMPLICATIONS FOR PSYCHOTHERAPY

Therapy with clients sexually abused by previous therapists is challenging and difficult; therapists need support and consultation to do this work. They also need to trust themselves and what they know about psychotherapy. These clients went to treatment originally needing therapy and instead were involved in a reenactment; they still need therapy.

The major task of the subsequent therapy is to establish and maintain a therapeutic alliance in a safe, respectful frame. In fact, for some clients the entire task of a subsequent therapy may be to detoxify and restore their faith in and thus their access to therapy. Ideally the subsequent therapy provides a frame that allows the client to process the previous therapy and to return to the goals that brought her to psychotherapy originally. It is helpful to anticipate the predictable difficulties, transferences, and countertransferences, both in consultation and with the client. The therapist should expect not to be trusted. She should expect the specific abuse to be represented in the transference and expect the client to fear the therapist's anger and sexuality. She can expect the client to expect abandonment, betrayal, blame, and censure. The therapist should also be aware that these fears will intensify with any change in the frame.

The elaboration and exploration of the therapeutic relationship with these clients also include the identification of parallels to earlier relationships, and examination of identity and relational patterns for the survivor. Ultimately, the therapist's influence is in the therapeutic realm with the client; she cannot free the world of exploitive people, but she can help her client develop capacities for making self-protective judgments, including the ability to recognize early warning signs of danger, to assert and maintain personal boundaries, to identify and leave a dangerous or exploitive interpersonal situation, and to use her fear and anger on her own behalf. Until the client feels she has the right and the ability to say no, her world cannot begin to have any safety. The therapist also needs to support the specific interpersonal skills that facilitate safety in all relationships; these skills include recognizing familiar emotional and interpersonal patterns and beginning to see reenactments and "rewrite the script." Using the new interpersonal relationship with the therapist as both an external and an internal resource is an important component of this development.

A therapist's courage to notice and name events in the therapeutic relationship, specifically to explore parallels to the prior abusive therapy relationship as well as to the client's abusive family, ultimately creates safety. As she is free to wonder aloud about what is happening in the room, about her client's feelings about her behavior and fantasies about her feelings, the therapist invites her client to be actively present in the relationship. Therapists should not underestimate the power of naming. As the therapist invites a client to notice and name her experience of the therapist, she communicates the importance of the client's awareness of her experience and knowledge of her truth. This active attention provides the opportunity for therapist and client together to acknowledge and explore her perceptions, noting reality in the current relationship and analyzing ways in which her past affects her experience of the therapist in the present. This commitment to acknowledging and validating reality and owning that we are part of the reality of the therapeutic relationship is what therapists owe their clients.

Part Three

VICARIOUS
TRAUMATIZATION
IN PSYCHOTHERAPY
WITH INCEST SURVIVORS

13

Vicarious Traumatization:
How Trauma Therapy
Affects the Therapist

TRAUMA THERAPY profoundly changes the therapist. We give up our familiar way of being and beliefs about the world when we embark on this work
with survivors of traumatic life events. These changes are both inspiring
and disturbing, involving gains and losses. Rarely do therapists enter the
field of trauma therapy with full understanding of the implications of their
choice. This chapter describes the impact of vicarious traumatization on the
self and life of the therapist.

VICARIOUS TRAUMATIZATION: THE CONCEPT

Vicarious traumatization is a process through which the therapist's inner
experience is negatively transformed through empathic engagement with
clients' trauma material (McCann & Pearlman, 1990a). While we acknowledge here and in chapter 19 the many rewards of doing trauma therapy, the concept of vicarious traumatization focuses specifically on the
negative aspects of the transformation. The therapist is a witness to his
clients' traumas, through their vivid descriptions of traumatic events, reports of intentional cruelty and sadistic abuse, and experiences of reliving
terror, grief, and yearning. He is both a witness to and a participant in
traumatic reenactments within and outside of the therapy relationship.

Some aspects of vicarious traumatization, such as experiencing intrusive imagery, are more likely to be present earlier in the therapist's work with survivors. Others, such as changes in frame of reference, occur over time, after extended empathic engagement. Just as the task of psychotherapy is to contextualize events in order to understand their process, understanding vicarious traumatization requires that the therapist first notice it and connect it to its context, his work. Like countertransference, vicarious traumatization incorporates both a therapist's affective response to this emotional exposure and his conscious and unconscious defenses against those affects. Unlike countertransference, vicarious traumatization refers to the cumulative effect of doing trauma work across clients and to its pervasive impact on the self of the therapist.

Vicarious traumatization results in profound disruptions in the therapist's frame of reference, that is, his basic sense of identity, world view, and spirituality. Multiple aspects of the therapist and his life are affected, including his affect tolerance, fundamental psychological needs, deeply held beliefs about self and others, interpersonal relationships, internal imagery, and experience of his body and physical presence in the world.

Vicarious traumatization is a natural response to a very specialized kind of highly demanding work. Just as survivor clients have developed various styles of protecting themselves as a result of childhood victimization, so do therapists develop styles of protecting themselves from repeated exposure to trauma material and traumatic reenactments in the work. Unfortunately, these adaptations are not necessarily all in the best long-term interest of the therapist, the therapy, or the client.

Vicarious Traumatization: What It Isn't

Unlike countertransference, vicarious traumatization is not specific to one client or therapeutic relationship; rather, it takes place over time, across clients and therapeutic relationships. While there is some overlap with burnout (Gamble et al., 1994), vicarious traumatization is not simply "emotional exhaustion resulting from the stress of interpersonal contact" (Maslach, 1978, p. 56), nor is it a result of the gap between our expectations and aspirations on the one hand and the depleting conditions of the workplace on the other (Suran & Sheridan, 1985). Vicarious traumatization differs in its conceptual basis from "secondary traumatic stress disorder," "compassion fatigue" (Figley, in press), "traumatic countertransference" (Herman, 1992), and the observation of post-traumatic stress symptoms in therapists (Lindy & Wilson, 1994); specifically, vicarious traumatization has its foundation in a constructivist personality theory. Unlike the other constructs, vicarious traumatization emphasizes the role of meaning and adaptation, rather than symptoms. Secondary traumatic stress disorder and traumatic countertransference have their foundations in a symptom-based diagnosis—post-traumatic stress disorder (APA, 1994)—and thus focus primarily on a constellation of symptoms. Yet all of these concepts are related to vicarious traumatization in various ways.

Vicarious Traumatization: What It Is

Vicarious traumatization evolves from the complex interaction of central aspects of the individual therapist with aspects of the work (described in chapter 14). Its effects will be unique in each therapist, depending on his personality, defensive style, and resources. The concept of vicarious traumatization is based in constructivist self development theory (CSDT), a developmental, interpersonal theory explicating the impact of trauma on an individual's psychological development and adaptation (see chapter 3 and McCann & Pearlman, 1990b). Our understanding of vicarious traumatization is based in a growing empirical foundation (Gamble et al., 1994; Hollingsworth, 1993; Pearlman & Mac Ian, 1994; Schauben & Frazier, in press), extensive clinical and supervisory data, and discussions with trauma therapists and others who voluntarily enter the world of trauma survivors around the world.*

Given our understanding of psychological trauma and the self and of the interpersonal therapeutic process, from a theoretical perspective, vicarious traumatization is inevitable. It is unique to trauma work and its effects are specific, pervasive, and predictable according to its theoretical foundation and the psychology of the individual therapist. The effects of vicarious traumatization are widespread; its costs are immeasurable. We carry our experience of vicarious traumatization far beyond our therapy space. Because it changes the self of the therapist, it will inevitably affect all of our relationships—therapeutic, collegial, and personal.

Vicarious traumatization can leave the therapist serious, cynical, sad. He may develop an increased sensitivity to violence, or be prone to bouts of grief and despair for humanity. It can affect his ability to live fully, to love, to work, to play, to create. Unaddressed vicarious traumatization can lead the therapist to leave the field, whether because it sets the stage for burnout (Raquepaw & Miller, 1989), because of the therapist's lost sense of identity as an effective helper (Horner, 1993), or because of the demoralization

---

*Vicarious traumatization can affect anyone who engages empathically with trauma survivors—journalists, police, emergency room personnel, shelter staff, prison guards, clergy, attorneys, researchers, etc. Because of this book's focus on psychotherapists, our discussion is specific to vicarious traumatization in therapists.

and "soul sadness" (Chessick, 1978) that characterize the spiritual damage of vicarious traumatization.

The effects of vicarious traumatization may be permanent. We have experienced these effects ourselves and we observe them in trauma therapists with whom we work. In addition, in our research study of 188 trauma therapists (Pearlman & Mac Ian, 1994), we found significant disruptions in beliefs about self and others as well as distressing psychological and somatic symptoms that resulted from their clinical work with trauma survivors.

At the same time we are convinced that the effects of vicarious traumatization are modifiable when addressed actively (Pearlman & Saakvitne, in press). In the last section of this book, we discuss ways to moderate the impact of the trauma material to which one is exposed and ways to modulate vicarious traumatization.

EFFECTS OF VICARIOUS TRAUMATIZATION ON THE THERAPIST

In general, the therapist may experience many of the same signs and symptoms in himself that his client experiences, but at subclinical levels. These include symptoms of post-traumatic stress disorder (as observed and elaborated by others including Lindy & Wilson, 1994), in addition to other symptoms of anxiety and depression.

CSDT delineates aspects of the self that may be impacted by trauma. Parallel to our understanding of the impact of trauma on a client is the impact of vicarious traumatization on specific areas within the therapist. Some therapists will find certain aspects of the work more difficult and impactful than others; some will be more likely to experience disruptions in one area than others. These changes then color the therapist's experience and perception of all of his life experiences.

Frame of Reference

Perhaps the most disturbing and enduring alteration for the trauma therapist is the inevitable transformation in his identity, world view, and spirituality. These components of an individual's frame of reference provide the lens through which he views, experiences, and interprets his world. Any change in frame of reference reverberates throughout the self. Like vision, our frame of reference is the pane through which we view ourselves and our world. As our vision changes, we lose clarity and the ability to recognize familiar objects, and our perceptions change. While we can get corrective lenses, something is lost. We will now be conscious of the need to make adjustments as we view our world. We accommodate to the changes, but we no longer take our healthy eyesight for granted.

Identity

Vicarious traumatization causes disconnection from one's usual experience of oneself. Whenever a specific aspect of identity is challenged, the experience of oneself can be one of "not me." This alienation from oneself invariably translates into a sense of unrealness, affective numbness, and distance from others. It leads to rethinking one's basic beliefs about identity, role, and self-worth.

Many who become therapists consider themselves warm, optimistic, and compassionate people. A therapist may experience surprise and shame at his countertransference responses, especially if they include sadomasochistic impulses, sexual arousal, voyeurism, murderous vengeance (Wilson et al., 1994). A therapist who hears himself making callous or cynical retorts to clients or colleagues, has dreams in which he is engaging in sadistic behavior toward his clients' perpetrators or his clients, or finds his mind creating traumatic fantasies can feel alienated from himself.

Another identity issue for trauma therapists arises when a trauma therapist who is not aware of a personal abuse history asks himself, "Am I a survivor?" When clients come to therapy without conscious awareness of their abuse histories and we witness the emergence of this knowledge, we may struggle with doubt or nagging questions about our own early experiences. Whatever the outcome, this very process calls one's identity and key relationships into question.

Similarly, work with survivors of sexual abuse forces each therapist to examine his or her gender identity, what it means to be a man when so many men are perpetrators; to be a woman, when women have been victimized repeatedly throughout time and across cultures; to be a mother, as awareness of maternal abuse of children grows. A therapist will ask himself about his vulnerability to abuse and his capacity for cruelty and exploitation (Krystal, 1968). These questions may shake to the core long-standing beliefs about one's identity and self-worth.

Hearing about sexual abuse affects the therapist's sexual experience and integration of his sexuality into his identity. What does it mean to enjoy one's sexuality, to feel sexy or erotic, when so many do not have access to these feelings? What does it mean to enjoy sexual intimacy when so many people have been terrorized and abused sexually? These thoughts and feelings may emerge during the therapist's sexual activity with his partner. The impact then of vicarious traumatization on the therapist's intimate relationships and personal life is disturbing (Maltz, 1992). He may not know how to explain it to his partner, particularly when requirements of confidentiality prohibit detailed discussion, and the intimacy, intensity, and process of psychotherapy is little understood by those outside the field. These dilemmas press the therapist's identity as an open, sharing partner in an intimate relationship.

Equally basic to one's identity is one's sense of his body. It is all too easy to move into one's head, to become a thinking rather than a sensing creature, in order to manage the onslaught of emotions connected to trauma therapy material. It is not uncommon for trauma therapists to withdraw from their own sensuality as an unconscious way of protecting themselves from their sexuality or from strong feelings. Therapists can dissociate from their bodily experience within and outside of sessions. There is a danger in this strategy. Therapists cannot afford to lose track of who they are; one's body and bodily experiences are a core aspect of oneself in the world. The experience of childhood sexual abuse has a profound impact on the survivor's relation to her body (Attias & Goodwin, 1993; Saakvitne, 1992; van der Kolk, 1994). As a therapist explores these issues with clients, his awareness of and feelings about his body can change.

Over time, a therapist may rethink another aspect of his identity: what it means to be a trauma therapist. He may begin to wonder why he does this work, or question his competence (Herman, 1992; Putnam, 1989) and efficacy. Therapists may feel isolated when in social situations people recoil from them when they answer the innocent question, "What kind of work do you do?" Remembering that people's responses are part of their own denial and their need to distance from the possibility that trauma can touch their lives is helpful. Yet a trauma therapist then lives with the same silence and isolation his clients experience when they tell or choose not to tell their stories.

Our public identity as trauma therapists can also prevent us from taking a break from work. While some may recoil, others will pursue us with a morbid fascination, pressing endless questions about their friends, families, sexual abuse cases in the news, or about the work and its impact on us. A prominent colleague reported that she now tells people at parties, "I'm an interior designer." Another says he is an actuary. These encoded responses allow them to enjoy themselves in social situations without spending the evening talking about trauma.

When one's professional identity is a central component of one's overall identity, as it often is, these disruptions are severely distressing. To combat feeling uncertain about one's professional identity, a therapist may cling to his professional persona in private life, which creates a barrier to intimacy in interpersonal relationships. It is an impossible dilemma when the work which sustains someone is also harming him.

So many trauma clients live in a netherworld between life and death, in which thoughts of death serve a self-soothing function—the only imaginable release from the pain of living. As therapists, exposure to and participation in that tension exacts a toll from us. Preoccupation with our clients' distress, their grief, and their terror can interfere with our ability to engage fully in our own life experiences. This preoccupation may serve to give us a semblance of control when in fact we have little control over our clients' choices. On the other hand if we do not feel preoccupied, we may question our identity and worth as therapist, or fear we have abandoned our clients.

When unrecognized and unattended, this state of affairs can make the vicissitudes of a therapist's own life seem overwhelming and unmanageable—or trivial and insignificant. Without one's usual anchor of identity, it is difficult to accommodate new information, to integrate change. The therapist may feel overwhelmed by his personal life when its demands are added to the baseline of pain or despair he carries in his heart every day. Each of us chooses this work for particular and personal reasons; survivor therapists may carry both a higher tolerance for painful feelings and a greater capacity for empathy. These characteristics can increase our vulnerability to vicarious traumatization.

World View

The therapist's perceptions of the world, of how and why things happen, of people in general, and his values, moral principles, and life philosophy are inevitably challenged by working with adult survivors. The trauma therapist may feel confused, sorrowful, and often angry as his old world view no longer holds his experience; "no explanation integrates this new reality" (Wilson et al., 1994, p. 42).

As the therapist listens repeatedly to tales of intentional abuse of children, he may feel overwhelmed by the scope and prevalence of child abuse and cruelty. He may question the utility of addressing the aftermath of this massive social problem in individual psychotherapies. Yet when the therapist loses sight of the profound difference he and a single relationship can make, he has lost his therapeutic tools and zeal. This change in world view defeats the therapist's greatest therapeutic gift, his belief in the process and hope for healing.

Some questions which indicate a disrupted world view include, "Is every client a survivor of childhood sexual abuse?" "How can people be so cruel to one another?" "Are people fundamentally self-serving or evil?" The trauma therapist may find himself wondering for the first time whether people he knows and loves are victims or perpetrators. He may feel suspicious of every parent he sees with a child in a store or at a park.

Sadistic abuse can be administered in "small, hidden concentration camps created by tyrants who rule their homes" (Herman, 1992, p. 3), in homes where childrearing takes place in a "malevolent developmental context" (Gelinas, 1994), and in cults by organized groups using satanic rituals (Sakheim & Devine, 1992a). Such abuse can elicit a wide range of responses in the therapist. In addition to our countertransference responses, we are also left with incredulity that people are capable of such repeated acts of horrific cruelty and violence; an alteration of world view to encompass these behaviors is inevitable. Furthermore, if we are not appalled, we need to question the possibility of vicarious traumatization. At a trauma discussion group meeting, the presenter asked if people would be upset if he described some satanic ritual abuse material as part of his case presentation. A participant said, "I hope so."

This world view disruption also leads us to experience what was once ordinary in new ways. Listening to a parent harshly chastise his child in the grocery store, once an annoyance, becomes painful and perhaps even terrifying for the vicariously traumatized therapist who may wonder what this child will endure when alone with her parent. Visiting a pet store now may be followed by a rush of horrific imagery rather than gentle compassion for a fellow creature or loving awareness of the appealing animals.

The realities of those who relate to others through violence chip away at our tenuous belief in what Freud called "the thin veneer of civilization" (Freud, 1930). In defense, we can substitute a veneer of cynicism which can itself be unsettling. Within social learning theory (Rotter, 1954), cynicism is conceptualized as overgeneralized negative expectancies. We can shift from beliefs such as "Sometimes people do terrible things" to "People are terrible"; from "Parents can hurt their children" to "Parents are dangerous." These shifts reflect a profound loss of optimism, hope, and companionship with humanity, and an emotional constriction that can infuse and severely narrow one's life. A therapist may experience a loss of emotional spontaneity, generosity, and vulnerability that will deeply affect both his intimate relationships and personal spirituality.

Our life philosophies, including our values and moral principles, are called into question as we encounter the cruelty one person can intentionally inflict upon another. Therapists who enter the field in large part motivated by humanitarian values can find themselves filled with murderous wishes and fantasies directed at some perpetrators of childhood sexual abuse. Those who held a fundamental belief that no one should be harmed intentionally may be horrified at themselves as they struggle with their rage at perpetrators of sadistic sexual abuse.

Spirituality

The pathognomonic sign of vicarious traumatization is the disruption to the therapist's spirituality. We use the term spirituality broadly to encompass hope, faith, joy, love, wonder, acceptance, forgiveness, gratitude, creativity. Neumann & Pearlman (1994) have developed a psychological framework for understanding spirituality; in brief, we understand spirituality as an inherent human capacity for awareness of an elusive aspect of experience. The components of spirituality include beliefs about nonmaterial aspects of experience, about meaning and hope, about connection with something beyond oneself, and about awareness of all aspects of life.* These aspects of experience are invariably disrupted by trauma; so too are they disrupted by vicarious traumatization. We then struggle to find a source of hope to offer our clients in their work, and for ourselves and our loved ones.

As trauma therapists, our most subtle sensibilities are vulnerable to disruption. The work continuously calls into question issues of meaning; it is easy to join our clients in a state of meaninglessness or nihilism. Yet our "will to meaning" (Frankl, 1959) is essential to our psychological survival in the face of trauma. Thus, this aspect of vicarious traumatization is particularly insidious and dangerous to the therapist. We can easily enter a state of hopelessness or despair (Dyregrov & Mitchell, 1992; Fischman, 1991; Herman, 1992; Margolin, 1984; Wilson et al., 1994). We may feel profound existential isolation and loneliness (Moustakis, 1961). While we may disagree with our clients' beliefs about the world on the basis of our own experience, we can feel their despair. We may then experience confusion and helplessness. Scurfield (1985) warns that those who work with Vietnam veterans will face the darkest side of humanity, and be forever transformed by that experience. In fact, the precursors to the concept of vicarious traumatization came out of the examination of therapists' experience of doing psychotherapy with Vietnam veterans, whose material often contained graphic accounts of war atrocities and personal loss (Haley, 1974), and therapists' experience of working with survivors of the Nazi Holocaust (Danieli, 1982).

Emotional numbing is both a response to painful feelings, such as horror, grief, outrage, shock, and rage, and a sign of vicarious traumatization. The defenses against painful feelings are also part of the effects of vicarious traumatization (just as countertransference reflects both feelings and de-

---

*A copy of the Life Orientation Inventory, developed to assess disruptions in these four areas, is in the appendix.

fenses against those feelings and related conflicts). A therapist's insight and attunement to his innermost thoughts and feelings and willingness to be open to all aspects of life can diminish as he pulls back in order to protect himself. The defenses employed to protect oneself from knowledge of people's capacity for cruelty, of the agony and terror of young children who are being molested, of the systematic sadism of those engaging in ritualized destructive cult activities have their own costs. As a therapist comes to rely on denial, intellectualization, isolation of affect, dissociation, and projection, his capacity to connect to himself and others will diminish. This selective focus narrows a person's most subtle human sensitivities and represents a shift in his spirituality.

Self Capacities

Self capacities allow an individual to maintain a positive sense of self-esteem and a consistent sense of identity and to manage and modulate strong affect. When these capacities are impaired by vicarious traumatization, the therapist can be overwhelmed with dysphoric feelings, self-criticism, and anxiety. He may find it more difficult to be alone without feeling anxious, depressed, or lonely; to tolerate and integrate strong feelings; to hold on to images of loving others; to enjoy activities and people previously valued. The therapist may feel sorrow, grief, anger, or rage. His tears may be very close to the surface much of the time. He may feel unloving or unlovable. He may avoid difficult movies or the news because the experience of others' suffering is so much more intense when one's self capacities are impaired.

Impairments in self capacities imply difficulty in self-soothing. The traumatized therapist may find it more difficult to calm and comfort himself and may turn to external sources of comfort, relief, or numbing, such as alcohol consumption, overeating, overspending, overwork, and television. He may find himself craving caretaking from others but unable to ask effectively for what he needs. He may feel overwhelmed with his life outside of work, unable to respond to his loved ones' needs, and unable to set limits or obtain support.

Ego Resources

The particular ego resources that are most sensitive to the effects of vicarious traumatization include: the ability to make self-protective judgments, the ability to be introspective, the ability to establish and maintain boundaries, the ability to take perspective, including empathy and sense of humor, the ability to strive for personal growth, and an awareness of one's psychological needs. Cognitive processing, which is also sensitive to the effects of vicarious traumatization, can become clouded.

A variety of maladaptive or harmful behaviors can ensue when these resources are impaired, including: overwork, decision-making difficulties, a loss of sensitivity to our own needs, a lack of interest in others in our lives, and a truncation of our personal growth. One can easily take on one more client, add another evening hour, pick up another challenging client, agree to write one more paper or chapter or give one more talk or workshop, or assume other responsibilities without considering the impact on oneself and one's personal life. It is not uncommon for therapists new to trauma therapy to become very absorbed in learning more about the work; this curiosity can become an obsessive preoccupation that excludes other interests. When a therapist is less introspective and has less access to his cognitive and perspective-taking abilities, he can become myopic in his therapies. He may focus on content to the exclusion of process, and he may be unable to process his own contributions to conflict in the therapeutic relationship. The loss of empathy with clients poses a profound danger to any therapy and can result in retraumatization of survivor clients.

Psychological Needs

The same five psychological needs that are sensitive to disruption by trauma are susceptible to the effects of vicarious traumatization. Disruptions in these need areas translate into interpersonal difficulties.

Safety

Just as safety appears to be disrupted for most trauma survivors (Pearlman et al., 1992), so too is it the most vulnerable need area in trauma therapists (Pearlman & Mac Ian, 1994). A disrupted sense of safety implies increased fearfulness, a sense of personal vulnerability to harm, and increased fears for our children and other loved ones (Dyregrov & Mitchell, 1992). Therapists often report nightmares that reflect disrupted safety. Behavior changes reported by trauma therapists with safety disruptions* include: talking to themselves self-critically, rejecting their partners' sexual advances, avoiding having people walk behind them, being told by others that they are too self-critical, not trusting their instincts with clients, checking the doors and windows, avoiding crowded streets, and listening for unusual noises.†

A disrupted sense of safety can also translate into hypervigilance and an expectation of victimization. The loss of one's sense of security and safety

---

*As measured by the TSI Belief Scale, which is in the appendix.

†The behavior change data reported here and in the following sections are behaviors that were significant at the p < .001 level among a sample of 188 self-indentified trauma therapists (Pearlman & Mac Ian, 1994).

permeates one's daily life. While women in American society generally live with greater fear than men (Gordon & Riger, 1989), those fears can be heightened by trauma work. Male therapists may be unaccustomed to feeling such constant apprehension and find it leads to identity and world view disruptions.

Trauma therapists are likely to experience a greatly increased sense of vulnerability relative to their children. This can be one of the most painful and evident aspects of vicarious traumatization for therapists who are parents. It is easy to lose perspective on what constitutes excessive risk and to move to an overprotective stance with one's children.

Trust

When trust in oneself is disrupted, the individual feels less able to be independent. He no longer trusts his perceptions of other people, social situations, or his own feelings. He may rely more heavily upon others to meet his needs, no longer trusting himself to meet them.

The loss of trust in one's judgment decreases one's safety in the world. When an individual does not trust his judgment or ability to judge others, he may find himself trusting everyone. Indiscriminate trust can lead anyone into situations of danger. The less access one has to his feelings, the less information he has to assess situations and people and form appropriate judgments.

When our trust in others is disrupted, we, like our clients, may uniformly reject all external resources. Our counterdependent difficulty asking for help can hinder us in many aspects of our lives. We may be mildly suspicious of others' motives, unable to trust as fully as we once did, or anticipate betrayal in all situations. Our lives as intimate partners, as friends, and as parents may become more difficult as we view our loved ones with less innocence and trust than may be warranted.

Trauma therapists with disrupted self-trust schemas reported the following behavior changes: being self-critical, being told they are self-critical, avoiding looking at themselves in the mirror, avoiding having people walking behind them, and not trusting their instincts with clients (Pearlman & Mac Ian, 1994).

Disruptions in other-trust in our therapist sample correlated significantly with dropping out of community affairs, making excuses to avoid social situations, preferring to go to the movies or eat alone, avoiding having people walk behind themselves, feeling ready to leave social functions shortly after arriving, going long periods without seeing friends, waiting for the day's end in order to be alone, shopping to make themselves feel better, avoiding crowded streets, and listening for unusual noises.

Esteem

Disruptions in esteem that develop from vicarious traumatization can lead to a generalized more negative sense of self-esteem. One might question, "If I can't help other people, what good am I?" Our esteem can be affected in relation to ourselves as professionals (as therapists or colleagues), as human beings, as women or men, as friends, and so forth. In our trauma therapist sample (Pearlman & Mac Ian, 1994), those with disrupted self-esteem schemas reported the following behaviors as a result of their trauma work: being self-critical, being told they are too self-critical, avoiding looking at themselves in the mirror, and hurting or harming themselves.

Impairments in esteem for others are a likely outcome of work with survivors of sexual trauma as therapists hear story after story of people who acted selfishly, neglectfully, or cruelly. We may degrade and devalue others, or simply ignore or dismiss their interests, concerns, and needs when they differ from ours. Disruptions in other-esteem schemas in our trauma therapist sample correlated significantly with dropping out of community affairs, avoiding having people walk behind them, shopping to comfort themselves, and listening for unusual noises.

A therapist with disruptions in esteem for others may assume that anyone not working with survivors or on issues of social reform is shallow or ignorant. Alternatively, as a therapist loses respect for himself, he may unrealistically idealize others whom he perceives as stronger, more resilient, or more capable or talented than himself. Loss of self-esteem and of esteem for others both decrease the therapist's connection with self and others.

Intimacy

An awareness of pervasive human cruelty can lead to emotional numbing which, in turn, blocks feelings of intimacy with oneself and with others. Intimacy requires connection with one's innermost feelings and thoughts. When we block pain, we lose touch with other feelings as well. Loss of self-intimacy inhibits enjoyment of one's usual individual pursuits and creativity. In our trauma therapist sample, those with disruptions in self-intimacy reported going out to avoid being alone and avoiding looking at themselves in the mirror (Pearlman & Mac Ian, 1994).

Numbness also inhibits interpersonal (other-) intimacy as we pull back from others to avoid disappointment or loss. Some research has found therapists to be more distant emotionally than others from their families (Farber, 1983b, 1983c; Henry, Sims, & Spray, 1973) and more restricted in the number, range, and intensity of their friendships over the years (Cogan, 1978; Farber, 1983a). Our partners may perceive that our clients and/or colleagues are more important to us than they are, that others receive our best time, that we are more available to them emotionally and at times physically (when we, for example, as a matter of course interrupt dinner to take a work-related phone call). Therapists can feel caught between an angry partner and an anxious client and solve this dilemma by withdrawing from both of them.

We may move away from colleagues who do different types of work or who do not view our work sympathetically. Therapists working with adult survivors may find it difficult to work or socialize with colleagues who are unaware of the extent and seriousness of childhood sexual abuse, dissociative identity disorder, or organized sadistic abuse. We may find ourselves preoccupied with our work, which in itself distances us from others.

The therapists with disruptions in other-intimacy reported avoiding entering a room full of strangers, staying in bed to avoid seeing anyone, making excuses to avoid social situations, preferring to go to the movies or eat alone, avoiding having people walk behind them, going long periods without seeing friends, and shopping to make themselves feel better.

Control

Through the work of trauma therapy, a therapist can experience a diminished sense of self-control. He may identify with his clients' previous helplessness or become aware that his own life and future are subject to the actions of others in ways he cannot hope to predict or control. These beliefs lead to distress as we question our ability to take charge of our lives, to direct our future, to express our feelings, to act freely in the world.

Trauma therapists may experience disruptions in the realm of other-control, one manifestation of which is an attempt to exercise greater control over others. They may move to taking greater control in their personal relationships in order to compensate for their inability to control the events in their clients' lives. The impossibility of controlling others can then lead to a narrowing of one's world in an attempt to operate largely in a world which can be controlled. There is of course tremendous loss in this solution as well, as traumatized therapists restrict their lives and their opportunities out of fear.

Alternatively, disruptions in other-control can result in a surrender of control in situations where control is appropriate and possible. One can give up any sense of an ability to influence or lead others as one comes to accept the helplessness of clients in their experiences of abuse.*

---

*We do not have data on the behavior changes in those therapists with disruptions in control schemas.

Sensory System

Through exposure to clients' reported memories, therapists may experience disruptions in their own sensory systems. The possibility that clients' clinical material may activate personally traumatic or painful memories for the therapist (Catherall & Lane, 1992; Marvasti, 1992; Saakvitne, 1992) makes this experience additionally complex (see chapter 8).

Imagery

A hallmark of vicarious traumatization is the intrusion of clients' violent sadistic imagery into the therapist's own inner life. Images that clients report in detailed and vivid language can stay with the therapist long after the therapy hour. For therapists who work with survivors of sexual assault this often means dealing with intrusive, sometimes violent, sexual imagery in the therapist's personal life, and often in his sexual life, a process also noted by Maltz (1992). It is not uncommon for the trauma therapist to find his own sexual experience abruptly interrupted by the unbidden images or bodily sensations that were described by his client. This is a profoundly personal and distressing event, just as similar intrusions in the form of flashbacks can be terrifying for the survivor herself.

The images most likely to stay with, intrude upon, and distress the therapist are those that in some way connect with his salient psychological needs. Thus, for example, a client may relate a particularly vivid memory of abuse which contains a theme of abandonment. For a therapist with central dependency needs, themes of abandonment will be particularly meaningful. Thus the therapist's worst fears may be realized in his client's experience, and that identification will frame his response to the client, sometimes facilitating empathy, other times interfering with it. This image may return to haunt the therapist until he recognizes the central theme and works it through in an appropriate forum (such as supervision, a vicarious traumatization consultation, or his own therapy).

In our study of trauma therapists (Pearlman & Mac Ian, 1994), we found that therapists without a trauma history were more likely to report experiencing intrusive imagery as a result of exposure to clients' trauma material than were therapists with a trauma history. Perhaps therapists with a trauma history have developed ways of coping with traumatic imagery. Dyregrov and Mitchell (1992) have also noted that those working with traumatized children report experiencing intrusive imagery.

Bodily Experiences

It is not uncommon for therapists to experience bodily sensations which parallel those described by their survivor clients. Genital pain, numbing of various body parts, and strange physical sensations during sessions have all been reported by trauma therapists working with sexual abuse survivors and dissociative individuals. To the extent that these experiences are hidden in a cloak of confusion or shame, they cannot be addressed and resolved. Therapists sometimes carry these experiences out of the therapy office, and many trauma therapists report informally they are much more dissociative in everyday life than they were prior to doing trauma work.

Other Sensory Experiences

Many trauma therapists develop a sensitivity to other sensory experiences, such as certain sounds or smells. After hearing story after story about children being abused in basements, unexpected noises from one's own basement can lead to a startle response or racing heartbeat. The taste or smell of alcohol can become negatively conditioned simply through hearing stories of abusive drunken adults. These responses are more likely in individuals in whom these sensory modalities are more highly developed than the imagery system, which tends to be the most common sensory modality in individuals in our culture.

It is clear that unaddressed vicarious traumatization poses hazards to the therapist and all of his relationships, both personal and professional. As vicarious traumatization affects the self of the therapist, it will emerge in the therapeutic relationship directly and through countertransference. The recognition of vicarious traumatization is an essential first step to self-protection.

Concomitantly, this work provides therapists with unparalleled opportunities for personal and spiritual growth. When aware of the risks, therapists can work to minimize the deleterious effects and maximize the positive transformative effects of their profession on all aspects of their selves.

14

What Contributes to
Vicarious Traumatization?

VICARIOUS TRAUMATIZATION is ineluctable for trauma therapists. Therapists cannot do this work without experiencing assaults to their usual ways
of viewing themselves, the world, and other people. Some have suggested
that vicarious traumatization is the result of the therapist's unresolved psychological issues (Sakheim, 1995). While one's conflicts and vulnerabilities
do contribute to vicarious traumatization, we do not believe anyone, however psychologically healthy, can do this work and remain unchanged.
Experiencing disrupted beliefs and intrusive imagery as a result of the clinical material is both inevitable and normal. These responses reflect neither a
disorder in the therapist nor a bad deed on the part of the client. Rather, it
is part of the reality and process of trauma therapy. Denying vicarious
traumatization will only force it underground, causing damage to both
therapist and client, just as the social denial of childhood abuse has done
incalculable harm to countless individuals and to the society as a whole.

Neither therapist nor client can participate in these therapies without
being transformed in profound ways. Indeed, the possibility of entering
empathically into an intimate relationship with a sexual abuse survivor and
not being transformed by it belies the concept of the therapeutic relationship. When we understand the factors that contribute to vicarious traumatization, we are better able to address and minimize its negative effects,

individually and organizationally. In this chapter, we examine how specific aspects of the work and work context and specific qualities of the therapist contribute directly and indirectly to vicarious traumatization. In psychotherapy, a key medium for vicarious traumatization is the therapist's empathy; we start with a discussion of that relational context.

EMPATHY: A THERAPIST'S ASSET AND LIABILITY*

As therapists, one of our most valuable tools is our capacity to enter empathically into the experience of our clients. The therapist's empathy is essential to the creation of a therapeutic relationship and thus to the recovery of the sexual abuse survivor, as others have also noted (McCann & Colletti, 1994; Wilson & Lindy, 1994a). Yet empathy also puts us at risk for vicarious traumatization; in particular, a specific type of empathic connection with our clients can heighten vicarious traumatization.

We describe this vulnerable state in the context of a four-square model of empathy suggesting that empathy varies along two dimensions: type of empathic connection and time frame. We present this model for heuristic purposes; clinically, these divisions are not as distinct as this model suggests. The model is intended to provide a guide for the clinician to consider his empathic style and distance with clients. Unlike Wilson and Lindy's (1994a) model of four types of countertransference responses, our model describes four types of *empathic engagement* with survivor clients.

Empathic Connection

To understand the relation between vicarious traumatization and empathy, we describe two types of empathic connection. One form of empathy focuses on the cognitive understanding of what happened, what the client says she experienced, how it came about, what it meant to her, her narrative account of the abuse and its aftermath, and so forth. We refer to this as *cognitive empathy* or cognitive comprehension.

The other form of empathy is affective. We can feel some of the client's pain, her fear, her rage, her grief, the range of intense emotions connected with her experience. When we sense her experience at a feeling level, this is *affective empathy* or empathic comprehension.†

---

*We wish to acknowledge the contribution of Ervin Staub, Ph.D. to our thinking about the relation between empathy and vicarious traumatization.

†Certainly it could be argued that there are complex variations at unconscious and preconscious levels such as somatic empathy (having parallel bodily symptoms), identificatory countertransference responses, and interpersonal reenactments, and that these processes also set the stage for vicarious traumatization. However, they are not characteristically identified as empathy, and for the purpose of this discussion we will focus on the two more conscious processes.

Time Frame

In addition to two types of empathy, there are two meaningful time frames in which we experience the survivor's experience of her trauma: *past* and *present*.

At the time of the trauma, as a child, the client had both cognitive and affective experiences. Currently, as an adult survivor, she also has both cognitive and affective experiences of what happened to her. *Thus there are four realms into which we can enter empathically with our clients: the past cognitive experience, the present cognitive experience, the past affective experience, and the present affective experience.*

In the first (past cognitive), we become aware of and attempt to understand the thoughts the little girl had about the abuse while it was happening, how she made sense of it, how she viewed those around her, how she coped, whom she told (if she attempted to tell anyone). In the second, (present cognitive), we learn how the adult survivor understands her abuse experience and current life experiences, including her responses and those of others, and how the abuse has affected her adult life. In the third realm (past affective), we feel the little girl's terror, anger, vulnerability, and pain. In the fourth realm (present affective), we feel the pain, rage, and grief of the adult who is increasingly aware of what happened to her, of her lack of control over the abuse, of all of the resulting losses. We can feel an empathic connection to our client in each of these four realms.

We suggest that it is the third realm, the past affective or affective empathy with the client as a child, in which we are most vulnerable to vicarious traumatization. Our connection to and experience of the overwhelming feelings of a child being abused affects us most deeply as therapists and human beings, and may change our fundamental experience of ourselves and the world. While it could be argued that avoiding such empathic connection would protect the therapist, it is however a crucial aspect of the therapy. It is only through the therapist's empathic connection, that the client herself can come to connect with and understand the truth of her experience in its developmental context.

ASPECTS OF THE WORK

We have defined vicarious traumatization as a transformation in the inner experience of the therapist that results from empathic engagement with clients' trauma material. Specific aspects of trauma therapy with incest survivors that can contribute to vicarious traumatization include the nature of the therapy process with survivors, the nature of the clientele, the specific facts of childhood sexual abuse, and both organizational and social contextual factors.

Empathic Engagement with
Trauma Material

Three aspects of trauma therapy contribute directly to vicarious traumatization: exposure to graphic trauma material, exposure to the realities of people's cruelty to one another, and observation of and participation in traumatic reenactments.

Graphic Trauma Material

The graphic descriptions of rape and sadism that many survivors need to share with their therapists in order to heal can horrify and haunt the therapist. Their vivid imagery is often accompanied by specific details of smells, sounds, and bodily pain which can shock or disgust the therapist. These details challenge his self capacities, his ability to self-soothe and tolerate the powerful feelings of abhorrence, rage, grief. When a therapist holds these images somatically, he can be troubled by nausea, acute bodily pain, headaches, fatigue, or malaise. The therapist's body may be involuntarily recruited for affect management as he works with graphic details of bodily experience or his clients' somatic symptoms.

Intentional Cruelty

A therapist's fundamental frame of reference and schemas are repeatedly challenged by the material he hears from survivors of childhood sexual abuse. The undeniable realities of people's cruelty to one another; the horrific abuse, misuse, and neglect of children; and the vulnerability of children to untrustworthy adults overwhelm our defenses when we hear, hour after hour, the manifold ways in which our clients have been injured, humiliated, molested, and systematically dehumanized. If a therapist has the courage not to deny his clients' truth, these facts will invariably lead to disruptions in his frame of reference. In the face of this reality, it is very difficult for a trauma therapist to hold a view of others as well-intentioned, of childhood as a time of innocence and joy, of families as supportive and loving.

Clients' stories of terror often change the therapist's safety schemas. How can one hold the illusion of safety, which allows him to walk down the street alone, sleep in a house with his windows open, and drive at night with the doors unlocked, after daily confrontations with the dangers faced by women and children in this society? To deny this danger would be to engage in a social delusion (Herman, 1992; Sakheim & Devine, 1995); our work robs us of the luxury of choice about those illusions, just as trauma and victimization have robbed our clients of their sense of safety, of their illusions.

Clients' Reenactments

In psychotherapy, trauma survivors are likely to engage in reenactments of their traumatic histories. We view these reenactments as a form of memory, an interpersonal memory whose unconscious reliving informs the therapist about the client's early relationships and provides the client with opportunities to rework important early relationships (see chapter 6 for further discussion). These reenactments involve not only holding difficult transferences and projections, but struggling with assaults to one's identity and cherished beliefs. Over time and within and across therapies, therapist and client will each take multiple roles including (but not limited to) victim, perpetrator, and bystander as these reenactments unfold. These roles will challenge the therapist's identity, ego-ideal, and beliefs about himself and other (Horner, 1993), and these challenges are a step in the process of vicarious traumatization.

Reenactments occur outside the therapeutic relationship as well. At times, they result in our clients being exposed to danger. Revictimization is a well-documented sequela of childhood sexual abuse (Chu, 1992; Neumann, in press; van der Kolk, 1989). Some clients are in battering relationships, while others are still being approached by their childhood abuse perpetrators, and others continue to reenact abuse on themselves. Hearing about a survivor client's current abuse puts a therapist repeatedly in the role of helpless witness, a traumatic experience. It is more than painful for therapists to engage in the slow work of self-building psychotherapy while they see their clients' self-esteem and bodies abused by significant others or themselves.

The Nature of Trauma Therapy

For a psychotherapist, it is the process of the trauma therapy, including repeated exposure to trauma material in the context of empathic connection with the survivor client, that creates vicarious traumatization. To begin with, these therapies are often intense and very intimate. This intimacy and intensity is frequently terrifying for the client and her terror then heightens the therapist's vigilance and sense of responsibility. This tension creates an exacting environment for the establishment of a therapeutic relationship.

The intimacy of these therapies calls for authenticity and affective availability on the part of the therapist. His feelings are an invaluable guide to what is happening in the therapeutic relationship. However, given the powerful and often distressing affects stirred by the material, this openness also puts the therapist at risk for vicarious traumatization. Yet, modulating his feelings can result in withdrawing from his clients. In trauma therapies, clients will be particularly sensitive to any pretense, withholding, or falseness on the part of the therapist. "Having one's feelings available to this extent is at times a very great strain" (Little, 1957, p. 244). Yet, if the therapist resorts to numbness, he is not only unable to use his feelings to connect with his clients, he is unable to use his feelings to ascertain his needs and protect himself.

Other Contextual Factors of Trauma Therapy

The context of the trauma therapy can also contribute to vicarious traumatization. For example, many trauma therapists work long hours, schedule consecutive sessions with trauma survivors, and may not set adequate self-protective limits on their availability and stamina. As a therapist becomes experienced in trauma therapy, he may pick up clients who have been referred by therapists to a "specialist" or an "expert." Unless the therapist is able to set and maintain limits on time and caseload, he can develop a large, challenging caseload of long-term trauma clients.

Another contributing contextual factor is the confidentiality of the work; one cannot share with one's partner or friends the details of the day's experiences. For a trauma therapist, this stricture means holding alone particularly frightening or appalling images or stories. Sitting alone with unmetabolized trauma material is a primary contributor to vicarious traumatization.

The Nature of the Clientele

Trauma survivor clients and the adaptations they have made present particular challenges to the therapist and his world view. We want to emphasize that this statement is not an indictment of our clients. Their experiences have harmed them deeply, and the path to healing is to work within a caring relationship to explore this harm. Yet, there are facts about clients, their histories, their lives, their situations, and their adaptations, which when experienced across many trauma clients will affect the therapist deeply.

Yassen (in press) emphasizes that "secondary traumatization" is a response to the client's trauma, not to the client herself. Psychoanalytically informed trauma theory (CSDT) suggests that the trauma influences the person of the survivor, and that the client's adaptation to the trauma incorporates the potential for interpersonal reenactment. Trauma therapy provides an opportunity to sort out the past from the present, to distinguish between past and current situations which can give rise to the same feelings (for example, a client who is frightened may quickly move to feeling abused). However, in this process the therapist will be exposed to difficult interpersonal and affective experiences, which when repeated across clients can change his experience of self and schemas about others.

It is not wrong for clients to have an impact on their therapists (nor is it a matter of choice or clients), even when the impact is painful. In choosing to become trauma therapists, we have made a commitment to bear witness to human suffering. The trauma therapist's hope is that, by lending his self in empathic connection to his client, he can help transform the client's experience into one in which both can find meaning. Yet, he must acknowledge the painful process of that journey and the toll it takes on the therapist in order to have a hope of managing it in a way that benefits both therapist and client.

Even without active current abuse, many survivor clients live with chronically stressful life conditions, and woefully inadequate supports. Supportive family, safe housing, education, an adequate income, a meaningful job, friends, child care, and health insurance are resources that survivors particularly need and may have difficulty obtaining because of their abuse histories. When encountered across clients, these overwhelming needs can make a therapist feel inadequate and devalued, thus shaking his faith in himself and his profession, and perhaps in his society as well.

Clients' Adaptations

Suicidal Preoccupation. Many survivor clients are chronically suicidal. For many, suicide has been a constant companion and mode of self-soothing as it provides an illusion of control and escape. However, therapists are committed to affirming life and helping clients survive and thrive. Research consistently finds that suicidal statements and behaviors are the most stressful client behavior for therapists (Deutsch, 1984; Farber, 1983c; Menninger, 1990). A recent study has found that psychologists experience such behaviors more often with survivor clients than with nonsurvivors, and that when survivor clients engage in these challenging behaviors, psychologists experience them as more stressful than when nonsurvivor clients engage in the same behaviors (Gamble et al., 1994).

Therapists must adjust both their professional and personal beliefs about suicide and the value of life in order to hold with respect the importance of suicidal thinking for survivors. That adjustment coupled with the real stress of not knowing whether someone the therapist has come to care for will be safe and alive can take an enormous toll on his self capacities and spirituality. When many of his survivor clients struggle with self-loathing or intolerable rage or grief, his self capacities can be severely taxed. When several clients question the meaning of life, often concluding that there is no reason to live, his spiritual beliefs and foundation can be shaken. The therapist is called upon to hold clients' hopelessness while assessing immediate and real danger and respecting their adaptive strategies. Survivor clients need their therapists to understand the depth of their despair without acting out of the therapists' own anxiety to hospitalize or otherwise constrain them. Yet, of course, at times a therapist is called to action for his own sake as well as his client's. It is important to differentiate a client's wish to be dead from an intention to kill herself. To complicate the picture further, many survivor clients cut, burn, punch, or otherwise injure themselves with no intent to kill themselves (Calof, in press), behaviors which Kreitman (1977) termed "parasuicidal." All of these behaviors can wear down the therapist who cares about the safety and esteem of his clients and does not share their images of themselves as despicable or worthless.

Interpersonal Style. One of the factors that modifies vicarious traumatization is the therapist's satisfaction and sense of efficacy in his work. His self-esteem as a therapist is a buffer against the assaults of vicarious traumatization to his identity. Yet trauma clients may be frightened, reluctant, or initially unable to take in what the therapist is offering. Childhood abuse can result in deep narcissistic injuries to clients, who then may struggle with suspicion and feelings of entitlement along with their mistrust. This combination can lead a client to challenge the therapist endlessly, to view the therapist's every move with suspicion or contempt, while at the same time demanding attention in ways that inhibit empathic responding. The therapist is then vulnerable to feeling worn out and unappreciated or, worse still, accused of being a perpetrator or a bystander by someone he wants to help. There are few more difficult situations for the therapist than that in which he is not allowed to be therapeutic or is perceived as abusive.

The therapist's efficacy, worth, and identity are also challenged when he has to struggle with setting limits and negotiating his needs in these therapies. Some clients will experience therapists' limits or needs as selfish, withholding, or unempathic. These charges can disrupt the therapist's identity as helper; the therapist may wonder, "Am I really a giving helper?" "Why can't I accept everyone?" Alternatively, he may engage in questioning related to his intimacy needs: "Why can't I connect with this person despite my wish to do so?"

Aspects of the Work Context

The context of our work—organizational, professional, and social—influences our resilience or vulnerability to the effects of vicarious traumatization. Norcross and Prochaska's (1986) informative study highlights the significant role of the work context in the therapist's stress level. They asked 108 women counselors to identify the precipitants of their own worst period of distress over the past three years. Many of the counselors mentioned aspects of their work situations, including supervisors, policies, promotions, salaries; only a small number mentioned any particular patient problem. Research on factors influencing burnout generally support this finding as well (Edelwich, 1980). It seems clear that aspects of his work context will contribute to a therapist's vicarious traumatization. The specific contributions to vicarious traumatization will be unique for each therapist; however, there are three general contexts that may affect the therapist's vicarious traumatization.

Organizational Context

Trauma therapists work in a wide range of settings, which have implications for their clinical work. The mission of the organization and the way the clinical work fits into that mission also shape the support the therapist receives for his work. The staff constellation can increase or decrease a therapist's sense of isolation or connection. One's colleagues may all be trauma therapists or one may be the only trauma therapist in a large institution, which can lead to isolation or withdrawal (or to being identified with one's clients by the organization). Organizational politics often affect the work of trauma therapists. When survivor treatment programs are eliminated, for example, in favor of other, perhaps more traditional programs, both clients and therapists suffer.

Research has found that those working in agency or clinic settings are more stressed than those working in independent practice (Ackerley, Burnell, Holder, & Kurdek, 1988; Hellman & Morrison, 1987; Pearlman & Mac Ian, 1994; Raquepaw & Miller, 1989). This finding may relate to their lack of authority to limit their own caseloads, the short-term nature of the treatments, the difficult life conditions of the clinic patients, lower incomes in studies which did not control for this, or other aspects of clinic work.

Therapists who work in settings in which colleagues or administrative or clinical supervisors do not conceptualize trauma work as they do are often more vulnerable to vicarious traumatization. For example, when clients are conceptualized as "borderline" without an understanding of the likely underlying childhood trauma (Bryer et al., 1987; Herman et al., 1989; Westen et al., 1990), or where dissociation is overlooked as a natural solution to the impossibilities of severe childhood abuse (Putnam, 1989) in favor of traditional conceptual models, a trauma therapist can feel angry and protective or misunderstood, blamed, or shamed for his work.

Trauma therapists can feel more strain and a sense of isolation when there are few trauma-sensitive individuals or programs to whom to refer survivor clients for adjunctive treatments, including medication evaluations, self-help groups, group therapy, body therapies, expressive therapies, inpatient treatment, partial hospital programs, outpatient therapists, and substance abuse treatment programs that specialize in treating survivors.

A lack of funds for treatment beleaguers many survivors, and can leave therapists struggling with conflicting needs and ideals. Survivors with serious impairments in self-esteem, interpersonal skills, and cognitive functioning (including dissociation) can have a difficult time in the workplace. Without solid employment (and sometimes even with it), a survivor may not have health insurance or sufficient income to pay for treatment. Organizations that can support treatment for clients who have limited funds support their therapist employees as well by protecting them from ending therapy relationships prematurely and abandoning clients, reenacting childhood traumas with the therapist playing the part of perpetrator. These resources are rare, however, and without them therapists may struggle against their feelings of outrage for survivor clients, their wish to offer help, and their own needs for financial security, self-care, and recognition of the limits of their resources. Especially when a therapist works in isolation, he may come to feel responsible to and for all survivor clients and fail to attend to his needs, increasing his vulnerability to vicarious traumatization.

There are also subtle ways in which organizations can set the therapist up for increased vicarious traumatization. A lack of respect for clients and their struggles can be manifest in such realms as telephone interactions with them (are they addressed by first name and the therapists by a moniker such as Dr., Mr., or Ms.?); appointment management; observation of client confidentiality; availability of a physically safe, private, and comfortable therapy space; and respectful transfer of clients when necessitated by therapist training programs or job changes. When organizations do not treat clients respectfully, the therapist can experience great stress, setting the stage for vicarious traumatization.

Organizations can become involved in trauma reenactments, for example by becoming insensitive or abusive to clients or employees, or they may themselves reflect the effects of vicarious traumatization as a result of doing too much trauma work with too little support. These dynamics are dangerous, if unrecognized, for staff and clients alike, and require an awareness and a willingness to be open to addressing dysfunctional or traumatic organizational dynamics.

The history of the organization with survivor clients will inform the work. If the organization views its experience treating survivors positively, it will provide more support for the clinician than if the experience is viewed largely as one of treatment failures. Treatment successes and opportunities to share successes are one antidote to vicarious traumatization. The availability of good trauma therapy supervision and of colleagues with whom to consult formally and informally supports the therapist and may also ameliorate vicarious traumatization. Further, the acknowledgment by one's colleagues and administrators of the difficulty and unique challenges of the work, including the unique potential for vicarious traumatization, can make a significant difference in a therapist's vulnerability to vicarious traumatization.

Professional Context

The therapist may be working in clinical arenas, including incest, dissociative identity disorder, and ritual abuse, which are not widely recognized or validated by colleagues. There are therapists who do not perceive or acknowledge the wide prevalence of childhood sexual abuse survivors in the society or in their own caseloads. These colleagues will fail to support the trauma therapist by not acknowledging the special needs of this population.

As discussed in chapter 16, trauma therapy occurs in the context of a paradigm shift (Kuhn, 1970) in the field of mental health. A paradigm shift involves a change in frame of reference for all of us. This process is reflected in academic and clinical battles about terminology, labels, technique, and validity of constructs, and in economic and political battles about funding, reimbursement, and accreditation. The individual trauma therapist can feel buffeted in the turmoil and lose sight of his needs in the clinical work.

Social Context

Both trauma and trauma therapy occur in a social context. The social context for the trauma therapy can either support or drain the therapist. The way victims and victimization are viewed in the community will affect the support the therapist feels for his work. If the social climate is one of misogyny, in which women are often blamed and often blame themselves for their own victimization (Ryan, 1971; Saakvitne & Pearlman, 1993), it may be difficult for the therapist to obtain the support he needs to feel effective. Doing this work in a culture in which sexual exploitation of and violence against women is the basis of a billion dollar entertainment industry is profoundly demoralizing and undermines the empowering work we do in psychotherapy. It is unnerving and enraging to treat survivors of sexual assault all day, and to see violence against women touted as family entertainment on television and movie screens at night.

Contributors to Wilson and Lindy's (1994b) volume on countertransference includes several chapters which explore social forces that we believe can contribute to vicarious traumatization: patriarchy and sexism (Hartman & Jackson, 1994), racism and capitalism (Parson, 1994), systemic denial (Maxwell & Sturm, 1994), and society's contempt for victims (Op den Velde, Koerselman, & Aarts, 1994). Although these authors are writing about survivors of other traumatic experiences, the same social forces affect both incest victims and their therapists.

Part of the social climate in this country today is an increasing awareness of the logarithmic increases in health care costs and charges. In response to this, the insurance industry has attempted to limit reimbursement for psychotherapy. Survivors who rely on health insurance (or who have no health insurance) to pay for their psychotherapy may only have resources for limited treatment. Unfortunately, recovery from childhood sexual abuse is long-term work. The process of psychotherapy can allow the survivor the chance to become a fully developed adult with rewarding relationships, the ability to participate fully in society as worker and parent, and a capacity to give to others; however, these goals will not be accomplished in 12 sessions, or in 12 months (Saakvitne & Pearlman, 1992).

Short-term work with incest survivors, increasingly mandated by managed care and other social systems which seek to limit costs and therefore treatment, sets the therapist up for vicarious traumatization. Short-term work allows for a more limited therapeutic relationship. The therapist knows less about clients' resources and capacities, so it is more difficult to anticipate the ramifications of interventions. He is also likely to know much more about the client's pain and difficulties than about her strengths. In short-term treatment, there is less opportunity to see the positive impact of therapeutic interventions; the therapist bears witness to the pain but may not be around to celebrate the healing. It also means less effective, and sometimes harmful, treatment; when a survivor begins to open up her pain and then must abruptly end treatment, she may leave with more active symptomatology than that which brought her into treatment. This puts the therapist in the role of perpetrator, which is another set-up for vicarious traumatization. Settings that are defined by crisis work, including hotlines, many inpatient units, and partial hospitalization or day treatment settings are often vulnerable to this hazard.

The broader social and political climate also affects the level of support the therapist receives for the work. The issues surrounding the validity of sexual abuse survivors' memories have undermined the work of the many courageous survivors and their therapists who are attempting to rebuild lives shattered by sexual abuse. While trauma therapists must be careful to inquire about the client's history rather than to construct it for her (Pearlman & McCann, 1994), they must also not support the social denial of child sexual abuse that has sabotaged the treatment of survivors for decades (Herman, 1992).

ASPECTS OF THE THERAPIST

The second major contributing factor to vicarious traumatization is the therapist himself. It is the interaction of both work, or situation, and therapist, or person, variables that is key in the development of vicarious trauma-tization. Anything that compromises the therapist's ego resources, self ca-pacities, or any unresolved personal issues, can set the stage for vicarious traumatization. Again, the specifics of what contributes to each therapist's vicarious traumatization will depend on the individual. Below we discuss the therapist's self or personality, personal history, current personal circum-stances, and place in his professional development as they may contribute to vicarious traumatization.

The Self

Identity, World View, and Spirituality

It is virtually impossible for a self-reflective trauma therapist not to struggle with identity issues as a result of the work (see Chapter 13). To the extent that the therapist may already be asking identity questions arising from developmental transitions or personal crises, he is more susceptible to disruptions as a result of working with numerous incest survivors in his caseload who are struggling with various, often malevolent-perpetrator, transference issues. He can be more vulnerable to accepting an identity defined by his clients or his professional role and not recognize those roles as aspects rather than the totality of himself.

When identity overlaps with self-esteem, issues of professional compe-tence are salient. This work is challenging, the clients' anguish severe, and when therapists invite clients to notice how well their relationships are meeting their needs, their own ability as therapists is up for examination because noticing involves the therapy relationship as well as others. The constant questioning of the therapist's competence by both client and thera-pist is a stressor that can contribute to the therapist's vulnerability to vicari-ous traumatization.

A therapist's world view grounds him in a larger context of human existence and community. The therapist whose life philosophy is unclear, who holds external views of causality or struggles constantly with questions of causality may be at greater risk for vicarious traumatization. The risk is the confirmation of one's worst fears about humanity, and a resulting de-spair which impacts both the therapist in his personal life and the therapies. Therapists who entered the field without a clear sense of purpose or belief about psychotherapy, or whose psychotherapy training lacked a theoretical framework to conceptualize the process of psychological change and heal-ing are at particular risk to be thrown into despair by therapeutic impasses or failures or to feel bewildered and create magical explanations for thera-peutic successes.

Spirituality is an inherent human capacity for awareness of an elusive aspect of experience (see chapter 3). The therapist who is experiencing disruptions in meaning and hope, connection, awareness, and sense of non-material aspects of life will be more vulnerable to further disruption in these areas through the work. Individuals who are experiencing spiritual crises, for example, a loss of meaning in life, will find themselves at particular risk for vicarious traumatization. Therapists who have no room in their formulations of human experience for the nonmaterial, intangible aspects of human experience may be at a loss in the face of the deep spiritual wound experienced by survivors of traumatic life events.

Affect Style

Survivor work is affectively intense and demanding. If the therapist has difficulty tolerating strong affect, he may experience affective overload in therapy sessions. His comfort or discomfort with his own powerful, often primitive, and sometimes dystonic affects will influence his identity and esteem and often evoke a range of further feelings of anxiety, shame, or confusion.

If the therapist is struggling to maintain a sense of inner connection with others, he is open to feelings of isolation and existential abandonment. In this context, it is more difficult to hold the feelings and stories shared by survivor clients. High personal standards and harsh superego-laden self-criticism or self-blame leave a therapist's sense of self highly vulnerable to damage through vicarious traumatization. It can also influence identity questions as the therapist grapples with questions of his competence and identity as therapist/helper. Such countertransference responses within a session can be taken in by the vulnerable therapist at a deep level. When experienced across sessions, they increase vicarious traumatization.

A compromised ability to make self-protective judgments can lead a therapist to take on more clients or invite more graphic trauma material than he can manage. He may not know he needs to protect himself, may not pull back from affect or trauma material that he is unprepared to manage, thus increasing his exposure and the probability of vicarious trau-matization.

Self-awareness and introspection are essential tools to the therapist. A therapist whose self-attunement is inhibited or limited will be more vulnera-ble to vicarious traumatization. This lack of insight prevents a therapist from knowing and processing his countertransference or sorting out the reality content in a transference response. He may not know he needs consultation on a difficult case or to take a break (whether a coffee break or a vacation) from work. He may fail to separate his own affect from that which is being projected by the client or to recognize his own projections and transference to the client. This lack of awareness can be a starting point for the countertransference-vicarious traumatization cycle (see chapter 15), as it sets the stage for empathic failures, therapeutic impasses, and confusion in the therapy that erode a therapist's esteem and hope. Without awareness, he is less likely to seek personal therapy, supervision, or consultation, to read or to attend professional meetings to learn more about trauma therapy. Doing trauma work without these supports can result in increased vicarious traumatization.

Self-awareness is linked to sense of humor and empathy; the underlying thread is perspective. Without perspective, trauma therapy can become deadly; all human endeavors are enriched and made more bearable by a sense of context. In survivor work, this means understanding the resources of the client, the therapist's place in his clients' lives, and the importance of the work, among other things. Those contexts and perspectives help the therapist to hold the pain he witnesses; without them, the work can impact him more strongly.

Ability to Recognize and Meet One's Needs

When the therapist's needs are not balanced and when he is struggling and failing to meet these needs in mature ways, he is more vulnerable to vicarious traumatization. For example, the therapist who has disrupted safety schemas is likely to feel heightened fear and insecurity when working with trauma survivor clients. The therapist with trust disruptions can find his convictions about betrayal and abandonment confirmed in his clients' stories. When intimacy is an issue for the therapist, he may feel increased alienation or isolation in response to his clients' stories of disconnection and alienation. For therapists with esteem disruptions, stories of ridicule of children and examples of self-mockery in their clients may fortify their own devaluation of themselves or others. Finally, therapists with control disruptions will certainly find trauma work challenging, highlighting their concerns and limitations with control in interpersonal situations.

Personal History

Each therapist brings his own unique personal history to the therapy relationship; when that history includes traumatic life experiences, he may be more susceptible to vicarious traumatization. The material a therapist hears from clients will stir not only empathy, but also memory and personal pain. The membrane between his personal and professional selves will be stretched and he will have to work more vigilantly at times to remain clear, protected, and boundaried. In chapter 8, we discussed in depth countertransference issues for therapists who are survivors; in this section, we describe the vicarious traumatization implications.

Survivor therapists may be at special risk for vicarious traumatization. In our study of trauma therapists, we found significantly more psychological disruption in the 60% of therapists who stated they had a personal trauma history (Pearlman & Mac Ian, 1994).* In particular, those therapists with a trauma history had significantly greater disruptions in schemas related to safety, self-trust, other-trust, self-esteem, and other-intimacy, as measured by the TSI Belief Scale (Pearlman et al., 1992; see appendix); greater disruptions on the SCL-90-R, a scale that assesses general psychophysiological symptoms (Derogatis & Spencer, 1982); and more intrusive symptoms related to client trauma material, as assessed by a modified form of the Impact of Event Scale (Horowitz, Wilner, & Alvarez, 1979). These results suggest that therapists with a personal trauma history are at greater risk for vicarious traumatization. Of course, these results are preliminary and many questions are unanswered. Many mitigating factors, such as self-care, personal therapy, supervision, and specific client issues, may affect a survivor therapist's experience. Our current study (Gamble et al., 1994) may provide answers to some of these questions. However, these data clearly speak to the need for therapists with trauma histories to be especially attuned to their needs and feelings.

The risk of vicarious traumatization may be higher for survivor therapists for several reasons. Probably most obviously, survivor clients' material can reawaken the therapist's own memories and consequent strong feelings. While a personal history of childhood sexual abuse certainly can allow a therapist to understand his survivor client more deeply, it can become problematic, for both therapist and client, when the therapist fails to acknowledge to himself the significance and effect of his own history in his therapy relationships. If the survivor therapist has not done extensive work on his abuse in his own therapy, this can be extremely disruptive, and the therapist may need to employ a variety of defensive strategies in his work, some of which open him to further traumatization. For example, one survivor therapist found himself increasingly dissociated during sessions in which clients were describing abuse material. This left him unable to engage interpersonally with the client or to recall the content of many sessions, so he was unable to contextualize and work through the material in his own supervision or therapy.

---

*We did not ask about the type of trauma the therapist had experienced; those who stated they had a trauma history comprised both sexual abuse and other trauma survivors.

Survivor therapists may be more sensitive than non-survivor therapists to the inner torment of survivor clients. To the extent that they identify with their clients and empathize with the agony of a small child enduring sexual abuse, they may be more likely to suffer. In addition, observing clients repeatedly engage in self-destructive reenactments, and playing a role in those reenactments, may be more agonizing for the survivor therapist because for him, the role of victim is not only symbolic and transferential, but the roles of perpetrator and bystander may also be known through his personal experience. A perpetrator transference may be especially noxious to a survivor who swore throughout childhood that he would never be like his perpetrator. The therapist may feel deeply injured when such a transference inevitably emerges.

Finally, the survivor therapist may have worked hard to develop a personal spirituality that includes connection, hope, and meaning. Doing this work can assault any therapist's spirituality; it can be particularly destructive for someone whose spirituality is constructed upon a fragile foundation. Thus, the survivor therapist can be especially vulnerable to the erosion of hard won hope and optimism.

Current Personal Circumstances

A therapist's current psychological and interpersonal situation will influence his susceptibility to vicarious traumatization. Life stressors such as the complex demands of relationships and family; stressful or traumatic life events such as a pregnancy, illness, the death of a loved one, or a divorce; and the crises that take place in the lives of friends and families (Belle, 1982) are common in the lives of psychotherapists (Fromm-Reichmann, 1960; Norcross & Prochaska, 1986) and can all take a toll on the therapist. World and community events can affect both therapist and client (e.g., national disasters, youth abduction in local community, wars and genocide) and can make therapists more vulnerable to vicarious traumatization as they open themselves to the pain of the larger society as well as that experienced by their clients.

The therapist grappling with personal loss can be moved into despair or overwhelming grief as he hears individual clients' stories of loss or becomes aware of cumulative themes of loss across trauma clients. Personal life events also affect the ability to perceive transference as such, causing a therapist to feel like an inadequate mother, a passive bystander, or a perpetrator of neglect. Recent stressful or traumatic life events can lead the therapist to reinforce his clients' disrupted schemas. When a client says, "You shouldn't let yourself get close to people because they will leave you," the therapist who has just lost an important relationship may agree, rather than upholding the belief that, while loss is an inevitable part of life, intimacy may provide rewards that balance the loss.

Chronic life stressors, such as living or working in an unsafe neighborhood, managing a family with inadequate support (child care, money, health insurance, etc.), or chronic health problems, can make a therapist more vulnerable to vicarious traumatization as he overidentifies with his clients, joining them in their despair, or identifies with the child who was expected to be an adult with inadequate resources. Acute, lesser stressors, such as a health problem, overwork, hunger, fatigue, overscheduling, an impending examination, and being on call, can also contribute to vicarious traumatization. When a therapist's resources are impaired, he is more vulnerable to being affected by his clients' despair and by their vivid trauma material.

Ongoing, normal aspects of the therapist's personal life can also predispose him to vicarious traumatization. For example, therapists who have children are often vulnerable to the disruption of their other-safety schemas. It can be unbearable to learn of dangers to children when one is connected with and responsible for children on a full-time basis. Many trauma therapists report being overprotective or suffering acutely from intense anxiety for their children's safety.

Being a woman or gay or a member of a minority culture in our society means being vulnerable to discrimination, defamation, and assault. These factors can make the female, gay or minority therapist more vulnerable to vicarious traumatization because these individuals already live in a state of heightened vulnerability and because they are more likely to identify with marginalized and victimized groups.

Current Professional Circumstances

Training and Supervision

The appropriateness of one's training for the work is a factor in vicarious traumatization. Without specific trauma therapy training, therapists have no framework for understanding their own experience or that of their clients. In our study of trauma therapists, those with masters training reported more psychological distress than did those with doctoral training (Pearlman & Mac Ian, 1994). These effects were independent of income. Perhaps those trauma therapists with more education were better prepared to deal with the clinical work, whether because of the availability of a theoretical framework, more effective ways of managing boundary issues and thus protecting themselves, more supervised experience, or other factors in some way related to a higher level of education. Without access to continuing education, trauma therapists have greater difficulty doing their work. This field is young and we are still learning about the impact of psychological trauma and effective treatment for survivors and training and supervision for clinicians.

Therapists without regular, frequent, trauma-focused supervision may also be more vulnerable to vicarious traumatization. We found that fewer than 65% of the therapists (74% of females and 38% of males) were receiving supervision, and a smaller percentage was receiving trauma-related supervision (Pearlman & Mac Ian, 1994).

The therapist's expectations about the work also influence its effect upon him. Meaning systems are an important container for strong feelings for *all* persons; without an understanding of the intensity of the work, without a theoretical framework for understanding the psychological impact of trauma and the recovery process, the trauma therapist is open to feeling confused or harmed by the work.

Professional Identity

The meaning of the work to the therapist influences its impact upon him. If his identity is organized around being a trauma therapist, it can be especially painful to be playing the role of perpetrator in a reenactment with a survivor. If the work is a less central part of the therapist's life or identity, he may be less likely to experience vicarious traumatization. (On the other hand, people whose work is meaningful may be happier overall than those who experience their work as without meaning. The benefits may outweigh the hazards.)

Control

Just as there is a correlation between a perceived lack of control over one's work and levels of burnout (Ackerley et al., 1988), both perceived and actual control can also be factors in vicarious traumatization. In our study of trauma therapists, those working in clinic and hospital settings showed higher levels of distress than those working in independent practice or multiple settings, independent of the clinician's income (Pearlman & Mac Ian, 1994). If the therapist cannot limit his caseload, choose which clients he will work with, obtain adequate resources for the work, and make clinical decisions in the client's best interest, he will feel thwarted clinically, inadequate, resentful, or neglectful. These feelings feed into vicarious traumatization.

When we understand the contributing factors, we are more likely to be able to identify and ameliorate vicarious traumatization and its potentially harmful effects of therapist and client. We discuss ways of addressing vicarious traumatization in chapter 18.

Part Four

THE INTERACTION BETWEEN COUNTERTRANSFERENCE AND VICARIOUS TRAUMATIZATION

15

The Countertransference-
Vicarious Traumatization Cycle

A THERAPIST who is unaware of or unresponsive to either countertransference or vicarious traumatization experiences can be thrown into a cycle of reactivity, both within and across treatments. Countertransference can heighten a therapist's vulnerability to vicarious traumatization because of his affect, identifications, loss of perspective, or unconscious reenactments. Vicarious traumatization can diminish the therapist's attunement to his inner affective and associative process as well as his ability to notice and address transference, affect, nuance, and countertransference clues in the therapy hour. Without awareness and consultation, a therapist can embark on a bumpy ride of countertransference-vicarious traumatization cycles with a client that can leave them increasingly disconnected and misled by miscommunication, misunderstanding, and mutual projection.

This chapter examines the complex interaction between countertransference and vicarious traumatization. *Countertransference* is specific to a particular therapeutic relationship and *vicarious traumatization* is manifest across trauma therapies. In addition, certain therapists respond with similar countertransference to the same dynamic across therapies (e.g., a generalized countertransference response of activity in the face of any client's passivity), and particularly malevolent and frightening trauma material or transference responses on the part of one client can create a generalized

317

vicarious traumatization response in the therapist. Countertransference and vicarious traumatization can intensify, moderate, or set the stage for one another throughout these therapies, as Lindy and Wilson (1994) have also noted.

A therapist's decreased self-awareness leads to therapeutic errors and interpersonal misunderstandings or empathic failures. This scenario increases the risk for therapeutic impasses, which themselves both result from and increase the potential for countertransference and vicarious traumatization. Therapeutic frustration and failure increase the negative impact of the therapy on the therapist and increase the therapist's strong, often distorted, feelings toward the client in a given therapy. This process is the countertransference-vicarious traumatization cycle, which can result in a loss of important aspects of the client, the treatment, or the therapist.

How Countertransference Responses Set the Stage for Vicarious Traumatization
Countertransference Affect and Defenses

Affect and Identity

A therapist's countertransference can set the stage for particular vicarious traumatization responses in a variety of ways. For example, when immersed in a countertransference response or enactment with a client, a therapist's intense feelings may reduce his self-awareness. In such a state, a therapist is especially vulnerable to the erosion of his cherished beliefs and values, which is a hallmark of vicarious traumatization. In addition, when suffering from "cumulative countertransference," or the cumulative effects of experiencing multiple intense countertransferences across sequential sessions (e.g., an afternoon of consecutive sessions with challenging clients) (Kauffman, 1994), a therapist becomes fatigued and less self-protective, or overstimulated and less insightful and less alert to potential avenues for vicarious traumatization.

Strong affects challenge a therapist's identity, both personal and professional. A therapist with an identity as tough and resilient may feel distressed and ashamed to find himself undone with grief or identificatory feelings of helplessness as he listens to a client's experience of childhood trauma. A therapist with an identity as warm and compassionate may be deeply troubled by angry or punitive countertransference feelings, likely to arise with clients who were victims of harsh punishment. A trauma therapist whose work is based on his capacity for hope in the face of his clients' despair may be shaken when he finds himself joining with his client's hopelessness in an unconscious countertransference identification. When his feelings are unacceptable, he may deny them, thus blocking the opportunity to process and understand their sources and lessening his availability to himself and to the therapy.

Example   A therapist was working with a survivor client who had recently suffered a number of significant losses. He was himself anticipating the death of a loved one. Over time, he found himself feeling increasingly unable to maintain hope and a belief in his client's ability to heal from grief. As the client ruminated endlessly on potential losses and was unable to engage in life, the therapist found himself experiencing the client as physically different: pallid, grey, unappealing, unenlivened. As this perception emerged into the therapist's awareness and he sought consultation, he realized he was engaged in a multidetermined reenactment. He recognized in his perception the repetition of the client's life-threatening illness early in childhood, and the parallel in his response to the client's mother's disconnection and helpless despair. The therapist realized that there was a further parallel in his own history, in his experience of his own mother as helpless in the face of his own childhood medical trauma. As the therapist began to question the effectiveness of this particular therapy process, he became more reactive, less emotionally available, and more withdrawn with all his clients, and specifically less able to tolerate death themes and despair in all therapies. This generalization reflects the impact of the countertransference despair on the hope that maintains therapies, thus creating a vicarious traumatization response.

Psychological Defenses

Both the fact and the specific details of a client's experience of incest and childhood sexual abuse evoke a range of strong affective, spiritual, and identity countertransference responses in the therapist. The therapist will experience his powerful emotional responses in the context of his own self capacities. A therapist who is uncomfortable with strong feelings in general or certain feelings in particular, or whose affect tolerance is exceeded by specific feelings will draw upon his familiar protective defenses. These defenses can compromise his ability to remain affectively available and genuine to himself or his client.

For example, a therapist who prides himself on his assurance and freedom from fear may develop a counterphobic defensive style. When asked to sit with his trauma survivor client's terror, past and present, this therapist must either abandon his client affectively to protect himself from feeling fear, or abandon himself and tolerate a feeling that challenges his capacities (and may invite other feelings, associations, or memories).

A therapist is vulnerable to vicarious traumatization responses in several realms: less tolerance for strong affects, identity confusion, and disrupted safety, esteem, control, trust, and intimacy schemas. Many trauma therapists move defensively into a stance of emotional invulnerability which requires affective numbing. The denial of any affects that contradict a defensive identity then prevents other protective or supportive measures. One cannot soothe or protect oneself from affects one denies having; "you cannot heal what you cannot feel" (Gurudev, personal communication, 1993).

For the therapist, this affective numbing is ego-dystonic. A therapist may feel horrified when he feels little sadness or compassion in response to a client's traumatic memories, experiences, or self-destructive behaviors. Another therapist may feel appalled at his feelings of rage, arousal, or sadism in response to a trauma client. These feelings may clash with his therapist identity, ego ideal, and deeply held values and thus lead to a loss of self-esteem or self-trust and a conflict in identity. When distress prompts unconscious defenses, such as denial, projection, or dissociation, the therapist loses opportunities to process or work through the feelings, which sets the stage for symptom development, unconscious acting out, and changes in self capacities and frame of reference. A therapist must be attuned to his affect states to be able to identify early warning signs of distress, countertransference, and vicarious traumatization.

Countertransference Identities

A therapist who is deeply entrenched in a protective maternal countertransference toward a client struggling with memories and feelings about childhood abuse or neglect is especially vulnerable to traumatization by his client's self-destructive reenactments. To witness a client's self-harm is distressing at any time, but can be devastating when the therapist has moved unconsciously into the role of mother with the concomitant feelings of love, responsibility, and protectiveness. The therapist may find his ability to maintain an inner sense of connection with others (perhaps his maternal introjects) challenged, as remaining connected with this client calls up immense pain and parental culpability.

Whenever a therapist is in a parental countertransference, he may unconsciously become more active or directive with his client, thus accepting a literal rather than symbolic role. And when his parentified interventions do not change a client's experience in the world, interpersonal style, or capacity for impulse control, the therapist may experience shame or the wish to assign blame. Either shame or blame can become generalized responses across therapies as different clients bring similar conflicts or dynamics into their therapies.

One antidote to these unconscious processes of countertransference and vicarious traumatization is the judicial use of countertransference disclosure. When a therapist recognizes and understands his countertransference, there is an opportunity to examine an interactive process at work in the therapy by naming the countertransference in the context of the therapeutic relationship. This interpersonal framework provides a grounding that helps contain the therapist's response to the therapy, and allows the potential for therapeutic working through. Countertransference disclosure requires thoughtfulness (see chapter 7), and when framed in a relational, nonblaming way, invites further acknowledgment and deepening of the therapeutic relationship.

Example One therapist found himself repeatedly offering advice about self-care to a survivor of multiple childhood and adult traumas, especially at the end of sessions. The client, a person with multiplicity, would react in a variety of ways after sessions, often by hurting her body, sometimes resulting in hospitalization. The therapist felt increasingly ineffective across treatments and moved into a slump which was accompanied by feeling overwhelmed as a therapist. Once the therapist recognized the pattern, he began to talk to the client about his own tendency to make suggestions when he saw the client's difficulty caring for herself. He recognized that by doing so, he might have neglected to hear his client's despair and anger. The client acknowledged hearing the therapist's words as directives to "get over it" and assumed her feelings were intolerable to him. The therapist wondered if the client's self-harm was then also a way for her to convey her hurt and anger, and to communicate her pain to him. His disclosure of his countertransference response to the client's self-injurious behaviors allowed the therapist to move with the client to a new level of work related to self-harm and self-care.

Countertransference to Transference

Therapist countertransference responses to particular transferences also open the door to vicarious traumatization. A therapist's fundamental sense of identity is challenged as he holds the range of projective roles, complementary and concordant identifications, and unfamiliar feelings that characterize countertransference. Further, managing the countertransference responses to several clients' negative, hostile, shaming, or blaming transferences, or the countertransference evoked by holding life and death anxiety for one or more suicidal, self-destructive, or despairing client challenges the therapist's identity as helpful and effective, as well as his world view. These countertransference responses often leave a therapist open to vicarious traumatization responses of loss of hope or faith in the process or in himself as a therapist, or a shift in his identity. For each therapist, specific countertransference affects, identities (i.e., self as perpetrator, victim, or bystander), and conflicts set the stage for particular vicarious traumatization vulnerabilities. These interactions are determined by the therapist's affective and defensive style and the salient conflicts between a countertransference response and the therapist's ego ideal.

Example   One therapist felt caught in an endless pattern of disappointing and hurting a particular client. He felt that no matter what he did, she experienced him as a perpetrator. He became very sensitive to these dynamics in all his therapies. He moved from initial feelings of guilt to weariness, resentment, and anger. He became increasingly withdrawn and indifferent. Without recognizing how wounded he felt by the relentless transference, he was unconscious of the generalized defenses he employed. The therapist was alarmed when he recognized that he seemed to be losing his interest in his clients and in psychotherapy in general. This response was entirely inconsistent with his former caring and enthusiasm about his work.

These responses involve all aspects of the therapist's self. For example, when a therapist is responding to a positive paternal transference, he may feel protective and experience his client as vulnerable, dependent, and cherished. At this time, the traumatic impact of being a helpless witness to the client's self-harm, interpersonal reenactments, or bleak despair will be greater. The therapist's rescue fantasies and feelings of responsibility and belief in his power can be distorted, leading to shame, anger, and despair. As we know, countertransference responses are often unconscious and can emerge in subtle changes in response to the client, shifts in fantasy material available to the therapist during sessions, or imagery associated with the particular client and her material, and thus are easily overlooked or ignored.

How Vicarious Traumatization Sets the Stage for Countertransference

Concomitantly, vicarious traumatization inevitably sets the stage for particular countertransference responses. Vicarious traumatization affects the self of the therapist, the context for countertransference. Changes in the therapist's core beliefs, identity, world view, emotional responsiveness, or hope affect the interpersonal realm of the therapeutic relationship and the intrapsychic experience of the therapist. At the most basic level, vicarious traumatization depletes the therapist of physical, emotional, and intellectual energy, thus lessening the resources he brings to each therapy relationship. This depletion inhibits the therapist's awareness of and attunement to his countertransference. In addition, impaired therapists are those at greatest risk for harming clients, whether through sexual contact (Butler & Zelen, 1977; Keith-Spiegel & Koocher, 1985; Pope et al., 1986; Schoener et al., 1989; Zelen, 1985) or other inappropriate or harmful behaviors.

Changes in Frame of Reference

Identity

When a therapist is mourning the loss of a cherished aspect of his identity, his countertransference to a client who challenges him in that area may reflect anger, hurt, or defensive boredom.

Example   One therapist was feeling inadequate as a therapist and questioning the effectiveness of psychotherapy in general as he observed the depth and chronicity of his clients' difficulties and the very slow progress of the work. On several occasions he became profoundly sleepy in sessions with a client with whom he had worked for over two years. Initially he felt embarrassed and guilty, then angry at his client for being boring. After consultation, he realized he was both disappointed and angry with the client who was currently going through a difficult time and showing a recurrence of the same symptoms and feelings that brought her to therapy. He realized that when he started working with her, he had high hopes for rapid change. He remembered thinking that she was ready to explore her abuse history and to acknowledge her strengths and that she would blossom with his warmth and support. Her current presentation and pain challenged both his belief in himself and in the process of therapy and evoked anger that he unconsciously attempted to deny through sleepiness. His vicarious traumatization experience of diminished faith in psychotherapy interacted with his particular (grandiose) parental countertransference with this client to create a countertransference response of disappointment and emotional withdrawal.

The therapist may feel surprised, guilty, or ashamed at his vivid feelings about or toward the client. When a therapist's image of himself as an effective helper is challenged by vicarious traumatization responses, he will be more narcissistically vulnerable and thus open to countertransference responses with clients who are narcissistically vulnerable. He may project shame on to clients who reproach him for his failures, whether directly, with critical or angry words, or indirectly, with depression, despair, or increased symptoms. When a therapist is suffering from vicarious traumatization, he may need the reassurance and connection provided by certain transference responses. For example, a therapist who is experiencing disruptions in his identity as nurturant male as a result of vicarious traumatization may invite his client, overtly or subtly, to praise him for his warmth or supportive style as a way of shoring up this aspect of his identity.

Disruptions in his identity as a competent therapist can lead a therapist to change his style of work without reflection. A behavioral response may be to introduce therapeutic techniques (such as hypnosis, eye-movement desensitization reprocessing, or more directive cognitive-behavioral strategies) without a theoretical understanding of the whole person of the client, and the specific goals, timing, and meaning of a technique in the context of the therapeutic relationship. While potentially valuable within their own theoretical contexts, the use of these techniques at times may serve a countertransference anxiety, that is, to protect the therapist from the distressing emotions evoked by the relationship.

When a therapist overidentifies with his client's experience, he risks losing his unique identity and therapeutic role. For example, he may become enraged at his client's perpetrators and unwittingly inhibit her exploration of her ambivalence and confusion. Sensing the therapist's rage at her abusive stepfather, for example, the client may then refrain from telling the therapist that he was the person who taught her to ride a bicycle, the one who insisted she do well at school, who helped her with homework. In addition, the therapist's rage at perpetrators may inhibit the client from discussing her own acts of neglect or abuse of her own children, younger siblings, children for whom she baby-sat, pets, or herself, or her own desires to destroy herself or others. In this way, the therapist's own vicarious traumatization (manifest in an identity shift toward identification with clients resulting in rage at perpetrators) contributes to a countertransference response (rage at hearing a client's account) which inhibits the treatment.

World View

The loss of a benevolent world view is always painful and often confusing. When this loss comes about as a result of confronting the harsh realities of human behavior, one can react against the bearer of the bad tidings. It is not surprising that therapists sometimes feel angry at clients who continuously challenge their ways of viewing the world. Therapists whose world view is shaped by early experiences of trauma may find their attempts to claim hope for themselves challenged by survivor clients. If the therapist's sense of the world as a place where benevolence is possible is tenuous or has been altered by his work, he may affirm or not notice his client's cynicism and despair, seeing it as normal and realistic. The danger of unprocessed vicarious traumatization here is that the therapist will not recognize the true source of his angry countertransference response: the loss of the beliefs upon which he has built all of his relationships.

The therapist whose world view has been altered by vicarious traumatization may develop convictions about people that lead to a variety of countertransference responses. He may come to view all others with suspicion or contempt, believe that things happen at random, and/or conclude that moral principles are useless or only reflect self-interest. The therapist may fail to hear or allow the client to speak that which challenges his world view or may agree thoughtlessly with negative beliefs about others. Alternatively, the therapist may unconsciously encourage the client to talk about things to help restore his shattered world view, but may not allow the client to explore fully her own feelings and thoughts about moral principles, causality, humanity.

Example   One therapist with many survivor clients was struggling with a disrupted world view. One of his clients adapted to prolonged sexual abuse by withdrawing almost entirely from other people. In the early years of the treatment, the client's only relationship was with the therapist. Over time, as a result of his own vicarious traumatization, the therapist began to agree with this client that relationships were too risky, people too self-interested, and that social withdrawal was a reasonable solution. The therapist's early clue to this countertransference response came in the form of a fantasy: One day the client began to talk about finding a remote hideaway where she could live independently and without society; the therapist found himself imagining the client on this island, and enviously wishing for a similar island for himself to escape the painful complexities of relationships. Through reflection, he realized the extent of his wish to flee from a world that had been malevolently transformed for him by this work (world view disruptions), and the impact of these beliefs on this particular therapy.

Example   Another therapist had come to view victimization of children as almost inevitable, clearly a vicarious traumatization effect of her extensive work as a trauma therapist. In listening to a client recount his early, loving experience with a priest, the therapist found herself suspicious of the possibility of innocence and protection in such a relationship, and awaiting the negative turn in the client's story.

Spirituality

Detecting shifts in spirituality paradoxically requires the very attunement to one's inner processes that is often lost as a result of vicarious traumatization. For many, of course, spirituality is strengthened by working with trauma survivors. However, to the extent that one experiences a loss or a major shift in meaning and hope, interconnectedness, awareness of all aspects of life, or awareness of the nonmaterial, a therapist may experience deep sorrow, anomie, confusion, and despair in particular interactions with clients.

Example   A therapist reported that a client struggling against despair and hopelessness requested, half-jokingly, "therapy speech number 3471. You know, the one about how this helps, how I won't feel this way forever, and we can do this together. We will be able to work it out." The therapist did not realize how tired and demoralized she was feeling until she heard herself sigh and say, "I don't know. I hope we can." Her client was shattered and frightened; she was afraid she had worn out her therapist and destroyed her hope. As the two of them discussed the interaction, the therapist realized that while part of her fatigue stemmed from the particular interactions between herself and the client, she was also responding to feelings that did not originate in that relationship.

This cycle can deepen when, in response to such feelings, one experiences further shame, guilt, or sorrow.

Cynicism follows disillusionment; cynicism develops over time as a protection against hope when repeated disappointment or loss seem inevitable. As a therapist resists this loss of hope, he may discourage clients from sharing trauma material. In a particular therapy, this may induce a counter-transference response of minimizing or distancing. The retreat can be unconscious and subtle; for example, the therapist may follow alternative threads that are offered in the therapy session or become sleepy or bored as the client moves into talking about memories. The therapist may protect himself by telling the client he is not sure she is ready to tell him a particular memory, meaning he is not sure he is ready to hear it. The therapist may find himself dreading sessions with certain clients. He may agree too quickly with the client's expressions of cynicism and despair. While there are certainly times when clients attempt to disclose trauma material before they are ready to do so, it is important to be aware of who is not ready — the client or the therapist.

Changes in Self Capacities

Ability to Tolerate Affect

Whenever it is difficult to tolerate strong affect or one feels disconnected from a positive sense of self, interpersonal situations are arduous. For some, this results in avoidance and for others in interpersonal conflict. In clinical work, the therapist may avoid feelings, trauma material, or topics which evoke strong feeling in him, or he may become authoritarian, adversarial, or argumentative with clients.

Disruptions in the therapist's self capacities can lead to strong counter-transference responses to emotional or emotionally evocative clients. These responses may emerge in a variety of inappropriate or harmful behaviors in the therapy. If the therapist is having difficulty tolerating strong affect, he may be impatient with his rage toward perpetrators or his grief about his client's devastating losses. A therapist may become tearful with a client and fear losing control and sobbing in session. Self capacity impairments result in a heightened sensitivity to a client's pain which can tap into the therapist's personal emotional life. The therapist may then experience his feelings as out of control or they may emerge in a way that disconnects the therapist from his client.

Vicarious traumatization makes some therapists more susceptible to the rage of narcissistically injured clients who are exquisitely sensitive to changes in the therapist's vulnerability and who may need to injure the therapist as a reenactment of a childhood dynamic.

Example   One therapist whose self capacities were stretched by a demanding schedule of trauma therapies with little rest and inadequate supports experienced some major personal losses, which further taxed his self capacities. Upon returning to work after a family funeral, the therapist's first client was a challenging individual whose adaptation to her childhood abuse included defensive, angry entitlement, a response to the severe neglect, blaming, and shaming she had experienced in childhood. In this session, rescheduled because of his absence, the client, sensing the therapist's unavailability, raged at him for not being more present emotionally and for moving the session back a day. The therapist found himself unable to tolerate the rage and felt angry, defeated, and hopeless about his work with this client, further stirring her desperation to connect. Aware of a wish to lash out, the therapist decided to tell the client that he had just experienced a death in the family. The client expressed disbelief, suggesting the therapist had just made this up in order to save face. The therapist found that speaking his experience regrounded him sufficiently to see the distortion in the client's perception and to separate her rage from his culpability. In this example, vicarious traumatization, complicated by the therapist's current life stressors, created a potential for countertransference retaliation, which was averted by the therapist's disclosure. The therapist said, "It's difficult for you to see my vulnerability. Whenever you were vulnerable in the past, you got hurt and shamed." By stepping out of the attack-retaliation cycle, the therapist provided space for the client to reflect rather than react. After a few moments of silence, she began to talk about her fear that the therapist would be overwhelmed by her and her anger about that possibility. She agreed she was both angry about and frightened by the therapist's obvious fatigue.

Difficulties in affect tolerance can translate into difficulty enjoying time alone. When fleeing solitude himself, the therapist can become blind to the potential maladaptive implications of a client's avoidance of time alone, and encourage her to keep busy as a way of coping with her own impaired self capacities.

Example   One therapist listened to himself encouraging a survivor client to accept a prestigious offer to teach a course during a period in her psychotherapy when she was processing deep grief. The client stated that time alone was very difficult for her and that she was often overwhelmed with feelings of sadness and rage. During their discussion, the client noted wryly, "You probably think it's a good idea to take this offer because you work all the time." The therapist was startled and considered the truth of the statement. As he considered the ways he filled his time with work to avoid his own painful feelings, he was able to move to a more neutral, client-focused stance in the discussion. His response to vicarious traumatization was to overwork and avoid time alone; this response led to a countertransference alignment with one side of his client's ambivalence to the neglect of an exploration of the defense and ambivalence.

Ability to Maintain a Positive Sense of Self

A therapist having difficulty maintaining a positive sense of self becomes increasingly self-critical, with variable self-esteem and at times intense self-loathing; these latter states leave a therapist exquisitely vulnerable to countertransference.

Lacking a positive sense of self, a therapist may take responsibility for his client's behaviors and survival. He may accept negative projections, and fail to identify and work with transference. When a client says he has failed her, he may accept her assessment completely and not explore the transference aspects of the feeling.

Example   One sexual abuse survivor started almost every session for the second year of her treatment saying she thought perhaps she should end treatment because it wasn't helping her retrieve adult abuse memories. The therapist, whose sense of self had been affected by his work, struggled with questions of his own adequacy. With the support of supervision, he was able to continue to explore with the client what might be making it difficult to get to the memories. His continuing questions in supervision, however, were whether he was indeed an effective trauma therapist or an effective therapist with this client, and whether the client should be referred to another therapist. In time, the client expressed a belief that if she remembered what had happened to her, she would have to end her relationship with her mother, leaving her alone in the world. This realization reframed her lack of memory as a relationship protection rather than a failure or inadequacy. Had the therapist colluded with her blaming stance, he would have precluded the more complex understanding of memory, motivation, and adaptation that emerged.

Failure to address transference. To identify and understand transference dynamics, the therapist must be able to sort out aspects of a client's response to him that reflect the current therapeutic relationship from those that reflect internalizations of her past relationships and interpersonal experiences. When a client's transference interacts with a therapist's self-doubts or inner conflicts, the therapist may need supervision or consultation to become regrounded in the therapeutic relationship and task. This lack of resilience poses the particular danger to clients of allowing them to harm the therapist, which can lead to tremendous fear, self-reproach, and despair. The client can end up feeling too powerful, toxic, or destructive, which deprives her of the opportunity to work through the conflict and intrapsychic dynamics that led to the transference.

Ability to Maintain an Inner Sense of Connection with Others

When the third self capacity is impaired in a therapist, this may translate into an inability to remain available to his client when she most needs it: when she is distancing from the therapist for some reason. The therapist loses his grounding and sense of connection and holding that in turn allow him to provide the same for the client.

Self capacity disruptions and their effects on the therapist may be subtle. Yet survivor clients will feel them, and at times may be aware of them before the therapist is. Survival for many abuse victims required the development of a highly attuned awareness of even the finest shifts in interpersonal dynamics. We cannot overemphasize the importance of ongoing attention to the therapist's self capacities. A therapist needs to attend to his affective state, level of arousal, availability of self-soothing, inner connections to benevolent objects, and level of self-acceptance. It is helpful before and after a clinical session to notice one's emotional state and needs, particularly to notice what was difficult in the session; this information provides signposts to one's current vulnerabilities as well as to self-care.

Changes in Ego Resources

When vicarious traumatization affects the therapist's ability to make self-protective judgments and establish boundaries, there are several direct implications for therapeutic frame and countertransference. A therapist's inability to set limits often leads to resentment of those to whom commitments are made, including clients. This resentment can be expressed through missing appointments, not returning a client's phone calls, tuning out during sessions, responding irritably to a client, or violating the frame of therapy in other ways.

Vicarious traumatization can lead to impaired clinical judgment: taking on too many clients, underestimating one's need for supervision and consultation, losing empathy or humor, unwittingly inviting clients to traumatize or otherwise intrude upon one, and losing awareness of one's countertransference. When a therapist is less introspective and has less access to his cognitive and perspective-taking abilities, he can become myopic in his therapies. He can become content-focused to the exclusion of process, and perhaps unable to process his own contributions to conflict in the therapeutic relationship.

Disruptions in empathy can lead a therapist to retraumatize a client by, for example, failing to notice and address her shame in the treatment relationship. If his ability to strive for personal growth is impaired, he may find himself neglecting his professional development, not obtaining supervision, or failing a client by not consulting colleagues about difficult clinical issues. These are all manifestations of the impact of vicarious traumatization on countertransference vulnerability.

Changes in Psychological Needs and Cognitive Schemas

Vicarious traumatization impairs one's ability to meet psychological needs in mature ways and to balance one's different needs. Disrupted beliefs can blind the therapist to a client's disruptions, or prompt him to attend to his own salient needs rather than the client's. A therapist's disrupted schemas leave him feeling helpless with clients with the same (or opposite) needs and schemas from his own. In response, some clients will censor their material according to their perception of the therapist's needs and limits. It is particularly difficult to notice and address this dynamic when the therapist's needs and schemas are disrupted by vicarious traumatization.

Safety

Therapist safety disruptions can emerge in a variety of countertransference responses: Therapists can become fearful for or overprotective of clients, fearful for their own safety with clients, agree with a client's beliefs that there is no safety anywhere, or fail to notice unsafe situations in the client's life. The therapist may become preoccupied with his client's safety and well-being, attempt to direct her behavior, and lose sight of a larger therapeutic task of exploring meaning with the goal of self-empowerment. For example, a therapist struggling with his own anxiety about safety responded in a discussion of his client's holiday plans by urging the client not to visit her abusive family, thus assuming an authority role rather than facilitating the client's development of self-protection. While it is certainly often appropriate for the therapist to express his concerns about the client's safety, his own sense of personal vulnerability may activate him to say or do things which are not useful to the client. It is not helpful for the client to feel caught between the therapist and others in her life; this can occur when a therapist's safety schemas are disrupted through vicarious traumatization. Further, the therapist's singular attention to safety precludes his recognition of other needs.

Example   A survivor client who had experienced an adult rape was working with a therapist whose vicarious traumatization took the form of profoundly disrupted safety needs and schemas. The client, for whom self-control was most salient, was discussing how the rape had limited her sense of freedom. The therapist repeatedly urged her to put extra locks on her door, thus reinforcing her worst fears and frustrating her attempts to be understood.

Trust

Disruptions in self-trust that lead a therapist to doubt his professional judgment have clear countertransference ramifications. This mistrust can lead to anxiety-driven overuse of medication or hospitalization. It may emerge through projection, as a therapist encourages his client to depend upon others rather than herself. A self-doubting therapist may turn to inappropriate sources (such as his partner or friends) for case consultation, or utilize too many consultants, confusing himself on a particular case or issue.

Disrupted other-trust can inhibit the therapist's ability to help clients learn to discriminate between trustworthy and untrustworthy people and situations. Generalized mistrust of others can lead the therapist to underutilize potentially helpful referral resources (such as medication consultants and self-help groups), supervision, and consultation, and to encourage the client to overutilize or rely exclusively on the therapist. When a therapist mistrusts his client, this mistrust, combined with his wish to deny abuse and human cruelty, can lead to a retraumatizing disbelief in response to a client's trauma disclosure. The therapist may blame the client for her victimization or for her subsequent difficulties, not believe what she tells him, or see her as manipulative. He may judge or inappropriately reject or encourage the client's dependency needs as he assumes an identity as the only trustworthy person in the world. This identity has clear countertransference implications; the therapist will be unable to tolerate negative transferences and will require complementary transferences. Disrupted other-trust can lead to further vicarious traumatization because the therapist is likely to feel even greater stress, responsibility, and burden from the work.

Esteem

The greatest clinical difficulty a therapist may face when his self-esteem is impaired is struggling with the feeling that someone (or perhaps anyone) would be a better therapist than he. His resultant guilt, shame, or envy can lead to his acceptance of clients' negative projections or transference as truth. Alternatively, he may defensively reject and deny those projections, projecting blame onto the client and abandoning work on the relationship. Clearly a therapist with self-esteem disruptions will have a particularly tough time managing countertransference with clients who assault his esteem, for example, highly critical or shaming clients. He may use interpretations to bolster his self-esteem, whether through demonstrating his cleverness or injuring the client through a critical or shame-inducing interpretation.

Similarly he may fail to perceive or to accept and work through the client's idealization of him. He may reject out of hand a client's idealization rather than understanding it in the context of her needs; alternatively he may require that the idealization be regarded as fact. Taken further, a therapist uncomfortable with his importance to the client or needing idealization because of impaired self-esteem may move away from a therapeutic relationship toward friendship or a sexual relationship with a client. When a therapist depends on a client to bolster or maintain his self-esteem, he is at risk for countertransference enactments that can compromise or destroy a treatment.

Disruptions in esteem for others carry their own countertransference hazards. The therapist's disrupted esteem for others can emerge in his negative judgment or contempt for others in his client's life, thereby precluding the client's expressions of ambivalence about those important others. Disrupted other-esteem schemas can obstruct the therapist's perceptions of the client's strengths and resources. The therapist may devalue his client as weak or defective. His lack of respect for the client may be evident in a variety of ways, for example, by violating the frame of a particular therapy (running late, not managing the financial aspects of the therapy properly), violating a client's confidentiality (talking with administrative staff or one's partner about a client), or not taking the client's concerns seriously. Alternatively, the therapist may respond with reaction formation by idealizing the client and denying any critical feelings, which may also serve to maintain the therapist's identity as "good therapist." This solution prohibits the client from sharing sadistic, shameful, or other aspects of herself which may be dissonant with the therapist's idealization. It also interferes with the therapist's having a balanced view of the client and can blind him to client expressions of rage directed at him, at others, or at herself.

Example   In one such case, a therapist was feeling stuck in a therapy that had produced only the smallest improvement in the client's presenting difficulties over the course of two years of treatment. This client's diminutive size and girlish mannerisms evoked a protective countertransference response from the therapist who perceived her as fragile and vulnerable. With consultation, he began to realize he was allowing himself to see only the comfortable aspects of the client, and was disregarding the client's rage and self-destructive interpersonal behaviors (e.g., engaging in a series of sadomasochistic extramarital affairs) in order to preserve his waning esteem for others. These disallowed aspects of the client emerged in self- and therapy-defeating patterns that continued because they went unnamed and unaddressed.

Intimacy

Disruptions in self-intimacy can lead the therapist to avoid time alone. He is in danger of using certain clients to meet his intimacy needs, of filling his thoughts with his clients' dilemmas and struggles. A therapist can subtly invite his clients to be similarly preoccupied with him or their therapy regardless of their developmental needs.

Other-intimacy disruptions can result in the therapist conducting the sessions in a social rather than therapeutic manner, striving to meet his intimacy needs in the safety of the therapeutic relationship to make up for disruptions in intimate relationships in his personal life. The therapist may not recognize his countertransference wish, based in his need for connection, for his client to remain in treatment past the time it is useful for the client. He may fail to follow up on a client's references to termination, or actively argue with the client about her readiness. The therapist may fail to explore transference responses with the client, preferring to view the relationship as only a "real," present relationship. This failure not only denies his role and distance as therapist but also blocks the curative process of psychotherapy, the opportunity for a client to reconnect her past to her present.

The most destructive manifestation of this disruption is the formation of a sexual relationship with a client, which is never therapeutic (in addition to being unethical, according to professional guidelines, and illegal in some states). Because of the particularly intimate nature of their work, therapists have an obligation to remain aware of their own intimacy needs and to meet them in appropriate ways outside their psychotherapies.

Control

Disruptions in self-control needs and schemas are reflected in the therapist's countertransference experience of being out of control of his feelings or behaviors, or fearing loss of control. He may either work hard to maintain control or give up trying to control himself. In clinical work, the therapist may deny his part in interactions with a client, failing, for example to take responsibility for a mistake or for actions that may be hurtful to the client, refusing to tolerate a client who expresses feelings that seem "out of control," and being unable to perceive, understand, or accept his own vicarious traumatization or countertransference responses. He may feel intolerant of uncertainty, ambivalence, and the not knowing which is characteristic of these therapies.

Disruptions in other-control have two possible countertransference manifestations: requiring or surrendering control in interpersonal situations. A therapist may feel unable to tolerate surprises or setbacks; have difficulty accepting supervision or consultation; attempt to make the client over in his image; use interpretations as weapons of control; give ultimatums or maintain inappropriate, unreasonable, rigid, or punitive boundaries; impose upon the client the notion that the therapist is indispensable; or use his position as valued guide to influence or persuade the client rather than to create a protected space for her self-exploration (concerning, for example, relationships, values, life decisions). The therapist may feel helpless or "deskilled" in working with a survivor client whom he cannot influence (Herman, 1992; Putnam, 1989).

Changes in Sensory System

When the therapist's sensory system is disrupted, he may experience unusual sensations connected to countertransference responses during sessions. This may be an empathic response, but if chronic it may reflect vicarious traumatization-induced countertransference. The hazards here are obvious. If the therapist is not able to remain grounded in the current reality as a result of vicarious traumatization, he cannot reach out to a client who is dissociating and invite her back into the therapy room. If he is feeling somatically flooded, he may shut down and try to shut down his client out of a countertransference experience of the client's overstimulating assault on him.

Example   A therapist often felt very sleepy in sessions with a somewhat dissociative survivor client. The client confronted him about his sleepiness, saying she wanted to know if it had something to do with her. The embarrassed therapist began to look closely at what was going on at the points in the session at which his sleepiness began. He became aware that he would grow sleepy when the client talked rapidly and without affect about the activities and habits of other people in her life, during which process her eyes would defocus. He discussed this pattern with the client, and they were able to identify that the client would behave in this way when she felt the need to ward off thoughts or feelings about traumatic memories. The therapist's sleepiness represented his own desire to escape the trauma material and the strong feelings associated with it, a desire stemming from his vicarious traumatization. This discussion allowed them to move back into connection with one another and to explore the possibility that talking about the abuse while remaining connected to one another could protect both of them from feeling overwhelmed by the abuse material.

VICARIOUS TRAUMATIZATION CONTRIBUTIONS TO THERAPEUTIC IMPASSE

Because of the influence of vicarious traumatization on countertransference and vice versa, unacknowledged vicarious traumatization can be a source of therapeutic impasse. When the therapist is impaired by the work, he inevitably and instinctively moves to withdrawal or some other action to protect himself. To the extent that this movement is organized around the therapist's needs and does not consider the client's experience, the result is a disconnection and abandonment of the client and the relationship. If a therapist brings personal needs into his therapies because of breakdown of boundaries, the client may withdraw, consciously or unconsciously, to protect herself. If the pair cannot sort out the reasons for the client's withdrawal, the therapy will be stalemated. A therapeutic impasse taxes a therapist's already strained personal resources when he is overextended, seeing too many clients, treating too many trauma clients, or has too many life stresses and insufficient support and supervision for his work.

Awareness of the interaction between vicarious traumatization and countertransference broadens the therapist's framework for understanding his part of the therapeutic relationship. Understanding the distinction between vicarious traumatization and countertransference and their potentiating effects on one another supports the therapist and his therapies.

16

Countertransference and Vicarious Traumatization Across the Therapist's Professional Development

THE CONTEXT for all of our work as therapists is our continuously evolving professional and personal identities. Becoming a therapist is a reiterative developmental process of identity construction. Experience within and across therapies shapes one's identity which in turn informs one's experience. The work of psychotherapy is active and interactive: We conceptualize, experiment, observe, analyze, and make connections. We integrate each of these experiences into our developing therapist identity, through which all of our experiences in the therapeutic relationship are filtered. Our professional identity, that is, our "self as therapist," then is the context for our countertransference and vicarious traumatization. The ability to recognize and use countertransference and to heed vicarious traumatization varies significantly during our professional development.

A therapist's identity is a composite of the unique role as therapist within the relationship and frame of psychotherapy and the unique person of the therapist. Countertransference and vicarious traumatization are shaped within this process of identity development and influenced by the therapist's relative sense of comfort, competence, and esteem at each point in the process. In this chapter, we address the countertransference and vicarious traumatization issues related to professional development in a developing field. We address countertransference and vicarious traumatization issues for the new therapist, the experienced therapist new to trauma work, and the experienced trauma therapist.

PROFESSIONAL DEVELOPMENT IN
A DEVELOPING FIELD

Theoretical Implications

Psychological trauma as a field of study has only begun to come into its own. Theory is evolving, research is building, and clinical expertise is growing. We are in the midst of a major paradigm shift (Kuhn, 1970) in our field. As with the shift of tectonic plates, we are likely to be shaken and disoriented by changes in beliefs we had held as truths. It is challenging and exciting, but somewhat daunting, to come of age as a clinician during the development of a new field. One searches for knowledge that has not yet been recorded or codified; one works from hypotheses that have yet to be tested empirically. However, as we accept the new paradigm and we forget the old, we may assume mistakenly that what we now take for granted is common knowledge. Within the field of psychological trauma, this myopia can mean losing awareness that the majority of therapists probably still view most adult female sexual abuse survivors as "borderlines"; that there is a lack of awareness of the connection among sexual abuse, eating disorders, and dissociation (McCallum, Lock, Kulla, Rorty, & Wetzel, 1992); and that many clinicians do not share the trauma framework. Of course the complementary hazard is that we discard from traditional paradigms that which is helpful. An understanding of borderline pathology, for example, that is based in a trauma framework can be helpful; without that framework, the focus becomes a collection of difficult symptoms and the result too often is to blame the client for them.

The recognition of the centrality of childhood trauma to psychological identity and distress opens us to a dramatically different way of understanding psychopathology and symptoms. These shifts have inexorably changed the nature of our profession and our work. They include a move from an emphasis on psychopathology to etiology and meaning, from a model that emphasizes illness and symptoms to one that emphasizes adaptation and survival, and from a view of psychotherapy as a unidirectional, authoritarian process between the expert doctor and his patient to a view of therapy as mutual venture within an intersubjective field. We are part of those changes and profoundly influenced by them. Like any new generation, however, we are also cut off from our professional parents, from our teachers, mentors, early supervisors, therapists, and analysts, by our new vision.

Personal-Professional Implications

When we face clinical phenomena for which our training proves insufficient, we must move beyond our training. This is the very experience which
led to the development of CSDT (McCann & Pearlman, 1990b). Our
clinical observations of severely impaired psychiatric patients were not supported by theory or treatment recommendations in the literature in the early
1980s. Thus, we were led by our clients rather than our teachers into a new
level of understanding. Not only do our clients challenge us, but if we
listen, they teach us what we need to know to help them.

Taking a different path from one's mentors can leave the therapist feeling
orphaned, estranged, or guilty — and sometimes triumphant. In our progres-
sion toward the new paradigm, we may lose idealized professional parental
figures, and perhaps our sense of grounding in the theoretical models of our
training. Our clinical work is built upon and held by theory and training.
This perceived loss of grounding is part of a separation process; we do not
really lose what we have learned. We simply become more critical consum-
ers of traditional theory and wisdom.

Coming of age as a clinician in a developing field means there is a lack of
wise elders, role models, research, and more experienced people to consult.
A therapist may look to newer clinicians who are trained or experienced in
trauma, sometimes asking them to provide wisdom beyond their years and
experience. A more experienced therapist may feel uncomfortable asking a
more junior colleague for a consultation.

We need to integrate the wisdom of experienced clinicians with the understanding of trauma-specific dynamics offered by the new generation of
clinicians. To do so, we need a community of colleagues. While there is
both an active trauma community and a large community of thoughtful
well-trained psychotherapists, these communities (particularly trauma and
psychoanalytic) are often split from one another, with separate professional
forums including societies, conferences, and journals, and many practitioners do not feel a part of either community. Many therapists choose to
work alone, although this option seems to be less available as the early
rumblings of health care reform echo throughout the field. Part of our
commitment to survivors includes a desire to make trauma theory, research,
and training in treatment available to all clinicians who are interested. This
goal requires we come together to learn and share our collective experience
and knowledge.

Social and Political Implications

Psychotherapy with incest survivors intersects with social and political issues, as evidenced by the media coverage of specific topics related to trauma

therapy. The social context that allows and supports childhood sexual abuse is one of patriarchy (Mac Ian, 1992) and deeply entrenched misogyny (Herman, 1981; Saakvitne & Pearlman, 1993). Therapists who work with survivors are subversives, speaking the unspeakable and encouraging others to do the same. Encouraging women (the majority of survivors in treatment at this time) to speak is still incendiary activity in many quarters. As Demause (1991) implies, it is not incest which is taboo across cultures, but talking about incest. Thus, when we accept a trauma framework, we are breaking a deep and powerful cultural taboo. This awareness can emerge in countertransference and the therapeutic alliance. Fighting social oppression is heady work; therapist and client can feel mutually empowered by their commitment to speak the truth. On the other hand, incest is a deeply personal trauma and each client is an individual, not a symbol. The complexities of an individual's emotional response to the event and meaning of childhood sexual abuse are contextualized by, but not identical to, the anger and goals of social revolution. Politics requires clarity; psychotherapy invites complexity.

The social and political importance of our work can enter into the countertransference in a variety of ways. It is essential for us to remember that our role is to help our client discover her truth and to accomplish her goals. We may at times be mistakenly tempted to urge her toward social action. On the other hand, our awareness of the social and political context within which sexual abuse of children takes place is fundamental to helping the client in her struggle to understand why this happened and why it happened to her. This is a delicate balance, requiring clarity about our role and the client's concerns.

We may feel the political significance of our work not only in our offices, but in our social and professional lives. As any trauma therapist can attest, such a position carries with it an implicit invitation to go head to head with society — at social gatherings, in professional presentations, with one's friends and relatives, and often with one's teachers and mentors. Those who protest the pervasiveness and significance of the psychological trauma of incest are vocal and ubiquitous. Their strident denial interacts with our vicarious traumatization. When others do not understand, our sense of isolation and despair in the face of deeply troubling social ills increase. Changes in our beliefs about others as a result of vicarious traumatization influence our response to these critics; we may feel uncharacteristic rage, contempt, helplessness, or fear. Perhaps in our own parallel traumatic reenactment, unwilling to be victims or helpless bystanders, we enter into the fray with those who deny abuse whom we experience at the social level as perpetrators.

Therapists and scientists do have a role in educating the public, media, and policy makers. Our clinical experience and academic and scientific training put us in a unique position to provide useful and accurate information. The ethics of science, responsible journalism, and public policy can be influenced by our commitment to disseminating the information we have. Yet, as many remind us, these struggles are not simply about science and facts, but about social backlash and fears (Olio et al., 1994) and dissociative trauma responses on a societal level (Brett, 1993). To protect ourselves, each of us must recognize the limits of what we alone can do; we need one another and our professional organizations to educate and transform a culture rooted in denial.

The Contexts of Professional Development for Trauma Therapists

Personal Context

The larger process of developing a professional identity and the immediate tasks of doing trauma therapy take place in the context of our own personal development and personal lives. The 25-year-old right out of graduate school faces different life tasks from the 45-year-old new graduate or the 40-year-old who has practiced for 10 years and is shifting his theoretical perspective. Clinicians establishing a career who are simultaneously building a family have still different sensitivities and challenges. Personal life events enter the therapeutic relationship and influence countertransference. For example, therapists with young children are particularly vulnerable in work with survivors of early childhood sexual abuse, and often experience increased fears for their children's safety. Other life events, experiences, and processes, both historical and contemporary, are also important aspects of the context for the developing trauma therapist.

Work may be more central for the therapist whose career is at an earlier developmental stage. This may mean he spends more time reading, learning, attending conferences, writing, obtaining supervision, and so on. The therapist needs to shed the focus on unilateral achievement often developed in an academic career and accept the circuitous, failure-ridden process that is psychotherapy. He will face the paradox that a therapist's success will come as he accepts his failures. It is important for a new therapist to monitor his immersion in work. While engaging in a variety of tasks may be protective, taking on too many survivor clients is likely to increase one's vicarious traumatization.

Immersion in work gives rise to a variety of countertransference responses, including an inability to empathize with a survivor client who becomes easily overwhelmed and unable to function at work (when the therapist is overfunctioning), or difficulty slowing down enough to be fully present during therapy sessions and to match the client's pace rather than speeding along at one's own pace. For therapists without family or other significant personal relationships, work may be so central to their identities that their self-esteem is yoked to the success they perceive in their therapies. This need is problematic when working with survivor clients who may take years to develop self capacities, trust, self-esteem, and so forth. Countertransference responses of frustration or boredom may emerge with clients whose work requires a long time. The trauma therapist whose identity is built upon his work is vulnerable to vicarious traumatization, which may be especially evident in disruptions in identity, meaning, esteem, and control. Protection against these vulnerabilities includes maintaining a well-rounded life outside of work as well as developing balance and variety within work.

The lack of confidence we all experience in these therapies can dovetail with the self-doubt of the emerging professional and sometimes the immaturity of a young clinician. It takes time for a new clinician to integrate and use himself as a person in his therapies. New therapists are often self-conscious and cautious. They may hesitate to allow their spontaneous responses, humor, and warmth into the therapeutic relationship; alternatively, they may use themselves in anxious and defensive ways out of fear of intimacy and uncomfortable affect. It takes time and experience for the clinician to bring his feelings into the room in a way that respects the client's needs for both connection and safety. Integrating aspects of the self is a developmental identity task for the therapist, just as it is for the client. As such, it may evoke feelings from the therapist's other developmental transitions, which may have been celebrated or demeaned in his family of origin.

In contrast, an experienced therapist new to trauma therapy may have a well-established identity as therapist, and have familiar ways of working and interacting with colleagues that he now questions. Despite his comfort with certain groups of clients and expertise in many areas, he may feel like a novice in work with trauma survivors. He is likely to be in a position of learning from people younger than himself. He may feel confidence and doubt simultaneously in his professional work. In fact, experienced trauma therapists also often struggle with such contradictory feelings, but later in the work, as they emerge in relation to the developing therapeutic relationships. Earlier in a therapist's trauma therapy experience, the confusion is often located in the therapist's identity and self-esteem.

A therapist's relationship with his own therapist or analyst provides a key context for his work and his professional identity development. He may remember how his therapist responds (or responded) to questions, needs, feelings, pain, and how she used herself in the work, and often turn to those memories for permission, reassurance, and guidance. As he moves into territories that differ from his therapist's work, he may feel anxious, and perhaps sad, disappointed, or angry at lost opportunities.

The process of increasing competence and confidence increases the therapist's self-esteem and solidifies his professional identity. On the way, the gap between his perception of himself and his ego ideal can be large. Such a gap sets the stage for feelings of inadequacy and self-criticism if the therapist is not comfortable in the role of novice. Suran and Sheridan's (1985) model of professional development suggests that this phase, which they term "competence acquisition" (p. 745), can be characterized by overwork. This solution is particularly problematic for therapists working with trauma survivor clients because a few more trauma clients may mean far more distress for the therapist (Gamble et al., 1994; Schauben & Frazier, in press).

Organizational Context

The organizational context within which the therapist is developing his experience, skills, and identity will also influence the countertransference and vicarious traumatization he experiences in the work. If he is a trainee in a formal training program, he may feel more support and permission for learning, allowing him to be more genuine with his clients rather than assuming the mantle of "expert." If the organization acknowledges the difficulties of the work and the inevitable vicarious traumatization it creates, he may have more support for the work and be able to work as a therapist with less shame, anger, anxiety, and strain. As one's experience grows, organizations can affirm the emerging trauma therapist identity by providing and supporting opportunities to supervise, consult, teach, present, and publish.

Social Context

Therapists developing a professional identity as a trauma specialist or as a psychotherapist working with sexual abuse survivors do so in a society that celebrates violence. Violence in general and sexual abuse in particular are pervasive in our society; descriptions and depictions of violence against women, children, and men are in almost every news report, television talk show, and movie. The society is steeped in interpersonal violence and disrespect for human life and personhood; this is the context for the developing trauma therapist's countertransference and vicarious traumatization.

The pervasive presence of sexual violence in our professional and personal lives can feel overwhelming. We take in the big picture in society and the excruciating details in the office. For our clients, our empathic engagement is a prime ingredient of healing. Reading the newspaper, one may disengage in order to preserve some private space that is not over-whelmed by violence. This requires developing an awareness of one's re-sponses to violence in the culture and managing the very strong feelings one may have in order to remain open to clients. Our awareness and regulation of the nature of our empathic connection may help protect us to some degree from vicarious traumatization.

The delayed memory controversy, which is very alive at this writing, is another reflection of society's unwillingness to believe that children are sexually abused and that abuse is damaging. This controversy reflects the pendulum swing of societal denial of childhood sexual abuse (Brett, 1993; Demause, 1991; Herman, 1992). It is dismaying to enter a field in order to help people and then be accused of harming them. Individuals may hesitate to enter this field in this litigious climate. It is very difficult to do this demanding work in a social context that not only devalues the work, but in fact twists the context so that the therapist is viewed as perpetrator.

This social climate can lead to a variety of countertransference responses for the developing therapist. He may feel anxious about talking about child-hood sexual abuse memories with the client. He may deny his expertise as he puts together the pieces of what he is hearing and feel afraid to wonder about the possibility of sexual abuse. Rather than taking an appropriately nondirective position in the exploration of memories, he may avoid the topic, which conveys to the client the message that the abuse is too awful to be spoken, or perhaps that the client herself is responsible or should feel ashamed.

Economic and social factors also influence professional development. The social values reflected by the movement toward managed care as a way of making decisions about who receives treatment, how much, from whom, and in what setting are disturbing. Certainly, at this writing, there is a need to restructure our health care system. Yet relegating to administrators whose job is to save their businesses money the job of making decisions about how we as a society will tend the wounds of those we have sacrificed through our unwillingness to stop child abuse represents another cruel abuse and betrayal.

Working in a system that most generously rewards not doing the work creates difficulties for the developing trauma therapist (Saakvitne & Pearl-man, 1992). Part of this development includes a growing understanding of the pervasiveness of the impact of childhood sexual abuse. With that understanding comes a realization that the work requires time because its essence is helping survivors learn to have healthy relationships, with them-selves and with others. Relationships take time to develop. This is not to say that useful work cannot be done in short-term therapy with survivors.

TRAUMA AND THE THERAPIST

However, restoring a person to wholeness is not done in six sessions. Knowing that there is pressure to work quickly can move the developing therapist into a variety of hazardous situations, including premature exploration of trauma material, ignoring what is important to the survivor client, or conveying that the survivor's needs are insignificant, thereby retraumatizing her. The therapist may feel resentment toward the administrators who are attempting to tell him how to do the clinical work he is trained to do, or frustrated at futile attempts to collaborate with managed care reviewers. The triangle created by the involvement of managed care reviewers can replicate the abusive family dynamics, with the reviewer cast in the role of perpetrator, the therapist in the role of helpless bystander, and the client once again as victim (Saakvitne & Abrahamson, 1994).

Cultural Context

Professional identity development is also obviously affected by the cultural context. This culture, with its racism, sexism, heterosexism, misogyny, and victim-blaming, gives rise to many countertransference responses in the developing trauma therapist (Saakvitne & Pearlman, 1993). Committing oneself to helping those who are at the bottom rungs of society—women, people of color, victims, children—both stirs our compassion and challenges our own ignorance and learned bigotry. For example, the therapist may feel pity or outrage for a client arising from his feelings about the cultural ordeals this client has experienced, ordeals which made childhood sexual abuse possible and then impeded the survivor's attempts to get help. Concomitantly, he may collude with her view of herself as damaged or helpless through his pity and protectiveness rather than acknowledging that it takes time to help her transform her experience through collaboration and empowerment.

The psychotherapist is an agent for social change. Yet therapists must find a balance between modeling socially acceptable or desirable values and behaviors and helping the client sort out her own values and needs. The challenge to the developing trauma therapist is to integrate his culturally founded personal beliefs into his professional identity in a way that allows him to feel whole and genuine while at the same time open to his clients' beliefs, values, and experiences. At times as therapists we are called upon to take a stand, to express our views on moral issues. We are very comfortable saying, "No child is ever to blame for child sexual abuse," "The protection of children in society is everybody's business," "It is never appropriate for a therapist to engage in sexual behavior with a client." Taking such a position moves us into the role of active bystander (Staub, 1989, 1992) and alters conservative notions of analytic neutrality; yet, not being explicit, for example, that children are not responsible for abuse, would be taking the role of nonprotective bystander. In our opinion, in trauma therapies, moral neutrality about such issues is impossible and in fact a betrayal of ourselves, our clients, and our social responsibility. At other times, our values are not relevant to the therapy; their expression could inhibit or block the client's freedom to express and sort out her beliefs.

No therapy is value-free; the pitfall for the developing trauma therapist is to assume that he is not conveying his own values to the client. When our clients hold opinions or ideals that conflict deeply with our own, we sometimes struggle to discover a comfortable position. How does one respond to a survivor client who expresses racist or sexist views? We must provide a context that allows exploration of all of the client's views, even those that are antithetical to our own. Yet, as we strive to create a respectful therapeutic context, we must attend to and name the client's abuse toward herself and others, in action and language. The dangerous extremes are to ignore bigotry or simply to refute it without attempting to understand its origins.

COUNTERTRANSFERENCE AND VICARIOUS TRAUMATIZATION ISSUES FOR THE NEW TRAUMA THERAPIST

The countertransference and vicarious traumatization that arise early in the trauma therapist's professional development can be disturbing and anxiety-provoking. The therapist new to trauma therapy is highly focused on the client and on technique. Experiencing and understanding countertransference are new. These responses can be heightened by the intensity of the feelings that can be evoked by survivor clients, whether responses to the realities of child sexual abuse, to graphic trauma material, or to the powerful reenactments that take place in the therapy, often costarring the therapist. Anxiety about having strong responses to the work can lead to rigid, rule-based behaviors or to action.

In addition to being distressing, the therapist's strong feelings of outrage, disbelief, disgust, and sexual arousal as he listens to his client's story may be unfamiliar. The new therapist may feel confused at having such feelings or such strong feelings in therapy sessions. Guilt or shame can make it difficult for the therapist to talk to a supervisor or colleague about his work and his feelings about it. With little experience with the process of psychotherapy and with himself as a psychotherapist, the new therapist has little basis for contextualizing the many strong feelings, the fantasies, and the thoughts elicited by the work. In the absence of appropriate supportive trauma therapy supervision, this new therapist is at much higher risk for becoming caught in troublesome therapeutic situations, losing self-esteem, wounding clients, and experiencing vicarious traumatization.

In a study of 188 trauma therapists, Pearlman and Mac Ian (1994) found a strong correlation between general symptoms of vicarious traumatization as measured by a symptom checklist and newness to doing trauma work. They also found that newer trauma therapists (and in particular those without a personal trauma history) were more likely to experience intrusions of clients' trauma imagery.

Unwitting participation in or unformulated observation of traumatic reenactments can have a profound effect on the therapist's frame of reference. Without the experience base to contextualize these events in the therapeutic relationship and progressively unfolding dynamics, the therapist will take the events more literally and personally and have fewer conceptual resources for his response.

Self-Confidence

Early in the course of his work as a trauma therapist, the individual faces two tasks: the development of a professional identity and of self-confidence. Developing appropriate expectations of one's clients and oneself is an important part of developing self-confidence. Many survivor clients have lived for years with severe personal and interpersonal difficulties, struggled against and at times acted on suicidal thoughts, and used a wide range of survival strategies, many of which are self-destructive (see chapter 3). The novice therapist may have high expectations for his efficacy and success in helping the client change these behaviors quickly. Such unrealistic expectations give rise to a number of countertransference responses such as frustration, anger, blaming, shaming, and guilt, all of which hinder the therapeutic relationship and the healing it can create.

Establishing appropriate expectations is an important part of the developmental process for the new trauma therapist. For some survivor clients, staying out of the hospital is a major accomplishment; the therapist and client may not realize major changes in self-destructive behaviors for a very long time. Most therapists learn in their training that a client's talk about death signals an emergency. It takes a long time to learn to distinguish among issues common to many survivors: the wish not to live, the wish to be dead, and the intention to kill oneself (all of which differ from thoughts and feelings that motivate self-mutilation and other self-destructive behaviors [Calof, in press]). It may take even longer to learn to sit with the client's despair and torment without moving to precipitous or preemptive action.

Newer trauma therapists may underestimate the survivor's difficulty developing trust. This failure to comprehend can translate into inappropriate expectations of oneself, the client, and the process, which leads to frustration, anger, puzzlement, and envy of more experienced colleagues, and potentially self- or client-blaming. Related to these issues of appropriate expectations is the strong need not to fail the client (Neumann & Gamble, 1994). Such anxiety can lead the new therapist to be too active or to withdraw. If not strongly supported at this point, he may experience seriously negative effects on his self-esteem, self-confidence, and hope for healing. When disillusioned so early in one's career, some people abandon psychotherapy and move to less complicated, less emotionally taxing, often symptom-focused approaches that protect them from anxiety and disappointment. Alternatively, these disillusioned therapists may leave the field. This may be one reason that newer therapists appear to have more signs of vicarious traumatization: Perhaps those who are suffering most leave the field and the more experienced therapists have found ways of successfully addressing vicarious traumatization.

The new therapist's understandably tentative self-confidence can invite a parallel process in therapy with survivors whose developmental context often required them to grow up too fast, to know more than they could know at a given age or stage of development. Traditionally, new therapists are discouraged from revealing to clients their student or training status, and most new therapists do not want their inexperience to be a topic of discussion in the therapy. The therapist then unconsciously invites his client not to notice, ask, or know the truth. The therapist may try not to know himself.

Example   A new therapist in training was working with a female client who was skeptical about therapy. This woman grew up in an abusive family in which she had been given early responsibility for taking care of younger siblings, and had suffered repeated enemas from one parent and sexual abuse from the other. The client repeatedly asked the therapist to tell her exactly how psychotherapy worked. The therapist acknowledged to herself that she wondered the same thing. With her client, however, she responded formally with a standard answer and then brought in some scholarly articles on the action of psychotherapy. It did not occur to the intern or her supervisor to notice the parallel process: The client was asking the therapist to know something she could not yet know developmentally, just as the client had been repeatedly asked to know and do more than was developmentally appropriate. The professional stance taught to trainees, to act assured and confident, served to create a stable dissociation within this therapeutic relationship and deprived both members of an opportunity to recognize an important developmental pattern.

The newer trauma therapist faces a number of possible pitfalls. Having discovered the trauma perspective, he may for a period of time be on the lookout for evidence of childhood sexual abuse, dissociation, dissociative identity disorder, and ritual abuse. This may take the form of making assumptions about the client and her history, diagnosing without appropriate supportive evidence, or pursuing memories too aggressively. Neumann and Gamble (1994) point out that newer trauma therapists may be more likely to engage in rescue fantasies. The newer trauma therapist may also be more likely to dismiss the issues of non-survivor clients or of non-trauma-related issues for the survivor, focusing primarily on trauma for a time. He may underestimate the importance of the traumatic context versus the traumatic events.

Frame Issues

As noted in chapter 7, there is often a greater demand by childhood trauma survivors on the frame of the therapy, specifically on the role and person of the therapist. The complex negotiation of frame issues will elicit different feelings for the newer therapist, the experienced therapist new to trauma work, and the experienced trauma therapist. A new therapist who learned in his training to take a neutral stance, to respond to questions with silence or with his own questions, may feel uncomfortable, guilty, and confused. An experienced therapist new to trauma therapy may feel more reluctant to change a familiar therapeutic style and may pathologize the client's needs. It is challenging to find a way of being with clients that feels both genuine and comfortable for therapist and client and models a healthy negotiation of interpersonal relationships and needs. While confusion is inevitable and in fact paradigmatic in these treatments, it can be difficult for the newer trauma therapist to assess whether this confusion stems from behaviors of the client, interpersonal processes between therapist and client, or his own ineptitude (Neumann & Gamble, 1994).

Each therapist finds his own comfort with countertransference disclosure over time. A therapist needs to learn by experimenting. Newer therapists are often uncertain about whether to disclose their responses and how and when to do so. The newer therapist may fear injuring his client by bringing too much of himself or his perceptions into the therapy. While respect is essential, it is important to remember that clients are resilient; they have withstood far worse than a therapist's well-intentioned errors. A feeling evoked in a therapy is not an assault or abuse. One of our former supervisors often would quote Harry Stack Sullivan, who said to his students, "A patient will always forgive you a mistake of the head; what is dangerous is a mistake of the heart." We must engage in a realistic assessment of the reality and limits of our power and responsibility as we experiment with countertransference disclosure.

The more experienced therapist faces the danger of not being open to discussing a frame change because he has always done things in a particular way. While there may be very good reasons for a certain frame, the importance of a discussion in which both parties are truly open to one another's perspectives is invaluable in building the therapeutic relationship and the survivor's trust in herself and others. With increasing experience, we must be very aware of the importance of allowing each interaction to remain fresh and genuine.

Advantages of Being New to Trauma Therapy

So far, we have focused on the potential hazards and challenges facing the therapist new to trauma therapy. There are also many benefits to the client and to the work. The newer trauma therapist brings idealism, energy, and a fresh perspective. He generally brings fewer assumptions about survivors and healing, and is more flexible because he has fewer theoretical and technical preconceptions. As a learner, he brings an investment in learning and in the clients which is likely to benefit the client and to energize those around him. We have found in our own postdoctoral fellowship training program that therapists in training challenge our assumptions in ways that lead to more solid thinking and greater understanding of the therapy process. For the developing therapist, there is a sense of wonder, awe, and deep satisfaction that can come through learning and working within a framework that provides hope for people who may have otherwise had none.

COUNTERTRANSFERENCE AND VICARIOUS TRAUMATIZATION ISSUES FOR THE EXPERIENCED THERAPIST NEW TO TRAUMA PARADIGMS

The experienced clinician who is new to trauma therapy struggles with the contradictions between his sense of competence as a therapist and his sense of bewilderment with trauma clients. A paradigm shift is unsettling for anyone; one must rethink assumptions and accommodate changes in one's basic frame of reference. For a therapist whose work is grounded in theory, the change of these premises often results in his feeling deskilled for a time until he has integrated the new ideas into his existing knowledge and conceptual base. The specific theory base the clinician brings also informs his countertransference responses. Coming to trauma therapy from a psychoanalytic perspective requires a shift in understanding and technique with transference, adopting a psychoeducational stance at times, and altering one's understanding of therapeutic neutrality, among other things. This may mean becoming more active and emotionally present, which can feel uncomfortable. Coming to trauma therapy from a cognitive-behavioral perspective, on the other hand, requires expanding one's focus to include the importance of the past and personality development, interpersonal reenactments, and a far greater understanding and acknowledgment of transference and countertransference. This therapist will probably need to become more neutral, less active, and more patient.

The experienced therapist is also susceptible to powerful emotional responses to the trauma material and traumatic reenactments, but may not expect, or have a theoretical understanding of, these responses. If his traditional way of practicing was more intellectual or contained, he may feel self-critical or ashamed of his emotionality. Without a frame for his responses, he may try to shut them down, override them, or screen them out, all of which compromise the therapy and the therapist's self-care.

Another issue for the therapist who has been in the field for some time is the recognition of what he did not know with prior clients. This recognition can set the stage for regret, guilt, or shame as he becomes aware that he may have failed certain clients or have been less helpful than he wanted to be. Regret and sorrow are also responses to our growing awareness of the historical limitations and failures of our profession and colleagues.

Guilt or shame over past therapies may lead the therapist to overcompensate by picking up too many survivor clients or by overbooking himself with clinical and other work. He may become harshly self-critical or even decide to leave the field. We have to accept at any given point in our careers that we knew what we knew at the time and did the best work given our understanding. In this vein, British psychoanalyst Margaret Little describes her experience of her two analytic treatments. She believed the first failed largely because her analyst did not know enough. When she said to her second analyst, Donald Winnicott, that she regretted not having found him sooner, Winnicott responded that it would not have done her any good, because earlier he "would not have known enough" (Little, 1981, p. 300).

COUNTERTRANSFERENCE AND VICARIOUS TRAUMATIZATION ISSUES FOR THE EXPERIENCED TRAUMA THERAPIST

The experienced trauma therapist has different countertransference responses and vicarious traumatization hazards. Because the dynamics and patterns of these therapies are familiar, he can be at risk for moving too fast with his survivor clients, particularly with new clients. As two therapists who do primarily long-term work with survivors and thus rarely pick up new clients, we have both had the experience of starting with a new client and forgetting how slowly the therapeutic relationship must develop, how painful the process of developing trust is, how fearful new survivor clients can be of the therapy process.

Another hazard for the experienced trauma therapist is that he may jump to conclusions based upon experiences with other clients. He may be less responsive to the personal meanings of the abuse for this client or assume he knows what is important to her. Alternatively, the therapist may focus on the interpersonal events of the trauma and forget what he knows about intrapsychic life. Trauma clients are not less complex than clients with whom we have always explored fantasy, dreams, superego dynamics, and other complicated intrapsychic systems of meaning-making.

Example   A new client readily presented with little affect her memory of a single episode of childhood sexual abuse. She then spoke about her emotional neglect in childhood and severe criticism by her older siblings. The therapist focused on the emotional abuse, and said little about the sexual abuse. Several weeks later the client asked whether the therapist thought the sexual abuse was important. In discussion, it became clear that the therapist's lack of response to the client's account of the abuse was hurtful and conveyed dismissal to the client. Therapists have been making this kind of error for years, but it was repeated here in part because the therapist was inured to the impact of single episode of abuse, which was not overtly violent, because he had become accustomed to graphic descriptions of violent, sadistic, and repeated abuse.

The more experienced trauma therapist, with a reputation as an expert, may draw a different transference from his survivor clients, who may idealize and expect him to be perfect. This can elicit a variety of countertransference responses, including discomfort, the desire to live up to the idealization, the inability to see it as a transference—perhaps resulting in a self-congratulatory response, and so forth.

Example   One experienced trauma therapist received a referral of a very challenging person with dissociative identities. Enjoying the idealized transference (albeit somewhat nervously), the therapist had difficulty setting appropriate expectations for himself and the client for the treatment. The client insisted that the therapist be able to understand her quickly and completely because of his expertise, an expectation the therapist shared. Within several months, the treatment broke down as the client became enraged that the therapist had not resolved her presenting problems of dissociation and marital discord.

Experienced trauma therapists may also feel special, powerful, or privileged. This can lead to difficulties in treatments that are proceeding slowly (as most do) or in other ways running counter to the therapist's identity.

When we think we know, we may stop being open to learning. On the other hand, as happens in other arenas, one often realizes just how little one knows with more experience. This can have the positive effect of opening us to new ideas, but it can also create inner confusion or a lack of self-confidence or trust in one's judgment. Another potential hazard of the "expert" role is the narrowing focus of one's work and thinking. It is easy to stop attending professional meetings that do not focus on trauma, to stop attending meetings at which one is not presenting, to stop hearing the importance of non-trauma material in the stories of our survivor clients.

As one accrues experience with sexual abuse survivor clients, one may increasingly be viewed as an expert. While this can feel gratifying, it has other ramifications as well. One may take on too many clients and too many trauma clients, for a variety of reasons. In most areas of the country, there is a dearth of therapists who are experienced with trauma clients. This may mean that one receives a disproportionate percentage of very difficult referrals, clients who have been through unsuccessful treatments. Whatever else it implies, this usually suggests that establishing a therapeutic relationship will be even more challenging. Particularly if the client has been abused or felt hurt, abandoned, or betrayed by, or experienced a therapeutic impasse with another therapist, developing trust will be more challenging.

Experienced and recognized trauma therapists may receive more referrals of clients who have extremely violent or sadistic abuse histories. These therapies can pose more challenges to the therapist's frame of reference and may also include more graphic trauma imagery such as that of cult or ritual abuse, contributing to the therapist's vicarious traumatization. To compound the difficulties, supervision may not be readily available to the more experienced trauma therapist. Some therapists address this problem through regular telephone supervision with colleagues around the country.

Far too many experienced therapists forego regular supervision out of a misguided belief that it is unnecessary after licensure, simply a luxury, or necessary only in the event of a therapy crisis or an impasse. The failure to treat with respect the complexities and real risks in this work is short-sighted and dangerous.

An experienced trauma therapist may find it difficult to allow himself to feel confused or afraid. Yet these feelings are inevitable in this work, and to the extent that we inhibit them, we are likely to move to other, less immediate feelings, possibly to the detriment of our therapies and ourselves. If we act like experts when we don't feel like experts, we do a disservice to clients and colleagues who can feel relief that we too have times of uncertainty, confusion, or fear.

Example   One client, after alternatively pleading and insisting that her therapist explain what was going on in a particular interaction, was startled when her therapist replied, "I don't know what's going on right now. I have faith, however, that together, in time, we will understand both your feelings and what's happening between us." The client returned often to the relief she felt that the therapist did not know either, and admitted that she was harshly self-critical whenever she did not understand instantly what she was feeling and why. The client continued, "You didn't even seem bothered that you don't know, you don't seem ashamed. You seem to think it's normal for understanding to take time."

Assaults to one's frame of reference have cumulative effects. In particular, the shifts in the therapist's identity may increase over time as he adjusts his expectations of what he can accomplish as a therapist. Whatever help we may offer to our survivor clients, we are helpless witnesses to their traumatic pasts. An altered sense of hope and meaning and a different relationship with one's awareness of all aspects of life are not uncommon long-term sequelae of working as a trauma therapist. In addition, the rage and outrage the therapist feels at perpetrators and about child sexual abuse continue to grow.

Advantages for the Experienced Trauma Therapist

As there are benefits for the newer trauma therapist, there are many benefits available to the more experienced trauma therapist and his clients. Doing this work over time provides the therapist with enormous satisfaction of accompanying survivor clients on a healing journey, and knowing that he has contributed to the process. With experience, the therapist can come to trust his knowledge, his judgment, his instincts, and the therapy process. This can hold him through some very tenuous moments (and sometimes weekends) in these therapies. It also seems likely that some of the therapist's schemas that are disrupted by the work early on may recover over time. Many therapists find their world view badly assaulted in their early years as trauma therapists; over time, however, many cherished beliefs about the fundamental goodness of most people may be restored. Time and success in these therapies are powerful healing forces.

The integration of one's general psychotherapy experience and one's experience working with sexual abuse survivors elucidates complexities in both areas and creates a rich, fascinating, theoretically compelling field. We are all part of this developing field and our new understandings enrich the entire field of practice.

Another advantage of being a more experienced trauma therapist is our increasing awareness of the types of transferences we pull for in our survivor clients. We learn more about ourselves, including our psychological needs and areas of primary vulnerability (Elkind, 1992) and how these interact with the selves of our clients (Jacobs, 1991; Pearlman, 1993). We become more skilled at sorting out complex transference-countertransference interactions, to the great benefit of client and therapist alike. In addition, we develop greater comfort talking about the therapeutic process and relationship with our clients. We may experience more freedom in the relationship, both to notice our own reactions and to speak. We may become freer to be ourselves, for example, using our humor, our warmth, our inquisitiveness.

Finally, becoming an experienced trauma therapist is a process that takes place in a context. Ideally, our experience base develops in the context of relationships with colleagues, and we may have a sense of belonging to a profession, to a network, and to a significant social movement. This context may be more attainable by the experienced trauma therapist whose more solid professional self-esteem may allow him to achieve greater success in discovering or creating the collegial relationships he needs to support the work he wants to do.

DEVELOPMENTAL ISSUES FOR SURVIVOR THERAPISTS*

Some therapists who are new to trauma work will discover their personal trauma histories for the first time through doing the work. A client's memories may stir powerful feelings in the new therapist; he may find himself having incomprehensible dreams or uncanny experiences of reliving something he did not know was part of his history. The realization that he is a survivor may give meaning to many previously incomprehensible experiences. This realization often occurs when the therapist is exposed to multiple survivor clients. It can be extremely confusing, and not always clear whether it is simply a strong countertransference/vicarious traumatization reaction or a dawning awareness of one's own trauma history. Good personal therapy and sensitive therapy supervision can help the therapist sort out these processes.

*For further discussion of therapists who are survivors of childhood sexual abuse, see chapter 8.

Neumann and Gamble (1994) point out an additional issue for the newer survivor trauma therapist. Initially, like all new therapists, he may identify more with the client than with the therapist role. For the survivor therapist, this may mean experiencing parallels between his own history and the clinical material as well as the reawakening of his own pain. This can obviously interfere with his ability to hear what the client is saying, to feel helpful or hopeful, as well as contribute to his own vicarious traumatization. The newer survivor therapist may also have a greater sensitivity to the enormous challenges survivor clients face in their healing journeys and a more immediate appreciation of their tremendous courage.

TRAINING AND SUPPORT IN THE PROFESSIONAL DEVELOPMENT OF A TRAUMA THERAPIST

Ideally, the therapist new to trauma therapy will have coursework in trauma theory and therapy that will include a focus on therapist issues such as countertransference and vicarious traumatization. Unfortunately, such training is still uncommon in professional graduate programs. Some institutions offer postdoctoral and other advanced training in trauma therapy. Advanced professional training is also available through many training centers, both in the form of ongoing seminars and one-time conferences and workshops. Many conferences provide audiotapes, which can be very informative. At least two major professional societies devote themselves to promoting the understanding of survivors of childhood sexual abuse and trauma: the International Society for Traumatic Stress Studies and the International Society for the Study of Dissociation.

Adequate support for the new trauma therapist includes a great deal of supervision; in our experience, two hours of individual supervision per week plus one or more hours of group supervision is an ideal minimum for a new therapist with a caseload of 12 to 15 clients. Those new to trauma therapy may need additional forums for checking out their experience with others, for accelerating their learning about trauma theory and therapy, and for examining the transference, countertransference, and vicarious traumatization issues raised in these therapies. This may mean resources for outside supervision if the organization is not able to provide sufficient experienced supervisors, and resources for attending conferences and workshops to further the new therapist's training.

In addition to professional support, the therapist new to trauma therapy will need personal support; we will discuss this in chapter 18. The new therapist may also need to develop ways of helping his friends and family members understand what he is experiencing without violating the confidentiality of his clients. A support group of therapists new to the work, which could for example grow out of the attendees at a trauma conference, could be very important.

Given the special issues for therapists who are survivors (Pearlman & Mac Ian, 1994), and for new therapists in particular, we strongly support Schatzow and Yassen's (1991) suggestion that every survivor therapist have at least one place where he feels comfortable acknowledging his survivor history and where he can talk about the interaction of his history with his work. We address these issues in more depth in chapter 8.

Part Five

THERAPIST SELF-CARE

17

Supervision and Consultation for Trauma Therapies

A TRAUMA THERAPY SUPERVISION or consultation is always a consultation on a therapy relationship, not a client. Throughout this book we have underscored the necessity for therapists who work with trauma survivor clients to have ongoing supervision and consultation for their work. We believe that such collaboration, evaluation, and support are essential, not a luxury or indulgence.

Yet, unsupervised trauma therapy seems to be all too common. In our study of 188 trauma therapists, only 64 percent reported receiving any kind of supervision, although 82 percent of those receiving trauma-related supervision found it helpful (Pearlman & Mac Ian, 1994). This work cannot and should not be done alone, not only because it is emotionally

In this chapter we will use the terms supervision and consultation interchangeably. One school of thought is that supervision implies a hierarchical relationship between a senior supervisor and a junior or training therapist. There is an equally strong tradition of supervision referring to the process of a therapist presenting clinical work to another clinician for the purpose of thinking together about the work and its process. We do not make the distinction between senior and junior therapist; like psychotherapy, we view supervision (or consultation) as a relational process whose focus depends on the needs of the person seeking help, the resources of the helper, and the interpersonal styles of both (Sarnat, 1992).

taxing and intellectually challenging, but because it is not possible for us to remain clear and boundaried in the face of the complex mix of levels of meaning and awareness and intense affective and fantasy arousal on the part of both participants in the therapeutic process. Linehan (1993) notes that the supervision or consultation team provides the context for the treatment. We believe all therapists have an ethical as well as personal responsibility to engage in regular, frequent clinical consultation on their psychotherapeutic work; a minimum of an hour weekly for an experienced clinician and more for newer clinicians is invaluable to the therapist and his therapies.

This chapter will address the technique and practice of supervision and consultation for trauma therapies, identify essential components for a trauma therapy supervision, and discuss some broader training and education needs.

COMPONENTS OF TRAUMA THERAPY SUPERVISION

Just as good trauma therapy is good psychotherapy with heightened attention to specific issues and techniques, trauma therapy supervision is clinical supervision with specific modifications. We recommend four components be included in a trauma therapy supervision:

1. A solid theoretical grounding, including a theoretical understanding of psychotherapy in general and trauma therapy in particular, a theory of the psychological responses to interpersonal violence, and an understanding of normal child development
2. A relational focus that attends to both conscious and unconscious aspects of the therapeutic relationship and the treatment process
3. A respectful interpersonal climate that allows attention to countertransference and parallel process
4. Education about and attunement to the therapist's vicarious traumatization.

While these components may not be part of each supervision session, all will be needed at different points in the work.

Theoretical Grounding

For the same reasons that all trauma therapy needs to be theory-based, a supervisor needs a theoretical framework through which to hear the clinical material presented by the therapist. Without theory, trauma therapies can easily become a series of crisis interventions or symptom-driven responses with no unifying concept of the person of the client and the context for the emergence of particular symptoms at particular times in his life and therapy. This fragmentation leads to the therapy becoming a re-creation of the client's internal state, and to frustration and failure for both the client and therapist.

A supervisor has the task of holding a theoretical container for the interpersonal intricacies of the therapeutic relationship. Thus, the supervisor can provide the holding for the therapist and the therapeutic relationship that allows the therapist to regroup and in turn hold the client and the relationship. The supervisory provision of a theoretical frame shores up the therapeutic frame. Holding within a theoretical developmental frame organizes what may feel like random, disconnected, or primary process material into a coherent, sensible, connected narrative that facilitates the therapist-client connection and thus the client's intrapersonal connections. The provision to the therapist of a sense of context and meaning lessens his anxiety and increases his genuine connection to his client. This connection decreases the existential or annihilatory anxiety that is so often the hallmark of these treatments.

Theory is essential in three general areas:

- Psychotherapy
- Responses to trauma
- Child development

Theory of Psychotherapy

One aspect of theory-based supervision is attention to the theory of psychotherapy. Clinical theory is based on assumptions and research about the curative aspects and the effects of the therapy process. Trauma therapy interventions presuppose a theory of change and healing; it is important that a supervisor be able to articulate the rationale and theoretical premises for the techniques of the therapy. This arena also includes education about therapeutic frame, boundary management and rationale, and other aspects of therapeutic technique such as neutrality, interpretation, working through, transference analysis, countertransference; stages of treatment, and the development of the therapeutic relationship.

Theory of Responses to Trauma

A developmental theory of personality that addresses the impact of psychological trauma on survivors (such as CSDT) is essential in supervision of trauma therapies. Information about normal responses to abnormal events helps therapists make sense of their clinical observations and experience.

Survivor clients often present with severe and confusing patterns of dissociation, self-mutilation, suicidal preoccupations, severe anxiety, depression,
flashbacks, fragmented memories, identity disorders, and existential despair. The supervision must include a way of understanding dissociation
and retraumatization. Again, there is a parallel to the trauma therapy itself;
just as the therapist is called upon by the client to give information to help
normalize and make sense of his experience, so the supervisor is called upon
by the therapist.

For example, having an understanding of the various forms of traumatic
memory allows therapist and client to understand tactile or olfactory sensations as possible body or sensory memories rather than as idiosyncratic
psychotic symptoms. Further, in the context of reenactments or interpersonal memory, both therapist and client can benefit enormously from at-
taching meaning to painful recurrent interpersonal patterns that emerge
within and outside of the therapy. A conceptualization that describes a
client with strong ego resources and undeveloped self capacities, that is, a
client who can present simultaneously as highly competent and functioning
in the world and as struggling with infantile dependence and a lack of
self-cohesion, can make the difference between therapeutic holding and
empathic failure. A theory that identifies central psychological needs which
can be disrupted by trauma helps the therapist and client sort out otherwise
confusing relationship difficulties and to connect them to specific traumatic
antecedents.

Child Development

A key educational task within both the supervision and the therapy is developmental education; therapist and client need to be able to understand the
developmental factors in a childhood sexual abuse survivor's history and
current presentation. Understanding the developmental level of the child at
the time of a traumatic event is crucial to understanding and developing
effective interventions for the later manifestations of that trauma. Survivor
clients often do not have any idea about what a child of a given age is
actually capable of or how that child would think about and understand a
confusing and frightening event. Likewise, if a therapist does not take into
account the developmental and cognitive level at which a client is functioning in a particular memory or reenactment, he can misinterpret and miss
opportunities for helpful interventions. Part of what is healing is for the
client and therapist together to understand how the client's childhood development was disrupted by trauma, what developmental tasks (such as developing the capacity to manage strong affect) were interrupted by the trauma,
and how the therapeutic environment can help the client build what is

underdeveloped. This theoretical framework can ameliorate the anxiety and feelings of helplessness and hopelessness that are constant occupational hazards for therapists in this work.

A Focus on the Therapeutic Relationship

Consistent with our basic premise that the healing of interpersonal trauma occurs in the context of the interpersonal relationship between the client and therapist, the supervision of trauma therapy must address and conceptualize the unfolding and development of the therapeutic relationship. The supervisory task is to help the therapist notice nuances of the therapeutic relationship and utilize his experience in the relationship. This is done by inviting exploration of the therapist's subjective experience, inviting trial identification with the client's experience, and listening to the client's words and other forms of communication about his interpersonal experience in the therapy. Such a relational approach encourages the therapist's progress toward genuineness and authenticity in the therapy (Jordan et al., 1991). The supervisory relationship therefore also provides an important realm in which to explore the transference dynamics and expectable relational paradigms likely to emerge in the therapy. As discussed elsewhere (chapter 5), the transference responses can be difficult for a therapist to hold and understand without a relationship-based model.

The technical approach to transference in trauma therapies is also somewhat different from more traditional psychotherapies. Rather than encouraging a transference to unfold completely (into a transference neurosis), one brings the real therapeutic relationship into the discussion earlier in the service of modulating the anxiety of a trauma-based transference and of developing self-protective interpersonal skills. To be able to work in this way, a therapist first needs to know himself: his manner, style, and presence as a therapist in general and with this particular client, his transference valence—that is, what transferences does he commonly "pull for" (maternal, authority, protector, judge), based upon his way of being in the world and in a therapy relationship? Second, he may have some ideas about what transference responses he can expect from this particular client given his experiences and adaptations. In both these arenas the supervisor can be an invaluable resource. When the supervisor invites the therapist to notice his experience in the room with the client, to notice details of his presence, behavior, style, and impact on the client, she opens these issues up for examination and discussion and teaches the therapist to use himself as his best therapeutic tool.

The relational focus of the supervision is further enhanced by attention to parallel process (Doehrman, 1976) between the supervisory relationship and the therapeutic relationship. The parallelism is inevitable and useful. It can be as straightforward as the therapist who wants to know what to do with an inconsolable, anxious client, yet rejects every suggestion made by the supervisor until the parallel process is pointed out. Sometimes it is more subtle, as when the supervisor participates in an empathic failure by repeatedly responding to content and focusing on therapeutic action rather than simply sitting with a therapist's affective experience. Through recognition and discussion of the process within the supervisory relationship, supervisor and therapist can recognize unconscious patterns in the therapeutic relationship.

A supervision must be supportive for a therapist to feel comfortable bringing his client's evaluative experience to the supervisor. The supervisor can model exploration of interpersonal interactions by her willingness to notice, name, and discuss interactions in the supervision. A supervisor must be nondefensive in response to the therapist's questions, disappointments, anger, hurt, or anxiety, just as the client needs the therapist to hear his experience without becoming defensive. One contribution to making trauma supervision and therapy safe is the acknowledgment of what goes on in the relationships, the validation of perceptions. This counteracts the phenomenon in abusive families of secrecy and denial, the invalidation of the child's perceptions.

Sarnat (1992) describes in detail the negotiation of a conflict and parallel process in a supervisory relationship in which her willingness to acknowledge her contribution to the subsequent therapeutic impasse allowed her supervisee to reexamine the therapeutic interaction that led to the impasse. When supervisors feel the need to be infallible, how can supervisees be open to mutual negotiation of conflict in their therapies?

A Focus on Countertransference

Ideally, supervision provides a respectful forum in which therapist and supervisor can identify and examine possible countertransference dynamics. As we have discussed throughout this book, these responses are complicated, personal, and often painful or embarrassing. It is important for the supervisor to normalize countertransference, and then facilitate the therapist's abilities to make clinical and personal use of his responses. This process includes interpreting countertransference, focusing on what clues or information the countertransference provides the therapist about himself, the client, and the therapeutic relationship.

It is important to be clear about the boundary between supervision and personal psychotherapy (Sarnat, 1992). While each supervisor-therapist pair negotiates the intimacy and content of the supervision according to their style and needs, there are clear differences between the tasks of the two relationships.* A supervisor does not have license to make interpretations, yet is inviting the therapist to reflect on his countertransference. This is a fine line, and each pair will find its own comfort level, which may shift as they come to know and trust one another over time. When a supervisor invites a therapist to notice his countertransference thoughts, feelings, associations, and behaviors, the framework for working with that material needs to be clear. Specifically, a supervisor should be open to and educative about the expectable countertransference responses to childhood sexual abuse, as well as to particular client factors.

It is not the supervisor's role to invite transference. While transference responses to the supervisor are inevitable, the supervisory contract is generally not to invite or explore them in depth, except as they reflect a parallel process with the therapy. At times, a supervisor recommends a therapist enter or resume personal therapy when issues beyond the scope of supervision seem to be relevant in his psychotherapies.

Therapists who are themselves survivors of childhood sexual abuse should have at least one supervision in which they can openly discuss relevant effects of their personal history on their clinical work. If the therapist has told the supervisor that he is a survivor, the supervisor should be attentive to the possibilities for retraumatization of the therapist and for the therapist to identify with the client (see chapter 8).

A Focus on Vicarious Traumatization

Finally, we consider it imperative that any supervision of trauma therapy include education about, awareness of, and attunement to the effects of vicarious traumatization. A supervisor may invite the therapist to notice changes in his behavior, identity, world view, and spirituality and in his beliefs about safety, trust, esteem, control, and intimacy, and to notice intrusions of traumatic imagery into his personal life. In particular, a supervisor must be alert to the effects of vicarious traumatization on the therapy.

Supervision is also a forum for developing strategies to address and ameliorate the effects of vicarious traumatization. A supervisor may suggest that the therapist explore professional, organizational, and personal strategies for self-care and self-protection. She may observe vulnerabilities for the therapist and encourage him to notice potential blind spots, emotional

---

*There are different perspectives on this matter, which are discussed in the supervision literature and reviewed by Sarnat (1992).

vulnerabilities, or failures to be self-protective. Sometimes a supervisor needs to work with the therapist on particularly troublesome trauma material, encouraging him to understand what about the material he finds particularly salient and troubling, and inviting him to explore ways of transforming the imagery and distressing associations, thoughts, and feelings. In addition, the supervisor's awareness of potential interactions between vicarious traumatization and countertransference (see chapter 15) can provide a helpful safeguard against therapeutic impasses and therapist distress. A supervisor can anticipate with the therapist potential unfolding relational and affective patterns in the therapy.

Most of all, a supervisor is always supervising the therapeutic relationship—never just a case or a client or a therapist. The supervisor helps the therapist keep the big picture in mind. She is constantly trying to fit the pieces of clinical material she hears into its historical, traumatic, interpersonal, therapeutic, and personal contexts. Holding the four threads—theory, therapeutic relationship, countertransference, and vicarious traumatization—allows the supervisor to draw upon a wealth of possible ways to elucidate meaning and context for the therapeutic relationship to which she is consulting.

SPECIAL ISSUES IN SUPERVISION OF TRAUMA THERAPIES

Within the framework suggested above, some particular issues are likely to arise in trauma therapy supervisions. In addressing them, we will explore the role of consultant and the supervisory relationship. For each of these issues, the consultant's task is to help the therapist manage his feelings and responses, and to facilitate the growth and progress of the therapeutic relationship.

Witnessing

Managing Chronic Suicidality and Despair

One of the most difficult and painful tasks of many trauma therapies is holding the client's existential despair and often chronic suicidality. These clients often require their therapists to walk through the valley of the shadow of death with them, and it is a long, arduous journey. The therapist is at times left with almost unbearable life and death anxiety, not knowing if his client will live through the process. It is not possible, nor would it be therapeutic, for most chronically suicidal trauma survivors to be hospitalized for the duration of their therapy process, and it is certainly not helpful for the entire treatment to be organized around crises and suicide assessments. Each therapeutic dyad needs to work out ways of addressing these issues in the context of the particular client and therapist-client fit. However, the consultant plays an important role.

Foremost, the consultant keeps an eye on the therapeutic process and asks the question, How does this particular suicidal feeling relate to current events in the therapy and the client's life? A therapist can be swept up in the immediacy of the crisis and stop noticing process, or he may become worn down and forget to look for variations in a pattern that can feel monotonously repetitive. Why now? When did these feelings start this time? What is the interpersonal context? What is the communication to the therapist in particular? A central thread is to remain aware of the meaning of suicide to this particular client, historically and in the present.

The consultant helps the therapist separate the meaning of suicide to him from its meaning to his client. For the client whose childhood context was one of entrapment, pain, and powerlessness, suicide may have become the embodiment of choice or freedom. For the client whose childhood context was one of intense loneliness, deprivation, and neglect, suicide may have become a soothing substitute for a mother figure. For the client in a family in which secrets were a source of power, suicide may have become a powerful secret, a reserve secret weapon against a world that can turn on someone at any time. For some clients chronic suidicality is a reenactment of their childhood experiences living with an unpredictable, abandoning, or actually suicidal parent. Each of these conceptualizations allows the therapist a way to connect and understand his client. The supervisor can create space in the therapeutic relationship by making room for meaning when the therapist is in an anxiety-driven action mode.

On the other hand, at times a therapist needs help from the consultant not to understand the meaning, but to hold the despair and fear. In part, this task is one of managing anxiety in the face of the limitations of control and influence over another person, and in part one of connecting with one's spirituality in a way that acknowledges the choices clients have to make between life and death. A therapist may simply need a place to take the pain of being a relatively helpless witness to his client's struggle with life and death. The consultant can offer empathy and respect and, in a sense, offer to hold vigil with the therapist. These are times when therapists need to be especially attuned to their own needs for emotional and spiritual nurturance. The consultant's job is to hold the therapist's anxiety and despair so the therapist can hold the client in his pain without moving to futile, potentially retraumatizing, action or indifference, without giving up hope or being harmed by the client.

Managing Self-assault, Self-loathing, and Reenactments

The therapist is also often a helpless witness to a trauma client's vicious self-assaults. The therapist may need to use consultation to voice his strong feelings about what he is witnessing and use the theoretical framework provided within the consultation to understand what the client is communicating about himself and about the therapeutic relationship. How is self-abuse a relational event, and how can the therapist move the behavior into the relationship of the therapy so that it can be worked on differently? The consultant's openness to using the supervisory relationship as a forum for exploring relational dynamics can help set the stage. Rice (1992) identifies psychotherapy as an apprentice profession and emphasizes that supervision is therefore the central component of training. He recognizes three ways in which supervision serves therapist education and training: by modeling appropriate boundaries, modeling a respectful, open therapeutic stance, and providing a holding environment. The consultant cultivates a therapeutic stance by modeling in the supervision a respectful openness to feelings, meaning, and communication.

The supervision also provides perspective on the interpersonal reenactments within the therapy. Whenever the therapist is feeling like a victim, a perpetrator, or a helpless witness, the supervisor may help therapist and client together examine the possibility that this is part of a process of interpersonal memory and often projective identification within the therapy, in which the client is exploring and teaching the therapist about his early experience.

The Holding Environment

Managing Intense Affect and Transference Feelings

The role of holding means the therapist must hear and reflect the client's material without retaliation and without being destroyed in order to detoxify the unmanageable affects and malevolent self and object representations that the client experiences as lethal. A consultant serves several functions with respect to the therapist's struggle to manage the range of intense, often primitive or disturbing, affects expressed in trauma therapy. When the client's feelings are expressed in the transference, they are more difficult to hold as they more directly challenge the therapist's affective and interpersonal style and identity; a consultant's respectful inquiry aids a therapist to notice and articulate his feelings without having to either act on or deny them. The theoretical framework that conceptualizes the therapeutic task in relation to affect is key. The concept of self capacities implies a therapeutic task of developing affect management skills which informs the therapist's response: to provide developmentally appropriate steps for the client to better identify his affect, context, needs, subjective experience, and choices. A developmental perspective on psychological trauma allows the therapist to understand that the high-functioning businessman sitting in the room with him may at times have a degree of affect tolerance that resembles the two-year-old boy he was when he was first sexually molested.

Likewise, a thorough understanding of the concept and process of transference greatly enhances a therapist's ability to hear and accept rather than react to a client's strong feelings toward the therapist. Creating safety for the expression of feelings is a therapeutic task that can be modeled and discussed in consultation. No matter how theoretically sophisticated or experienced a therapist is, he can forget the concept of transference in the intensity of his affective countertransference. This pattern is part of the inevitable reenactments and enactments in psychotherapy with trauma survivors.

Managing Content of Trauma Memories

The therapist's management of and responses to a client's trauma memories relate to his own affect tolerance. The therapist will be called upon to manage not only the affects stirred in response to the traumatic memories and images shared in the therapy, but also the impact of imagery itself and the meaning to the therapist of the abusive events. Thus it will be helpful for the consultant to provide not only affective holding and theoretical conceptualizations, but also information about vicarious traumatization and self-care. The consultant can also be helpful by listening for themes in the trauma material that may suggest transferences and countertransference likely to emerge in the therapy. This anticipation can help the therapist prepare and listen for repetitive interpersonal patterns in the therapy which then provide important opportunities for reworking traumatic object relationships.

Boundaries

As noted previously, the negotiation of boundaries in trauma therapies is both crucial and difficult and relies on principles of clarity and respect. Consultation is an effective forum in which to address boundary issues. This efficacy, however, relies on the safety of the consultation relationship and mutual respect and acceptance. Because many of the countertransference feelings evoked in trauma therapies feel shameful, therapists are often reluctant to report them to supervisors (Adler, 1992).

The role of the supervisor or consultant as "other" or "third," an outsider yet part of the therapeutic dyad, has interesting implications in a trauma therapy in which themes of safety, exclusivity, secrecy, and absent parents may be central. The client may have a transference to the supervisor or a fantasy about the role of the supervisor that elucidates important relational patterns. The supervisor may also have to negotiate boundary issues; for example, a client's request to speak with the supervisor. The therapist may need to negotiate responses to clients' questions about the content of the supervision hour, or the client's request or demand that he not discuss their work in supervision. These requests open the way for the therapist to educate the client about the purpose of consultation, its confidentiality, and its role in protecting the therapy. These discussions provide useful opportunities to examine the process of reenactment, and to again clarify and negotiate respectful, appropriate boundaries that serve the needs of both client and therapist.

Managing Erotic Feelings

A consultant can provide invaluable assistance in creating an atmosphere where the therapist can talk about the predictable erotic, voyeuristic, and sexual feelings that emerge in these therapies. Therapists are undertrained in understanding and working with their own erotic feelings in their psychotherapies, and concomitantly therapeutic consultations often fail to address and work with a therapist's erotic feelings and responses. Gorkin (1987) states,

> It is worth noting that, in spite of the burgeoning interest in countertransference issues, scant attention has been paid in the literature to the therapist's feelings and fantasies toward patients. . . . it is more comfortable nowadays for a therapist to fantasize throwing a patient out of the office than it is to imagine joining the patient on the couch (p. 108).

Gorkin's discussion of sexualized countertransference is one of the few in-depth discussions of the topic in the current literature (Schoener et al., 1989). Therapists need to examine what prevents them from acknowledging and exploring erotic transference and countertransference feelings. The relationship with the consultant is an important part of what can inhibit or facilitate the discussion of erotic feelings in the therapy. If the consultant is comfortable with her own sexuality and sexual feelings, with a range of responses, and with the boundaries around the consultation and the therapy, she can convey a greater openness for the therapist's feelings.

It is inevitable that therapies involving childhood sexual abuse will at times stir sexual feelings, including sexual feelings that may be dystonic to the therapist, such as sexual attraction to or fantasies about clients, arousal in response to sexual trauma material, emergence of unfamiliar bisexual urges and feelings, identifications with sexual aggressors, and voyeuristic fantasies. These feelings and fantasies occur not in a vacuum, but in the context of a complex, intimate therapeutic relationship, and therefore they have many levels of meaning. Certainly a therapist should examine and understand his personal context (historical experiences, sexual identity issues, current sexual relationship issues, etc.), but he must also ask how these feelings are a response to the conscious and unconscious communications of this client. To what in the client's presentation, material, and experience is the therapist responding? How can he appropriately bring the unconscious aspect of this communication into the shared conscious awareness of the therapeutic relationship? A trusting supervisory relationship can allow for an open exploration of these questions.

Example   A male therapist presented three recent sessions with a female client to his female supervisor. He mentioned that in the middle session his client related an erotic dream she had about him. He continued to present a detailed discussion of the subsequent session in which she discussed childhood isolation and loneliness. He spoke at more length than usual. When he finished, the supervisor invited him to return to the dream and asked him if the client had given him details. He said yes and looked embarrassed. She invited the therapist to note his flight from the dream and asked what feelings he had about it. He acknowledged that he felt embarrassed, uncomfortable because he felt flattered, and ashamed to tell his supervisor for fear she would think he had been seductive with his client. His supervisor normalized his responses and the emergence of the dream at this point in the development of the therapy. She also helped the therapist contextualize the dream relative to the earlier session and link both the dream and his countertransference-driven response (or lack of response) to the themes of the subsequent hour.

Texts addressing sexual misconduct and boundary violations by professionals emphasize the important preventive role of supervision and consultation and stress the need for a forum in which to address the therapist's sexual and erotic feelings outside of the therapy relationship (Folman, 1991; Schoener et al., 1989). In their volume on psychotherapists' sexual involvement with clients, Schoener et al. discuss specific signs of potential sexual boundary violations, including seductive behavior and game playing on the part of the therapist, unattended or unaddressed seductive behavior on the part of the client, and therapies that become stalled or ineffective because of failure to discover or address underlying feelings of sexual attraction. They recommend specific supervisory intervention, with the supervisor inquiring explicitly about boundary issues including outside-of-session contacts, therapist disclosure of sexual feelings, and changes in frame or boundaries.

Consultation is a forum to examine other kinds of boundary dilemmas as well, including issues of physical touch, gifts, personal questions, telephone contact, and other issues common in these treatments. For a survivor of childhood sexual abuse, all boundaries have a sexual meaning; when any boundary is breached or violated, the event raises the fear and expectation that bodily and sexual boundaries will also be violated. Therefore, the open exploration of countertransference factors in boundary negotiations and unconscious sexualization of nonsexual events in the therapy is an important consideration for the therapy consultation.

Therapeutic Impasse

We have written in chapter 10 about countertransference responses that relate to therapeutic impasses. Here we want to note the important role of the consultant in helping resolve therapeutic impasses (Elkind, 1992). Specifically with regard to a psychotherapy with a survivor of childhood abuse, the model of collaboration between therapist and consultant can be very powerful in and of itself. Seeking a consultation is ideally framed as the therapist and client being stuck and needing help figuring out what isn't working. This is a significant shift away from a family history in which problems may have been blamed on the child or ignored. When the consultant is viewed as a collaborator, someone who has the best interest of the therapy relationship foremost in her mind, the client may feel held in a unique way: The people who are supposed to help him are doing their jobs and doing them in a respectful, cooperative way.

If the therapist, client, and consultant decide that the consultant will meet with the client or will sit in on a session, it is important for the consultant to invite the therapist to discuss all of his feelings about these sessions, both before and after them.

It is also important for the consultant and therapist to be clear in advance about the purpose of the session and what each of their roles is, who will run the session, what they hope to accomplish, and so forth. Of course it is important to work out boundary issues in advance as well: whose office will they use, who will start and end the session and when, who will pay whom what fee—and what are all of the implications of each decision.

When the consultant meets with the client and therapist, the therapist may feel abandoned by the consultant as the consultant works to understand the client's experience. If the outcome of the consultation is a decision that the therapist and client should end their work together, consultant and therapist should generate a list of possible new therapists for the client. Although they may be tempted to have the consultant become the next therapist, this role shift is not recommended for any of the parties involved. It undermines the boundary and role clarification that is part of a therapy consultation and can lead to the therapist feeling abandoned or betrayed and the client feeling unsafe or involved in a reenactment.

Parallel Process

One realm within supervision in which boundary issues and other therapeutic processes will emerge is in the parallel process. While both therapist and consultant hope ultimately to serve the best interests of the client, the primary function of the supervisory relationship is to provide support and education for the therapist. In this context, parallel process enactments commonly reflect dynamics around dependence, boundaries, self-esteem, safety, and control. When a therapist prefers to use a consultation hour to discuss many clients, therefore focusing on brief specific questions or problems, it may reflect a reality of too many clients and not enough supervision, or the therapist's feeling overwhelmed. It may reflect a conscious or unconscious avoidance of certain affective material or countertransference responses in his therapies. If the focus on several clients is initiated by the supervisor, it may reflect her lack of comfort with the therapist's work. Moving through many cases in a supervision hour is more common among newer therapists, whose anxiety often focuses on technique and specific interventions. It may also reflect a personal or therapeutic style of avoiding affect or intimacy. Or it may reflect anxiety about esteem issues, a fear of disclosing details of the therapeutic process.

The supervisory relationship can allow for the expression of these issues and the freedom to notice relational patterns in the supervision (such as chronic lateness, sessions running over their allotted time, forgetting notes or clinical material, filling the hour with detailed reports of clinical material and leaving no time for the supervisor's response, etc.). This requires some active structuring on the part of the supervisor, especially early on in the relationship, including asking questions, making observations, and inviting the therapist to notice his own experience, both in the therapy and in the consultation.

FRAME FOR TRAUMA THERAPY SUPERVISIONS

Just as in the psychotherapy relationship, a supervisory relationship has boundaries and a frame. The specifics of the frame will vary based upon the contract and the therapist's and supervisor's needs, resources, and roles, which should be delineated explicitly at the outset of the supervision. Therapist and supervisor need to address such issues as confidentiality, legal responsibility, evaluation, time, fee, frequency, and availability of the supervisor.

The interpersonal climate of the supervision is also crucial. In order for a supervisee to be able to address his insecurities, confusion, and complicated feelings, the relationship must focus on safety, trust, respect, and clear boundaries.

Confidentiality

The parameters of confidentiality should be negotiated at the outset of the supervisory relationship and, like all frame issues, discussed over time as they arise in various overt and disguised forms.

If a therapist is to share his most intimate feelings, he will need to know that the supervisor is not discussing them elsewhere. This boundary is especially sensitive in training and organizational settings where the awareness of and respect for boundaries and confidentiality may not be as great as the therapist would require to feel safe.

Evaluation

Ideally, evaluation should not be conducted by the supervisor. It is not uncommon in training programs, such as internships or postdoctoral fellowship programs, for the supervision to include an evaluation component. The conflict inherent in the roles of supervisor and evaluator is also experienced by many therapists in agencies where the supervisor is also the boss. The ideal trauma therapy supervision is one in which the therapist feels free to share all of his thoughts, feelings, and fantasies about the client, all of his struggles about the work, and to explore his unconscious associations to the client and his material. This kind of freedom is rare in a situation where the therapist is also being evaluated. Where they converge, it is imperative that both the supervisor and therapist know the boundaries of the relationship, for example: What is the basis for the evaluation? What are the limits of confidentiality in the relationship? Who else has access to the evaluation? What will it include? The supervisor should be attuned to themes in the therapist's material that relate to issues of judgment and evaluation and name these themes as they arise, both to increase the safety of the supervisory relationship and to model the naming of issues related to esteem and trust.

MODELS OF SUPERVISION

There is a movement in the field of clinical supervision away from an authoritarian, expert-based model of supervision toward a more relational, interactive model (Jordan, 1990; Rosica, 1993; Sarnat, 1992; Slavin, 1993). This model enables the supervisor to participate with the clinician in an examination of the process of the therapy. It allows both parties not to know and encourages them to use their relational experience as part of the relevant data—a very appropriate model for the therapeutic relationship with survivor clients. This approach often increases anxiety for both, but it is also a more genuine reflection of the gradual process of knowing that is psychotherapy. It can enhance the therapist's connection to the client rather than invite the therapist to assume a false self modeled on the supervisor which will inevitably be experienced as an abandonment by the client. Newer therapists or those with little training in psychological trauma may want and need a more didactic style in the beginning. Yet, an interpersonal focus is essential to convey the importance of a relational approach to trauma therapy. This model goes a step further in that it contains within it the implicit premise that in order to teach, to facilitate growth or change in another in a relational context, the teacher or supervisor must be open to being changed and taught (Elliott, 1994).

Most clinicians are familiar with a traditional one-to-one model of supervision in which a more experienced therapist acts as the supervisor or consultant. However, because the field of trauma therapy is new, it is not uncommon for a therapist to have useful ideas about a more experienced therapist's work with a trauma survivor client. A rewarding alternative one-to-one model is a peer consultation where two clinicians consult to one another; we find this works best when clearly structured so each person has a period of time in which to present and discuss his clinical work.

Other supervision takes place in small groups, either peer supervision groups or groups of clinicians meeting with a more experienced consultant or supervisor. Groups can function according to a rotating presentation structure, by topics (such as dissociation, hypnosis, dissociative identity disorder), or as continuing case presentation (where one clinician presents detailed process material from his work with a particular client over a period of several weeks or months). Therapists in training benefit from a format in which the more experienced consultant presents her case; not only does she teach from her own work, giving trainees a rare opportunity to see how an experienced trauma therapist works, but she also models her openness to learning through consultation and normalizes the strong countertransference and vicarious traumatization responses all therapists have in this work.

When a group of people first come together for the purpose of supervision, their focus is often initially on clients rather than on the therapy relationships or the therapist. It is helpful for participants to discuss early on what frame and structure would enhance each person's comfort for sharing his struggles and feelings about the therapies he is discussing. Talking about the process among the group members can help set the stage for discussing the process of the therapies, as well as the more personal issues of countertransference and vicarious traumatization.

Vicarious Traumatization Consultations

From time to time, or on a regular and more frequent basis, therapists may benefit from a consultation that focuses specifically on vicarious traumatization. This can be helpful to a therapist who is experiencing a particular intrusion of clients' material, who has a large survivor caseload, whose own trauma history is being activated by the work, or who is experiencing changes in his personal or professional life which he relates to his work as a trauma therapist. We discuss vicarious traumatization consultations in chapter 18.

Consultation for Group Therapies

Consultation for group therapies for trauma survivors is extremely important. We recommend that such groups have two cotherapists, and that the consultation is most helpful when it addresses the cotherapists' working relationship as well as the other components of a trauma therapy consultation already discussed. Consultation is important on an ongoing basis, and especially helpful when the group is in transition (forming, adding members, experiencing a crisis or an impasse, and ending).

ETHICAL ISSUES IN SUPERVISION OF TRAUMA THERAPIES

A psychotherapy consultation is also a forum for identifying, clarifying, and addressing ethical issues that arise from time to time. It is not uncommon for complicated ethical issues to emerge, given the intensity and potential for reenactment in therapies with clients who have been violated physically, psychologically, ethically, morally, and legally in the past. Such issues might include a client urging physical contact, a client making a homicidal threat, constant changes in boundaries such as meeting time or place, third party contacts, a family member seeking treatment with the same therapist, contact with the client outside of the therapy relationship or office, and so forth. The negotiation of these matters can provide critical reparative experiences in the therapy. Any persistent questioning of the frame which does not resolve through discussion with the client or in which the therapist feels uncertain about how to proceed should be discussed in supervision, and may benefit from the input of an ethics consultant. It is risky to try to figure out these issues alone because the clinical situation is rife with opportunities for parallel process and unconscious reenactments.

PROFESSIONAL AND TRAINING ISSUES

Supervision and case consultation are key components of every therapist's professional development and identity formation. Psychotherapy is an apprenticeship trade in some ways, and we all have mentors and teachers whom we have viewed as master therapists. Supervisors and consultants become internalized and made part of our "internal supervisor" (Casement, 1991). Casement uses the term *supervision* to refer to the process of the therapist stepping back from his experience of the therapeutic work in order to have an overview of the process in the context of the particular client and his history and character. He advocates the development of an "internal supervisor," that is, an observing part of the therapist that incorporates an internalization of his supervisor(s) with "trial identifications" (Fleiss, 1942) with the client and self-knowledge and autonomy.

Impediments to Seeking Supervision

It is often easier for students and newer clinicians to seek supervision because they feel more justified in their anxiety, given their lack of experience and information. It is a dangerous side effect of the medical model that as therapists we hold an unrealistic notion that we are supposed to know what is going on and to understand our clients and our clinical interactions with them at all times. Traditionally, students alone have the license not to know, although many still succumb to pressures that prompt them to strive to appear certain, as if that were a mark of competence. The experienced therapist or analyst, by contrast, has to make an effort to preserve an adequate state of not knowing if he is to remain open to fresh understanding (Casement, 1991).

In confusing not knowing with ignorance, a therapist runs the risk of imposing on a client the "self-deception of a premature understanding, which achieves nothing except to defend the therapist from the discomfort of what he does not know" (Casement, 1991, p. 9). Instead, Casement encourages holding a creative tension between what one knows and does not know in the therapeutic situation. We have spoken elsewhere of the dangers of assuming we know what our clients cannot yet know and of the essential need to be with our clients in their experience of not knowing and trying to learn.

Clinical supervision is required or expected as part of the job or training position for some therapists. For many other therapists, after one or two years of postgraduate practice, consultation is voluntary and may be difficult to pursue for a number of reasons. Many therapists come to believe they should not need consultation because they erroneously believe supervision is only for beginning therapists. The licensing rules in many states augment this fantasy because licensure granted after one or two years of supervised practice after receiving one's degree means a therapist can legally practice independently, that is, without supervision. Therapists then fall into an age-old fallacy of mistaking what is legally required with what is ethical, necessary, or right. This dangerous belief can be further supported by the natural tendency for many therapists to be independent and to value autonomy and competence, which increases the resistance to acknowledging the need for or seeking help.

Training programs often encourage therapists to presume their own mental health, knowledge, expertise, and authority. The implicit expectation is that the therapist should be unfailingly confident (the "if you don't know, fake it" mentality). In fact, however, therapists must learn therapy anew with every new client. We are always learning from our clients what it is they need us to know.

For a therapist, seeking consultation means opening up the private relationships of one's therapies for scrutiny and observation. This process may bring up feelings of shame or loss of something special and intimate. Therapists may fear they are betraying their clients' trust (this can also be a projection of the therapist's reluctance to relinquish the privacy or secrecy of the relationship). If a therapist believes he is supposed to know what is going on in a therapy at all times, admitting to a consultant that it is not always clear can be very difficult and painful. If the therapist believes he is not supposed to have feelings about the work, he will not comprehend his need for support.

It is important to examine one's reasons for avoiding consultation. While there are important issues of availability of competent, appropriate supervisors and of cost, there are different ways to address those, as discussed above. What might the reasons for not seeking consultation reflect about the therapist's identity, about his psychological needs? Is he unable to acknowledge his need for consultation because he feels he should be able to figure it out on his own? What might the reasons for not seeking consultation reflect about a particular client or his feelings about that client? Is he experiencing sexual arousal, anger, disgust, envy, competition, or voyeurism with respect to this client? Is he afraid the treatment is failing, ashamed of something he has said or done?

Another deterrent for therapists seeking consultation is negative prior experiences with supervision. Few supervisors have been taught to supervise and many clinicians have had negative experiences of supervision. Whether the experience was simply useless, or humiliating or damaging to a therapy relationship, these negative experiences strongly influence later decisions about seeking consultation. Just as clients should interview prospective therapists and make choices, so too should therapists interview and choose their consultants. These are important relationships and need to be created deliberately.

ORGANIZATIONAL ISSUES

Organizations have a responsibility to create a climate that supports the pursuit of learning through consultation and supervision. If organizations have the resources to offer consultation in-house, roles and boundaries should be explicit and lines of confidentiality discussed. Munroe and his colleagues (in press) have written about a trauma treatment team approach whose purpose is both to provide therapists with support in their work and to prevent secondary or vicarious traumatization.

From time to time, a clinician may need to consult with someone outside the organization for expertise not available among the staff of the organization or to free himself from organizational dynamics that may be affecting the therapy relationship deleteriously. Certainly those who provide supervision and consultation within an organization also have their own supervision and consultation, both for their own clinical work and to keep them attuned to issues of shame and anxiety in being supervised and presenting one's clinical work.

There are times in the life of an organization when a trauma-focused consultation, conducted by an outside consultant, may be in order for the entire organization. An example of this would be a critical incident debriefing or an opportunity for staff to process thoughts and feelings following a traumatic event in the organization. It may be a mixture of clinical and consulting roles, as in a consultation and processing meeting in the wake of a client committing or attempting suicide or a clinician committing an ethical violation, such as breaching a boundary with a client (Schoener et al., 1989). Or it may be a consultation concerning its management of vicarious traumatization. At times human services organizations have benefitted from consultations when things weren't working properly (e.g., high staff turnover, low morale, significant interpersonal conflict) because of vicarious traumatization which permeates the staff.

Organizations have a powerful influence on therapists they employ and on the therapeutic relationships that exist within the organization. Sensitivity on the part of members, and particularly leaders, of the organization to times when organizational dynamics call for an external consultation will allow those involved to develop a clearer sense of the dynamics and options for change.

Training for Trauma Treatment

Although there is a paucity of attention to trauma theory and therapy in most professional training programs, the trend is slowly changing. There continues to be a great need both for academic and professional courses that address specific clinical and theoretical issues related to psychological trauma and for a commitment to integrate trauma theory and therapy techniques into all clinical coursework. Likewise, there is a serious need for practicum, internship, residency, and other training positions that provide didactic and practical training opportunities that focus on trauma. We support the development of postgraduate (postdoctoral and postmasters) organized trauma training programs. We have developed a postdoctoral training program at the Traumatic Stress Institute (TSI) to provide advanced training in theory, research, and treatment of trauma survivors. Danieli (1994) has written a chapter outlining a specific approach to the training of trauma therapists which emphasizes attention to countertransference. The International Society for Traumatic Stress Studies (ISTSS) has developed a core curriculum in trauma theory, research, and treatment which stands as a model and a practical tool for institutions undertaking the development of trauma training (Danieli & Krystal, 1989). TSI has developed its own trauma training curriculum to provide a theory-based companion to the ISTSS curriculum.

Continuing Education in Trauma Work

Most mental health disciplines require continuing education and clinicians know the importance of keeping abreast of new ideas and specialized training opportunities in their fields through the literature, tapes, and conferences. The high attendance at trauma-focused conferences, workshops, and continuing education opportunities speaks to the great need for similar opportunities, and for less experienced clinicians to have access to basic and advanced training in trauma-specific topics. These trainings also provide important opportunities for collegial networking and support. Trauma therapists and others working with trauma survivor clients need one another for support, education, consultation, and resources. In our study of trauma therapists, attending workshops was the top-rated item in a list of behaviors therapists found helpful in addressing the stresses of trauma work (Pearlman & Mac Ian, 1994).

ISSUES FOR SUPERVISORS

We want to conclude this chapter by examining the effect of the supervisor on the supervision process and the effect of trauma supervision on the supervisor. The role of supervisor is quite different from that of a therapist; one listens differently, responds differently, and has different responsibilities. Nonetheless, there are also parallels, including potential transference from the therapist to the supervisor and countertransference from the supervisor to both the therapist and the client. Supervision is hard work; the supervisor will be aware of multiple levels of meaning and patterns of relationships. She will hear both the client's and the therapist's feelings and distress and may feel pulled to respond to their wish for relief and helpful intervention on her part. The wish for the supervisor to be an expert can interact with her self-expectations.

The new therapist or the therapist new to trauma work may experience more anxiety and is more likely to form an idealized transference to the supervisor. These dynamics invite the supervisor to be more active, more reassuring, and more directive, all of which may be appropriate and helpful if maintained within the larger goal of helping the therapist trust himself and use himself in the therapy. It also invites the supervisor into the expert role, which may or may not be comfortable for her and which, if accepted unquestioningly, can preclude the unfolding of the therapeutic relationship.

Supervision of trauma therapies can be taxing and difficult work; supervisors are asked to hear difficult trauma material and often hear more about clinical crises than clinical progress. At times, the need to support the trauma therapist can conflict with the supervisor's personal needs. A supervisor can be vulnerable to vicarious traumatization from trauma material presented in the context of a supervision, without the context of really knowing the client, which is part of what makes it easier to hear difficult trauma material.

The supervisor will want to consider the structure and scheduling of supervisions and to select those therapists to whom she feels comfortable consulting. It is much more difficult to consult to a clinician who does not share one's theoretical orientation, treatment philosophy, and basic values about the work. The consultation is more likely to be satisfying and successful for all parties if the supervisor thinks in advance about how to structure it, both to meet her needs and to facilitate the therapist's growth and his therapeutic relationships with clients. Consultation can be enormously rewarding and a wonderful learning experience for both the consultant and the therapist. It is a way we all have of working in connection with others, of sharing the power of this meaningful work, of honoring the complexity of the process, of validating our needs for support, and of sharing wisdom and experience.

18

Addressing
Vicarious Traumatization

IN THIS CHAPTER, we discuss strategies for working and living which we have found helpful in protecting our ability to remain available to our clients, our colleagues,˙ our friends and families, and ourselves. The strategies we recommend here serve to counter the spiritual damage—the loss of meaning and hope, connection, and awareness of all aspects of life and the nonmaterial—that can come about through unaddressed vicarious traumatization.*

Three primary concepts in vicarious traumatization interventions are awareness, balance, and connection (what one colleague called the ABCs of VT). Successful interventions restore and renew the therapist in general and address the specific psychological impact of working with survivors.

An *awareness* of oneself, one's needs, limits, and resources, is essential to living fully. Awareness of what is going on within oneself, where changes have taken place, is required to develop personal intervention strategies. Interventions to restore one's emotional equilibrium, for example, differ from those employed to rework changed beliefs about the world. Maintaining attunement to one's inner life is vital here. Just as they are clues to our

---

*See McCann and Pearlman (1990b) for strategies to be used by consultants, and Pearlman and Saakvitne (in press) for strategies to be used by therapists of traumatized therapists.

countertransference, our dreams, fantasies, associations, affects, and bodily sensations connect us to our wholeness and complete experience.

It is imperative to create *balance* among work, play, and rest, as well as balance among a variety of activities within one's work life and within one's personal life. Balance can be a powerful antidote to the bleakness that can entrap a therapist who has severely restricted the scope of his interests and, in effect, withdrawn from life.

Connection with oneself and others is the antidote to the isolation that can come about through vicarious traumatization. Such connection is absolutely necessary for us both professionally and personally. Connection allows one to identify personal needs and to meet them.

We now turn our attention to specific strategies for addressing vicarious traumatization within both professional and personal realms. In general, we encourage therapists to do for themselves the self-affirming, self-protecting, and self-nurturing things they encourage their clients to do. While many of these strategies are general approaches that would benefit all therapists, some have been developed specifically to address vicarious traumatization.

PROFESSIONAL STRATEGIES

Recognize and Accept
Vicarious Traumatization

The recognition that vicarious traumatization is a natural outcome of trauma work, a sort of occupational hazard, is an essential first step. Accepting our responses as normal allows us to explore their intricacies and address them without blame, shame, or pathologizing, both alone and in conjunction with others.

To recognize and accept vicarious traumatization requires a therapist to find a supportive environment in which to acknowledge, express, and work through clients' painful experiences and his responses to them. A confidential, professional relationship, whether with colleagues, a supervisor or consultant, or one's own therapist provides such a forum. Farber and Heifetz (1982) have written about the importance of therapists speaking openly about their negative feelings about their work. Not having a consulting relationship within which to speak these feelings leaves a therapist in a place of perpetual isolation, doubt, and shame.

Limit Exposure

Knowing about vicarious traumatization can allow us to give ourselves permission to limit our exposure to trauma material where possible; Maltz

(1992) notes the value of protecting oneself from "sexual abuse overdos-
ing" (p. 22). It may be essential to our clients that we hear their experiences, but we do not have to take on additional painful or graphic material
unnecessarily. For example, we can screen what we read (perhaps sometimes skimming or skipping case vignettes in certain books or journal articles); not attend, or allow ourselves to leave, certain sessions at professional
meetings; ask supervisees on occasion to limit the details they share about
their clients' abuse experiences; and so forth. The amount of trauma material we can manage varies from day to day and sometimes from hour to
hour.

In supervision, a supervisor's request of a supervisee not to give unnecessary details of a graphic trauma experience needs to be framed as self-care
and negotiated to address the supervisee's needs. Often the specific details
are essential to understanding the complex meaning of a traumatic event to
an individual; however, there are other times when there is much that is not
essential to share, and in supervision we have the luxury of saying so. This
is a delicate balance, and it is not traditional supervisory practice to contain
what the supervisee can explore. Each supervisor-therapist dyad will find
its own way of working with this issue; we are suggesting here that the
needs of the supervisor are an important component of the supervisory
relationship.

It is a different matter to limit that sharing in psychotherapy; however,
the continuous bombardment of the therapist by the client with graphic
trauma material is a matter that should be discussed in the treatment as it
can represent an acting out of aggressive or hostile feelings by the client, or
an unconscious reenactment of the client's overstimulation in childhood. In
our everyday work as trauma therapists, limiting exposure in psychotherapies generally takes the form of considered self-protection. As a client is
about to share a particularly horrific or graphic trauma memory, one may
choose to step back a bit. This can be done through a variety of strategies.
Imagining being surrounded by white light, or a bubble or cloud that will
absorb and protect you from pain, engaging in self-talk (e.g., "that was
then, this is now, he is safe now, I can listen to this now"), soothing
yourself with imagery (e.g., imagining that you and the client are surrounded by a community of loving people who will hold this with you, or
envisioning yourself and the adult self of the client with the child who is
being abused and stopping the abuse) can all make it easier to listen without
feeling overwhelmed. Bringing human connection into awareness counteracts some of the loss and some of the trauma; reminding yourself silently,
for example, "I care deeply about him, and our connection to one another
and to the larger human community can hold us in this experience." Thinking through this moment into the future can also be helpful; this involves

self-talk, such as, "Some day the client will be stronger and able to live the life he wants," "This is very difficult now, but eventually it will be easier," or "This acute pain or grief will not last forever for him."

Attend to Empathy

In chapter 14, we discussed the different ways we engage empathically with our clients. We noted the possibility of engaging with the child victim's and the adult survivor's cognitive and affective experiences, and that engaging with the child's affective experience makes the therapist most vulnerable to vicarious traumatization. It is beneficial to both client and therapist for the therapist to maintain a broader perspective than only that of the terror of the child. Helpful contexts include knowing that the child endured the pain both he and the therapist are now feeling, that he is now in at least one protected relationship, that he has resources that saw him through and that continue to be available to him, and that healing is possible. The therapist who is overwhelmed with grief and rage for and with a child who is being brutalized will not be as effective as the therapist who can keep one foot firmly planted in the present. It is always better for the client that we protect ourselves and not let ourselves be injured or overwhelmed by them or their feelings. This attention to empathy protects both the therapy and the therapist from some aspects of vicarious traumatization.

Name Reenactments

Another major contributor to vicarious traumatization is the therapist's involvement in reenactments with clients. Reenactments are inevitable. Our participation in reenactments is inevitable. As clients struggle to communicate and to master their earlier experiences, they will engage us as victim, perpetrator, and bystander in a variety of painful and sometimes traumatic reenactments. One way to reduce our vicarious traumatization from this source is to be ready to notice and name and explore reenactments with our clients. We should also remind ourselves that our clients are not engaging in these behaviors in a sadistic or malicious way in order to undermine the therapies (although these motives can certainly be a part of a reenactment). We find it helpful to remind ourselves that our client is teaching us what it was like to be him growing up, giving us a sampling of his family of origin experiences. This conceptualization frees us to work together on the meanings of the reenactments with the client, rather than feeling controlled or victimized by them. Our freedom to work with reenactments as such can lead to therapeutic change, which also ameliorates vicarious traumatization.

Set Limits

In chapter 7, we discussed creating and maintaining a therapeutic frame primarily for the sake of the client and the therapeutic relationship. Here we underscore the value of the frame in protecting the therapist. Maintaining a consistent therapeutic frame and knowing and conveying respectfully one's own limits to clients are ways to prevent some vicarious traumatization. When we overwork, we are endlessly available to clients between sessions, ignore session starting and ending times, wear ourselves down, we send confusing messages to clients about the boundaries and safety of the therapy relationship. We send mixed messages that undermine the therapy when we encourage clients to set limits in relationships but fail to do so in our relationship with them. For example, many therapists assume that they must be on 24-hour call for their clients. We encourage therapists to de-velop alternative arrangements, perhaps sharing weekend coverage with colleagues. One trauma therapist of our acquaintance lets her clients know that she is available from 9:00 a.m. to 9:00 p.m., Monday through Friday, and that if they need help on an emergency basis at other times they may use a local crisis line or the hospital emergency room. We remind ourselves of our human limitation when we set and hold to such limits. When we mistake our clients' needs for mandates about our responsibilities, we are at risk for greater vicarious traumatization. Further, we endanger our clients by allowing ourselves to be harmed by the relationship.

Maintain Professional Connection

Building a network of professional connection serves many valuable func-tions, a fact noted by others as well (e.g., Freudenberger & Robbins, 1979; Kaslow & Schulman, 1987). It counteracts the isolation in which many trauma therapists work and which others may experience as they withdraw from people in response to vicarious traumatization. The community also gives us opportunities to reality-test our negative beliefs about others devel-oped in the course of doing trauma therapy, to restore our sense of connec-tion with others, and to allow us to normalize our responses to the work as we talk with colleagues who share these responses. One can build profes-sional connection in a variety of ways, including attending workshops or training seminars, using support groups to talk about the effects of the work, discussing trauma cases with colleagues, and giving and receiving supervision.

Professional Education

Trauma therapists will find it useful to attend professional training meet-ings on non-trauma- as well as trauma-related topics. While trauma presentations provide opportunities to learn about new ways of working and to connect with other clinicians who are doing similar work, the non-trauma presentations allow us to continue to develop broader therapy skills and interests, to take a break from trauma work, and to meet different people, as well as to evaluate our own approaches from a different perspective (Freudenberger & Robbins, 1979; Kaslow & Schulman, 1987). In our study of trauma therapists, 76 percent listed attending workshops as a way of balancing the demands of their work (Pearlman & Mac Ian, 1994). Freudenberger and Robbins have also noted the restorative value of continuing informal training.

Support Groups

Groups of trauma therapists can provide a place to talk about the impact of the work, to obtain peer supervision, and to exchange ideas about clinical work, professional development opportunities, and therapist self-care. Groups of general therapists may be an alternative for therapists who are working in small communities without other trauma therapist colleagues. The group may consist of others doing similar but not identical work (e.g., people working with survivors in a variety of settings, therapists of other trauma survivors as well as those working with incest survivors) as a way of providing balance and perspective. Others have suggested professional support groups as a way of reducing individuals' discontent and alienation, as well as providing ways for professionals to learn from one another (Farber & Heifetz, 1982; McCarley, 1975; Sarason, Carroll, Maton, Cohen, & Lorentz, 1977). Such groups need not be large; a few people meeting together monthly can provide enormous support.

Supervision and Consultation*

All trauma therapists need someone with whom they can discuss without shame their many reactions to their work. A sensitive supervisor can help the clinician understand his experiences of vicarious traumatization and begin to develop ways of managing it. As previously mentioned, supervision is also a way of expanding one's sense of professional connection.

Vicarious Traumatization Consultations

As a supplement to traditional therapy consultations, we have developed a new type of collaboration which we call a vicarious traumatization consul-

---

*We use the terms supervision and consultation interchangeably here in order to emphasize our belief that all trauma therapists should have ongoing contact with an experienced trauma therapist. See chapter 17 for an in-depth discussion of supervision.

tation. Such a consultation provides a forum for talking more about our clinical work than we might choose to in our own psychotherapy and more about our personal life, both past and present, than we might in therapy supervision. Many therapists in our research sample report talking about the effects of their work in their personal psychotherapies (Pearlman & Mac Ian, 1994). This finding may indicate a need for additional forums for addressing the impact of these therapies.

A vicarious traumatization consultation can provide opportunities to address several issues. First, for the many therapists who are themselves survivors, a vicarious traumatization consultation provides a place where a therapist can address ways his own history may be interacting with his work (Schatzow & Yassen, 1991). This helps protect against the intrusion of the therapist's own issues into his therapies, and it also gives the therapist a place to talk about the reactivation of his own history. Because many clinicians receive their only supervision from people who are also their administrative supervisors, or from people not of their own choosing, a special consultation relationship may feel more comfortable for a more personal level of self-disclosure.

A second important way of using a vicarious traumatization consultation is to identify the therapist's most salient need areas that have been disrupted by vicarious traumatization. One way of managing some of these disruptions is to identify the particular needs (trust, control, intimacy, esteem, safety) represented in the trauma material the therapist finds most distressing. In addition, aspects of the therapist's identity, world view, and spirituality will be disrupted by working with trauma survivors. If he can identify specific aspects of the work (such as specific trauma images) that are especially distressing to him within this framework, he can detoxify some of the imagery or traumatic interactions that may be haunting him. For example, a story that contains vivid descriptions of the client's helplessness and/or the helplessness of bystanders may disturb the therapist who has strong needs for self-control or whose identity rests primarily in being a helper. Identifying what is salient to the therapist in a particularly distressing image or account provides the framework for working through this issue, work which can take place in the vicarious traumatization consultation, in the therapist's individual therapy, or in other ways and places that feel appropriate and helpful to the therapist. An additional bonus of this work is that in the future it allows the therapist to process more quickly and protect himself more readily from the painful impact of troubling traumatic imagery.

Another use of the vicarious traumatization consultation is as a forum for reality checks. The therapist can check with his consultant about whether it sounds like he is changing the therapeutic frame, about whether he is at risk for acting out some of his needs or feelings in his therapies, and about whether he seems more cynical or alienated from others.

We conduct some vicarious traumatization consultations in individual sessions and others in group settings. The latter may be staff groups (McCann & Pearlman, 1990a) or groups of therapists from the community who come together regularly for this purpose. One of us conducts an ongoing group of community therapists that over time has created a foundation of trust, which provides many of the benefits of the individual vicarious traumatization consultation as well as those of a support group.

Create Balance

Balancing clinical work with other types of work is enormously helpful in managing vicarious traumatization; others have noted the value of such balance for therapists in general (Farber & Heifetz, 1982; Guy & Liaboe, 1986; Kaslow & Schulman, 1987). For this reason, we teach, write, supervise, and do research. These activities also give us a sense of contribution at a broader level than the individual therapy, a sense that our work is reaching, and we hope helping, more people. Maltz (1992) noted the value of engaging in income-producing work that is unrelated to working with survivors of sexual abuse. Potential benefits of engaging in nonclinical work derive from the ability to be active, to make professional connections, and to engage in work that may produce more tangible or immediate rewards or whose outcomes relate more directly to one's activity.

Within the clinical realm, to balance the isolation of individual therapy, it can be helpful in developing a caseload to work toward a mix of individual, couples, family, and group therapy or look for opportunities to work with a cotherapist. Seeing both trauma and non-trauma clients, or survivors of a variety of traumatic life experiences — chronic and some acute trauma clients, some men, women, adults, and children — varies the clinical issues and transference dynamics with which the therapist becomes engaged. Of course all of this must be done within the range of one's abilities and interests, but broadening and varying one's work can reduce the strain of working with only one type of client and the effects of repeated exposure to trauma material. To hear in session after session of incidents of childhood sexual abuse creates despair and a distorted perspective that everyone's life experience is traumatic.

Limiting one's caseload is also useful where it is possible; a little over half of our trauma therapist sample reported limiting their caseloads as a way of coping with the demands of trauma work (Pearlman & Mac Ian, 1994). Not only is the trauma material difficult in these therapies, but as we have emphasized throughout this book, the therapist is asked to be emotionally present in a way that is challenging and tiring. Relationally

based psychotherapy is more strenuous than more didactic, distant, or authoritarian models of treatment. We believe it is a far more effective approach, however.

While not every clinician has the option of saying no to a particular case
or to adding more cases, one must consider the clinical, ethical, and personal issues that are involved in taking on another potentially stressful case
when feeling depleted. When considering picking up a new client, one needs
to consider what additional resources might make the work less taxing;
these might include additional supervision, the ability to schedule the client
at a time that is convenient for the clinician, and giving up some other
responsibility or task. For those based in organizations, it is often necessary
to work to educate those in authority about the professional, ethical, human, and business reasons to create manageable caseloads. Therapists often
feel futile in the face of large unresponsive systems. However, it is valuable
to remember Margaret Mead's words, "Never doubt that a small group of
committed citizens can change the world. Indeed it is the only thing that
ever does." As trauma therapists we must educate our colleagues, bosses,
and organizations about the need for appropriate resources for survivors
and those who serve them.

For some clinicians, giving supervision offsets some of the demands of
direct clinical service. Just as we, as therapists, benefit from interactions
with our clients, so too can we learn and grow from our work as supervisors. Many clinicians are more active as supervisors than as therapists; for
them, supervising is a way to discharge some of the need for action and
perhaps to offset the sense of helplessness that can arise in trauma therapies.
Listening to our supervisees' struggles normalizes our own and balances
our sense of isolation, and vice versa. A supervisor's openness about her
experience normalizes for a supervisee the difficulty of the work. We may
feel more effective as supervisors than as therapists at times—a good antidote to the assaults on our identity as helper or our self-esteem schemas.

Balancing one's day and week is another important way of supporting
oneself and thereby ameliorating the impact of vicarious traumatization.
Self-care can be woven into one's workspace and workday. Where one has
the option, furnishing one's office with personal objects to serve as private
reminders of self, connections, personal meaning, therapeutic successes,
and life outside of work can be helpful. We find it helpful to attend to the
scheduling of clients: not scheduling difficult clients back to back, and
starting and ending the therapy week with clients with whom we feel most
effective. Using time between sessions to stretch, do yoga breathing, lie
down for 5 minutes, step outside, or call a friend can remind us that we
have bodies, serenity, and connections. We can use art work, perhaps
through our own drawing or painting, after a session or at the end of the

day to leave clients' trauma imagery behind.* It can be helpful to use music (sing, play, compose, listen) to heal, to recharge, and to connect with feelings. Scheduling breaks within long clinical days or arranging one's schedule in observance of one's natural rhythms can also be helpful. Some people do better scheduling some early morning clients and going home at 5:00, while others may prefer to have personal time in the morning and work later. One clinician arranges her workday with a 2-hour break in the middle so she can go home for lunch. Another schedules in a 1/2 hour break whenever she is seeing 5 or more clients in a day. Someone else finds it helpful to do most of her supervisions on one day, her administrative work on one day, and her therapies on the remaining days. One colleague takes a 3-day weekend every 6 weeks, and tries to plan her next vacation before the current vacation ends. Our own staff schedules a meeting, such as staff meeting, case conference, or seminar, in the middle of each of three days to provide everyone with a break from clinical work and some connection with colleagues during the day. The two of us colead two or three therapy groups on two or three different days to vary the rhythm and lessen the isolation of the individual psychotherapy work. The key is to attend to your own feelings and needs and to attempt to plan your work days and weeks in response to those needs.

Seek Spiritual Renewal†

Reminding ourselves of the importance and value of the work we do is a powerful antidote to the spiritual damage created by vicarious traumatization. Suran and Sheridan (1985) suggest that the failure to find meaning in one's work is associated with burnout. The loss of meaning and hope that can come about through vicarious traumatization can be countered by an awareness of the power of the work to transform the lives of survivors. Non-trauma therapists and friends sometimes ask us how we can do this work; the simple answer is that our clients heal and grow, and it is tremendously rewarding to be part of that process. We find it enormously helpful to identify and celebrate those moments of change with our clients, with our colleagues, and with ourselves. Discussing our successes in supervision is as important as discussing our difficulties.

The sense of connection with something beyond oneself, which is part of spirituality, can take the form of a connection with a healing mission and

---

*We thank Sandra Streifender, M.A. for her thoughts on addressing vicarious traumatization.
†We presented an in-depth discussion of the impact of trauma work on the therapist's spirituality in chapter 13. In chapter 19, we discuss the rewards of doing trauma therapy.

with others—both clients and colleagues—who share the mission. Sharing one's clients' journeys from paralysis and despair to life and hope is a source of unending wonder, a great gift and privilege. As we engage in this journey with our clients, our own hope is renewed.

Others have found that maintaining a focus on the larger purpose of one's work is valuable and significant for trauma workers of all sorts (Dyregrov & Mitchell, 1992). As therapists, we may lose sight of our purpose at times, but reminding ourselves of why we are engaging in therapy with survivors provides a holding context of meaning that renews us. Holding hope with and for our clients is an essential part of their healing. In order to sustain that ability, we need to be aware of subtle shifts in our own capacity for hope. Allowing ourselves to notice when things go well, when our clients do better, when our work feels useful can be restorative to an assaulted sense of hope. Through research with 243 psychologists, Medeiros and Prochaska (1988) found a strategy of "optimistic perseverance" most helpful for therapists in their work with difficult clients.

So many therapists are guided to the work of psychotherapy by their optimism, and so many become disillusioned and eventually cynical in the course of their careers. It *is* hard to hold a sense of optimism about human nature in the face of the realities of child sexual abuse. As we find ourselves expressing cynical views, it can be helpful to allow ourselves to explore that loss of optimism. How and when did it begin? What has contributed to it over time? How does cynicism serve to protect us from disappointment? As we explore our disillusionment or cynicism and become acquainted with it, it may begin to diminish.

Organizational Strategies*

People do trauma therapy in a variety of settings. It is important for both client and therapist to have a safe, private, comfortable space in which to work. The physical safety of the therapist's office space and the confidentiality a private space allows are essential to minimize the negative effects of the work.

Therapists need a variety of resources to do this work effectively. Organizational resources include adequate pay and time off. Health insurance with mental health benefits is important. Access to continuing professional education and weekly clinical supervision with an experienced clinician

---

*These remarks are primarily written for those who are working within organizational settings, such as public or private clinics or hospitals. Many of these suggestions, however, can pertain equally to the solo practitioner.

reflect an organizational recognition of the challenges of the work. Maintaining an environment that shows respect for clients through observing confidentiality, frame, and boundaries (e.g., telephone contacts, appointment hours, and confidentiality of client files) supports the respectful holding of the clients and their therapies. It is critical for an organization to provide adequate vacation time and for the clinician to use it. We recommend that therapists take vacations, including at least one extended vacation (two to three weeks) per year to get away from the work and its intensity and to renew themselves. Organizations also support clinicians in this work by developing community support networks for referrals to adjunctive services (individual, group, and family therapy; medication consultation; physical health care; specialized outpatient, partial hospital, and inpatient services; substance abuse treatment; body therapies; expressive therapies; self-help resources, including libraries and support groups).

Through collaboration, organizations can also engage in social action directed toward ending violence and victimization, increasing the rights of victims, and monitoring the behavior of professionals in their interactions with survivors; help develop effective child protection services; provide community education programs geared toward prevention of violence and support for survivors, and understanding and acceptance of diversity (racial, sexual, cultural); and so forth. These activities can create a climate that supports the trauma therapist, thereby ameliorating the negative impact of the work.

Personal Strategies

Probably the most important recommendation we make to our colleagues about their personal lives is to have one. When we say this at presentations, it is invariably met with uneasy laughter; too many trauma therapists have given up their personal lives. Again we want to emphasize the importance of balance—balancing work with play and rest. Our trauma therapist sample noted travel, spending time with family, exercising, and socializing as ways of balancing the demands of their work (Pearlman & Mac Ian, 1994). Others have also written about the importance of maintaining balance between work and private time (Farber & Heifetz, 1982; Freudenberger & Robbins, 1979). Strategies that strengthen our resources and address our spiritual needs are most likely to counter the negative impact of the work in our personal lives. In our personal lives we need to nurture all aspects of ourselves. In the following sections, we discuss some general self-care strategies, and then look at strategies for addressing vicarious traumatization within each individual's frame of reference and the specific need areas that may be affected.

General Self-Care

Personal Psychotherapy

The importance of personal therapy for the therapist cannot be overemphasized, and has been recommended by others as a way of remaining open to ourselves and our clients (e.g., Farber, 1983b; Freud, 1937; Guy & Liaboe, 1986; Kaslow & Schulman, 1987). It is not only essential, however, as preparation for the responsible role of therapist, but also as a place in which to process the impact and effect of our therapeutic work on ourselves, to take all of our needs, our wishes, our fears, all of our feelings and thoughts. Psychotherapy is a way of understanding and nurturing oneself, a gift one can give oneself whose benefits also ripple outward to family, friends, clients, and colleagues.

Ideally, survivor therapists will have the option of a psychotherapy group for therapists who are survivors of childhood sexual abuse. Incest survivor groups in general provide important forums for healing by decreasing the great isolation many survivors feel and normalizing their range of feelings, reactions, symptoms, and experiences. A therapist survivor group offers a place for therapist survivor clients to address the complicated issues of being a therapist and an incest survivor, issues of shame and self-esteem, the issues involved in showing competence and need. Such a group can provide a safe place for connection and validation that can be invaluable in the healing process.

Rest and Play

The concept of rest may be alien to some therapists. It can include sleep, sitting or lying down and doing nothing, reading a magazine or a novel, listening to music, and so forth. Vacations are important and may involve rest (lying on the beach) and play (touring an unfamiliar city). Playing with a pet, engaging in sports activities, attending concerts are examples of restorative activity; Freudenberger and Robbins (1979) have noted the restorative value of activities such as tennis, long walks, and visiting museums. Both rest and play can allow us to connect with interests and parts of ourselves not present in our work (Louden, 1992). Hobbies and avocations such as gardening, playing music, drawing, and hiking all allow for the fuller expression of oneself. Laughter is a powerful antidote to the gravity of our work, the use of humor a kind of restorative exercise in perspective-taking.

Sometimes a therapist will require a break from doing therapy (Freudenberger & Robbins, 1979). Taking a sabbatical can provide renewal, or may allow the therapist to decide again whether he wants to continue to work as a trauma therapist. It is essential to notice when the short breaks and other ameliorative strategies are not working. We need to be able to give ourselves permission to speak when we feel depleted, and when we see our colleagues heading for trouble. Therapists who do not notice and act to counter their vicarious traumatization are at risk for harming their clients, as well as causing serious physical health, mental health, and relationship problems for themselves. None of us can do this work alone, and we depend upon one another to help us take care of ourselves (Herman, 1992; Munroe et al., in press).

Frame of Reference

Identity

It is essential that we allow ourselves to recapture and continuously evolve all aspects of our humanity. This means engaging in relationships in which we are experienced as human, soft, playful, passionate, sexual, demanding, inquisitive, intellectual, frightened, vulnerable, and so forth. It is important to nurture nonprofessional aspects of our identities, such as mother, partner, sister, son, tennis partner, student, lover of literature, music, artist, dancer, swimmer, runner, hiker, gardener. As therapists, we strive to be always thoughtful and careful; we need places and activities where we can be spontaneous and playful and let go of our self-consciousness and responsibility.

Our identities include the reality of our bodies. It is not uncommon for traumatized therapists to move out of their bodies into their minds. The experience of doing talk therapy all day can be one of sensory deprivation. Being aware of one's body is closely linked to being aware of one's feelings. An automatic response to vicarious traumatization can be to shut down feelings, which means not noticing one's body. Reconnecting with one's body frequently is essential to restoring oneself to full humanity. This can take a variety of forms: Yoga, conscious breathing, exercise, movement, dance, stretching, massage, and touch are all ways of reminding ourselves that we have bodies.

As we withdraw from our feelings and bodies through vicarious traumatization, we may forget to feed and nurture our bodies adequately. Eating properly and attending to our physical health should not be secondary considerations for any therapist (Kaslow & Schulman, 1987). Trauma therapists can be at risk for unconscious use of food, drugs, or alcohol to maintain numbness or feed depletion. Being rested, fit, and healthy sends strong messages to clients about what they might choose for themselves; it also contributes to our own mental health and well-being, and allows us to be there for our clients over the long haul.

Spirituality

As we have described in previous chapters, much of the damage of trauma and of vicarious traumatization is spiritual damage. We have written in more depth elsewhere about this issue (Neumann & Pearlman, 1994); here we discuss specific antidotes to the difficulties in areas we include within spirituality: connection, meaning and hope, awareness, and the nonmaterial.

Suran and Sheridan (1985) note that spiritual development is central to self-development, and can help therapists find self-worth that is not based in their professional achievements. It is essential to develop and nurture spiritual lives outside of our work.

Connection. Developing a sense of connection with something beyond oneself is an essential part of countering the spiritual damage of vicarious traumatization. This might mean developing a sense of community, of history, or belonging to all of humanity or to life itself. It can take the form of engaging in religious practices, yoga, or meditation, or connection with nature or a higher power.

Meaning and Hope. Discovering what is meaningful to oneself and pursuing it is another aspect of spiritual renewal. Again, this is a very personal, individual matter. For some it may be living according to certain principles; for others, it may mean devoting time to certain activities; for yet others, it may mean taking time regularly to contemplate one's life and life in general and making whatever adjustments seem appropriate.

Expecting good things to happen is a personal matter, and the ability to hope may be impacted by doing trauma work. Hope, after all, carries the risk of disappointment, and one cannot help but be affected by the countless stories of children's hopes dashed. Yet our own ability to hope for ourselves and our loved ones is central to our optimism and joy.

Awareness. As our awareness of human cruelty increases through our work, so too can our awareness of the incredible strength our clients have developed to survive. Committing and recommiting ourselves to remain aware of all aspects of life, both the painful and the joyful, is another way of sustaining and asserting our humanity, and countering the numbing that can signal vicarious traumatization. The diminished ability to tolerate strong affect, a hallmark of both psychological trauma and vicarious traumatization, can make it difficult to open ourselves to additional pain. Limiting our exposure to violence on television and in the movies can help us to be present for our clients in bearing witness to their traumatic experiences and may be one way of protecting ourselves from further disillusionment and intrusive imagery. Alternatively, when we notice we are protecting ourselves from tenderness, hope, idealism, and love in self-protection, we have to examine the cost of our strategies.

Acceptance of human suffering, of the effects of the work, of our own needs allows us to move toward life-enhancing activities. Struggling against our pain slows our own healing; accepting it enables us to move through it. Our clients struggle continuously with accepting and forgiving themselves, for what they did and did not do in response to the sexual abuse. As trauma therapists, we too can find ourselves regretting what we have and have not done for and with our clients. Worrying about our shortcomings can serve many psychological functions, but it clearly disconnects us from our full range of feelings and from others. Accepting our limitations and errors and forgiving ourselves opens us to working honestly and without shame with our clients, and models something we want our clients to emulate. Bringing creativity and beauty into one's life is part of expanding our frame of reference to include all of life.

Nonmaterial. An awareness of the nonmaterial aspects of life is an essential part of spirituality, and, again, one that may be assaulted by doing trauma work. Remaining attuned to ephemeral aspects of life requires our most delicate sensibilities, which may be the first to shut down as a result of vicarious traumatization. Reawakening ourselves to beauty, grace, joy, and love is essential to the restoration of our full humanity. Here is another place for pursuing and expressing our own creativity through whatever channels appeal to each of us.

World View

Our life philosophies, moral principles, notions of causality, and values are all susceptible to the effects of vicarious traumatization. Continuous examination of these, alone and with others, can keep our world views fluid and up to date, consonant with our experience and needs. Remaining open to new ideas is one way of reestablishing a full and balanced world view.

An essential part of world view is perspective. Placing ourselves and our work in various contexts can help us rebuild a disrupted frame of reference. Useful perspectives include the personal (seeing our work as only one aspect of our lives), the relational (remembering that we are working in collaboration with our clients), the professional (being part of a broad network of colleagues who are engaged in similar work), the social (addressing important social and public health problems—violence and victimization), and the historical (knowing this moment is but a snapshot in time, a long history during which people have struggled with many of the same issues).

Working for social justice can provide a way of restoring a positive world view, as well as lending balance to the therapist's neutrality and bystandership. Comas-Diaz and Padilla (1990) have written about the restoration of a sense of purpose which can come about through social action by therapists. Such activity can help us overcome our sense of helplessness and deal with the rage we may feel toward our society. We believe it is not generally helpful to urge clients to action, but rather it is our task to provide clients with an accepting, open space for the exploration of their own needs. Thus, we may need to discharge some of our own outrage through working for social change. As this work is often done through organizations, it is also another way to connect with other like-minded people.

Example   One of us felt the need to channel her outrage at clients' experience of relentless abuse and became involved in a community group organized to address issues of social justice for adult rape victims and for victims of childhood sexual assault. Joining this group allowed her to channel her anger constructively and to do something to try to prevent abuse and punish offenders, while freeing her as a therapist from the pressure of these intense feelings in the psychotherapy. One of us became active organizing a self-help group for a different group of traumatized people—the HIV positive and their caregivers. We have participated in marches, protests, walks, and swims for action and spoken out at public forums on issues important to us. As an organization, we at the Traumatic Stress Institute strive to identify ways to speak out on issues of victimization and mental health through media, public education, professional education, and political forums.

Intrusive Traumatic Imagery

At times our clients' graphic descriptions of their experiences of violence and victimization can become vivid images in our own minds. These images can intrude upon our awareness when we least expect them and rob us of serenity, pleasure, and personal time. One approach to decreasing the intrusiveness of these images is to connect the psychological need themes embedded in the image with one's own experience, and to work on the personal issues represented by these themes. For example, for a therapist with salient safety needs, intrusive imagery may reflect themes of danger and vulnerability. In understanding this and then working on these issues in his own therapy or vicarious traumatization consultation, the therapist can rapidly and markedly diminish the power of the imagery.

A second approach is to change the scene in ways that can help detoxify the imagery. This may mean introducing other persons into the scene, creating magical transformations of terrifying or disgusting aspects of the image, changing the outcome, or developing alternative ways for the scene to unfold.

Another approach, particularly helpful when the imagery intrudes into one's interpersonal sexual activity, is to speak. The power of the imagery in part comes from the fact that we hold it alone. Just as clients experience relief when they speak and explore their terrifying images with a concerned and caring person, so too will the therapist feel some relief by letting his partner know he is distracted by something horrible and that he needs to stop until the images and accompanying affect pass. Of course, the dictates of confidentiality prohibit the therapist from sharing the specifics of clients' imagery with his partner. However, it is possible to let his partner know that a particular scene came to mind related to his work which included sexual torture, and then to find an appropriate forum (supervision, vicarious traumatization consultation, personal psychotherapy) to explore the specifics of the image and what about it was particularly meaningful to the therapist.

We cannot approach our work as a sprint and continue the race; it is a marathon and requires pacing and ongoing rest and rejuvenation. Our willingness to address vicarious traumatization allows us to protect our physical and psychological health as well as our professional and personal health and fulfillment. Attention to the person of the therapist serves not only ourselves, but also our clients, colleagues, relationships, and profession.

The commitment to doing excellent trauma therapy requires much of us. We must be open, aware, knowledgeable, available, hopeful. In order to do our best work, we must nurture ourselves so we can be all of these things for our clients and for ourselves. The work of trauma therapy can enrich our lives; yet we must tend to our own needs in order not to be depleted by it. In addition to preserving our own humanity, we have a responsibility to our clients to address vicarious traumatization.

19

The Rewards of
Doing Trauma Therapy

TRAUMA THERAPY WORKS. When treated within a trauma framework, incest survivors can resolve long-standing intrapsychic and interpersonal difficulties and discover meaning and hope in their lives. This fact is at the root of many of the rewards of doing trauma therapy.

Sometimes when people ask us, "How can you do this work?" we think, "How could we not?" How could we have the ability to contribute to a journey of hope and healing and not use it? There is no other work that we would find this meaningful, challenging, and rewarding. What other work would allow us to engage fully—our minds, our hearts, our spirits? How could we choose not to do something that demands our creativity, all of our intellectual capacity, all of our feelings, our whole humanity?

Sometimes people ask, "How can you stand to hear such pain? Don't you get depressed?" The act of listening is part of the process of healing. It is personally transformative, inspiring, and rewarding to witness and be part of people's healing. All therapists who work with trauma survivor clients have been or will be asked how they can do this work. This chapter is a response to that question. We both feel that the work has deeply transformed us, as therapists, as women, as people, and as members of society. In this chapter, we want to express our gratitude to our clients, our colleagues, and our teachers, for those transformations.

TRANSFORMATION OF OUR CLIENTS

When our clients grow and heal, we are rewarded. Survivor clients often come to therapy with debilitating symptoms, painful self-loathing, agonizing loneliness, and despair. We sit with them in their enormous pain, often for months and years. When our clients are able to make even subtle shifts in their previously fixed patterns, the relationship deepens and the relief is felt by both.

On a daily basis, we can hear signs of minor and major changes in our clients' relationships with themselves and others, in their feelings and affect tolerance, in their beliefs and awareness of their needs, in their compassion for themselves and others, in their judgment and choices. We need to remember to listen for these phrases and hold on to the enormity of their significance.

> I can't believe I'm saying this, but I am glad to be alive and glad to be feeling. The feelings aren't all good by any means, but they are real. (Spoken by a client who had refused to have the "f-word" [feelings] spoken by her therapist for months)

> It was the best ice cream I had ever had. (Spoken by a man who had denied any child-like feelings and tortured himself by deprivation and humiliation, after stopping for ice cream on impulse after a therapy session)

> I thought of the group and I didn't feel so alone. (Spoken by a group member who remained silent for months and felt that she did not belong and was not liked)

> It wasn't my fault. I was a kid. (Spoken by a male survivor who had consistently blamed and shamed himself for childhood sexual abuse at the hands of a neighbor that occurred over several years)

> I feel sad for that little girl. (Spoken by a client who had always angrily refused to have anything to do with the image of the little girl she was when she was sadistically abused)

> I am not crazy. I had no choice. I was surviving. (Spoken by a client who dissociated frequently in childhood and then decided the abuse happened because she dissociated and was "weird")

> My mind is pretty clever. It was protecting me. Imagine that. (Spoken by a client who tentatively revealed the "psychotic belief" that she had been abducted by aliens. When she and her therapist explored the meaning of the "memory," she began to understand it as a way both

to know and not know, thus protecting her sanity and her life since the man who sexually abused her told her to "forget it" and threatened her life if she did not)

I never imagined sex could be in the context of loving. I never would have believed it if anyone had tried to tell me. (Spoken by a gay survivor who had never allowed himself any feelings when being sexual with a partner)

When our clients let us know what is helpful, they teach us. When a client says, "I heard your voice. You were giving me permission to have my feelings," we understand the power of our presence, often when we were beginning to feel powerless or useless. When a client who initially needed extra sessions or phone calls to hear the therapist's voice is now able to evoke a memory of the therapist's voice when needed, we understand the therapeutic process is working. When a client who spent a session in despair tells his therapist in the next session, "I felt better after I left. Thank you for hearing me out," we come to appreciate the power of being emotionally present to someone in pain. Our clients' change is an affirmation of the process of psychotherapy and of our hope for them.

Our clients' willingness to seek help reminds us not to do the work alone. Both of us have a strong sense of community with other trauma therapists. We also feel a strong connection with our clients as individuals and as a group. Sharing in such an intimate process provides a deep, satisfying, and extensive sense of connection that is rare in most professional or work contexts.

TRANSFORMATION OF THE THERAPIST
AS THERAPIST

As therapists who have a trauma framework, we have worked with many survivors who have struggled for years within and against a mental health system which had not only not yet learned to help, but in many instances harmed its clients. We find that we have something to offer that is helpful to these clients. The availability of a theory which allows survivors who were previously labeled "damaged" or "hopeless" to claim or reclaim their lives and pride allows us to offer a different kind of psychotherapy experience. Participation in a psychotherapy process based upon relational principles, to which we bring our genuine selves and invite our clients to bring their whole selves, allows a deep and meaningful connection of two people with different roles, and a mutual goal. It is deeply rewarding to be able to offer a theory that provides a new way to understand the past, and a relationship that provides a new way to experience the present.

Intellectually, this work is both demanding and rewarding. It is fascinating to discover how the human mind works, how creative and resourceful children can be, and the many natural mechanisms that can be activated to protect the self. The symbolism of dreams and fantasies, the complex interconnections of different experiences and various aspects of the self, are remarkable. Within the therapeutic process, the possibilities of deeper and deeper understanding that unfold over time in a therapeutic relationship, and the interactions of conscious and unconscious processes are awesome. Our intellects are actively and constantly engaged by this work, and we are always learning. While it means we must live with the anxiety of the new and the unknown, the truth is that we must learn from each client how to do psychotherapy with him. We are always beginners in some essential ways. Our willingness to learn with the client sets the stage for the unfolding of the psychotherapy.

We will continue to be challenged by our clients to grow as therapists. Many teachers of psychotherapy (Fromm-Reichmann, 1960; Kaiser, 1965; Searles, 1975; Sullivan, 1953) have taught that a client will transform his therapist so the therapist can give the client what he needs. Our clients have invited and demanded, directly and indirectly, that we move forward in our professional growth. They have often taught us what we need to know to help them. Their courage to face themselves has given us courage to face ourselves, our strengths and limitations.

TRANSFORMATION OF THE THERAPIST AS PERSON

These therapies are often characterized by a unique depth of intimacy. The connection we have with our clients, through humor, love, and pain, can be profound. We feel nourished by such connections. They recognize the participants' shared humanity; therapist and client share experiences as humans, women or men, parents and children, witnesses, and members of families, communities, and society.

Sharing in the growth and development of another person is an honor. Participating in the transformation of a client's despair is a life-altering, spiritual experience for those therapists who are open to it. Our clients' resilience and capacity to heal and to grow are powerful antidotes to the creeping cynicism that characterizes vicarious traumatization. These observations promote our increased respect for the human spirit (Herman, 1992), a powerful bequest of this work.

When a survivor client makes the first phone call to a therapist, or walks into the therapy office, it is an acknowledgment of the truth of sexual abuse. The client is breaking the silence.

Example   A client showed anxiety every time she heard the sound of a fire engine or ambulance siren when in a therapy session. As she and her therapist explored her associations she said with angst that she became focused on the experience of terror that the waiting victim would be feeling. She repeated again and again, "It means someone is in trouble, in pain, hurting." Her therapist reminded her gently that the siren also meant someone was getting help.

Over a year later, when the client was visiting a friend on an inpatient psychiatric unit she saw someone she knew and liked from several years back. When telling her therapist about it the next week, she said, "Initially I felt terrible. I thought it must mean she's in terrible trouble if she's here. It must be really bad. Then your words came back to me. They didn't help at the time, but last week I found myself thinking, it also means she's getting help."

By entering our office, the survivor client is profoundly changing something in his life experience: He is no longer trying to do it alone. As we enter into a therapeutic relationship with that client, we feel privileged and deeply moved to be part of such a significant process.

Our clients' courage and determination may inspire us to press forward in our own continuing personal growth. These therapies often lead therapists to go back to their own personal therapy, to the benefit of themselves and their clients. As therapists we can be humbled by our clients' courage to take emotional and interpersonal risks with which we struggle in our own therapeutic work.

Psychotherapists have the experience of knowing intimately people they would otherwise not have known, and of sharing vicariously in others' life choices and struggles, their most intimate feelings, needs, and concerns (Mahoney, 1991). These intimate relationships contribute enormously to our growth as individuals, add complexity to our lives, and increase our capacity for empathy and understanding.

The awareness of the fragility of current experience that results inevitably from our exposure to trauma, invites us to ask, "Is this how I want to be spending my time?" as well as "How important is what I'm so concerned about right now?" This awareness heightens our gratitude for good fortune and allows us to reorder priorities, and to say yes to the lives we are creating for ourselves on a daily basis. We frequently ask our clients, "What will you be needing over the hours and days ahead?" We remind ourselves likewise to remain attuned to our needs and feelings and to make our choices for the future conscious.

Part of our therapist role is the role of witness. Bearing witness to our clients' struggles and traumas has given us an increased appreciation of the many gifts and privileges in our own lives. We feel more grateful for the loving relationships in our lives, for our ability to enjoy our private time, for our connections with family and friends, for our creature comforts, autonomy, and safety. We no longer take for granted beauty, joy, nature, love. The value of these gifts is more apparent to us as a result of doing this work.

At times, we have had glimmers of wisdom resulting from our work. Wisdom, like empathy and humor, requires perspective on the situation at hand, oneself, and the larger context. Our clients teach us the things we might have learned from grandparents, wise elders. Sharing joy and sorrow, laughter and pain, wisdom and ideas with another person is at the heart of what it means to be human. The many moments of such connection in therapy deepen our own humanity.

Rewards for the Therapist
as a Member of Society

The work of the trauma therapist is the work of a revolutionary. We are willing to speak the silent shameful secret of society: that children, whom society professes to value and protect, are commonly violated, assaulted, molested, and neglected. As therapists working with survivor clients, we confirm that child abuse exists and that it leaves extensive damage in its wake. Speaking out as an advocate for those who have been harmed and working to restore their sense of value and connection is a major social contribution. This work is demanding and important, and satisfying because it makes a difference, both to the individual clients and to society.

Our work serves not only to heal those who have been harmed, but also to protect their children and to break the cycle of abuse that silence and shame engender. Survivors who are parents have more options in responding to their own children once they have addressed their own trauma histories. They may not be able to undo the injuries their children have already experienced, but they can respond more quickly and appropriately if they have an understanding of their own childhood abuse experiences. It is deeply satisfying to contribute to breaking a malignant cycle by doing trauma therapy with survivor parents and therapists.

One significant reward of doing trauma therapy has been our increased sense of connection with people who suffer everywhere, across time and across cultures. People who are able to complete graduate training and become therapists in this country are relatively privileged. We give back something meaningful from this place of privilege when we choose to enter the world of pain and to acknowledge our deep human connection with those who suffer. While it is a dark path, it is a spiritual journey, into the darkest recesses of people's private experiences, and one which deepens our humanity in increasing our awareness of all aspects of life. In this way, it is indeed a gift, a reward of doing this work.

Appendix

This appendix contains two measures developed at the Traumatic Stress Institute. The first, the TSI Belief Scale, is a measure of disrupted cognitive schemas. It assesses disruptions in the five psychological need areas (safety, trust, esteem, intimacy, and control) identified by CSDT as sensitive to the effects of trauma. Within each area, the scale contains items intended to assess disruptions related to self and to other. This measure has been described by Pearlman et al. (1992) and Stamm, Bieber, and Pearlman (1991). Normative data from four criterion groups are available.

The second measure is the Life Orientation Inventory, a measure of spirituality based in a broad, nontheistic notion. It assesses the respondent's beliefs in four areas: meaning and hope, nonmaterial, awareness, and connection. It has been described by Neumann and Pearlman (1995).

For additional information (including scoring and reliability data) on these measures, please contact Laurie Anne Pearlman, Ph.D., Traumatic Stress Institute/Center for Adult & Adolescent Psychotherapy, 22 Morgan Farms Drive, South Windsor, CT 06074.

ID _____   Sex (circle one) F M   Your age _____   Date _____

TSI BELIEF SCALE

Revision L©

This questionnaire is used to learn how individuals view themselves and others. As people differ from one another in many ways, there are no right or wrong answers. Please place next to each item the number from the scale below which you feel most closely matches your own beliefs about yourself and your world. Try to complete every item.

1	2	3	4	5	6
Disagree strongly	Disagree	Disagree somewhat	Agree somewhat	Agree	Agree strongly

_____ 1. I generally feel safe from danger.
_____ 2. People are wonderful.
_____ 3. I can comfort myself when I'm in pain.
_____ 4. I find myself worrying a lot about my safety.
_____ 5. I don't feel like I deserve much.
_____ 6. I can usually trust my own judgment.
_____ 7. I feel empty when I am alone.
_____ 8. I have a lot of bad feelings about myself.
_____ 9. I'm reasonably comfortable about the safety of those I care about.
_____10. Most people destroy what they build.
_____11. I have a difficult time being myself around other people.
_____12. I enjoy my own company.
_____13. I don't trust my own instincts.
_____14. I often think the worst of others.
_____15. I believe I can protect myself if my thoughts become self-destructive.
_____16. You can't trust anyone.
_____17. I'm uncomfortable when someone else is leading the group.
_____18. I feel good about myself most days.
_____19. Sometimes I think I'm more concerned about the safety of others than they are.
_____20. Other people are no good.
_____21. Sometimes when I'm with people, I feel disconnected.
_____22. People shouldn't place too much trust in their friends.
_____23. Mostly, I don't feel like I'm worth much.
_____24. I don't have much control in my relationships.
_____25. My capacity to harm myself scares me sometimes.
_____26. For the most part, I like other people.
_____27. I deserve to have good things happen to me.
_____28. I usually feel safe when I'm alone.
_____29. If I really need them, people will come through for me.

1	2	3	4	5	6
Disagree strongly	Disagree	Disagree somewhat	Agree somewhat	Agree	Agree strongly

_____30. I can't stand to be alone.
_____31. This world is filled with emotionally disturbed people.
_____32. I am basically a good person.
_____33. For the most part, I can protect myself from harm.
_____34. Bad things happen to me because I'm bad.
_____35. Some of my happiest experiences involve other people.
_____36. There are many people to whom I feel close and connected.
_____37. Sometimes I'm afraid of what I might do to myself.
_____38. I am often involved in conflicts with other people.
_____39. I often feel cut off and distant from other people.
_____40. I worry a lot about the safety of loved ones.
_____41. I don't experience much love from anyone.
_____42. Even when I'm with other people, I feel alone.
_____43. There is an evil force inside of me.
_____44. I feel uncertain about my ability to make decisions.
_____45. When I'm alone, I don't feel safe.
_____46. When I'm alone, it's like there's no one there.
_____47. I can depend on my friends to be there when I need them.
_____48. Sometimes I feel like I can't control myself.
_____49. I feel out of touch with people.
_____50. Most people are basically good at heart.
_____51. I sometimes wish I didn't have any feelings.
_____52. I'm often afraid I will harm myself.
_____53. I am my own best friend.
_____54. I feel able to control whether I harm others.
_____55. I often feel helpless in my relationships with others.
_____56. I don't have a lot of respect for the people closest to me.
_____57. I enjoy feeling like part of my community.
_____58. I look forward to time I spend alone.
_____59. I often feel others are trying to control me.
_____60. I envy people who are always in control.
_____61. The important people in my life are relatively safe from danger.
_____62. The most uncomfortable feeling for me is losing control over myself.
_____63. If people really knew me, they wouldn't like me.
_____64. Most people don't keep the promises they make.
_____65. Strong people don't need to ask for others' help.
_____66. Trusting other people is generally not very smart.
_____67. I fear my capacity to harm others.
_____68. I feel bad about myself when I need others' help.
_____69. To feel at ease, I need to be in charge.
_____70. I have sound judgment.
_____71. People who trust too much are foolish.
_____72. When my loved ones aren't with me, I fear they may be in danger.
_____73. At times my actions pose a danger to others.
_____74. I feel confident in my decision-making ability.
_____75. I can't work effectively unless I'm the leader.

1	2	3	4	5	6
Disagree strongly	Disagree	Disagree somewhat	Agree somewhat	Agree	Agree strongly

_____76. I often doubt myself.
_____77. I can usually size up situations pretty well.
_____78. I generally don't believe the things people tell me.
_____79. Sometimes I really want to hurt someone.
_____80. When someone suggests I relax, I feel anxious.

_____

ID _____   Sex (circle one) F M   Your age _____   Date _____

LIFE ORIENTATION INVENTORY

Revision B ©

This questionnaire is used to learn how individuals view themselves in relation to various aspects of life. Each person has unique views and there are no right or wrong answers. Please place next to each item the number from the scale below which you feel indicates to what extent the item is true for you.

1	2	3	4	5	6
Not at all true	Somewhat true	Moderately true	Quite true	Very true	Extremely true

_____ 1. I celebrate my bond to the entire creation.
_____ 2. I have hope for the future.
_____ 3. I believe in the supernatural.
_____ 4. Experiences make a big impression on me.
_____ 5. I fit in with the universe.
_____ 6. I try to fit in with the universe.
_____ 7. I block some experiences from my awareness.
_____ 8. There is something beyond the worldly.
_____ 9. All living things are interconnected.
_____10. I notice and attend to what's going on inside me.
_____11. I am connected with all others.
_____12. I'm hopeful that things can change.
_____13. I have had experiences which go beyond physical reality and rational thought.
_____14. I am a very perceptive person.
_____15. There is life after death.
_____16. I am part of an interactive cosmos.
_____17. Life can be understood.
_____18. My life has meaning.
_____19. I expect the best.

1	2	3	4	5	6
Not at all true	Somewhat true	Moderately true	Quite true	Very true	Extremely true

_____20. I am affected by all my experiences.

_____21. I believe in the unity of all living things.

_____22. Something positive will happen.

_____23. We are part of a larger whole.

_____24. I belong in the natural world.

_____25. Knowing too much about life is a burden.

_____26. I believe in the paranormal.

_____27. There is an unseen dimension of being beyond rational explanation.

_____28. I identify with all of humanity.

_____29. Existence is patterned in a way that can be understood.

_____30. People can connect with something that is beyond mind and matter.

_____31. I attempt to be aware in all the different circumstances of life.

_____32. All beings are related.

_____33. I'm not open to new experience.

_____34. I believe in "a better tomorrow."

_____35. There are experiences that cannot be grasped by the mind or physically sensed.

_____36. I am responsive to my experiences.

_____37. I believe in a divine being such as God or a higher power.

_____38. Things that seem senseless at first can be understood, if we make an effort to understand them.

_____39. Reality is limited to what I can see and feel.

_____40. I like to be in control of what I experience.

References

Abney, V. D., Yang. J. A., & Paulson, M. J. (1992). Transference and counter-transference issues unique to long-term group psychotherapy of adult women molested as children: Trials and rewards. *Journal of Interpersonal Violence, 7*(4), 559–569.

Ackerly, G. D., Burnell, J., Holder, D. C., & Kurdek, L. A. (1988). Burnout among licensed psychologists. *Professional Psychology: Research and Practice, 19*(6), 624–631.

Adler, G. (1992, May). The therapist's shame. In J. Grunebaum (Chair), *Training for treatment: How can it help?* Symposium conducted at the Meeting of the Massachusetts House of Representatives Committee on Sexual Misconduct by Physicians, Therapists, and other Health Professionals, Boston, MA.

Adler, G., & Buie, D. (1979). Aloneness and borderline psychopathology: The possible relevance of child development issues. *International Journal of Psycho-analysis, 60*, 83–96.

Adler, P. (1993, May). *Male therapists treating female incest survivors.* Grand Rounds presentation at Holyoke Hospital Center for Psychiatry, Holyoke, MA.

American Psychiatric Association (1994). *Diagnostic and statistical manual of mental disorders* (4th ed.). Washingon, DC: Author.

Armsworth, M. W. (1989). Therapy of incest survivors: Abuse or support? *Child Abuse and Neglect, 13*, 549–562.

Armsworth, M. W. (1993, October). *Trauma and the body.* Paper presented at the 9th Annual Meeting of the International Society for Traumatic Stress Studies, San Antonio, TX.

Attias, R., & Goodwin, J. (1993, October). *Distortion of body image in childhood survivors of incest.* Paper presented at the 9th Annual Meeting of the International Society for Traumatic Stress Studies, San Antonio, TX.

Atwood, G. E., Stolorow, R. D., & Trop, J. L. (1989). Impasses in psychoanalytic therapy: A royal road. *Contemporary Psychoanalysis, 25,* 554–573.

Balint, M. (1969). Trauma and object relationship. *International Journal of Psychoanalysis, 50,* 429–435.

Banning, A. (1989). Mother-son incest: Confronting a prejudice. *Child Abuse and Neglect, 13,* 563–570.

Bard, M., & Sangrey, D. (1986). *The crime victims' book* (2nd ed.). New York: Brunner/Mazel.

Basescu, S. (1990). Tools of the trade: The use of the self in psychotherapy. *Group, 14*(3), 157–165.

Bass, E., & Davis, L. (1988). *The courage to heal: A guide for women survivors of child sexual abuse.* New York: Harper & Row.

Bateson, G., Jackson, D., Haley, J., & Weakland, J. (1956). Toward a theory of schiozphrenia. *Behavioral Science, 1,* 251–264.

Beere, D. (1989, August). *The experience of shame and traumatization.* Paper presented at the 97th Annual Meeting of the American Psychological Association, Atlanta, GA.

Belle, D. (1982). The stress of caring: Women as providers of social support. In L. Goldberger, & S. Breznitz (Eds.), *Handbook of stress: Theoretical and clinical aspects* (pp. 496–505). New York: Free Press.

Benedek, T. (1953). Dynamics of the countertransference. *Bulletin of the Menninger Clinic, 17,* 201–208.

Benjamin, J. (1988). *The bonds of love: Psychoanalysis, feminism, and the problem of domination.* New York: Pantheon.

Benson, G., Apfel, R., Grossman, F., Benjamin, B., & Howe, O. (1992, May). Prevention, collusion, and indifference in the training system. In J. Grunebaum (Chair), *Training for treatment: How can it help?* Symposium conducted at the Meeting of the Massachusetts House Committee for Sexual Misconduct by Physicians, Therapists, and other Health Professionals, Boston, MA.

Bion, W. R. (1961). *Experiences in groups.* New York: Basic.

Black, A., & Pearlman, L. A. (1994). *Self-esteem as a mediator between beliefs about self and beliefs about others.* Manuscript in preparation.

Blank, A. S. (1985a). Irrational reactions to post-traumatic stress disorder and Vietnam veterans. In S. M. Sonnenberg, A. S. Blank, & J. A. Talbot (Eds.), *The trauma of war: Stress and recovery of Vietnam veterans* (pp. 71–98). Washington, DC: American Psychiatric Press.

Blank, A. S. (1985b). The unconscious flashback to the war in Vietnam veterns. In S. M. Sonnenberg, A. S. Blank, & J. A. Talbot (Eds.), *The trauma of war: Stress and recovery of Vietnam veterans* (pp. 295–308). Washington, DC: American Psychiatric Press.

Blatt, S. J., & Erlich, H. S. (1982). Levels of resistance in the psychotherapeutic process. In P. L. Wachtel (Ed.), *Resistance: Psychodynamic and behavioral approaches* (pp. 69–91). New York: Plenum.

Blatt, S. J., & Ford, R. Q. (1994). *Therapeutic change: An object relations perspective.* New York: Plenum.

Bloch, D. (1978). *So the witch won't eat me: Fantasy and the child's fear of infanticide.* New York: Grove.

Blumenfeld, W. J. (Ed.). (1992). *Homophobia: How we all pay the price.* Boston: Beacon.

Bollas, C. (1987). *The shadow of the object: Psychoanalysis of the unthought known.* New York: Columbia University Press.

Borys, D. S., & Pope, K. S. (1989). Dual relationships between therapist and client: A national study of psychologists, psychiatrists, and social workers. *Professional Psychology: Research and Practice, 20*(5), 283–293.

Boston Lesbian Psychologies Collective. (Ed.). (1987). *Lesbian psychologies.* Chicago: University of Chicago Press.

Bowlby, J. (1988). *A secure base.* New York: Basic.

Braun, B. G. (Ed.). (1986). *Treatment of multiple personality disorder.* Washington, DC: American Psychiatric Press.

Braun, B. G. (1988a). The BASK model of dissociation. *Dissociation, 11*(1), 4–23.

Braun, B. G. (1988b). The BASK model of dissociation. Part II: Treatment. *Dissociation, 11*(2), 16–23.

Brazelton, T. B., & Cramer, B. G. (1990). *The earliest relationship: Parents, infants, and the drama of early attachment.* New York: Addison-Wesley.

Brett, E. A. (1993, April). Pros and cons of psychoanalytic views on trauma. In S. Phillips (Chair), *Violence, aggression, and psychic trauma: Psychoanalytic perspectives.* Symposium conducted at the Western New England Psychoanalytic Institute, Yale University, New Haven, CT.

Brett, E. A., & Ostroff, R. (1985). Imagery and posttraumatic stress disorder: An overview. *American Journal of Psychiatry, 142,* 417–424.

Breuer, J., & Freud, S. (1893–1895). Studies on hysteria. In J. Strachey (Ed. and Trans.), *The standard edition of the complete psychological works of Sigmund Freud* (Vol. 2). New York: Norton.

Briere, J. (1989). *Therapy for adults molested as children: Beyond survival.* New York: Springer.

Briere, J. (1992). *Child abuse trauma: Theory and treatment of the lasting effects.* Newbury Park: Sage.

Briere, J., & Zaidi, L. Y. (1989). Sexual abuse histories and sequelae in female psychiatric emergency room patients. *American Journal of Psychiatry, 146*(12), 1602–1606.

Brown, G. R., & Anderson, B. (1991). Psychiatric morbidity in adult inpatients with childhood histories of sexual and physical abuse. *American Journal of Psychiatry, 148,* 55–61.

Brown, L. S. (1989). New voices, new visions: Toward a lesbian/gay paradigm for psychology. *Psychology of Women Quarterly, 13,* 455–458.

Brown, L. S., & Ballou, M. (Eds.). (1992). *Personality and psychopathology: Feminist reappraisals.* New York: Guilford.

Browne, A., & Finkelhor, D. (1986). Impact of child sexual abuse: A review of the research. *Psychological Bulletin, 99*(1), 66–77.

Brownmiller, S. (1975). *Against our will: Men, women, and rape.* New York: Simon & Schuster.

Bryer, J. B., Nelson, B. A., Miller, J. B., & Krol, P. A. (1987). Childhood sexual and physical abuse as factors in adult psychiatric illness. *American Journal of Psychiatry, 144*(11), 1426–1430.

Bulman, R., & Wortman, C. B. (1977). Attributions of blame and coping with the "real world": Severe accident victims react to their lot. *Journal of Personality and Social Psychology, 35,* 351–363.

Burgess, A. W. , & Holmstrom, L. L. (1974). Rape trauma syndrome. *American Journal of Psychiatry, 131,* 981–985.

Burgess, A. W., & Holmstrom, L. L. (1979). Adaptive strategies and recovery from rape. *American Journal of Psychiatry, 136,* 1278–1282.

Butler, S., & Zelen, S. L. (1977). Sexual intimacies between therapists and patients. *Psychotherapy: Theory, Research, and Practice, 14,* 139–145.

Calof, D. L. (1993). *Traumatic amnesia: The dissociation of knowledge.* Unpublished manuscript.

Calof, D. L. (1994). *Chronic self-injury and self-mutilation in adult survivors of incest and childhood sexual abuse: Etiology, assessment, and intervention.* Unpublished manuscript.

Cardena, E. (in press). The domain of dissociation. In S. J. Lynn, & J. W. Rhue (Eds.), *Dissociation: Clinical, theoretical, and perspectives* (pp. 15–31). New York: Guilford.

Carlson, K. (1990). *In her image: The unhealed daughter's search for her mother.* Boston: Shambhala

Casement, P. J. (1991). *Learning from the patient.* New York: Guilford.

Catherall, D. R., & Lane, C. (1992). Warrior therapist: Vets treating vets. *Journal of Traumatic Stress, 5*(1), 19–36.

Chessick, R. D. (1978). The sad soul of the psychiatrist. *Bulletin of the Menninger Clinic, 42,* 1–9.

Chodorow, N. (1989). *Feminism and psychoanalytic theory.* New Haven, CT: Yale University Press.

Chu, J. A. (1988). Ten traps for therapists in the treatment of trauma survivors. *Dissociation, 1,* 24–32.

Chu, J. A. (1992). The revictimization of adult women with histories of childhood abuse. *Journal of Psychotherapy: Research and Practice, 1*(3), 259–269.

Cogan, T. (1978). A study of friendship among psychotherapists (Doctoral dissertation, Illinois Institute of Technology, 1977). *Dissertation Abstracts International, 38,* 4445.

Cohen, M. B. (1952). Countertransference and anxiety. *Psychiatry, 15,* 231–243.

Comas-Diaz, L., & Padilla, A. (1990). Countertransference in working with victims of political repression. *American Journal of Orthopsychiatry, 60,* 125–134.

Cooperman, M. (1969). *Defeating processes in psychotherapy.* Presentation to Topeka Psychoanalytic Institute, Topeka, KS.

Courtois, C. (1979). Victims of rape and incest. *The Counseling Psychologist, 8,* 38–39.

Courtois, C. (1988). *Healing the incest wound: Adult survivors in therapy.* New York: Norton.

Courtois, C., & Chefetz, R. (1993). *The erotic and traumatic transference and countertransference matrices.* Paper presented at the Eastern Regional Conference on Abuse and Multiple Personality, Alexandria, VA.

Danieli, Y. (1982). Therapists' difficulties in treating survivors of the Nazi Holocaust and their children (Doctoral dissertation, New York University, 1981). *Dissertation Abstracts International, 42,* 4947–4948.

Danieli, Y. (1984). Psychotherapists' participation in the conspiracy of silence about the Holocaust. *Psychoanalytic Psychology, 1,* 23–42.

Danieli, Y. (1985). The treatment and prevention of long-term effects and intergenerational transmission of victimization: A lesson from Holocaust survivors and their children. In C. R. Figley (Ed.), *Trauma and its wake: The study and treatment of post-traumatic stress disorder* (pp. 295–313). New York: Brunner/Mazel.

Danieli, Y. (1994). Countertransference, trauma, and training. In J. Wilson, & J. D. Lindy (Eds.), *Countertransference in the treatment of PTSD* (pp. 368–388). New York: Guilford.

Danieli, Y., & Krystal, J. H. (1989). *The initial report of the Presidential Task Force on Curriculum, Education and Training of the Society for Traumatic Stress Studies*. Chicago: International Society for Traumatic Stress Studies.

Davies, J. M., & Frawley, M. G. (1991). Dissociative processes and transference-countertransference paradigms in the psychoanalytically oriented treatment of adult survivors of childhood sexual abuse. *Psychoanalytic Dialogues, 2*(1), 5–36.

Davies, J. M., & Frawley, M. G. (1994). *Treating the adult survivor of childhood sexual abuse: A psychoanalytic perspective*. New York: Basic.

Demause, L. (1991). The universality of incest. Journal of *Psychohistory, 19*(2), 123–164.

Derogatis, L. R., & Spencer, P. M. (1982). *The Brief Symptom Inventory (BSI): Scoring, administration and procedures*. Baltimore, MD: Clinic Psychometric Research.

Deutsch, C. J. (1984). Self-reported sources of stress among psychotherapists. *Professional Psychology: Research and Practice, 15*(6), 833–845.

Dick, R., Lessler, K., & Whiteside, J. (1980). A developmental framework for cotherapy. *International Journal of Group Psychotherapy, 30*, 273–285.

Doehrman, M. (1976). Parallel processes in supervision and psychotherapy. *Bulletin of the Menninger Clinic, 40*, 9–104.

Dutton, M. A., Burghardt, K. J., Perrin, S.G., Chrestman, K. R., & Halle, P. M. (1994). Battered women's cognitive schemata. *Journal of Traumatic Stress, 7*(2), 237–255.

Dyregrov, A., & Mitchell, J. T. (1992). Work with traumatized children: Psychological effects and coping strategies. *Journal of Traumatic Stress, 5*(1), 5–17.

Edelman, M. W. (1987). *Families in peril: An agenda for social change*. Cambridge, MA: Harvard University Press.

Edelwich, J. (1980). *Burnout: Stages of disillusionment in the helping professions*. New York: Human Sciences Press.

Ehrenberg, D. B. (1987). Abuse and desire: A case of father-daughter incest. *Contemporary Psychoanalysis, 24*(4), 593–604.

Ehrenberg, D (1992). *The intimate edge*. New York: Norton.

Elkind, S. N. (1992). *Resolving impasses in therapeutic relationships*. New York: Guilford.

Elliott, D. E. (1994, November). Organizational and relational contexts for training. In K. W. Saakvitne (Chair), *Training trauma professionals: Organizational, clinical and research components*. Symposium conducted at the 10th Annual Meeting of the International Society for Traumatic Stress Studies, Chicago, IL.

Elliott, D. M., & Guy, J. D. (1993). Mental health professionals' versus non-mental health professionals' childhood trauma and adult functioning. *Professional Psychology: Research and Practice, 24*(1), 83–90.

Elliott, M. (Ed.). (1993). *Female sexual abuse of children*. New York: Guilford.

Epstein, L. (1987) The problem of the bad-analyst-feeling. *Modern Psychoanalysis, 12*(1), 35–45.

Epstein, S. (1985). The implications of cognitive-experiential self-theory for research in social psychology and personality. *Journal for the Theory of Social Behavior, 15*, 283–310.

Epstein, S. (1991). The self-concept, the traumatic neurosis, and the structure of personality. In D. Ozer, J. M. Healy, Jr., & A. J. Stewart (Eds.), *Perspectives on personality* (Vol. 3). Greenwich, CT: JAI Press.

Epstein, S. (1994). Integration of the cognitive and psychodynamic unconscious. *American Psychologist, 49*(8), 709–724.

Fairbairn, W. R. D. (1954). *An object relations theory of the personality.* New York: Basic.

Fancher, R. E. (1973). *Psychoanalytic psychology: The development of Freud's thought.* New York: Norton.

Farber, B. A. (1983a). The effects of psychotherapeutic practice upon psychotherapists. *Psychotherapy: Theory, Research and Practice, 20*(2), 174–182.

Farber, B. A. (1983b). *Stress and burnout in the human service professions.* New York: Pergamon.

Farber, B. A. (1983c). Psychotherapists' perceptions of stressful patient behavior. *Professional Psychology: Research and Practice, 14*, 697–705.

Farber, B. A., & Heifetz, L. J. (1982). The process and dimensions of burnout in psychotherapists. *Professional Psychology: Research and Practice, 13*, 293–301.

Fast, I. (1985). *Event theory: A Piaget-Freud integration.* Hillsdale, NJ: Lawrence Erlbaum.

Fenichel, O. (1941). *Problems of psychoanalytic technique.* Albany, NY: The Psychoanalytic Quarterly, Inc.

Ferenczi, S. (1949). Confusion of tongues between adults and the child: The language of tenderness and of passion. *International Journal of Psychoanalysis, 30*, 225–230.

Ferenczi, S. (1950). *Further contributions to the theory and technique of psychoanalysis.* London: Hogarth Press.

Field, C. L. (1990). *On working with trauma survivors who form negative therapeutic reactions.* Paper presented at the 98th Annual Meeting of the American Psychological Association, Boston, MA.

Figley, C. R. (1991, October). *Treating traumatized therapists: Professional realities of trauma in everyday life.* Symposium presented at the 7th Annual Meeting of the International Society for Traumatic Stress Studies, Washington, DC.

Figley, C. R. (Ed.). (in press). *Compassion fatigue: Secondary traumatic stresss disorder from treating the traumatized.* New York: Brunner/Mazel.

Figley, C. R. (1994). *Compassion fatigue.* Presentation in the Premeeting Institute, "Intergenerational Effects of Trauma," at the 10th Annual Meeting of the International Society for Traumatic Stress Studies, Chicago, IL.

Finell, J. S. (1987). A challenge to psychoanalysis: A review of the negative therapeutic reaction. *Psychoanalytic Review, 74*(4), 487–515.

Finkelhor, D. (1979). *Sexually victimized children.* New York: Free Press.

Finkelhor, D. (1986). *A sourcebook on child sexual abuse.* Beverly Hills: Sage.

Finkelhor, D., Hotaling, G., Lewis, I. A., & Smith, C. (1990). Sexual abuse in a national survey of adult men and women: Prevalence, characteristics, and risk factors. *Child Abuse and Neglect, 14*, 19–28.

Finkelhor, D., & Russell, D. (1984). Women as perpetrators. In D. Finkelhor (Ed.), *Child sexual abuse: New theory and research* (pp. 171–185). New York: Free Press.

Fischman, Y. (1991). Interacting with trauma: Clinicians' responses to treating psychological aftereffects of political repression. *American Journal of Orthopsychiatry, 61*, 179–185.

Fleiss, R. (1942). The metapsychology of the analyst. *Psychoanalytic Quarterly, 11*, 211–227.

Follette V. M., Polusny, M. M., & Milbeck, K. (1994). Mental health and law enforcement professionals: Trauma history, psychological symptoms, and impact of providing services to child sexual abuse survivors. *Professional Psychology: Research and Practice, 25*(3), 275–282.

Folman, R. Z. (1991). Therapist-patient sex: Attraction and boundary problems. *Psychotherapy, 28*(1), 168–173.

Fraiberg, S. H. (1959). *The magic years: Understanding and handling the problems of early childhood.* New York: Charles Scribner's Sons.

Frankl, V. (1959). *Man's search for meaning: An introduction to logotherapy.* New York: Washington Square Press.

Freud, A. (1963). The concept of developmental lines. *Psychoanalytic Study of the Child, 18*, 242–265.

Freud, A. (1967). *The ego and the mechanisms of defense* (rev. ed.). New York: International Universities Press.

Freud, S. (1896). The aetiology of hysteria. In J. Strachey (Ed. and Trans.), *The standard edition of the complete psychological works of Sigmund Freud* (Vol. 3, 189–221). New York: Norton.

Freud, S. (1905). Fragment of an analysis of a case of hysteria. In J. Strachey (Ed. and Trans.), *The standard edition of the complete psychological works of Sigmund Freud* (Vol. 7, pp. 3–122). New York: Norton.

Freud, S. (1909a). Analysis of a phobia in a five-year old boy. In J. Strachey (Ed. and Trans.), *The standard edition of the complete psychological works of Sigmund Freud* (Vol. 10, pp. 3–151). New York: Norton.

Freud, S. (1909b). Notes upon a case of obsessional neurosis. In J. Strachey (Ed. and Trans.), *The standard edition of the complete psychological works of Sigmund Freud* (Vol. 10, pp. 153–318). New York: Norton.

Freud, S. (1910). The future prospects of psychoanalytic therapy. In J. Strachey (Ed. and Trans.), *The standard edition of the complete psychological works of Sigmund Freud* (Vol. 11, pp. 139–151). New York: Norton.

Freud, S. (1915). Observations on transference-love. In J. Strachey (Ed. and Trans.), *The standard edition of the complete psychological works of Sigmund Freud* (Vol. 12, p. 159). New York: Norton.

Freud, S. (1920). Beyond the pleasure principle. In J. Strachey (Ed. and Trans.), *The standard edition of the complete psychological works of Sigmund Freud* (Vol. 18, pp. 3–64). New York: Norton.

Freud, S. (1923). The ego and the id. In J. Strachey (Ed. and Trans.), *The standard edition of the complete psychological works of Sigmund Freud* (Vol. 19, pp. 3–69). New York: Norton.

Freud, S. (1930). Civilization and its discontents. In J. Strachey (Ed. and Trans.), *The standard edition of the complete psychological works of Sigmund Freud* (Vol. 21, pp. 59–146). New York: Norton.

Freud, S. (1937). Analysis terminable and interminable. In J. Strachey (Ed. and Trans.), *The standard edition of the complete psychological works of Sigmund Freud* (Vol. 23, pp. 216–253). New York: Norton.

Freud, S. (1939). Moses and monotheism. In J. Strachey (Ed. and Trans.), *The standard edition of the complete psychological works of Sigmund Freud* (Vol. 23, pp. 3–137). New York: Norton.

Freudenberger, H. J., & Robbins, A. (1979). The hazards of being a psychoanalyst. *Psychoanalytic Review, 66*(2), 275–296.

Fried, E. (1971). Basic concepts in group psychotherapy. In H. I. Kaplan, & B. J. Sadock (Eds.), *Comprehensive group psychotherapy*. Baltimore, MD: Williams & Wilkins.

Friedrich, W. M. (1990). *Psychotherapy of sexually abused children and their families*. New York: Basic.

Fromm, M. G., & Smith, B. (Eds.). (1989). *The facilitating environment: Clinical applications of Winnicott's theory*. Madison, CT: International Universities Press.

Fromm-Reichmann, F. (1960). *Principles of intensive psychotherapy*. Chicago: The University of Chicago Press.

Gabbard, G. O. (1991). Technical approaches to transference hate in the analysis of borderline patients. *International Journal of Psychoanalysis, 72*, 625–638.

Gabbard, G. O. (1993). An overview of countertransference with borderline patients. *Journal of Psychotherapy Practice and Research, 2*(1), 7–18.

Gabbard, G. O. (1994a). Sexual excitement and countertransference love in the analyst. *Journal of the American Psychoanalytic Association, 42*(4), 1083–1106.

Gabbard, G. O. (1994b). Reconsidering the American Psychological Association's policy on sex with former patients: Is it justifiable? *Professional Psychology: Research and Practice, 25*(4), 329–335.

Gabbard, G. O. (1994c). On love and lust in erotic transference. *Journal of the American Psychoanalytic Association, 42*(2), 385–403.

Gamble, S., Pearlman, L. A., Lucca, A. M., & Allen, G. J. (1994, October). *Vicarious traumatization and burnout among Connectiuct psychologists: Empirical findings*. Paper presented at the Annual Meeting of the Connecticut Psychological Association, Waterbury, CT.

Ganzarain, R., & Buchele, B. (1986). Countertransference when incest is the problem. *International Journal of Group Psychotherapy, 36*, 549–566.

Ganzarain, R. C., & Buchele, B. J. (1988). *Fugitives of incest: A perspective from psychoanalysis and groups*. Madison, CT: International Universities Press.

Gay, P. (1988). *Freud: A life for our time*. New York: Norton.

Gelinas, D. J. (1983). The persisting negative effects of incest. *Psychiatry, 46*, 312–332.

Gelinas, D. J. (1994). *Malevolent families: A traumatic developmental context*. Manuscript submitted for publication.

Gelinas, D. J., Goodwin, J. M., Sachs, R. G., & Taylor, C. (1991). *Malevolent development contexts and transgenerational trauma: Theory and intervention frameworks*. Paper presented at the 7th Annual Meeting of the International Society for Traumatic Stress Studies, Washington, DC.

Geller, J.D. (1990, November). Transference and countertransference issues in psychotherapy supervision. In S. Teitelbaum (Chair), *Transference and countertransference: Pivotal issues in psychoanalysis supervision*. Symposium conducted at the Meeting of the Post-Graduate Center for Mental Health, New York, NY.

Gill, M. M. (1954). Psychoanalysis and exploratory psychotherapy. *Journal of the American Psychoanalytic Association, 12*, 632–649.

Gill, M. M. (1979). The analysis of the transference. *Journal of the American Psychoanalytic Association, 27* (Suppl.), 263–288.

Gill, M. M. (1982). *Analysis of transference* (Vol. 1). New York: International Universities Press.

Gill, M. M. (1983). The interpersonal paradigm and the degree of the therapist's involvement. *Contemporary Psychoanalysis, 19*, 200–237.

Gitelson, M. (1952). The emotional position of the analyst in the psychoanalytic situation. *International Journal of Psycho-Analysis, 33,* 1–10.

Gleser, G. C., Green, B. L., & Winget, C. M. (1981). *Prolonged psychosocial effects of disaster: A study of Buffalo Creek.* New York: Academic Press.

Goodwin, J. (1989). *Sexual abuse: Incest victims and their families* (2nd ed.). Chicago, IL: Year Book Medical Publishers.

Goodwin, J. (Ed.). (1993). *Rediscovering childhood trauma: Historical casebook and clinical applications.* Washington, DC: American Psychiatric Press.

Gordon, M. T., & Riger, S. (1989). *The female fear.* New York: Free Press.

Gorkin, M. (1987). *The uses of countertransference.* Northvale, NJ: Jason Aronson.

Greenacre, P. (1954). The role of transference: Practical considerations in relation to psychoanalytic therapy. *Journal of the American Psychoanalytic Association, 2,* 671–684.

Greenson, R. R. (1967). *The technique and practice of psychoanalysis.* New York: International Universities Press.

Greenson, R. R. (1971). The "real" relationship between the patient and the psychoanalyst. In M. Kanzer (Ed.), *The unconscious today* (pp. 213–232). New York: International Universities Press.

Grellert, E. A. (1992). Sources of countertransference in the treatment of MPD for never-multiple and once-multiple therapists. *Treating Abuse Today, 2*(1), 5–8.

Greven, P. (1991). *Spare the child: The religious roots of punishment and the psychological impact of physical abuse.* New York: Knopf.

Guy, J. D. (1987). *The personal life of the psychotherapist.* New York: Wiley.

Guy, J. D., & Liaboe, G. P. (1986). The impact of conducting psychotherapy on psychotherapists' interpersonal functioning. *Professional Psychology: Research and Practice, 17*(2), 111–114.

Haley, S. A. (1974). When the patient reports atrocities. *Archives of General Psychiatry, 30,* 191–196.

Hartman, C. R., & Jackson, H. (1994). Rape and the phenomena of countertransference. In J. P. Wilson, & J. D. Lindy (Eds.), *Countertransference in the treatment of PTSD* (pp. 389–394). New York: Guilford.

Heimann, P. (1950). On countertransference. *International Journal of Psychoanalysis, 31,* 81–84.

Hellman, I. D., & Morrison, T. L. (1987). Practice setting and type of caseload as factors in psychotherapist stress. *Psychotherapy, 24*(3), 427–433.

Henry, W., Sims, J., & Spray, S. L. (1973). *Public and private lives of psychotherapists.* San Francisco: Jossey-Bass.

Herman, J. L. (1981). *Father-daughter incest.* Cambridge, MA: Harvard University Press.

Herman, J. L. (1992). *Trauma and recovery: The aftermath of violence from domestic abuse to political terror.* New York: Basic.

Herman, J. L., Perry, C., & van der Kolk, B. A. (1989). Childhood trauma in borderline personality disorder. *American Journal of Psychiatry, 146*(4), 490–495.

Heyward, C. (1993). *When boundaries betray us.* San Francisco: HarperCollins.

Hollingsworth, M. A. (1993). Responses of female therapists to treating adult female survivors of incest. (Doctoral dissertation, Western Michigan University, 1993). *Dissertation Abstracts International, 54,* 3342.

Holt, J. (1974). *Escape from childhood: The needs and rights of children.* New York: Dutton

Horner, A. (1986). *Being and loving*. Northvale, NJ: Jason Aronson.

Horner, A. (1993). Occupational hazards and characterological vulnerability: The problem of "burnout." *American Journal of Psychoanalysis, 53*(2), 137–141.

Horowitz, M. J. (1979). Psychological response to serious life events. In V. Hamilton, & D. M. Warburton (Eds.), *Human stress and cognition: An information-processing approach* (pp. 235–263). New York: Wiley.

Horowitz, M. J. (1986). *Stress response syndromes* (2nd ed.). Northvale, NJ: Jason Aronson.

Horowitz, M. J., Wilner, N., & Alvarez, W. (1979). Impact of event scale: A measure of subjective stress. *Psychosomatic Medicine, 41*(3), 209–218.

Jacobs, T. J. (1991). *The use of the self: Countertransference and communication in the analytic situation*. Madison, CT: International Universities Press.

Jacobs, T. J. (1994, March). *Impasses and progress in analysis: Working through and its vicissitudes in patient and analyst*. Keynote address at Countertransference and Therapeutic Impasse, conference sponsored by the Karen Horney Institute for Psychoanalysis, New York, NY.

Janet, P. (1919). *Psychological healing: A historical and clinical study*. (E. Paul, & C. Paul, Trans.). (Vol. 1, pp. 661–663). New York: Macmillan.

Janoff-Bulman, R. (1985). The aftermath of victimization: Rebuilding shattered assumptions. In C. R. Figley (Ed.), *Trauma and its wake: The study and treatment of post-traumatic stress disorder* (Vol. 1, pp. 15–25). New York: Brunner/Mazel.

Janoff-Bulman, R. (1989a). Assumptive worlds and the stress of traumatic events: Applications of the schema construct. *Social Cognition, 7*(2), 113–136.

Janoff-Bulman, R. (1989b). The benefits of illusions, the threat of disillusionment, and the limitations of inaccuracy. *Journal of Social and Clinical Psychology, 8*(2), 158–175.

Janoff-Bulman, R. (1992). *Shattered assumptions: Towards a new psychology of trauma*. New York: Free Press.

Jones, E. (1953–57). *The life and work of Sigmund Freud, in three volumes*. New York: Basic.

Jordan, J. (1990). *Courage in connection: Conflict, compassion, creativity*. Wellesley, MA: Stone Center Working Paper Series.

Jordan, J. V., Kaplan, A. G., Miller, J. B., Stiver, I. P., & Surrey, J. L. (1991). *Women's growth in connection: Writings from the Stone Center*. New York: Guilford.

Kahana, B., Harel, Z., & Kahana, E. (1988). Predictors of psychological well-being among survivors of the Holocaust. In J. P. Wilson, Z. Harel, & B. Kahana (Eds.), *Human adaptation to extreme stress: From the Holocaust to Vietnam* (pp. 171–192). New York: Plenum.

Kahn, M. (1991) *Between therapist and client: The new relationship*. New York: Freeman.

Kaiser, H. (1965). Emergency. In J. D. Geller & P. D. Spector (Eds.), *Psychotherapy: Portraits in fiction* (pp. 59–93). Northvale, NJ: Jason Aronson.

Kaslow, F. W., & Schulman, N. (1987). *The family life of psychotherapists: Clinical implications*. New York: Haworth.

Kauffmann, C. M. (1993, August). Feeling like a hostage: Countertransference paralysis and loss of frame. In K. W. Saakvitne (Chair), *Countertransference in analytic psychotherapy with adult incest survivors*. Symposium conducted at the

101st Annual Meeting of the American Psychological Association, Montreal, Canada.

Kauffman, C. (1994, November). Discussant in K. W. Saakvitne (Chair), *Advanced issues in trauma therapy: Countertransference and dissociation*. Symposium conducted at the 10th Annual Meeting of the International Society for Traumatic Stress Studies, Chicago, IL.

Keane, T. M., Fairbank, J. A., Caddell, J. M., Zimering, R. T., & Bender, M. E. (1985). A behavioral approach to assessing and treating post-traumatic stress disorder in Vietnam veterans. In C. R. Figley (Ed.), *Trauma and its wake: The study and treatment of post-traumatic stress disorder* (pp. 257–294). New York: Brunner/Mazel.

Keane, T. M., Zimering, R. T., & Caddell, J. M. (1985). A behavioral formulation of post-traumatic stress disorder in Vietnam veterans. *Behavior Therapy, 8,* 9–12.

Keith-Spiegel, P., & Koocher, G. P. (1985). *Ethics in psychology: Standards and cases*. New York: Random House.

Kernberg, O. (1975). Borderline personality organization. *Journal of the American Psychoanalytic Association, 15,* 641–685.

Kilpatrick, D. G., Veronen, L. J., & Resick, P. A. (1982). Psychological sequelae to rape: Assessment and treatment strategies. In D. M. Doleys, R. L. Meredith, & A. R. Ciminero (Eds.), *Behavioral medicine: Assessment and treatment strategies* (pp. 473–497). New York: Plenum.

Kinsey, A. C., Pomeroy, W. B., Martin, C. E., & Gebhard, P. (1953). *Sexual behavior in the human female*. Philadelphia, PA: Saunders.

Klein, M. (1975). *The writings of Melanie Klein* (Vols. 1–4). London: Hogarth.

Kluft, R. P. (Ed.). (1985). *Childhood antecedents of multiple personality disorder*. Washington, DC: American Psychiatric Press.

Kluft, R. P. (Ed.). (1990a) *Incest-related syndromes of adult psychopathology*. Washington, DC: American Psychiatric Press.

Kluft, R. P. (1990b). Incest and subsequent revictimization: The case of therapist-patient sexual exploitation, with a description of the sitting duck syndrome. In R. P. Kluft (Ed.), *Incest-related syndromes of adult psychopathology* (pp. 263–287). Washington, DC: American Psychiatric Press.

Kluft, R. P. (1994). Countertransference in the treatment of multiple personality disorder. In J. P. Wilson, & J. D. Lindy (Eds.), *Countertransference in the treatment of PTSD* (pp. 122–150). New York: Guilford.

Kohut, H. (1971). *The analysis of the self*. New York: International Universities Press.

Kohut, H. (1977). *The restoration of the self*. New York: International Universities Press.

Kreitman, N. (1977). *Parasuicide*. Chichester, England: Wiley.

Krystal, H. (Ed.). (1968). *Massive psychic trauma*. New York: International Universities Press.

Krystal, H. (1978). Trauma and affects. *Psychoanalytic Study of the Child, 33,* 81–116.

Kuchan, A. (1989) Survey of incidence of psychotherapists' sexual contact with clients in Wisconsin. In G. R. Schoener, J. H. Milgrom, J. C. Gonsiorek, E. T. Luepker, & R. M. Conroe (Eds.), *Psychotherapists' sexual involvement with Clients: Intervention and prevention* (pp. 51–64). Minneapolis, MN: Walk-In Counseling Center.

Kuhn, T. S. (1970). *The structure of scientific revolutions* (2nd ed.). Chicago: University of Chicago Press.

Kus, R. J. (1990). *Keys to caring: Assisting your gay and lesbian clients.* Boston: Alyson.

Lane, F. M. (1986). Transference and countertransference: Definitions of terms. In H. C. Meyers (Ed.), *Between analyst and patient: New dimensions in counter-transference and transference* (pp. 237–256), Hillsdale, NJ: Analytic Press.

Langs, R. J. (1973). *The technique of psychoanalytic psychotherapy* (Vol. 1). New York: Jason Aronson

Langs, R. J. (1974). *The technique of psychoanalytic psychotherapy* (Vol. 2). New York: Jason Aronson.

Langs, R. J. (1975). The therapeutic relationship and deviations in technique. *International Journal of Psychoanalytic Psychotherapy, 4*(1), 6–14.

Laub, D., & Auerhahn, N. C. (1993). Knowing and not knowing massive psychic trauma: Forms of traumatic memory. *International Journal of Psychoanalysis, 74*, 287–302.

Laub, D., & Auerhahn, N. C. (1994). Decontextualizing the context: What do we learn about trauma from our patients? In N. C. Auerhahn (Chair), *Intergenerational memory of trauma: Methods of inquiry.* Symposium conducted at the 10th Annual Meeting of the International Society for Traumatic Stress Studies, Chicago, IL.

Lebowitz, L., & Roth, S. (1994). I felt like a slut: Cultural constructions and women's response to being raped. *Journal of Traumatic Stress, 7*(3), 363–390.

Lerner, H. G. (1988). *Women in therapy.* New York: Harper & Row.

Levine, H. B. (Ed.). (1990). *Adult analysis and childhood sexual abuse.* Hillsdale, NJ: Analytic Press.

Lewis, H. B. (1976). *Psychic war in men and women.* New York: New York Universities Press.

Lifton, R. J. (1979). *The broken connection.* New York: Simon & Schuster.

Lindy, J. (1988). *Vietnam: A casebook.* New York: Brunner/Mazel.

Lindy, J. D., Green, B. L., Grace, M., MacLeod, J. A., & Spitz, L. (1988). *Vietnam: A casebook.* New York: Brunner/Mazel.

Lindy, J. D., & Wilson, J. P. (1994). Empathic strain and countertransference roles: Case illustrations. In J. P. Wilson, & J. Lindy (Eds.), *Countertransference in the treatment of PTSD* (pp. 62–85). New York: Guilford.

Linehan, M. M. (1993). *Cognitive-behavioral treatment of borderline personality disorder.* New York: Guilford.

Little, M. (1957). 'R'—The analyst's total response to his patient's needs. *International Journal of Psychoanalysis, 38*, 240–254.

Little, M. (1981). *Transference neurosis and transference psychosis.* New York: Jason Aronson.

Loewenstein, R. J. (1993). Posttraumatic and dissociative aspects of transference and countertransference in the treatment of multiple personality disorder. In R. P. Kluft, & C. G. Fine (Eds.), *Clinical perspectives on multiple personality disorder* (pp. 51–85). Washington, DC: American Psychiatric Press.

Loftus, E. F. (1993). The reality of repressed memories. *American Psychologist, 48*(5), 518–537.

Loris, M. (1994). Countertransference love, hate, and empathy. *Developments: The newsletter of the Center for Women's Development at HRI Hospital, 3*(1), 1,4.

Louden, J. (1992). *The woman's comfort book: A self-nurturing guide for restoring balance in your life*. New York: HarperCollins.

Luborsky, L., Chandler, M., Auerback, A. H., Cohen, J., & Bachrach, H. M. (1971). Factors influencing the outcome of psychotherapy: A review of the quantitative research. *Psychological Bulletin, 75*, 145–185.

Luborsky, L., & Spence, D. P. (1978). Quantitative research on psychoanalytic therapy. In S. L. Garfield, & A. E. Bergin (Eds.), *Handbook of psychotherapy and behavior change: An empirical analysis*, 2nd ed. (pp. 331–368). New York: Wiley.

Mac Ian, P. S. (1992). *Gender, family autonomy, and acceptance of incest*. Unpublished master's thesis, University of Connecticut, Storrs, CT.

Mac Ian, P. S., & Pearlman, L. A. (1992). Development and use of the TSI Life Event Questionnaire. *Treating Abuse Today, 2*(1), 9–11.

MacKinnon, C. A. (1987). *Feminism unmodified: Pornography*. Cambridge, MA: Harvard University Press.

MacKinnon, C. A. (1989). *Toward a feminist theory of the state*. Cambridge, MA: Harvard University Press.

Mahler, M. S., Pine, F., & Bergman, A. (1975). *The psychological birth of the human infant: Symbiosis and individuation*. New York: Basic.

Mahoney, M. J. (1981). Psychotherapy and human change process. In J. H. Harvey, & M. M. Parks (Eds.), *Psychotherapy research and behavior change* (pp. 73–122). Washington, DC: American Psychological Association.

Mahoney, M. J. (1991). *Human change processes: The scientific foundation of psychotherapy*. New York: Basic.

Mahoney, M. J., & Lyddon, W. J. (1988). Recent developments in cognitive approaches to counseling and psychotherapy. *Counseling Psychologist, 16*(2), 190–234.

Malcolm, J. (1980). *Psychoanalysis: The impossible profession*. New York: Vintage.

Maltz, W. (1992). Caution: Treating sexual abuse can be hazardous to your love life. *Treating Abuse Today, 2*(2), 20–24.

Maltz, W., & Holman, B. (1987). *Incest and sexuality: A guide to understanding and healing*. Lexington, MA: Lexington.

Marcus, B. F. (1989) Incest and the borderline syndrome: The mediating role of identity. *Psychoanalytic Psychology, 6*, 199–215.

Margolin, Y. (1984). *What I don't know can't hurt me: Therapist reactions to Vietnam veterans*. Paper presented at the 92nd Annual Meeting of the American Psychological Association, Toronto.

Maroda, K. (1991). *The power of countertransference*. New York: Guilford.

Marvasti, J. A. (1992). Psychotherapy with abused children and adolescents. In J. R. Brandell (Ed.), *Countertransference n psychotherapy with children & adolescents* (pp. 191–214). Northvale, NJ: Jason Aronson.

Mas, K. (1992). *Disrupted schemata in psychiatric patients with a history of childhood sexual abuse on the McPearl Belief Scale*. Unpublished doctoral dissertation, California School of Professional Psychology, Fresno, CA.

Maslach, C. (1978). Job burnout: How people cope. *Public Welfare, 36*, 56–58.

Masson, J. M. (1984). *The assault on truth: Freud's suppression of the seduction theory*. New York: Farrar, Straus, & Giroux.

Masters, W. H., & Johnson, V. E. (1966). *The human sexual response*. Boston: Little, Brown.

Maxwell, M. J., & Sturm, C. (1994). Countertransference in the treatment of war veterans. In J. P. Wilson, & J. D. Lindy (Eds.), *Countertransference in the treatment of PTSD* (pp. 288–307). New York: Guilford.

Mayman, M. (1967). Early memories and character structure. *Journal of Projective Techniques and Personality Assessment, 32,* 303–316.

McCallum, K. E., Lock, J., Kulla, M., Rorty, M., & Wetzel, R. D. (1992). Dissociative symptoms and disorders in patients with eating disorders. *Dissociation, 5*(4), 227–235.

McCann, I. L., & Colletti, J. (1994). The dance of empathy: A hermeneutic formulation of countertransference, empathy, and understanding in the treatment of individuals who have experienced early childhood trauma. In J. P. Wilson, & J. D. Lindy (Eds.), *Countertransference in the treatment of PTSD* (pp. 81–121). New York: Guilford.

McCann, I. L., & Pearlman, L. A. (1990a). Vicarious traumatization: A contextual model for understanding the effects of trauma on helpers. *Journal of Traumatic Stress, 3*(1), 131–149.

McCann, I. L. & Pearlman, L. A. (1990b). *Psychological trauma and the adult survivor. Theory, therapy, and transformation.* New York. Brunner/Mazel.

McCann, L., & Pearlman, L. A. (1991). Constructivist self development theory as a framework for assessing and treating victims of family violence. In S. Stith, M. B. Williams, & K. Rosen (Eds.), *Violence hits home* (pp. 305–329). New York: Springer.

McCann, I. L., & Pearlman, L. A. (1992). Constructivist self development theory as a framework for assessing and treating adult survivors of ritual abuse and other severe childhood traumas. In D. K. Sakheim, & S. E. Devine (Eds.), *Out of darkness: Exploring satanism and ritual abuse* (pp. 185–206). New York: Lexington.

McCann, L., Pearlman, L. A., Sakheim, D. K., & Abrahamson, D. J. (1988). Assessment and treatment of the adult survivor of childhood sexual abuse within a schema framework. In S. M. Sgroi (Ed.), *Vulnerable populations: Evaluation and treatment of sexually abused children and adult survivors* (Vol. 1, pp. 77–101). Lexington, MA: Lexington.

McCann, I. L., Sakheim, D. K., & Abrahamson, D. J. (1988). Trauma and victimization: A model of psychological adaptation. *Counseling Psychologist, 16*(4), 531–594.

McCarley, T. (1975). The psychotherapeutic search for self-renewal. *American Journal of Psychiatry, 132,* 221–224.

McDougall, J. (1989). *Theaters of the body.* New York: Norton.

McGee, T. F., & Schuman, B. N. (1970). The nature of the cotherapy relationship. *International Journal of Group Psychotherapy, 20,* 25–36.

Medeiros, M. E., & Prochaska, J. O. (1988). Coping strategies that psychotherapists use in working with stressful clients. *Professional Psychology: Research and Practice, 1,* 112–114.

Menninger, W. W. (1990). Anxiety in the psychotherapist. *Bulletin of the Menninger Clinic, 54*(2), 232–246.

Merwin, M., & Smith-Kurtz, B. (1988). Healing of the whole person. In F. M. Ochberg (Ed.), *Post-traumatic therapy and victims of violence* (pp. 57–82). New York: Brunner/Mazel.

Meth, R. L., Pasick, R. S., Gordon, B., Allen, J., Feldman, L. B., & Gordon, S. (1990). *Men in therapy: The challenge of change.* New York: Guilford.

Meyers, H. C. (Ed.). (1986). *Between analyst and patient: New dimensions in countertransference and transference*. Hillsdale, NJ: Analytic Press.

Miller, A. (1981). *The drama of the gifted child: The search for the true self*. New York: Basic.

Miller, A. (1984). *Thou shalt not be aware: Society's betrayal of the child*. New York: Farrar, Straus, & Giroux.

Miller, A. (1988). *Banished knowledge: Facing childhood injuries*. New York: Doubleday.

Miller, D. (1994). *Women who hurt themselves: A book of hope and understanding*. New York: Basic.

Miller, J. B. (1976). *Toward a new psychology of women*. Boston: Beacon.

Miller, J. B., Jordan, J. V., Kaplan, A. G., Stiver, I. P., & Surrey, J. L. (1991). *Some misconceptions and reconceptions of a relational approach*. Wellesly, MA: Stone Center Working Paper Series (no. 49).

Mitchell, J. (1974). *Psychoanalysis and feminism*. New York: Pantheon.

Money, J. (1987). Sin, sickness, or status?: Homosexual gender identity and psychoendocrinology. *American Psychologist, 4*, 384–399.

Montgomery, J. D., & Greif, A. C. (Eds.). (1989). *Masochism: The treatment of self-inflicted suffering*. Madison, CT: International Universities Press.

Morrison, A. (1989). *Shame, the underside of narcissism*. Hillsdale, NJ: Analytic Press.

Moustakis, C. (1961). *Loneliness*. New York: Prentice-Hall.

Munroe, J.F. (1990). Therapist traumatization from exposure to clients with combat related post traumatic stress disorder: Implications for administration and supervision (Doctoral Dissertation, Northeastern University, 1990). *Dissertation Abstracts International, 52*(03), 1731.

Munroe, J. F., Shay, J., Fisher, L., Makary, C., Rapperport, K., & Zimering, R. (in press). Preventing traumatized therapists: A team treatment model. In C. R. Figley (Ed.), *Compassion fatigue: Secondary traumatic stresss disorder from treating the traumatized*. New York: Brunner/Mazel.

Murray, H. A. & Kluckhohn, C. (1953). Outline of a conception of personality. In C. Kluckhohn, & H. A. Murray (Eds.), *Personality in nature, society, and culture* (2nd ed. rev., pp. 3–49). New York: Knopf.

Nathanson, D. L. (Ed.). (1987). *The many faces of shame*. New York: Guilford.

Neumann, D. A. (in press). The long-term sequelae of childhood sexual abuse. In J. Briere (Ed.), *Violent victimization*. San Francisco: Jossey-Bass.

Neumann, D. A., & Gamble, S. (1994). Issues in the professional development of psychotherapists: Countertransference and vicarious traumatization in the new trauma therapist. Submitted for publication.

Neumann, D. A., & Pearlman, L. A. (1994). *Toward the development of a psychological language for spirituality*. Manuscript in preparation.

NiCarthy, G. (1982). *Getting free: A handbook for women in abusive relationships*. Seattle: Seal.

Nicholas, M., & Collins, J. (1992). *The co-therapist relationship in group psychotherapy*. Presentation at the Annual Meeting of the Eastern Group Psychotherapy Association, New York, NY.

Norcross, J. C., & Prochaska, J. O. (1986). Psychotherapist heal thyself: The psychological distress and self-change of psychologists, counselors, and laypersons. *Psychotherapy, 23*(1), 102–114.

Ogata, S. N., Silk, K. R., Goodrich, S., Lohr, N. E., Westen, D., & Hill, E. M.

(1990). Childhood sexual and physical abuse in adult patients with borderline characteristics. *American Journal of Psychiatry, 147*(8), 1008–1013.

Ogden, T. H. (1986). *The matrix of the mind.* Northvale, NJ: Jason Aronson.

Olio, K. (1993, September). Countertransferential desperation: Impact on treatment choices, magic cures, inherent obstacles, and misuses of effective techniques. In *Countertransference in therapy with survivors of childhood sexual abuse.* Conference sponsored by Holyoke Hospital Center for Psychiatry, Holyoke, MA.

Olio, K. (1994). Truth in memory: Comments on Elizabeth Loftus's "Reality of Repressed Memory." *American Psychologist, 49*(5), 442–443.

Olio, K., Schwartz, M., Courtois, C., & Bloom, S. L. (1994, November). *The delayed memory controversy: Politics, validity, and clinical implications.* Symposium conducted at the 10th Annual Meeting of the International Society for Traumatic Stress Studies, Chicago, IL.

Op den Velde, W., Koerselman, G. F., & Aarts, P. G. H. (1994). Countertransference and World War II resistance fighters: Issues in diagnosis and assessment. In J. P. Wilson, & J. D. Lindy (Eds.), *Countertransference in the treatment of PTSD* (pp. 308–327). New York: Guilford.

Ormont, L. R. (1991). Use of the group in resolving the subjective countertransference. *International Journal of Group Psychotherapy, 41*(4), 433–447.

Ormont, L.R. (1992). Subjective countertransference in the group setting: The modern analytic experience. *Modern Psychoanalysis, 17*(1), 3–12.

Parson, E. R. (1984). The reparation of the self: Clinical and theoretical dimensions in the treatment of Vietnam combat veterans. *Journal of Contemporary Psychotherapy, 4*, 4–56.

Parson, E. R. (1986). Transference and post-traumatic stress: The intersecting point in psychotherapy. In C. R. Figley (Ed.), *Trauma and its wake: The study and treatment of post-traumatic stress disorder* (pp. 314–337). New York: Brunner/Mazel.

Parson, E. R. (1994). Inner city children of trauma: Urban violence traumatic stress response syndrome (U-VTS) and therapists' responses. In J. P. Wilson, & J. D. Lindy (Eds.), *Countertransference in the treatment of PTSD* (pp. 151–178). New York: Guilford.

Paulson, I., Burroughs, J. C., & Gelb, C. B. (1976). Cotherapy: What is the crux of the relationship? *International Journal of Group Psychotherapy, 26*, 213–224.

Pearlman, L. A. (1993, August). Countertransference responses to dissociation in psychotherapy with adult trauma survivors. In J. Darwin & K. W. Saakvitne (Chairs), *Countertransference in analytic psychotherapy with adult incest survivors.* Symposium conducted at the 101st Annual Meeting of the American Psychological Association, Toronto, Canada.

Pearlman, L. A., & Deiter, P. J. (1995). *The TSI feeling style inventory.* Manuscript in preparation.

Pearlman, L. A., & Mac Ian, P. S. (1994). *Vicarious traumatization in therapists: An empirical study of the effect of trauma work on trauma therapists.* Submitted for publication.

Pearlman, L. A., Mac Ian, P. S., Mas, K. Stamm, B. H., Bieber, S., & Johnson, G. (1992). *Understanding cognitive schemas across groups: Empirical findings and their implications.* Paper presented at the 8th Annual Meeting of the International Society for Traumatic Stress Studies, Los Angeles, CA.

Pearlman, L. A., & McCann, I. L. (1992). Constructivist self development theory: A theoretical framework for assessing and treating traumatized college students. *American Journal of College Health, 40*(4), 189–196.

Pearlman, L. A., & McCann, I. L. (1994). Integrating structured and unstructured approaches to taking a trauma history. In M. B. Williams, & J. Sommer, Jr. (Eds.), *Handbook of post-traumatic therapy* (pp. 38–48). Westport, CT: Greenwood.

Pearlman, L. A., & Saakvitne, K. W. (in press). Constructivist self development theory approach to treating therapists with secondary traumatic stress disorder. In C. R. Figley (Ed.), *Compassion fatigue: Secondary traumatic stresss disorder from treating the traumatized.* New York: Brunner/Mazel.

Peck, M. S. (1983). *People of the lie.* New York: Simon & Schuster.

Peterson, M. (1992). *At personal risk: Boundary violations in professional-client relationships.* New York: Norton.

Piaget, J. (1971). *Psychology and epistemology: Towards a theory of knowledge.* New York: Viking.

Pleck, J. (1981). *Men and masculinity.* Boston: MIT Press.

Pope, K. S. (1994). *Sexual involvement with therapists.* Washington, DC: American Psychiatric Association.

Pope, K. S., & Bouhoutsos, J. C. (1986). *Sexual intimacy between therapists and patients.* New York: Praeger.

Pope, K. S., & Feldman-Summers, S. (1992). National survey of psychologists' sexual and physical abuse history and their evaluation of training and competence in these areas. *Professional Psychology: Research and Practice, 23*(5), 353–361.

Pope, K. S., Keith-Spiegel, P., & Tabachnick, B. G. (1986). Sexual attraction to clients: The human therapist and the (sometimes) inhuman training system. *American Psychologist, 41,* 147–158.

Pope, K. S., & Vetter, V. A. (1991). Prior therapist-patient sexual involvement among patients seen by psychologists. *Psychotherapy: Research, Theory, and Practice, 28*(3), 429–438.

Putnam, F. W. (1989). *Diagnosis and treatment of multiple personality disorder.* New York: Guilford.

Racker, H. (1957). The meaning and uses of countertransference. *Psychoanalytic Quarterly, 26,* 303–357.

Raquepaw, J. M., & Miller, R. S. (1989). Psychotherapist burnout: A componential analysis. *Professional Psychology: Research and Practice, 20*(1), 32–36.

Reich, A. (1951). On counter-transference. *International Journal of Psychoanalysis, 32,* 25–31.

Reik, T. (1937). *Surprise and the psychoanalyst.* New York: Dutton.

Reik, T. (1948). *Listening with the third ear.* New York: Farrar, Straus, & Giroux.

Reis, B. E. (1993). Toward a psychoanalytic understanding of multiple personality disorder. *Bulletin of the Menninger Clinic, 57*(3), 309–318.

Reis, B. E. (in press). Time: The missing dimension in traumatic memory and dissociative subjectivity. In J. Alpert (Ed.), *Delayed memories of childhood abuse: Essential papers for the clinician.* New York: Jason Aronson.

Renshaw, D. (1982). *Incest: Understanding and treatment.* Boston: Little, Brown.

Rice, C. (1992, May). Creative approaches to prevention through training: Understanding and responding to issues of sexuality and power in treatment. In J. Grunebaum (Chair), *Training for treatment: How can it help?* Symposium sponsored by Massachusetts House Committee for Sexual Misconduct by Physicians, Therapists, and other Health Professionals, Boston, MA.

Rich, A. (1986). *Of woman born: Motherhood as experience and institution* (rev. ed.). New York: Norton.

Rogers, C. R. (1951). *Client-centered therapy: Its current practice, implications, and theory.* Boston: Houghton Mifflin.

Rosica, K. (1993, August). Supervision: Reality as a collective hunch. In H. Yershalmi (Chair), *What does the supervisor know? Supervision in a constructive perspective.* Symposium conducted at the 101st Annual Meeting of the American Psychological Association, Toronto, Canada.

Ross, C. A. (1989). *Multiple personality disorder: Diagnosis, clinical features, and treatment.* New York: Wiley.

Roth, S. (1987). *Psychotherapy: The art of wooing nature.* Northvale, NJ: Jason Aronson.

Roth, S. (1989). *Coping with sexual trauma.* Unpublished manuscript.

Roth, S., & Cohen, L. J. (1986). Approach, avoidance, and coping with stress. *American Psychologist, 41,* 813–819.

Roth, S., & Lebowitz, L. (1988). The experience of sexual trauma. *Journal of Traumatic Stress, 1,* 79–107.

Rotter, J. B. (1954). *Social learning and clinical psychology.* Englewood Cliffs, NJ: Prentice Hall.

Rotter, J. B. (1966). Generalized expectancies for internal versus external control of reinforcement. *Psychological Monographs, 80* (1, Whole No. 609).

Russell, D. E. H. (1984). *Sexual exploitation: Rape, child sexual abuse and workplace harassment.* Newbury Park, CA: Sage.

Russell, D. E. H. (1986). *The secret trauma: Incest in the lives of girls and women.* New York: Basic.

Ryan, W. (1971). *Blaming the victim.* New York: Pantheon.

Saakvitne, K. W. (1990, August). Psychoanalytic psychotherapy with incest survivors: Transference and countertransference paradigms. In K. W. Saakvitne (Chair), *Psychoanalytic views of trauma: Clinical, theoretical, and research perspectives.* Symposium conducted at the 98th Annual Meeting of the American Psychological Association, Boston, MA.

Saakvitne, K. W. (1991, August). *Psychoanalytic psychotherapy with incest survivors: When the therapist was abused.* Paper presented at the 99th Annual Meeting of the American Psychological Association, San Francisco, CA.

Saakvitne, K. W. (1992, August). Incest and feminine identity: Shame, sexuality, and rage. In K. W. Saakvitne (Chair), *Unconscious shame, guilt, and psychoanalytic considerations of trauma.* Symposium conducted at the 100th Annual Meeting of the American Psychological Association, Washington, DC.

Saakvitne, K. W. (1993a, May). Psychoanalysis and trauma theory: Parallel developmental lines. In I. Moses (Chair), *Psychoanalytic perspectives on the treatment of trauma.* Symposium conducted at the Annual Meeting of the Connecticut Psychological Association, Stamford, CT.

Saakvitne, K. W. (1993b, August). Double jeopardy: Countertransference with patients sexually abused by previous therapists. In K. W. Saakvitne (Chair), *Countertransference in analytic psychotherapy with adult incest survivors.* Symposium conducted at the 101st Annual Meeting of the American Psychological Association, Toronto, Canada.

Saakvitne, K. W. (1993c, August). Eroticized maternal transference in psychoanalytic treatment of female incest suriviors. In M. C. Buttenheim (Chair), *Sexuality and intimacy in the adult relationships of childhood incest survivors*. Symposium conducted at the 101st Annual Meeting of the American Psychological Association, Toronto, Canada.

Saakvitne, K. W. (1995). Therapists' responses to dissociative clients: Countertransference and vicarious traumatization. In L. M. Cohen, J. N. Berzoff, & M. R. Elin (Eds), *Dissociative identity disorder: Theoretical and treatment controversies*. New York: Jason Aronson.

Saakvitne, K. W., & Abrahamson, D. J. (1994). The impact of managed care on the therapeutic relationship. *Psychoanalysis and Psychotherapy, 11*(2), 181–197.

Saakvitne, K. W., & Pearlman, L. A. (1992, October). Response to M. J. Bennett, Managed care and the sexual abuse victim, *Berkshire Mental Health Review: A Quarterly Newsletter for Health Professionals*, II(1), pp. 3,5.

Saakvitne, K. W., & Pearlman, L. A. (1993). The impact of internalized misogyny and violence against women on feminine identity. In E. Cook (Ed.), *Women, relationships, and power: Implications for counseling* (pp. 247–274). Alexandria, VA: American Counseling Association.

Sakheim, D. K. (1995). Vicarious actualization: Therapist's self-development through working with trauma survivors. *Raising Issue, 1*(6), 1–5.

Sakheim, D. K., & Devine, S. E. (Eds.). (1992a). *Out of darkness: Exploring satanism and ritual abuse*. New York: Lexington.

Sakheim, D. K., & Devine, S. E. (1992b). Bound by the boundaries: Therapy issues in work with individuals exposed to severe trauma. In D. K. Sakheim & S. E. Devine (Eds.), *Out of darkness: Exploring satanism and ritual abuse* (pp. 279–299). New York: Lexington.

Sakheim, D. K., & Devine, S. E. (1995). Trauma related syndromes. In C. A. Ross & A. Pam (Eds.), *Pseudoscience in biological psychiatry: Blaming the victim* (pp. 255–272). New York: Wiley.

Salisbury, J., Ginorio, A. B., Remick, H., & Stringer, D. M. (1986). Counseling victims of sexual harassment. *Psychotherapy, 23*, 316–324.

Sarason, S. B., Carroll, C. F., Maton, K., Cohen, S., & Lorentz, E. (1977). *Human services and resource networks*. San Francisco: Jossey-Bass.

Sargeant, N. M. (1989). Spirituality and adult survivors of child sexual abuse: Some treatment issues. In S. M. Sgroi (Ed.), *Vulnerable populations: Sexual abuse treatment for children, adult survivors, offenders, and persons with mental retardation* (Vol. 2, pp.167–202). New York: Lexington.

Sarnat, J. E. (1992). Supervision in relationship: Resolving the teach-treat controversy in psychoanalytic supervision. *Psychoanalytic Psychology, 9*(3), 387–403.

Schafer, R. (1983). *The analytic attitude*. New York: Basic.

Schatzow, E., & Yassen, J. (1991). *Specialized treatment models for clinicians with a history of trauma*. Workshop at the 7th Annual Meeting of the International Society for Traumatic Stress Studies, Washington, DC.

Schauben, L. J., & Frazier, P. A. (1995). Vicarious trauma: The effects on female counselors of working with sexual violence survivors. *Psychology of Women Quarterly, 19*(1), 49–64.

Schoener, G. R., Milgrom, J. H., Gonsiorek, J. C., Luepker, E. T., & Conroe, R. M. (1989). *Psychotherapists' sexual involvement with clients: Intervention and prevention*. Minneapolis, MN: Walk-In Counseling Center.

Schwaber, E. (1993, March). Impasses and their manifestations: Further reflections on analytic listening. In *Countertransference and therapeutic impasse*. Symposium conducted at the Meeting of the Karen Horney Center for Psychoanalysis, New York.

Schwartz, D. P. (1988, March). *On caring and its troubles*. Presented at the Friday night lecture series at the Austen Riggs Center, Stockbridge, MA.

Scurfield, R. M. (1985). Post-trauma stress assessment and treatment: Overview and formulations. In C. R. Figley (Ed.), *Trauma and its wake: The study and treatment of Post-Traumatic Stress Disorder* (pp. 219–256). New York: Brunner/Mazel.

Searles, H. F. (1959). The effort to drive the other person crazy: An element in the aetiology and psychotherapy of schizophrenia. In *Collected papers on schizophrenia and related subjects* (pp. 254–283). New York: International Universities Press.

Searles, H. F. (1975). The patient as therapist to his analyst. In P. L. Giovacchini (Ed.), *Tactics and techniques in psychoanalytic therapy* (Vol. 2, pp. 95–151). New York: Jason Aronson.

Searles, H. F. (1979). *Countertransference and related subjects*. New York: International Universities Press.

Sgroi, S. M. (1982). *Handbook of clinical intervention in child sexual abuse*. Lexington, MA: Lexington.

Sgroi, S. M. (1988). *Vulnerable populations: Evaluation and treatment of sexually abused children and adult survivors* (Vol. 1). Lexington, MA: Lexington.

Sgroi, S. M. (1989). *Vulnerable populations: Sexual abuse treatment for children, adult survivors, offenders, and persons with mental retardation* (Vol. 2). Lexington, MA: Lexington.

Shengold, L. (1989). *Soul murder: The effects of childhood abuse and deprivation*. New Haven, CT: Yale University Press.

Shevrin, H. (1980). The psychological unconscious: A necessary assumption for all psychological theory? *American Psychologist, 35*(5), 421–434.

Shevrin, H. (1992). Event-related potential indicators of the dynamic unconscious. *Consciousness and Cognition: An International Journal, 1*(4), 340–366.

Silverman, L. H. (1985). Research on psychoanalytic psychodynamic propositions. *Clinical Psychology Review, 5*(3), 247–257.

Slavin, J. (1993, August). Construction of the therapist's responsiveness: Supervision and the development of trust. In H. Yerushalmi (Chair), *What does the supervisor know?: Supervision in a constructive perspective*. Symposium conducted at the 101st Annual Meeting of the American Psychological Association, Toronto, Canada.

Spiegel, D., & Cardena, E. (1991). Disintegrated experience: The dissociative disorders revisited. *Journal of Abnormal Psychology, 100*(3), 366–378.

Stamm, B. H., Bieber, S. L., & Pearlman, L. A. (1991, October). *A preliminary report and general scale construction and generalizability of the TSI Belief Scale*. Paper presented at the 7th Annual Meeting of the International Society for Traumatic Stress Studies, Washington, DC.

Staub, E. (1989). *The roots of evil: The origins of genocide and other group violence*. New York: Cambridge University Press.

Staub, E. (1992). Transforming the bystander: Altruism, caring, and social responsibility. In M. Fein (Ed.), *Genocide watch*. New Haven, CT: Yale University Press.

Stiver, I. (1992). *A relational approach to therapeutic impasse.* Wellesley, MA: Stone Center Working Paper Series (no. 58).

Stolorow, R. B., Brandchaft, B., & Atwood, G. (1987). *Psychoanalytic treatment: An intersubjective approach.* Hillsdale, NJ: Analytic Press.

Sullivan, H. S. (1953). *The interpersonal theory of psychiatry.* New York: Norton.

Suran, B. G., & Sheridan, E. P. (1985). Management of burnout: Training psychologists in professional life span perspectives. *Professional Psychology: Research and Practice, 16*(6), 741–752.

Tansey, M. J., & Burke, W. F. (1989). *Understanding countertransference: From projective identification to empathy.* Hillsdale, NJ: Analytic Press.

Terr, L. C. (1990). *Too scared to cry.* New York: HarperCollins.

Terr, L. C. (1994). *Unchained memories: True stories of traumatic memories, lost and found.* New York: Basic.

Ulman, R. B., & Brothers, D. (1988). *The shattered self: A psychoanalytic study of trauma.* Hillsdale, NJ: Analytic Press.

van der Hart, O., Brown, P., & van der Kolk, B. A. (1989). Pierre Janet's treatment of post-traumatic stress. *Journal of Traumatic Stress, 2,* 379–395.

van der Kolk, B. A. (Ed.). (1984). *Post-traumatic stress disorder: Psychological and biological sequelae.* Washington, DC: American Psychiatric Press.

van der Kolk, B. A. (Ed.). (1987). *Psychological trauma.* Washington, DC: American Psychiatric Press.

van der Kolk, B. A. (1988). The biological response to psychic trauma. In F. M. Ochberg (Ed.), *Post-traumatic therapy and victims of violence* (pp. 25–38). New York: Brunner/Mazel.

van der Kolk, B. A. (1989). The compulsion to repeat the trauma: Re-enactment, revictimization, and masochism. *Psychiatric Clinics of North America, 12*(2), 389–411.

van der Kolk, B. A. (1994). The body keeps the score: Memory and the evolving psychobiology of posttraumatic stress. *Harvard Review of Psychiatry, 1,* 253–265.

van der Kolk, B. A., & Greenberg, M. S. (1987). The psychobiology of the trauma response: Hyperarousal, constriction, and addiction to traumatic reexposure. In B. A. van der Kolk (Ed.), *Psychological trauma* (pp. 63–87). Washington, DC: American Psychiatric Press.

van der Kolk, B. A., & McFarlane, E. C. (in press). *The black hole of trauma: Human adaptations to overwhelming experience.* New York: Guilford.

van der Kolk, B. A., & van der Hart, O. (1991). The intrusive past: The flexibility of memory and the engraving of trauma. *American Imago, 48,* 425–454.

Vissing, Y. M., Straus, M. A., Gelles, R. J., & Harrop, J. W. (1991). Verbal aggression by parents and psychosocial problems of children. *Child Abuse and Neglect, 15,* 223–238.

Wachtel, P. (1982). On the limits of therapeutic neutrality. *Contemporary Psychoanalysis, 22,* 60–70.

Wagner, A. W., Linehan, M. M., & Wasson, E. J. (1989). *Parasuicide: Characteristics and relationship to childhood sexual abuse.* Poster presented at the Annual Meeting of the Association for Advancement of Behavior Therapy, Washington, DC.

Waites, E. A. (1993). *Trauma and survival: Post-traumatic and dissociative disorders in women.* New York: Norton.

Walker, L. (1985). The battered woman syndrome study. In D. Finkelhor, R. J. Gelles, G. T. Hotaling, & M. A. Strauss (Eds.), *The dark side of families* (pp. 31–48). Beverly Hills, CA: Sage.

Westen, D., Ludolph, P., Misle, B., Ruffins, S., & Block, B. (1990). Physical and sexual abuse in adolescent girls with borderline personality disorder. *American Journal of Orthopsychiatry, 60*(1), 55–66.

White, M. T., & Weiner, M. B. (1986). *The theory and practice of self-psychology*. New York: Brunner/Mazel.

Williams, L. M. (1992, Summer). Adult memories of childhood abuse: Preliminary findings from a longitudinal study. *The APSAC (American Professional Society on the Abuse of Children) Advisor*, 19–21.

Williams, T. (1988). Diagnosis and treatment of survivor guilt: The bad penny syndrome. In J. P. Wilson, Z. Harel, & B. Kahana (Eds.), *Human adaptation to extreme stress* (pp. 319–336). New York: Plenum.

Wilson, J. P., & Lindy, J. D. (1994a). Empathic strain and countertransference. In J. P. Wilson, & J. D. Lindy (Eds.), *Countertransference in the treatment of PTSD* (pp. 5–30). New York: Guilford.

Wilson, J. P., & Lindy, J. (Eds.). (1994b). *Countertransference in the treatment of PTSD*. New York: Guilford.

Wilson, J. P., Lindy, J. D., & Raphael, B. (1994). Empathic strain and therapist defense: Type I and II CTRs. In J. P. Wilson, & J. D. Lindy (Eds.), *Countertransference in the treatment of PTSD* (pp. 31–61). New York: Guilford.

Wilson, J. P., & Raphael, B. (1993). *International handbook of traumatic stress syndromes*. New York: Plenum.

Winnicott, D. W. (1949). Hate in the countertransference. *International Journal of Psychoanalysis, 30*, 69–74.

Winnicott, D. W. (1958). The capacity to be alone. *International Journal of Psychiatry, 39*, 416–420.

Winnicott, D. W. (1960). The theory of the parent-child relationship. In *The maturational process and the facilitating environment*. Madison, CT: Interational Universities Press.

Winnicott, D. W. (1965). *The maturational process and the facilitating environment: Studies in the theory of emotional development*. New York: International Universities Press.

Winter, S. (1976). Developmental stages in the roles and concerns of group leaders. *Small Group Behavior, 7*, 349–363.

Wolf, E. K., & Alpert, J. L. (1991). Psychoanalysis and child sexual abuse: A review of the post-Freudian literature. *Psychoanalytic Psychology, 8*(3), 305–327.

Wolstein, B. (Ed.). (1988). *Essential papers on countertransference*. New York: New York University Press.

Wong, M. R., & Cook, D. (1992). Shame and its contribution to PTSD. *Journal of Traumatic Stress, 5*(4), 557–562.

Yalom, I. D. (1975). *The theory and practice of group psychotherapy* (3rd ed.). New York: Basic.

Yassen, J. (in press). Prevention of secondary traumatic stress in individuals. In C. Figley (Ed.), *Compassion fatigue: Secondary traumatic stresss disorder from treating the traumatized*. New York: Brunner/Mazel.

Zelen, S. L. (1985). Sexualization of therapeutic relationships: The dual vulnerability of patient and therapist. *Psychotherapy, 22*, 178–185.

Index

435

NAMES